BLACK WOMEN'S ART ECOSYSTEMS

SITES OF WELLNESS AND SELF-CARE

TANISHA M. JACKSON

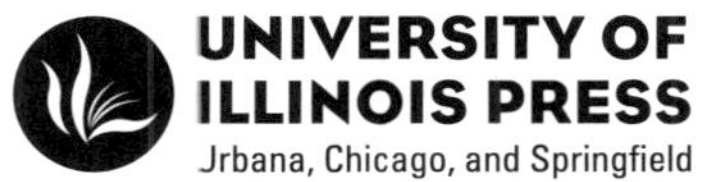

© 2025 by the Board of Trustees
of the University of Illinois
All rights reserved
Manufactured in the United States of America
1 2 3 4 5 C P 5 4 3 2 1
♾ This book is printed on acid-free paper.

Library of Congress Cataloging-in-Publication Data
Names: Jackson, Tanisha M. author
Title: Black women's art ecosystems : sites of wellness and self-care /
    Tanisha M. Jackson.
Description: Urbana : University of Illinois Press, [2025] | Series:
    The new Black studies series | Includes bibliographical references
    and index.
Identifiers: LCCN 2025025183 (print) | LCCN 2025025184 (ebook)
    | ISBN 9780252046841 cloth | ISBN 9780252088940 paperback |
    ISBN 9780252048388 ebook
Subjects: LCSH: African American women artists—Social networks
    | Art and society—United States
Classification: LCC N6538.B53 J33 2025 (print) | LCC N6538.B53
    (ebook) | DDC 709.73/082—dc23/eng/20250618
LC record available at https://lccn.loc.gov/2025025183
LC ebook record available at https://lccn.loc.gov/2025025184

THE NEW BLACK STUDIES SERIES

Edited by Darlene Clark Hine
and Dwight A. McBride

*For a list of books in the series, please see
our website at www.press.uillinois.edu.*

BLACK
WOMEN'S
ART
ECOSYSTEMS

This book is dedicated to my mother, Rea Jackson, and my grandmother,
Evangelist Annetta Yvonne Avery (1937–2020):
The effectual fervent prayers of a righteous (wo)man avail much (James 5:16)

8578462

Contents

Foreword

DINDGA McCANNON

This book is, first of all, so overdue!

Black women have long been said to be "strong women." (I interpret that as being thought of as "Super Women.") In my time (late 1950s, early '60s), Black women were expected to cook, clean, take care of our families (sometimes other people also), and manage households—all the while wearing a smile.

But after we finish taking care of others, who takes care of us? And how do we use our art to help the communities we are part of? This book shows how many women have done it.

As founding members (along with Kay Brown and Faith Ringgold) of Where We At Black Women Artists in 1971, we didn't think of many of the things *Black Women's Art Ecosystems* speaks about. Although wellness and self-care were not formally in our conversations, we became a sisterhood. We nurtured each other through being able to talk about things of concern to us as Black women and as artists (and having others listen and comment); babysitting for one another so we could have uninterrupted studio time; occasionally loaning or giving each other overdue rent money; educating each other about where to find artist work opportunities and exhibits; planning retreats where we could rest, rejuvenate, and invite guest speakers on herbology, yoga, and vegetarianism; and more. We understood the power that art brought to us as artists, and we saw how having access to artmaking empowered others in the communities where we lived and taught. When we went into the prison system, we were loved and respected because we had come from the same neighborhoods as some of the inmates but without the attitudes the prison employees came with. The prisoners understood that we understood how important it was to us to come into their space and unselfishly share our knowledge of various arts; it gave many of them something positive to do while serving time. We would go into shelters and not only teach art but also gave workshops on preparing your own baby food and healthy eating. (At that time, if you were a vegan, or non–meat eater, you were thought of as very strange.) We would teach the children, who found outlets for freely expressing themselves. We often used art to teach math, reading, and science. We became wellness workers. Although we didn't have a formal title for what we were doing, we wanted to be able to create our art and share the love of creating with our community. Much of what we did organically at the time is what this book discusses.

Indeed, as Dr. Jackson stated, 2022 marked a pivotal moment for Black women artists: finally we were allowed, in significant numbers, into the art world of mainstream America. I, who had been working as an artist for fifty-five years, had been discovered! (Actually, I was *re*discovered, as my work had been well known in Brooklyn and Harlem for fifty years.) I went from having works in the collections of two museums to having works in thirteen. Like many others, I am now finally able to make a decent living on what I create.

I remember going to the Venice Biennale and refusing to look at any other work until I had seen Simone Leigh's installation—and Sonia Boyce's work right next to hers. Other countries decided to exhibit more works by women that year (finally they were letting more of us out into the daylight) but it was those two who took home the top prizes. For a Black woman artist in the 1970s, this was an amazing, surreal moment. And I continue to be amazed at the sheer number of not only African American women artists being shown in America but also other women of color. All of these events make the publication of this book right on time. It discusses how we have been able to sustain ourselves until this moment and by using these same tools, how the Black women artists of the future might be able to sustain themselves going forward.

Another thing I love about *Black Women's Art Ecosystems* are the interviews with the Black women artists. Outside of artists' talks and exhibition catalogs, we rarely hear Black women artists speaking about their work. I knew little about the artists interviewed in the book, but their stories and their discussions of their work made me want to know and see more. As I was introduced to each artist, I was inspired to Google them and look at more work. The work collectively is strong, innovative, inspiring, beautiful! And the inclusion of the abstract artists . . . wonderful! This is another group usually left out of conversations about Black women artists as well as conversations about Black art.

While reading this manuscript, I realized how connected we all are in the Black arts community. I have interacted with at least ten of the people mentioned in this book: Deborah Willis, as an artist associate; I'm mentioned in Lisa Farrington's book *Creating Their Own Image: The History of African-American Women Artists*; Nell Painter used my quilt *Wedding Party No.1* on the cover of one of her books. I was one of the first members of the Weusi Artist Collective in 1965; and Kay Brown and I were the only women members until three years ago. (The group is still active.) I am friends with many of the members of AfroCobra, and we have exhibited in the same spaces. One of my men friends worked and traveled with the Urban Bush Women in the 1990s. I've exhibited at The Colored Girls Museum when it first opened. Lavett Ballard (featured in chapter 4) was one of the under-fifty artists when I curated an exhibition titled "Generations 7."

"Generations 7" paired seven Black women artists under age fifty with seven Black women artists over sixty-five at the Rush Arts Gallery in Philadelphia. I have worked and still do work with Souleo from time to time; he is an amazing curator. Danny Simmons, an artist associate, is president of the Rush Arts Gallery in Philadelphia, an incredible artist, and a major voice in the New York Art scene. At Weeksville I have just curated one of two exhibitions for some of the "Where We At" Black Women Artists who are still living and honored those who are no longer with us.

As an elder artist, I am so proud of this book. It shows and speaks about a very important part of our lives. We Black women artists really are wellness workers. We understand that through our art and our reaching out and commitment to our communities that we can help make a difference. This book and all the research that went into it will be a guide to those who come after us. It will open the door for more cultural transformation, more healing, more advocacy for social justice, influencing the changing political landscape and hopefully inspire more Black Women artists to form collectives. Although we live in a digital world that often separates us, we still can effect change by coming together. The doors have opened. To make sure that they don't close again, we must join forces.

Preface

In narrating the story of Black women artists as wellness workers, I think it is also essential to share my personal journey and how art has been integral to my life, as well as a source of healing for me. My earliest memory of creating art dates back to when I was five. At the time, I was an only child living with my mother—my parents had recently divorced—and I sat in my new surroundings: a Pound Puppies–themed bedroom. These toys, created by Tonka in the 1980s, were a line of plush stuffed-dog dolls that captured my imagination and sparked my creative spirit. On my fifth birthday, I received my first Pound Puppy, which inspired me to replicate their images through drawing. This early experience marked the beginning of my identity as a creative individual. At some point, while I was sitting in my room, the thought came to me to try and draw a Pound Puppy. I remember first studying the images of the dogs on my comforter. I noticed that every dog was a collection of geometric shapes connected to develop a complete picture. At the time, I didn't know that what I was discovering was composition and form; that would come many years later in a high school art class. Yet this awareness prompted me to try to replicate the images on my bed comforter through drawing. I picked up a pencil, and on a piece of white paper, I began drawing a single shape, the dog's ear, and then connecting the other shapes that made up its eyes and a nose. I drew the image very carefully to ensure its form was proportional and correct in scale, and soon I completed the picture of a Pound Puppy. I had excellent hand-eye coordination for a five-year-old and recognized that I had natural talent; I remember thinking, *I can draw*. My mother came into my room to check on me at some point, and I proudly showed her my drawing. She was amazed at my picture's quality and affirmed me by saying, "Nisha, you're an artist!" My mother's praise and affirmation confirmed what I already knew about myself, and it was from this point that I would hold on to the identity of a creative artist while navigating life.

As I grew older, societal expectations shaped my perceptions of success and career goals. Despite my natural talent for art, I pursued a path toward becoming a medical doctor, influenced by the notion that careers in engineering, law, and medicine were more prestigious and lucrative. However, my passion for the humanities led me to major in English, where I discovered a love for literature and writing. My undergraduate years were enriched by courses in Black studies, which fueled my interest in the African diaspora and my appreciation for Black culture.

My journey took a significant turn when I enrolled in the Master of Arts program in the Department of African American and African Studies at The Ohio State University. This decision marked a departure from my initial career aspirations and ignited my passion for research and teaching. However, during my first quarter of graduate school, I faced a debilitating illness. This illness brought immense physical challenges, but I persevered, determined to complete my studies despite the pain and fatigue.

Art became a crucial part of my healing process. During my recovery from surgery, I rediscovered my love for painting. Using art supplies I had stored away, I began creating figurative images of Black people, scenes of Black women in meditation, and still-life compositions. This meditative practice of painting helped me regain my strength and confidence, affirming my identity as an artist.

After completing my graduate program, I embarked on a path that combined my interests in art, Black studies, and community engagement. My doctoral studies in art education allowed me to merge these passions, focusing on the representation of Black women in art and visual culture. This journey led me to my current roles as a professor in Black studies at Syracuse University and executive director at the university's Community Folk Art Center, where I explore the transformative power of art within the context of wellness.

My dual engagement with academia and community-based arts has provided a dynamic platform for studying the impact of art on individual and collective well-being. The Community Folk Art Center, with its emphasis on African diaspora arts, is a living laboratory for understanding how the creative practices of Black women artists contribute to community wellness. Through my research, I aim to amplify the voices of contemporary Black women artists, examining how their work fosters resilience, empowerment, and healing within their communities.

In writing about Black women artists as wellness workers, I draw inspiration from my own experiences and the works of the fourteen Black women creatives featured in this book. Their ability to blend cultural narratives, spirituality, and community engagement resonates deeply with my commitment to fostering cultural pride and self-empowerment. By bridging the gap between academia and community engagement, I strive to highlight the vital role that Black women artists play in promoting wellness and resilience, not only within their own communities but beyond.

Acknowledgments

My journey in exploring the work of Black women in visual culture and art began with my dissertation, "Defining Us: A Critical Look at the Images of Black Women in Visual Culture and Their Narrative Responses to These Images." This research sparked years of scholarship dedicated to amplifying the voices and artwork of Black women creatives. I am grateful to my advisor, Dr. Vesta A. H. Daniel, who guided me through my early scholarship and reminded me to ask the right critical questions.

Financial support for this book came from the Syracuse University Humanities Center Manuscript Development Workshop Grant, and I thank Alan Middleton and Sarah Workman for their support. I owe tremendous thanks to Drs. Georgene Bess, Yolanda Covington-Ward, Stephanie Y. Evans, and Kwasi Konadu for their critical feedback as preliminary reviewers, which strengthened my research.

I appreciate the American Association of University Women for supporting me through the American Fellows Program, providing a fellowship year to finish this book. The writing community I developed as a participant in the National Center for Faculty Development & Diversity (NCFDD) was invaluable, offering resources and support for navigating the publishing process.

I am grateful for fellow interlocutors: Drs. Osei Appiah, Scot Brown, Mary Phillips, Jeffrey Squire, and Guillaume Youbué. Your feedback, support, and the writing group were essential in keeping me accountable and focused on telling these artists' stories.

Much of what keeps me grounded is my family. I want to thank my mother, Rea Jackson, who has been a constant reminder of the wellness work Black women do, through her ministry and the care she has provided for our family. Mom, you inspired my love for Black people, Black history, and learning from a young age. I remember vividly the day you sat me in our kitchen when I was five years old to memorize a passage from Frederick Douglass's slave narrative for Black History Month. You were also the first to recognize and nurture my creativity.

My heartfelt thanks go to my father, Reuben Jackson Paygai, and my step-mother, Gertrude Paygai, whose support and encouragement were constant in the completion of this book. My scholarly focus on the African diaspora is deeply connected to our Liberian heritage and the pride you instilled in me as a Bassa woman.

I am also grateful to my grandmother, Annetta Yvonne Avery, who understood the importance of this book more than anyone. Before her death, she constantly reminded me to "write the book," and her words have been a guiding force. To my grandfather, Robert Earl Avery, your confidence in me has been a driving force. I hope I've made you proud, and I appreciate all your advice and stories, which encouraged me throughout the writing process.

To my Aunt Darla, Uncle Chauncey, my sister Christiana, and my brothers—Jordan (who reminds me to G.O.T.G.N.), Navaronne, Reuben "Trocon," Austin, Kevin—and other extended family members, thank you for the sparks of joy and balance you bring to my life.

I am thankful for my church family in Columbus, Ohio, at the Church of Christ of the Apostolic Faith (CCAF), and especially my Sunday-school sisters, who have prayed for me and celebrated my accomplishments. My church family in Syracuse, New York, at Holy Temple Church and Apostolic Church of Jesus Christ, has also been a source of support.

To my homegirls, who have been incredibly uplifting: Jill, Alicia, Marissa, Nichole L., Jonataye, and Cjala, I deeply appreciate our sisterhood and your grounding presence.

Thank you to Arielle Elle Spears-Hay and Ryan Hay for your visual and technical expertise in the digital production of my scholarship, photo shoots, graphics, and visual-content editing. Your support has been invaluable.

My amazing editors, Dr. Vonda Morton, who has been with me from the beginning, working on every iteration of this book, and Barbara Curialle: Thank you for your dedication.

I also thank the University of Illinois Press and the acquisition editors Dominique Moore and Leigh Ann Cowan for their enthusiasm for this project from the start. To the blind reviewers, thank you for reading my work and providing invaluable feedback.

I want to express my gratitude to the College of Arts and Sciences and my colleagues and staff in the Department of African American Studies at Syracuse University for their support in my professional development, mentorship, and resources allocated to complete this book.

Thank you to the incredible team at the Community Folk Art Center. Your support and professionalism allowed me to devote more attention to my scholarship.

My Frank W. Hale Jr. Black Cultural Center family has been supportive from the time I walked through the doors as a work-study student, matriculated through graduate school, to now. Special thanks to Larry Williamson, LaShalle Johnson, and Lee Smith for your continued support.

I am especially grateful to the permissions team at the Schomburg Center for Research in Black Culture, the Brooklyn Museum, the estate of Kay Brown, the Union Art Gallery, the Kasim Art Gallery, Galerie Myrtis, The Colored Girls Museum, House/Full of Blackwomen, Ashara Ekundayo Gallery, and Where We At: Black Women Artists for their support and participation in completing this project.

Most important, I want to thank the artists featured in this book, who allowed me to interview them and showcase their artwork, and who entrusted me with their personal stories on wellness, healing, and art: Lavett Ballard, Tawny Chatmon, Vashti DuBois, Ashara Ekundayo, Shanequa Gay, vanessa german, Vanessa Johnson, Dindga McCannon, Delita Martin, Amber Robles-Gordon, Tokie Rome-Taylor, Dianne Smith, amara tabor-smith, and Lava Thomas. Your willingness to share your communities, family stories, art-making processes, and lived experiences has been invaluable. Your art demonstrates the power of Black women's art ecosystems as sites of wellness.

BLACK
WOMEN'S
ART
ECOSYSTEMS

The Intersection of Black Women's Artistic Ecosystems and Wellness

Let frustration fuel inspiration.
—Sonia Boyce

The year 2022 marked a pivotal moment for Black women artists, as numerous exhibitions featuring their work emerged in mainstream art institutions.[1] Sonia Boyce's phrase "Let frustration fuel inspiration" perfectly encapsulates the transformative potential of converting negative emotions into positive outcomes.[2] This theme is often reflected in the art of many Black women artists. These exhibitions culminated when the multimedia artist and pioneer of the British Black Arts Movement Sonia Boyce's award-winning British Pavilion exhibition *Feeling Her Way* won the prestigious Venice Biennale's Golden Lion for best national exhibition.[3] Boyce's exhibition featured the voices of Black women through harmonious choruses and sometimes unharmonious clashing sounds "set against tessellating wallpaper and golden 3D geometric structures."[4] Her sonic ambiance amplified Black women's voices in ways that "embod[y] feelings of freedom, power, and vulnerability," according to the British Council, which commissioned Boyce's work.[5] Her collaborators' performances were inspired by a single question: "As a woman, as a Black person, what does freedom feel like? How can you imagine freedom?"[6] The artwork that developed from these creative collaborations demonstrates that Boyce is a wellness worker whose sonic installation speaks volumes about the important work Black women artists offer to the world. A juror of the Golden Lion committee tweeted that through Boyce's work with other Black women to create a visual and auditory narrative that centers Black women's experiences, she "unpacks a plenitude of silenced stories."[7] This acknowledgment of Boyce's work and Black women's silenced stories on a global stage is a hopeful sign that people are starting to listen to Black women and that through visual art, people are beginning to see Black women in meaningful ways that give credence to our humanity. This is an important step toward Black women's collective healing and wellness.

This book sets out to bridge the seemingly disparate fields of Black women's mental health and their visual art to think critically about how contemporary Black women artists have been making art as a sociopolitical strategy to save themselves and others in their respective communities. Analogously, within the framework of *Black Women's Art Ecosystems* (BWAEs), the notion of wellness pertains to the physical, emotional, and creative well-being of individual artists. The flourishing of the entire artistic ecosystem is contingent on the state of wellness experienced by its constituent artists, encompassing acknowledgment, support, and provisions for self-care. This accentuation of wellness underscores the intrinsic interdependence between the health of individual artists and the vibrancy of the collective artistic community. Specifically, through an analysis of visual narratives, personal narratives, historical archives, and art-making practices, *Black Women's Art Ecosystems* determines how Black women artists facilitate wellness through creative expression and cultural knowledge. Furthermore, it explores how Black women artists strategically organize and mobilize in collectives and Black art spaces to facilitate a system of support and the overall sustainability of their work. In the broadest terms, Black women making art, in Black art spaces that engage communities and that speak to their own personal healing and wellness, are participants in what I call Black Women's Art Ecosystems (BWAEs). To continue this discussion, it is important to define Black women's wellness.

Wellness and Black Women's Health Disparities

The National Wellness Institute defines wellness as "an active process through which people become aware of, and make choices toward, a more successful existence."[8] This definition connotes a sense of agency and self-determination connected to wellness. However, it is important to explore how Black women secure wellness for themselves, given that the overall state of Black women's health faces critical disparities at a national level. Black women's health is worse in comparison to that of others when one takes systemic barriers into consideration. Also, this definition of wellness suggests that through self-determination and strategic actions, one can empower oneself to acquire a state of wellness. This book expounds on the ways Black women artists express that self-determination through their art. However, we must consider the massive challenges of race- and gender-based health disparities affecting Black women that self-determination alone cannot eradicate.

In an open letter to President Joseph R. Biden, Vice President Kamala Harris, and members of the National Health Care Team, four Black women CEOs of some of the nation's leading health care organizations, the Black Women's Health Imperative pointed out that in addition to the global COVID-19 pandemic, the Black community continues to experience health care disparities across all generations, from birth to death.[9] Some of these health disparities include chronic illnesses such as diabetes, cardiovascular disease, obesity, reproductive health issues, and mental health issues. The letter also explains that the social determinants of health are shaped by the distribution of money, power, and resources and that the lack thereof is mostly responsible for health inequalities. Adding to this list of health care disparities, the Black feminist scholar Treva Lindsey asserts, "Our health outcomes are historically bound and socially constructed by medical violence. It's not about social predisposition; it's about a nation's medical system being built on violence against, exploitation of, and contempt for Black feminized flesh and bodies."[10] All things considered, Black women cannot necessarily address these issues solely through determination and agency; it takes structural change and policy reform. The engagement of the four Black women CEOs with top government officials exemplifies how Black women have persistently advanced and maintained optimal health through policy efforts. These efforts span various roles, including academic positions, congressional roles, research foundations, nonprofits, and appointments ranging from grassroots to national levels.[11] This multifaceted approach demonstrates the strategic influence Black women exert across different spheres to advocate for health equity. Their leadership not only highlights their commitment to systemic change but also emphasizes the importance of diverse representation in policy making.

According to the World Health Organization founding document, the primary determinants of a person's quality of health are based on social, economic, and physical environments, as well as a person's individual characteristics and behaviors.[12] Advocates and health practitioners investigate Black women's health in the United States through an array of categories: access to affordable health care, disease prevention, mental health care, equitable responses to public health emergencies, sufficient diversity in clinical research, and legislative agendas that stymie the progression of Black women's health. National organizations such as the Black Women's Health Imperative report that the Federal Government has decreased investments in the care of women of color in general and Black women specifically.[13] This organization and others focused on Black women's health are committed to building institutional strategies and national policy agendas that advocate for Black women's health. Despite these organizations' efforts, there has been little conclusive progress in improving the overall health of Black women in the United States, a conclusion the Heckler Report on Black and Minority Health reached in 1985 but that remains true today.[14] Notwithstanding the slow progress on Black women's health, 9.5 million Black women are reported to be in good health, meaning they have access to resources and/or have developed and implemented skills allowing them to overcome physical and mental health barriers.[15] This glimmer of light begs the question, What specific strategies are Black women employing to develop wellness? For the purposes of this book, I explore how Black women artists contribute to these strategies, given that many of these artists demonstrate cultural grounding and social awareness in their art as commentary on the Black diasporic experience.

Culturally Appropriate Models for Mental Health Practices

As wellness workers, Black women artists challenge the structural and institutional race and gender inequity that has a direct impact on their overall health disparity. To gain a better understanding of this connection, we must first look at the mental health field and culturally appropriate approaches to therapy. For example, collectives of Black feminist scholars and various kinds of wellness workers deploy culturally appropriate models of mental health practices that positively affect Black women's mental health and wellness. Mental health practitioners focusing on institutional strategies and culturally conducive therapy see value in centering a discussion on Black women's wellness, but often this approach is facilitated by clinical or structured health care and community agencies. Both approaches to Black women's wellness, though necessary, do not necessarily consider how Black women have facilitated their own wellness in the past and present, as well as creating opportunities for wellness in their respective communities at a grassroots level. Carmen Braun Williams and Marsha I. Wiggins have determined that both Afrocentric and feminist models of therapy fail to consider Black women's diversity and intersectional identities.[16] Thus, traditional research on the relationship between Black women's mental health and wellness relies on challenging mental health care practices that are not culturally inclusive of Black women's unique experiences by providing models that are.

Indeed, the assumption that Black women share a common identity has long been the basis for mental health care practitioners who seek to provide services through a culturally conducive framework. Black feminist therapy and womanist therapy employ "strategies that integrate multiple cultural variables into a coherent sense of self."[17] Thelma Bryant-Davis and Lillian Comas-Díaz explore the psychology of African American women and Latinas from theory to practice. The psychologies of both groups "centralize the need to focus on the self-definition and art of healing of Black women and Latinas as they strive to survive, grow, and thrive in the face of multiple intersecting forms of oppression."[18] Culturally aware mental health practitioners provide services that speak to the experiences of Black women in the belief that race and gender are distinct. Janis Sanchez-Hucles posits that "Black women live in a world that still stigmatizes race and gender and other social distinctions that have led to the development of womanist therapy to encompass Black women who embody multiple cultural identities."[19] Expressive arts are one strategy that mental health practitioners use to integrate cultural nuances in practice.

When we consider the centrality of the arts in Black culture, "creativity has historically been manifest in African indigenous healing practices that . . . incorporate multiple uses of the arts in healing."[20] Danielle Drake-Burnette, Bravada Garrett-Akinsanya, and Thelma Bryant-Davis explain that "expressive arts have the ability to engage all the senses toward precisely clarifying the experience, which can be communicated through one or multiple creative modalities."[21] Similarly, Shanee Stepakoff argues that although many therapists find that the expressive arts are efficacious in helping patients identify and express underlying emotions, visual arts in particular have also been used to treat both physical and mental health issues.[22] John Bowles's research finds that Black feminist or womanist visual art has been used as a form of self-reflection for Black women while also stimulating viewer self-reflection on issues of race and gender.[23] Self-reflection is a significant strategy for Black women's self-care as they navigate trauma and oppression brought on by issues of identity.

Hence, *Black Women's Art Ecosystems* analyzes the representation of wellness in Black women's artwork, and how the contexts of their art and art-making process are strategies for healing. Most important, this book explores the impact of Black women artists on facilitating wellness for others by addressing socio-economic and political interests and demands through collective work and by creating safe spaces that support Black women artists and their communities. Drawing on both archival and ethnographic research, along with visual analysis of artwork created by contemporary American Black women artists, this book illustrates how they construct a practical model for achieving wellness that is versatile and demonstrates the significant role Black women artists and art, in general, have in Black communities in ways that prioritize Black people's interests. A practical theme among many of the artists discussed in this book is the opportunity for Black women to just breathe and take up space.

One incredibly important model that informs this study's understanding of Black women's mental health care is Stephanie Evans, Kanika Bell and Nsenga Burton's BREATHE model.[24] Their scholarship illuminates and broadens existing concepts of Black women's wellness applied by mental health care practitioners who are invested in centering Black women's voices and experiences.

BREATHE is an acronym for the defining principles Balance, Reflection, Energy, Association, Transparency, Healing, and Empowerment and is a womanist model for Black women's mental health.[25] By providing a breath or a life force to women who have been crippled under the weight of stress, depression, anxiety, abuse, trauma, and oppression, the BREATHE model builds on a metaphor of Black women's need to exhale to heal and thrive.

The key principles of this model give Black women the tools to engage in the process of restoration, a life-cycle change, and an increased understanding of Black women's mental health.[26] The principles of the BREATHE model help to identify what optimal mental health care for Black women looks like and how to contextualize Black women artists as wellness workers. Examples of all these principles are found within the interviews and visual narratives of the Black women artists in this book. However, both the Association and Healing principles are the most present in the analysis of Black women artists and wellness.

The Association principle includes Black women "creat[ing] and maintain[ing] social networks that promote, affirm, and encourage wellness."[27] Association is an undercurrent in understanding the impact of Black women artists' work in communities and artists' collectives. Black women artists create what are culturally referred to as "sister circles" to affirm and encourage wellness within the art community.[28] The appropriateness of using a Black feminist epistemology and a womanist mental health model to expand the conversation of Black women's wellness beyond clinical approaches supports the idea that Black women artists and wellness workers articulate shared values. It also informs questions such as "What is wellness? Why do Black women have health disparities compared with other groups of people? What are some culturally conducive models of mental health practices that can narrow those disparities? How do Black women artists cultivate wellness as contributors to culturally conducive wellness practices?" Similarly, the Healing principle has relevance in identifying Black women artists as wellness workers and how they look for ways to cultivate wellness for themselves and others. Taking these two principles into consideration, as well as how wellness is defined, it is equally important to locate where Black women artists' wellness work takes place. This research has identified that location and sustainability of Black women artists' wellness work resides in BWAEs.

Alternative Ecologies and Ecosystems

This book's use of ecosystems as a metaphor to describe the process of Black women's wellness work can be performed only through what the physicist Fritjof Capra describes as "systems thinking." Capra writes, "To understand the lessons of ecosystems and apply them to our human communities, we need to learn the principles of ecology. . . . The principles of ecology are, if you wish, the patterns of life."[29] The botanist A. G. Tansley, introduced the term *ecosystem* in a seminal 1935 publication centered on vegetational concepts.[30] In rudimentary terms, an ecosystem, or ecological system, comprises a geographical expanse wherein plants, animals, and various other organisms, alongside meteorological and topographical elements, harmoniously converge to constitute a sphere of life.[31] Within this framework, ecologists categorize living entities as biotic factors, delineating their roles as competitors, pollinators, dispersers, predators, prey, disease-causing agents, or mates. In contrast, abiotic factors encompass nonliving components such as temperature, moisture, light, and soils.[32]

Beyond its inaugural application to describe natural systems, the term *ecosystem* has found pervasive utility across diverse subfields of ecology and adjacent disciplines, serving as a metaphor to elucidate disparate community configurations. In the domain of Black studies, Nathan Hare introduced the term *Black ecology* to delineate the "ecological ordeal" that African Americans face in relation to their physical and social milieus within urban settings.[33] Hare contends that the authentic resolution to the environmental crisis lies in the decolonization of the Black race. Keelah Williams, Oliver Sng, and Steven Neuberg assert that ecology exerts an influential force, engendering stereotypes that, in the American context, supplant racial stereotypes by presuming characteristics tied to home ecologies.[34] Justin Hosbey and J. T. Roane examine marronage as Black ecologies and counter settler-colonial ideologies of ecological degradation, extraction, and accumulation by scrutinizing the land stewardship and environmental practices of Black communities in the American South.[35]

Malcom Ferdinand and Romry Opperman posit a stance in favor of a decolonial ecology as opposed to a decolonizing ecology. They advocate for a comprehensive reconfiguration, contending that ecological concerns are inherently intertwined with sociopolitical considerations. This perspective challenges the conventional dichotomy that historically has isolated ecological issues from antiracist movements, Afrofeminist demands, and the broader struggle against gender discrimination. In contrast to the more limited approach of decolonizing ecology, which involves modifying existing understandings, a decolonial ecology seeks a fundamental transformation of the conceptual frameworks that traditionally have compartmentalized ecological and sociopolitical realms.[36]

In the realm of racial ecologies, Tiffany Lethabo King explores Black life and ecosystems through the lens of Black fungibility. She contends that an eighteenth-century map of South Carolina and Georgia offers a platform for reimagining Blackness "as a set of ecotones, or transitional processes," fostering Black escape.[37]

An understanding of eco art is incredibly helpful in making metaphorical connections for BWAEs. *Eco art*, or *ecological art*, is an artistic practice that integrates ecological ethics into both its content and materials. Emerging in the late 1960s and gaining formal recognition in the 1990s, it is distinct from related movements such as land art and environmental art due to its deliberate focus on ecological systems and sustainability.[38] Ann T. Rosenthal aligns with Capra's perspective on "systems thinking" and explains that eco art inherently embodies a multidisciplinary and pedagogical approach. According to Rosenthal, eco artists integrate insights from various fields, including art, ecology, landscape architecture, urban planning, and history. Their endeavors encompass activities such as the restoration of impaired ecosystems, the interpretation of environmental and cultural histories, and the illumination of systemic challenges and potential solutions, such as remediating water systems within a city bioregion.[39]

Françoise d'Eaubonne coined the term *ecofeminism* in her book *Le féminisme ou la mort* (*Feminism or Death*). She argues that significant parallels exist between the patriarchal suppression of women and the subjugation of nature, resulting in environmental degradation.[40] Likewise, Greta Gaard defines ecofeminism as a movement establishing connections among gender, race, and class, critiquing ideologies that endorse the exploitation and degradation of the environment.[41]

The confluence of women, art, and the environment constitutes a pivotal intersection within contemporary discourse, illuminating intricate relationships among creativity, gender, and the natural world. Some scholars and practitioners have argued that ecofeminist art should focus on "Eurocentric capitalist patriarchal culture built on the domination of nature and the domination of woman 'as nature'."[42] Nonetheless, it is disconcerting to observe the conspicuous absence of environments shaped and cultivated by Black women from prevailing narratives characterizing the current state of this field. In contrast, *ecowomanism* is a theology that uses the experiences and cosmologies of Black and indigenous women to address climate and social injustice.[43] Ecowomanist scholars have carved a pathway that centers intersections of race and gender in relation to the environment.[44] For example, Melanie L. Harris posits that the theoretical framework "centers the perspectives of women of African descent in environmental justice and reflects upon these women's activist methods, religious practices and theories on how to engage earth justice."[45] Yet Black women artists' nuanced perspectives on and contributions to ecological dialogues, social justice initiatives, and community spaces are frequently marginalized or overlooked. Their artistic ecosystems, intricately weaving together cultural heritage, activism, and environmental consciousness, are vital components for a more inclusive and comprehensive understanding of the dynamic interplay of women, art, and the environment. Rectifying this gap is not merely an effort to address historical oversights but also a crucial step toward acknowledging the diverse voices and experiences enriching the broader landscape of environmental aesthetics and artistic expression.

Introducing the concept of Black women's art ecosystems as a theoretical framework, this book seeks to comprehend the interconnectedness of Black women's artistic practices, community building, and wellness. By scrutinizing the landscapes shaped by Black women artists and the narratives embedded in their art, this research expands traditional notions of environmental justice to include cultural, emotional, and mental dimensions of well-being. As a metaphor, Black women's art ecosystems extend the conversation of Black ecologies in Black studies and optimal mental health practices in mental health care and wellness disciplines.

Drawing Parallels between Ecological Principles and Black Women's Art Ecosystems

At the macro level, Black women artists participate in a mainstream art ecosystem. Yet at a micro level, they belong to Black women's art ecosystems. Metaphorically, BWAEs operate like natural ecosystems to the degree that these spaces are controlled by external and internal factors. Like natural ecosystems, BWAEs are "dynamic entities—they are subject to periodic disturbances and are in the process of recovering from some past disturbance."[46] Building on these basic definitions, the remainder of this book is guided by the concept of BWAEs, which helps to identify Black women artists' wellness work. Metaphorically, BWAEs draw parallels to ecological principles.

Six ecological principles help establish a connection between BWAEs and ecosystems in general: Biodiversity and Intersectionality, Interconnectedness and Collaboration, Adaptability and Resilience, the Cyclical Nature of Creativity, Cultural Conservation and Preservation, and Environmental Justice and Representation.[47] The parallels are as follows:

- **Biodiversity and Intersectionality:** Biodiversity and intersectionality are critical for the health and resilience of an ecosystem. Incorporating an intersectional approach to biodiversity is crucial for understanding the complex interactions between different species, as well as the human impact on ecosystems. The intersectionality of biodiversity encompasses the interconnectedness of various species and their roles within an ecosystem. The diverse interconnections within an ecosystem contribute to its overall health and resilience, highlighting the importance of considering biodiversity from an intersectional perspective. The complexities of biodiversity and intersectionality can be seen as key factors in the maintenance of healthy ecosystems. In ecological modeling, biodiversity is emphasized due to its strong correlation with ecosystem balance, resilience, and sustainability.[48] Similarly, within BWAEs, diversity in perspectives, experiences, and artistic expressions plays a vital role in contributing to the richness and vitality of the community. BWAEs encompass a vibrant and diverse network of artists, curators, collectors, scholars, and institutions that support and promote the creative expressions of Black women artists.

These ecosystems are vital spaces for artistic exploration, empowerment, and cultural exchange. At the core of BWAEs are the artists themselves, who artistically express their positionality as it relates to race, gender, and other identity markers. Their intersectional experiences create a diverse tapestry of artistic voices, mirroring the diversity found in ecological systems. Within these ecosystems are dedicated galleries, museums, and exhibition spaces that showcase and celebrate the artwork of Black women artists. These venues are abiotic platforms where these artists gain visibility among diverse audiences while contributing to ongoing conversations in the art world. Furthermore, exhibitions and shared studio spaces foster a sense of community among artists, allowing collaborations, mentorship, and networking opportunities among peers.

- **Interconnectedness and Collaboration:** Ecological systems thrive on interconnectedness, where different species collaborate with and depend on each other. This interconnectedness is not limited to the relationships between species but also extends to the relationships between ecological systems and human societies. Interconnectedness in ecological systems is further emphasized by the concept of socio-ecological systems, which acknowledges the close interdependence and interactions between natural elements and human societies.[49] Analogously, in BWAEs, collaboration and interconnectedness among artists, curators, critics, and audiences are essential. Curators and art professionals play an essential role in curating exhibitions, organizing events, and advocating for recognition and inclusion within mainstream art institutions. Curators also actively look out for emerging talent by actively seeking it out—fostering career development opportunities while prolonging Black women artists' artistic contributions for years to come. Additionally, BWAEs are supported by collectors and patrons who invest in and acquire artwork created by Black women artists. Their support not only ensures financial stability for these practices but also validates them as important artistic practices by showing them to wider audiences. Collectors and patrons play an essential role in raising the visibility and impact of Black women artists through actively engaging with their work and sharing it. Similarly, scholars and researchers also contribute by researching the artists' history, aesthetics, and cultural significance. Their work strives to acknowledge and preserve the contributions made by Black women artists, elevating their narratives and cultivating greater appreciation of their creative processes. The support and interdependence within the community form a network that sustains and enhances the entire artistic ecosystem.

- **Adaptability and Resilience:** Ecological systems are adaptable and resilient in the face of challenges. This is a topic of particular interest to researchers and policy makers alike, garnering attention from various sectors. One approach is through the lens of socialecological resilience. Some researchers, such as those at the Stockholm Resilience Centre, view resilience as the adaptive capacity of a system to recover from a disturbance.[50] Moreover, the concept of resilience in urban ecology highlights the system's ability to withstand stress and absorb disruptions while maintaining its essential structure and ecological processes.[51] Similarly, BWAEs demonstrate resilience by adapting to societal changes, addressing issues of representation, and overcoming obstacles. This adaptability ensures the sustainability of the artistic community and its ability to navigate and respond to external pressures.

- **Cyclical Nature of Creativity:** Ecological systems follow cyclical patterns, such as the water and carbon cycles. These patterns have a profound impact on interactions, population dynamics, abundance, and richness in various ecological systems.[52] Creativity in BWAEs is cyclical in nature, so ideas, influences, and inspiration circulate within the community. This cyclical exchange fosters growth and evolution, akin to the natural cycles that sustain ecosystems.

- **Cultural Conservation and Preservation:** Ecological principles emphasize the conservation of biodiversity and the protection of ecosystems. Biodiversity is at the core of ecological principles, as it encompasses the variety of ecosystems, species, populations, and genes in different geographical locations and their evolution over time.[53] Additionally, biodiversity is crucial for the functioning of ecosystems and provides ecosystem services that are essential for human well-being.[54] BWAEs require the conservation and preservation of cultural heritage and artistic contributions. Recognizing, celebrating, and preserving the cultural contributions of Black women artists ensures the continuity and vibrancy of this artistic ecosystem.

- **Environmental Justice and Representation:** Ecological justice involves the fair distribution of environmental benefits and burdens, taking into account various dimensions of justice such as distributive or distributional justice, recognitional justice, intergenerational justice, and reparational justice.[55] Ecological justice seeks to address the unequal and unfair distribution of environmental impacts, resources, and risks among different social groups. Moreover, ecological justice also encompasses the recognition of diverse cultural perspectives and the fair representation of these differences in environmental decision-making processes. Furthermore, ecological justice is concerned with ensuring that future generations are not unduly burdened by current environmental actions and that historical injustices are redressed to the fullest extent possible. The realm of Black women's art has a parallel concept of artistic justice, emphasizing fair representation, recognition, and support. This ensures that the benefits of the artistic ecosystem are equitably distributed among its members.

By framing BWAEs within the framework of ecological principles, we can appreciate their complexity and interconnectedness, and the need for conservation and sustainability. This theoretical concept highlights the importance of nurturing and valuing the diversity and contributions of Black women artists within a broader artistic ecosystem.

Overall, BWAEs are vibrant and thriving spaces that support and celebrate the artistic excellence and cultural contributions of Black women artists. Through their creativity, resilience, and innovative approaches to art making, Black women artists continue to shape and redefine the art world by challenging dominant narratives while inspiring future generations of artists. This understanding of BWAEs bolsters the argument that they are conducive to cultivating wellness.

Snowball Sampling: A Methodology for Wellness

The genealogy of my academic work began with my interests in visual art and the African diaspora. As a self-identifying creative who has made visual art since the age of five, I am intrigued by how people can create visual material from their imaginations. Applying this same level of interest to Black studies, I have similar memories from around the same age of being read stories about Black historical figures that fostered a love for the study of Black people and the African diaspora. Throughout my academic journey, spanning both undergraduate and graduate studies, I developed a sustained fascination with both art and Black studies, both informal and formal. Within the intersections of these disciplines, I honed my research focus, delving into the intricate realm of identity construction for Black women. My particular emphasis lies in exploring the broader issues surrounding our representation in visual spaces, encompassing art, visual culture, and mass media. Consequently, my interests in the topic of contemporary Black women artist wellness workers defines the methods from which I analyzed archival sources and chose fourteen Black women artists and curators to interview for this study.[56] Currently, I am a professor in African American studies and the gallery curator and executive director of the Community Folk Art Center, an African diaspora arts center located in Syracuse, New York. My work situates me in a community of national and international African diaspora artists. As a member of this community, I initially approached one Black woman artist, Lavett Ballard, whose artwork clearly reflected narratives of Black women's wellness. She and I worked on an exhibition in 2021 that led to introductions to and conversations with other Black women artists in her community. Ballard recommended other artists and artwork to examine, which in turn led to other conversations and recommendations from those artists, ultimately snowballing into collecting data from Black women artists who live across the United States. The snowball sampling method applied to selecting the artists interviewed is organically aligned with the BWAEs conceptual framework and its principle of interconnectedness. Parker, Scott, and Geddes explain that in a snowball sampling methodological approach, "researchers usually start with a small number of initial contacts (seeds) who fit the research criteria and are invited to become participants within the research. The agreeable participants are then asked to recommend other contacts who fit the research criteria and who potentially might also be willing participants, who then in turn recommend other potential participants, and so on."[57] Some of the Black women artists discussed in this book have collaborated in group exhibitions or are within six degrees of separation. Furthermore, snowball sampling is a convenient means of recruiting research participants when seeking access to hard-to-reach populations.[58] One of the major challenges that arises when trying to recruit artists in research that reflects the biodiversity of BWAEs is that they are geographically scattered. For this book, snowball sampling allowed me to penetrate a community of artists who are not only dispersed but whose vulnerability is often displayed visually, but with no guarantee that they would be willing to share such vulnerabilities in an interview.[59] My initial encounters with artists unfamiliar to me or with whom I had not previously collaborated became a conduit through which I could cultivate the requisite level of trust essential for securing their willingness to participate in interviews. What was most valuable about this method is that it proved the presence of the association principle and the interconnectedness of BWAEs, where each artist interviewed operates fluidly and demonstrates a shared value for Black women and Black community wellness.[60]

The biodiversity of Black women artists and their interconnectedness are guiding determinants of which artists are explored in this book. Formally and informally, Black women artists come together at exhibitions, conferences, residencies, and other supportive networking spaces and have established Black women's artist collectives modeled on their progenitor, "Where We At" Black Women Artists (1971–85), one of the earliest formally organized Black women's artist collectives in the United States.[61] Similarly, contemporary artists live during a time when technology allows them to be more connected and their work more accessible. Consequently, I was not restricted to a particular geographical space in conducting research. I was able to connect online with many of the artists highlighted in this book, in addition to meeting many in person. Technology provided easier accessibility to these artists, but I had other reasons for choosing them.

When I use the term *Black women artists*, I am talking about people who identify as Black and female, and this is limited to cisgender Black women. Also, the term *art* specifically refers to the visual arts, including painting, drawing, sculpture, printmaking, photography, video, filmmaking, architecture, design, mixed media, murals, and computer-generated art. Other artistic disciplines such as the performing arts, textile arts, and conceptual arts employ visual art elements that this book takes into consideration. Shelley Esaak posits that visual arts "are created to stimulate us through a visual experience. When we look at them, they often provoke a feeling of some sort."[62] I found it important to examine women who collectively represent most media found in visual arts in order to have a diverse representation of visual artists that matches the intensity engendered by these art forms. Further, I determined that I had interviewed enough artists to address the topic of Black women artist wellness workers when I realized that the Black women artists in this book provided representation for each principle identified in BWAEs.

BWAEs: Engaging Theories of Memory, History, and Visual Culture

In her book *Beyond Respectability: The Intellectual Thought of Race Women*, the scholar Brittany Cooper contends "that if we actually want to take Black women seriously as thinkers and knowledge producers, we must begin to look for their thinking in unexpected places, to expect its incursions in genres like autobiography, novels, news stories, medical records, organizational histories, public speeches, and diary entries."[63] *Black Women's Art Ecosystems* adds to this list the voices of artists, their artwork, and Black women art scholars. The scholarship on BWAEs is a critical endeavor that engages with the rich tapestry of Black art and visual culture. I explore the intersection of my work with the theoretical frameworks and critical voices proposed by Leigh Raiford, Cheryl Finley, Sarah Elizabeth Lewis, Deborah Willis, Krista Thompson, Lisa Farrington, and Nell Painter. By examining Raiford's theory of critical black memory, Finley's concept of symbolic possession of the past, Lewis's notion of groundwork, Willis's insights on photography, Thompson's scholarship on Afro-Caribbean art, Farrington's historical exploration of African American women artists, and Nell Painter's memoir on being old in art school, this review highlights how these scholars' insights enrich our understanding of Black women artists' contributions to contemporary art and culture.

Leigh Raiford's theory of critical black memory articulates the ways in which Black communities use visual culture to engage with their past and to shape collective memory. Raiford argues that photographs and other forms of visual art are repositories of cultural memory, allowing Black individuals and communities to reclaim and reinterpret their histories.[64] This critical engagement with memory challenges dominant narratives that have historically marginalized or erased Black experiences. Raiford's work emphasizes the power of visual culture to act as a site of resistance and empowerment for Black communities. Black women artists, through their creative practices, exemplify Raiford's concept of critical Black memory by using their art to document, reinterpret, and preserve the histories and experiences of Black communities. Their work often becomes a visual archive that challenges dominant historical narratives and asserts the significance of Black women's contributions to cultural memory.

Cheryl Finley's concept of symbolic possession of the past delves into the ways in which African American artists reclaim historical narratives through their work. Finley posits that Black artists engage in a symbolic repossession of history by reinterpreting and re-presenting elements of the past in their art. This process not only asserts ownership over Black history but also disrupts and challenges prevailing historical narratives.[65] By embedding historical symbols and references into their work, Black artists create a dialogue between the past and the present, highlighting the continuity and resilience of Black cultural heritage. In line with Finley's symbolic possession of the past, Black women artists frequently incorporate historical symbols, motifs, and references into their work, engaging in a form of symbolic reclamation. This artistic practice not only honors the past but also reclaims it from erasure and misrepresentation. By doing so, these artists assert their agency and reshape collective understandings of history.

Sarah Elizabeth Lewis introduces the concept of groundwork to describe the foundational role of visual art in shaping and reflecting cultural and social movements. Lewis argues that art is a critical foundation for societal change, providing a means of envisioning and articulating new possibilities for the future.[66] Through visual art, Black artists lay the groundwork for new narratives, identities, and cultural expressions that challenge and expand existing frameworks. Lewis's theory articulates the transformative potential of art in fostering social justice and cultural renewal. Lewis's notion of groundwork is evident in the ways Black women artists use their work to envision and advocate for new futures. Their art often addresses themes of social justice, identity, and community, preparing the way for cultural and societal transformation. Through their creative practices, Black women artists create spaces for dialogue, reflection, and activism, fostering a deeper understanding of the intersections of race, gender, and culture.

Deborah Willis's scholarship on photography explores the significance of photographic images in documenting and shaping African American history and identity. Willis emphasizes the role of photography in both personal and collective memory, highlighting how Black photographers and subjects use the medium to assert their presence and articulate their experiences.[67] Willis's work underscores the importance of photography in constructing and preserving visual histories that counter dominant, often exclusionary, narratives. She also explores how Black women photographers rehistoricize visual memory.[68] Her insights reveal the importance of photography as a tool for empowerment and cultural affirmation within Black communities. Willis's scholarship on photography resonates with the work of Black women artists in this book who use the medium to capture and convey their lived experiences. These artists leverage photography's documentary power to assert their presence and articulate their narratives, contributing to a visual history that challenges exclusionary representations.

Krista Thompson's scholarship on Afro-Caribbean art examines the unique cultural expressions and artistic practices of artists from the Afro-Caribbean diaspora. Thompson highlights how these artists draw on their rich cultural heritage to create works that address themes of identity, migration, and resistance.[69] Her research emphasizes the intersectionality of race, culture, and history in Afro-Caribbean art, showcasing the ways in which these artists navigate and negotiate their multifaceted identities. Thompson's work contributes to a broader understanding of Black visual culture by incorporating the diverse perspectives and experiences of Afro-Caribbean artists. Her insights further enrich our understanding of Black women's art ecosystems by highlighting the cultural diversity and complexity within the African diaspora. In this book, Afro-Caribbean artists' exploration of identity, migration, and resistance parallels the themes found in the broader context of Black women's art, illustrating the interconnectedness of these artistic expressions.

Lisa Farrington's scholarship focuses on the contributions of African American women artists, exploring how their work intersects with issues of race, gender, and identity. Farrington provides a comprehensive analysis of how African American women artists navigate the art world, challenge stereotypes, and create spaces for their voices to be heard. Her work emphasizes the importance of understanding the unique experiences and perspectives of Black women artists within the broader context of American art history.[70] Farrington's research highlights the resilience and creativity of these artists, as well as their ability to address social and political issues through their art. Farrington's analysis provides a crucial lens through which to examine the unique challenges and contributions of Black women artists. Her emphasis on the intersections of race, gender, and identity aligns with the broader themes of this book, highlighting the resilience and creativity of Black women artists as they navigate and challenge the art world.

Adding to this rich tapestry, Nell Painter's memoir *Old in Art School* provides a personal narrative that intersects with these theoretical frameworks. Painter's reflections on her experiences as an older Black woman in the predominantly white art world offer valuable insights into the challenges and triumphs of navigating artistic spaces that are often exclusionary. What is most revealing is how art school and being an artist changed her thinking as a historian. She writes, "Now what history means to me in images is freedom from coherence, clarity, and collective representation. My images carry their own visual meaning, which may or may not explicate history usefully or unequivocally."[71] Painter's memoir highlights the importance of perseverance, self-discovery, and the transformative power of art at any stage of life. This perspective supports this scholarship by highlighting Black women artists' use of art to transcend conventional historical narratives and create new and liberating spaces for personal and collective expression.

Although these scholars provide invaluable insights into various aspects of Black art and visual culture, my scholarship on Black women's art ecosystems addresses several critical gaps. Specifically, this book focuses on the interconnectedness of Black women artists within their communities and the ways in which these ecosystems foster wellness and resilience. By examining the collective and collaborative nature of these ecosystems, I highlight the importance of community-based art practices and the role of Black women artists as wellness workers. Furthermore, this book emphasizes the therapeutic and healing potential of art within these ecosystems, particularly for Black women who have historically faced marginalization and trauma. This focus on wellness and healing through art provides a unique contribution to the existing literature, offering new perspectives on the transformative power of Black women's creative practices.

The scholarship on Black women's art ecosystems is enriched by the theoretical contributions of Black women art scholars. By engaging with these scholars' insights on memory, history, cultural transformation, photography, Afro-Caribbean art, and the experiences of African American women artists, this book situates Black women artists within a broader context of visual culture and social change. These artists not only document and reinterpret the past but also envision new possibilities for the future, highlighting the critical role of art in shaping cultural and social landscapes. Through their creative practices, Black women artists continue to assert their presence, reclaim their histories, and lay the groundwork for a more inclusive and equitable cultural narrative. *Black Women's Art Ecosystems* builds on these foundations, addressing gaps in the existing literature by emphasizing the collective, community-based nature of BWAEs and their role in fostering wellness and resilience.

Exploring Wellness through Black Feminist and Womanist Epistemology

In an article derived from my doctoral research, "MeTelling: Recovering the Black Female Body," I wrote, "One of the major objectives of this study was to let multiple voices of Black women be heard through narrative writing and digital video art and to shed light on how they perceive their collective selves to be visually represented in popular visual culture."[72] I advocated for Black women to engage in a pedagogical practice I term MeTelling Narratives to challenge and correct the misrepresentations of Black women in visual culture by creating more affirming images. Black feminist theory significantly influenced my interpretation of how Black women artists reframe race, gender, and other "controlling images" in art.[73] *Black Women's Art Ecosystems* continues this exploration and articulation. Patricia Hill Collins's groundbreaking scholarship on Black feminist epistemology has been a guiding beacon in my analysis of Black women's art ecosystems and the wellness endeavors of Black women artists. Collins emphasizes the role of epistemology in examining the standards used to evaluate knowledge and the reasons behind our beliefs.[74] She contends that Black women act as agents of knowledge, challenging a "matrix of domination through counter-hegemonic knowledge" that enables them to define themselves.[75] The strategy of self-definition, a theme explored by all the artists in this book, aligns with Collins's framework.

Black women's practice of centering themselves is connected to *standpoint theory*, whereby theorists emphasize the utility of an everyday experiential concept of knowing. Thus standpoint theory supports strong objectivity, or the notion that the perspectives of marginalized and/or oppressed individuals can help to create more objective accounts of the world.[76] Standpoint theory also asserts that Black women are in a unique position to examine and critique their collective experiences in ways that members of other cultures, and particularly the dominant group culture, cannot. Black women can be and often are agents of knowledge regarding their experiences and can effectively challenge the status quo as outsiders within.[77] Patricia Hill Collins posits that individual African American women show varying types of consciousness regarding Black women's shared angle of vision. Yet, by aggregating and articulating individual Black women's expressions and consciousness as a collective, focused group consciousness becomes possible.[78] As an example, this book looks at individual Black women artists who articulate their collective experiences as Black women in the United States through art. Their standpoint is displayed through images and visual and performance-art storytelling, along with oral history narratives. Through my analysis of their artistic expressions, I find the collective group consciousness that Black feminist scholars describe.

In *Embodied Avatars: Genealogies of Black Feminist Art and Performance*, the Black feminist scholar Uri McMillan offers a profound contribution to the scholarship of BWAEs and Black feminist epistemology.[79] McMillan's work delves into Black women artists' performative strategies, examining how they use their bodies as sites of resistance and empowerment. His exploration of "embodied avatars" highlights the ways that Black women artists navigate and challenge oppressive structures through performance, creating new narratives and identities that defy stereotypical representations.

In *Embodied Avatars*, McMillan traces the genealogies of Black feminist art and performance, emphasizing the historical and cultural contexts that shape these artistic practices. This genealogical approach aligns with my research on Black women's performance art in this book, which also seeks to uncover the historical and sociocultural underpinnings of Black women's creative expressions. McMillan's analysis provides a framework for understanding how contemporary Black women artists draw on and transform past legacies to forge new artistic paths, resonating with my focus on the dynamic and evolving nature of Black women's art ecosystems. Furthermore, McMillan's emphasis on the body as a critical site of knowledge production and political intervention enriches the Black feminist epistemology that undergirds this book. By foregrounding the corporeal dimensions of Black women's artistic practices, McMillan underlines the importance of embodied knowledge and lived experience in shaping artistic and intellectual traditions. This perspective complements my examination of how Black women artists use performance to articulate and negotiate their identities, histories, and social realities within their ecosystems.

Both Collins's and McMillan's scholarship supports the importance of Black feminism in art education research and praxis that is explored in *Black Women's Art Ecosystems*. Furthermore, the art educator Joni Boyd Acuff argues that a Black feminist perspective in art education research "works to demystify the value of subjective theories and methods established by some traditional Eurocentric, Western paradigms and methodological approaches."[80] With that background, Black feminist theory paves the way for a deeper exploration of womanism, which further expands the discourse by encompassing the unique experiences and cultural contributions of Black women.

The term *womanist*, coined by Alice Walker, encapsulates "activism, spirituality, and relational empowerment" in a woman's commitment to herself, fostering personal growth and dedication to the well-being of her community and society at large.[81] Walker notably extends the definition of womanist to include not being a separatist from men, except in specific circumstances where it may be essential for one's own well-being or overall health. This perspective reflects a fundamental principle of womanism, which emphasizes the survival and well-being of the entire community, including men, while acknowledging the distinct experiences and challenges faced by women of color. This lends understanding to how Black women's wellness is connected to carving out time for the self.[82] In this book, I argue that Black women artists illustrate how their individual and perhaps separatist journeys to wellness are necessary and intricately linked to the collective well-being of their communities: the womanist theologian EbonyJanice Moore builds on the scholarship of Alice Walker; Dr. Delores Williams, the first person to publish the words womanist theology; Audre Lorde, who defines self-care as an act of political warfare; June Jordan, who recognized self-care as self-preservation; Roya Marsh, who writes poetically on Black joy as resistance; Angela Davis, who reflects on the importance of yoga and meditation as a form of self-care; and many other Black women practitioners of contemporary activism and wellness work. Moore contends that we are in a fourth wave of womanist thought that involves radical and revolutionary acts of Black women dreaming, resting, playing, and intentionally seeking the experience of bliss and pleasure. Her definition of womanism is "a sociopolitical and spiritual-religious practice that Black women use as a tool for both justice-making for our communities . . . and for ourselves."[83] Moore's definition provides context to the analysis of the art-making praxis and art content explored in *Black Women's Art Ecosystems*. These theoretical frameworks interconnect the discourse on Black women's art and mental health. My aim is to engender a comprehensive dialogue on the resourceful strategies employed by Black women artists to address their well-being, strategies often overlooked by health care professionals and systems. These strategies, along with collective consciousness, are often found at site-specific spaces: meaning their performances are created to exist in certain places that are considered when creating the artwork.[84]

Black Women's Artist Collectives and Art Spaces

Many of the artists explored in this book have shown in all–Black women exhibitions and also have been part of actual Black women's artist collectives. Taking it a step further, some of the women presented in this book have also established art studios, galleries, boutique museums, and Black women's art spaces in their neighborhoods. These provide not only a platform for Black women artists to display their work but also a space to address community needs through arts education and community-based art projects. I explore a few of these spaces in this book and provide details of how Black women artists engage in activism as well as creating spaces for healing that contribute to their wellness. Black women artists organizing informal and formal collectives is not new. The first documented Black women's artist collective in the United States, "Where We At" Black Women Artists, was founded during the Black

Arts Movement (1965–75) and the simultaneous feminist art movement. Black male patriarchy pervaded the Black Arts Movement and only grudgingly made space for Black women artists. Similarly, the (second-wave) feminist movement of the 1960s and 1970s was dominated by white women, who focused on issues and concerns that did not account for the unique experiences of inequity that Black women faced. To create a space for themselves, Black women artists who could not find opportunities or support in either movement formally organized professional Black women's art exhibitions. Another comparable Black women's art collective, Women of Visions, Inc., was founded in 1981 in the robust Black art community of Pittsburgh, Pennsylvania, and is the longest-running Black women's art collective in the United States. For over forty years, the members of this collective have engaged in a mission to promote the careers of and secure opportunities for Black women artists. Like Where We At, they have engaged the needs of the Black community through neighborhood collaborations and educational programming. Whereas newly formed collectives such as Tilla Studios (2017–present), located in Atlanta, are creating economic empowerment opportunities for Black women artists in the area as part of their central focus, all of the collectives mentioned as well as others demonstrate that "Black women's ability to forge this individual, unarticulated, yet potentially powerful expression of everyday consciousness into an articulated, self-defined, collective standpoint is key to Black women's survival."[85] The remaining chapters of *Black Women's Art Ecosystems* explore this articulation.

Chapter Summaries

The chapters in this book are designed and organized to provide a comprehensive exploration of the role of Black women artists as wellness workers. Each chapter contributes to a narrative that unfolds over the course of the book. The first three chapters explore artists' collectives and art institutions that represent larger concepts within BWAEs. This is followed by a more narrowly focused discussion of an individual artist's personal attainment of wellness through art and leads to other chapters focused on groups of artists creating wellness work that coincides with core principles within BWAEs.

When we examine contemporary Black women artists and their narratives on wellness in the twenty-first century, it is imperative to acknowledge the significant contributions of their forerunners. This particularly pertains to Black women artists who actively participated in the black power and women's rights movements, addressing sociopolitical challenges within the Black community that transcended gender considerations. These pioneering Black women artists constitute a crucial focal point for an enriched discourse.

Chapter 1 of this book amplifies the historical significance of the earliest Black women's art collective, Where We At (WWA, 1971–85), as an illustrative example of collective empowerment and wellness. It was a strategic response to the systemic barriers encountered by Black women artists within the art community, emanating from institutional racism and sexism. This exploration of WWA's community-based arts programming and artistic endeavors demonstrates how Black women artists have historically cultivated spaces of support, creativity, and advocacy to challenge exclusion and affirm their artistic and cultural contributions. This chapter also discusses the continuity of BWAEs and other twenty-first century collectives by looking at the House/Full of Blackwomen project, a Black women's artist collective in Oakland, California. Their practice of wellness also delves into Black women artists's agency in addressing individual wellness and the broader needs of the Black community through community-based art initiatives, underlining their commitment to social justice. Historical and current Black women's artist collectives are positioned as fundamental pillars of collective empowerment within BWAEs. These collectives are instrumental in creating collaborative spaces that facilitate resource sharing, mutual amplification of voices, and a profound sense of community and solidarity. The resultant empowerment and communal support contribute significantly to the well-being and agency of individual artists within these collectives.

The second chapter focuses on community engagement and environmental wellness. It begins with an examination of the history of African American art galleries and museums in response to the marginalization of Black artists in mainstream art spaces in the United States. Raymond Doswell explains that African American museums focus on African American culture and history, along with a mission of collecting and preserving material on Black history and cultural heritage.[86] Amina J. Dickerson makes them as much a political space as a cultural one.[87] Much of the writing on the history of Black art spaces focuses on museums, with the first one being the College Museum in Hampton, Virginia (1868). These spaces show the prevalent role that art has played in African Americans' development of formal education as well as in cultural uplift.

Building on this historical record, chapter 2 focuses primarily on African American art galleries and boutique art spaces that are either led by Black women or thematically showcase Black women artists and their work. Through the analysis of three site-specific BWAEs—The Colored Girls' Museum, Love Front Porch, and the ArtHouse—I argue that these spaces not only provide a platform for Black women artists to create and exhibit their work but also offer an opportunity for wellness, healing, and response to "disturbances" in the communities where they are located. Specifically, this chapter shows the significant influence stemming from Black women's boutique museums and other art spaces. Within the construct of Black Women's Art Ecosystems, a confluence of pivotal elements is discernible, notably evident in the integral roles of museums and galleries in Black communities in fostering new considerations of the meaning of environmental wellness. These institutions cultivate a harmonious environment where artistic expressions thrive. By providing a dedicated platform for the exhibition and preservation of Black women's art, these carefully curated spaces contribute substantially to the environmental wellness of the artistic community. They not only celebrate cultural diversity but also are sanctuaries that safeguard the vibrancy of Black women's artistic contributions, thereby enriching the overall environmental wellness of the broader artistic ecosystem. Chapter 2 sets the stage for the rest of the book, which analyzes the artwork and art-making experiences of contemporary Black women artists.

Chapter 3 continues the discussion on collective wellness with a focus on Black women artists whose sculpture and performance art are vehicles for memorializing Black people's collective experiences. These artists also use their media to usher in aspects of communal mourning that lead to healing. Some memorial art is a form of activism, advocating for social justice and change. Engaging with such art can contribute to a sense of empowerment and motivation for working toward a more just and equitable society. In this chapter, I expand the discussion of vanessa german's wellness-centered work, exploring how her *Power Figure* sculptures and performance art are powerful expressions of mourning and memorialization for collective Black experiences. This chapter also examines artwork by Lava Thomas, whose installations, sketches, and sculptures are resources to assist in grief and commemoration at the local and national level.

Chapter 3 offers an in-depth understanding of the important role of reflecting on and honoring the Black loss of life in facilitating healing and transformative social justice. During the early spring of 2020, most of the world was devastated by the global COVID-19 pandemic.[88] This virus is debilitating at best and deadly at worst. Like many other Americans in the United States, the curator and gallerist Myrtis Bedolla was unprepared for society to shut down in response to the virus. She was preparing to showcase an all-woman group exhibition, *Women Heal through Rite and Ritual*.[89] The exhibition was scheduled to open at Galerie Myrtis in Baltimore.[90] However, like many other public spaces, the gallery temporarily closed its doors under the state mandate and as part of the government's effort to control the spread of the deadly virus. This exhibition showcased seven women artists whose work reveals a confluence of African and Mexican diasporic spiritual and religious practices and approaches to restoring wellness on the physical and spiritual planes.[91] Although timely, the narratives and information on healing and wellness through "codified imagery and symbolism" became inaccessible to the public.

In her curatorial statement, Bedolla questioned the tenets of technological determinism that posit that technology develops independently from society.

Actually, when technology is taken up and used, it has a powerful effect on the character of society.[92] This theory overemphasizes the significance of modern technology by not considering more ancient and spiritual technologies rooted in "ancient and oral traditions, personal ruminations, and memories."[93] Bedolla endeavored to highlight an existence not driven by modern technology in *Women Heal through Rite and Ritual,* but how ironic that viewers could access the exhibition only online. For example, her website provided a digital art catalog and short videos of the artists discussing their work. The exhibition gained more exposure on social media platforms such as YouTube and Instagram.

While exploring the online images, I found a commonality among all the artists in the group exhibition. Chapters 4 and 5 analyze and discuss three artists from the exhibition—Lavett Ballard, Delita Martin, and Shanequa Gay. I credit Ballard with introducing me to the other two artists in the exhibition, and I collaborated with her in curating a solo exhibition. Chapter 4 explores Ballard's work and exhibition in detail as I analyze the interviews I conducted with Ballard about the works in the exhibition, along with art she has created subsequently that aligns with the concept of wellness. This chapter explores Ballard's attention to lineage and familial narratives, as she cultivates wellness through an exploration of self. In 2021, she showcased a series of artworks in two exhibitions that amplified her contribution as a Black woman artist and wellness worker. Continuing the conversation on *Women Heal through Rite and Ritual,* Chapter 5 offers a close reading of work by Delita Martin and Shanequa Gay, with a particular focus on how they use art to nurture cultural and spiritual wellness. Within the paradigm of BWAEs, artists play an active role in fostering and sustaining cultural and spiritual wellness. This symbiotic relationship is predicated on the interconnected roles of artists as cultural stewards, shaping and preserving narratives that resonate with the community's cultural identity. Artists also are spiritual facilitators, infusing their creations with symbolic depth and transcendent qualities that engender a sense of psychical resonance within the community. This interplay between artistic expression and the nurturing of cultural and spiritual wellness underscores the artists' pivotal role in shaping the holistic well-being of BWAEs. Recognizing the commonality of themes in their artwork, this chapter portrays each artist as a wellness worker who explores Black women's wellness in both the temporal and spiritual worlds.

Chapter 6 focuses on the specific medium of photography and how Black women artists create Black portraiture and use photography as a tool to foster wellness within an empowering aesthetic. Tawny Chatmon uses photography and mixed media to create portraits mainly of Black children in period clothing. She provides commentary on the vulnerability of Black childhood through the perspective of Black motherhood. Her photo-based portraits celebrate

Black youth while creating a space where they are protected and affirmed. Similarly, artist Tokie Rome Taylor also uses photography and mixed media to create portraits of Black children in regal attire as a means of affirming their identity and reclaiming their distorted representation in visual and popular culture. Taylor's narrative approach to creating a visual counternarrative considers African American Southern culture and the preservation of elements of African diaspora spirituality in the Black church as reference points of wellness. Both artists demonstrate how they use photography to address phenomena both past and present that affect the wellness of Black women and Black children. The representation of Black children in photography establishes a link to ancestral memory, creating a visual continuum of Black experiences that contribute to generational wellness, providing a sense of continuity and shared history. It reinforces the importance of preserving and passing down cultural narratives for the well-being of present and future generations.

Chapter 7 offers an analysis of Black women artists working in abstraction. Within the framework of BWAEs, abstract art is a conduit for cognitive wellness. The examination of nonrepresentational forms and expressions compels viewers to interact with art on a more profound intellectual and emotional plane. This cognitive involvement nurtures a disposition of curiosity and mental well-being within the community, promoting a plurality of perspectives and interpretations. Creating abstract art also offers a nontraditional approach to representing the African diaspora that influences the analysis and interpretation of wellness.

Amber Robles-Gordon is a multidisciplinary artist who works primarily with fiber arts to create a visual language. An analysis of her visual language is connected to her understanding of wellness as being an ongoing state of healing. Robles-Gordon's art also speaks to gender and race inequity. Originally from Puerto Rico, she immigrated to the United States at the age of five and lost aspects of her culture that she tries to recapture through artmaking. Dianne Smith is also a multidisciplinary artist of Afro-Caribbean descent. Although she was born and raised in the Bronx, her parents emigrated to the United States from Belize. Consequently, her artwork is heavily informed by the women in her family, who taught her basketry during her summer visits to Belize. An analysis of her work highlights how ancestral memory informs her abstract sculptures, created out of woven and knotted butcher paper to perpetuate what she calls newly assigned value when making art. Both artists in chapter 7 extend the conversation of BWAEs to transnational levels that deepen cultural interpretations of wellness and community through specific symbols and iconography.

Chapter 8 revisits an earlier conversation in this book, which began as an autobiographical and auto-ethnographic narrative of how visual art making and Black studies scholarship have been constant epistemological threads in my life. Both art and my passion for studying the African diaspora are conduits for my development of wellness. In this chapter I discuss how my experience as a Black studies professor, curator, and executive director at the Community Folk Art Center is another example of a site-specific space that supports (although not exclusively) Black women artists. In the context of BWAEs, the assimilation of community-based arts emerges as a notable contributor to the educational wellness of both individual participants and the broader communal framework. This symbiotic relationship encompasses a nuanced interplay of interconnected elements, which are subject to detailed examination.

The conclusion, Chapter 9, considers the implications of viewing Black women artists as wellness workers and the need to sustain BWAEs for the betterment of society at large. The conclusion also discusses the implication of major themes in the book and suggests future directions for the use of BWAEs as a paradigm to discuss the holistic health of African diasporic communities.

1

Collective Empowerment and Wellness

People always ask me where I have been this whole
time. I've been here all along. Whether through painting
or weaving, I'm interested in telling stories of Black
women who refuse to take no for an answer, who push
the limits of what's possible. The full breadth of their
stories is often cut short or overlooked.
—Dindga McCannon, cofounder of "Where We At"
Black Women Artists, Inc.

The Black women's artist collective "Where We At" Black Women Artists, Inc. (WWA) was established in 1971 and should be contextualized within the Black Arts Movement (BAM) and the women's liberation movement of the 1960s and 1970s. Dindga McCannon's statement that "People always ask me where I have been this whole time" reveals the political climate Black women found themselves in at the time.[1] Both movements came on the heels of an arduous civil rights movement, which focused on demanding racial equality and reforming the United States through the legal system. Although the pursuit of civil rights did not subside, by the late 1960s the black power movement was widely resonant. Black people shifted their focus to "racial pride, economic empowerment, and the creation of political and cultural institutions."[2] In response to racism and violence, Black artists were looking for ways to lend their voices to the movement. During this time the renowned Black artist Elizabeth Catlett was in exile in Mexico for her socialist affiliations. Catlett had been making politically charged art since the 1940s, during the Social Realism period, in various media such as figurative sculptures and had produced dozens of prints in support of the civil rights and Black Power movements in the United States.[3] In 1961, she asserted herself as a leader of the Black Arts Movement when she wrote a speech for the third annual meeting of the National Conference of Negro Artists. Her speech "The Negro People and American Art at Mid-Century" encouraged artists of color to reject the exclusionary and racially biased American museum and gallery system by creating their own all-Black exhibitions.[4] Her words would prove to be the catalyst for Black artist collectives like Spiral (1963). Spiral was a cooperative founded by eleven Black men, including Romare Bearden and Hale Woodruff, who later became juggernauts in the American art canon. Spiral initially formed as a response to the March on Washington for Jobs and Freedom in August 1963: "The artists came together to discuss their own role in the civil rights movement, the shifting landscape of American art, culture and politics, and to consider the role of the artist in the fight for social justice."[5]

The Harlem-based Weusi Artist Collective was founded after Spiral in 1965; its name means "black" in Swahili and is an example of how the collective embraced Afrocentric names, aesthetics, principles, and a focus on bringing art to the Black community.[6] The Weusi Artist Collective met Catlett's call to create Black art spaces and institutions when it established its own gallery, Weusi-Nyumba Ya Sanaa (Swahili for "black house of art" or "black gallery") and curated Black-centered art exhibitions for over a decade.

The Black Arts Movement was not confined to New York City. In Chicago a collective known as the Organization of Black American Culture (OBAC) formed in 1967. They are best known for creating the *Wall of Respect*, an eight-panel mural with fifty portraits paying homage to Black political leaders and entertainers. The mural was created by a group of local artists on an abandoned building on the South Side of Chicago. Creating the mural was also participatory, as members who lived in the surrounding community provided feedback, critiques, and support. The *Wall of Respect* and other activities inspired by OBAC reflect the collective's founding purpose and mission:

- To work toward the ultimate goal of bringing the Black Community indigenous art forms which reflect and clarify the Black Experience in America;
- To reflect the richness and depth and variety of Black History and Culture;
- To provide the Black Community with a positive self-image of itself, its history, its achievements, and its possibility for creativity.[7]

Similar trends reflecting race and community consciousness followed. Throughout the nation, murals such as the Detroit *Wall of Dignity* (1968); the *Wall of Truth* (1969), also in Chicago; and the Atlanta *Wall of Respect* (c. 1974) exemplified how artists of the Black Arts Movement created public art to reflect the political landscape and provide affirming images within Black communities.

In 1968 OBAC embraced Pan-African ideology, with an emphasis on Black solidarity and power. The collective changed its name to COBRA (Coalition of Black Revolutionary Artists) and changed its name a final time to AfriCobra (African Commune of Bad Relevant Artists). The collectives that developed during the civil rights and black power movements demonstrate how Black artists used art to participate in these movements. The arts were the soundtrack and backdrop to a shifting political climate. However, for Black women artists, the Black Arts Movement was heavily patriarchal and created minimal, if any, space for them to participate in collectives. As mentioned before, Spiral, one of the most prominent Black artist collectives, invited only one Black woman, Emma Amos, to join the group after one of the members, Hale Woodruff, showed examples of her work at a Spiral meeting in 1964. Amos, who had known Woodruff years before in her childhood and then as a master's student at New York University, reflected, "I'm not sure they invited other people by looking at their work, but they were very nervous about having a woman in their group, and they wanted to make sure I was a real artist and not a dilettante or something."[8] Amos's reflection on being the only woman invited to Spiral, and the group's nervousness about having women join, along with her having to prove she was a real artist, speaks to the marginalization Black women felt in the Black Arts Movement, where race was a more salient focus than women's rights.[9]

On the other hand, the women's liberation movement began in the 1960s as a second wave of feminism in much of the Western world. Women from diverse racial, cultural, and economic backgrounds joined to combat institutional sexism and advocate for equality for women through consciousness raising, protest, and reform. Although Black women joined ranks with white women, it became apparent that their issues with racism were not an area of concern for their white counterparts. Similarly, the women's liberation movement was harrowing to Black women's pursuit of equity. Although the movement sought gender equality, it often prioritized the concerns of white women, sidelining the racial and socioeconomic struggles that were central to Black women's experiences. This lack of intersectionality made it difficult for Black women to align fully with the movement, as their unique challenges were not always recognized or addressed. Black women "were often suspicious of the mainstream Feminist Movement, since its primarily White, middle-class membership was largely blind to its own racial biases and class privilege. Queer, transgender, and disabled women were even further sidelined."[10] Although not homogenous, Black women's shared collective marginal experiences spurred Black feminists into organizing and "[i]n response, Black women developed their own ways of fighting gender inequity and racism, creating organizations like the Combahee River Collective, the National Alliance of Black Feminists, the National Black Feminist Organization, and the Third World Women's Alliance."[11] These Black women's organizations and collectives began carving out a space for themselves from which they could communicate their distinctive experience, predominantly brought on by racism, sexism, and classism. For Black women artists in particular, actions aligned with the political protests of the time.

"Where We At" Black Women Artists:
Establishing Their Location

In the summer of 1971, the first formal Black women's artist collective, Where We At (WWA), was established. The group initially consisted of six women— Kay Brown, Jerrolyn Crooks, Pat Davis, Mai Mai Leabua, Dindga McCannon and Faith Ringgold—who met to plan the first Black women's art exhibition in known history. As a result, the group doubled in size to twelve Black women artists whose work included but was not limited to photography, sculptures, paintings, and mixed media. The exhibition ran from June through July at the Acts of Art Gallery, at 15 Charles Street in Greenwich Village. It was "a resounding success" according to Kay Brown, whose article in the *Feminist Art Journal* (April 1972) documented the group's founding and historical exhibition. Brown wrote:

> The theme of the show was: "WHERE WE AT"— BLACK WOMEN ARTISTS 1971. The title depicted the significant role of the Black woman artist and showed the community that we did exist—in numbers. Heretofore, the viewing public appeared to believe that the Black artist was synonymous with the Black male artist. Many of the artists who had worked for years had not been given opportunities for exhibiting their works.[12]

Brown's account of the founding of Where We At reveals a lot about the social climate that Black women artists faced during the Black Arts Movement. First, this collective's very existence was a political act that brought awareness to the fact that Black women artists were not merely the one or two who might be given space in predominantly male Black art exhibitions. In reality, Black women artists were both numerous and professional. The "Where We At" Black Women Artists collective also embodied many characteristics of a black power and nationalist perspective, one of which is self-determination. What is most instructive is how the group merged their artistic practices with community-based arts programming centered on social justice and transformative justice initiatives. When you consider the group's name, Brown clarifies, the exhibition was intended to emphasize the artists' close ties to the grassroots community, and its title was meant to evoke the show's general earthiness.[13]

The collective and the women's work mainly provided a visual narrative about issues affecting their community. The name of the collective also conveys the significance of Black women needing to emphasize their location. The group's proclamation continued the legacy of the Black liberation activist Anna Julia Cooper, who eighty years prior wrote, "Only the BLACK WOMAN can say when and where I enter, in the quiet, undisputed dignity of my womanhood, without violence and without suing or special patronage, then and there the whole Negro race enters with me."[14] During the first wave of feminism,

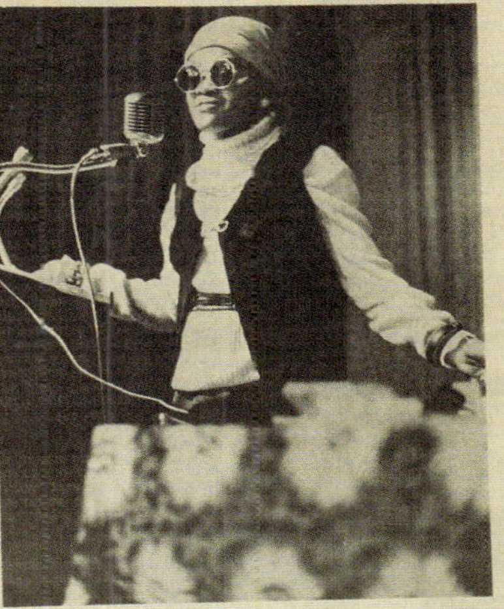

"Where We At" Black Women Artists

KAY BROWN

In the summer of 1971, six Black women artists: Kay Brown, Jerrolyn Crooks, Pat Davis, Mai Mai Leabua, Dindga McCannon and Faith Ringgold met together to plan the first Black women's art exhibition in known history.

The show was held during the months of June and July at the Acts of Art Gallery, 15 Charles Street in Greenwich Village. Interest in the exhibition was so great that within the few weeks before the show, the artists had doubled in number to twelve women artists including painters, sculptors, and photographers.

The theme of the show was: "WHERE WE AT" - BLACK WOMEN ARTISTS 1971. The title depicted the significant role of the Black woman artist and showed the community that we did exist--in numbers. Heretofore, the viewing public appeared to believe that the Black artists was synonymous with the Black male artist. Many of the artists who had worked for years had not been given opportunities for exhibiting their works.

The exhibition was a resounding success. The theme of the show was retained as the name of the group itself: "THE WHERE WE AT" BLACK WOMEN ARTISTS. The group was determined to stay together in unity to continue exhibitions and to develop projects to benefit the community.

At the time of this writing, the group numbers seventeen while inquiries for membership continue to pour in. The group wants to remain open to as many professional women artists as possible.

The members are:

Carol Blank	Iris Crump	Charlotte Richardson
Kay Brown	Pat Davis	Faith Ringgold
Vivian Browne	Doris Kane	Akweke Shingho
Carole Byard	Mai Mai Leabua	Ann Tanksley
Gylbert Coker	Dindga McCannon	Jean Taylor
Jerrolyn Crooks	Onnie Millar	

Since the first show at the Acts of Art Gallery, the WHERE WE AT group has had an exclusive show at the WEUSI-NYUMBA YA SANAA GALLERY, 158 West 132nd Street in Harlem. It was the first time in the gallery's eight year history that it had an organized group of artists exhibiting outside of WEUSI'S own group. The women artists also participated in the 1270 Women's art show dedicated to unwed Black mothers and the care of Black children, as well as the innovative PAX Bed-Stuy organization dedicated to the exposure, support and promotion of Black artists in Brooklyn. There are several other exhibitions in the near future, such as re-opening the EXPERIENCE GALLERY in Brooklyn, May of this year as well as the New York Public Theatre, the Community Gallery at the Community Church, the Langston Hughes Cultural Center, Corona Queens in April, and the Selma Burke Gallery in Pittsburgh as well as several others. The traveling exhibition is available for any persons interested. See below for inquiries.

The WHERE WE AT BLACK WOMEN ARTISTS is a real "coming together" of creative and talented Black women, unique in its philosophy of mutual support of Black women artists in the creative endeavor. The group is relevant to today's African-American women and is vital to the Black Community. The artists exchange information and resources for the mutual benefit of all and is dedicated to the cultural education and enrichment of the community.

For more information, contact:
Kay Brown
762 Halsey Street
Brooklyn, NY 11233

Dindga McCannon stating the six demands at the Open Hearing.

DEMANDS

We have six demands which we'd like to address to the Brooklyn Museum:

1. A Black Women's Exhibition
   --because there never was one
   --so that women should be recognized not only as Black artists, but also as women
   --because most Black women artists live in Brooklyn.

2. The museums should provide day-care centers or children's workshops so that mothers can attend classes.

3. The museums should underwrite projects and workshops relevant to the community.

4. The museums should provide part-time scholarships (as well as full-time) to women having to work during the day.

5. Any scholarship program should be publicized so that the artists could know about the program.

6. The museums should take an active part in helping the woman artist obtain living and working space.

Kay Brown's original article in *Feminist Art Journal* (April 1972), p. 25.

Cooper, often called the mother of Black feminism, insisted that women's rights and Black progress should be addressed concurrently. Her words above argue that gender and race "cannot be conflated except in the instance of a Black woman's voice and it is this voice which must be uttered and to which we must listen."[15] Furthermore, Cooper also understood that Black males modeled white male patriarchy and perpetuated the subjugation of women despite experiencing their own subjugation by white men. Fast forward to the Black Arts Movement and the women's liberation movement, and we find evidence of Black women still fighting for racial and gender equality. Despite both feeling the sting of patriarchy, one notable difference between Black feminism and mainstream feminism was Black feminists' willingness to include and work with Black men. Dindga McCannon notes that although WWA members were feminists, they didn't want to be segregated from men.

She recalls, "The main issue is that we were excluded from the Black art scene but also the world art scene. A lot of men didn't welcome us at the table but we didn't use that as a reason to exclude them from our lives."[16] Similarly, Kay Brown recounts distinctions between the content of art that radical, predominantly white feminists made, which "focused totally on sexism, in an often flagrant, bizarre fashion," like nudes with "blood seeping from their genitals," and artwork made by Black women at that time who did not identify as radical feminists.[17] Brown states, "In direct contrast, the paintings, graphics, and sculpture of the Black women artists related to issues defining the unity of the Black family . . . incorporated the idealism of the Black male-female relationship . . . [and] centered on African-related concepts."[18] Furthermore, WWA exhibited with Black men. According to the poster in the following figure, the 1972 exhibition *Cookin' and Smokin'* at the Weusi-Nyumba Ya Sanaa Gallery "finally made [it] clear that a cooperative spirit existed between women artists and their male counterparts."[19] The exhibition *Close Connections* (1985) featured WWA artists and eight Black male artists from the Weusi collective.[20] A year later, the exhibition *Joining Forces: 1 + 1 = 3* featured WWA artist members in collaboration with Black male artists from the New Muse Community Museum of Brooklyn. The title of the show "indicated an erotic symbol that suggested how the male-female relationship created a *third* thing that went beyond arithmetic."[21] WWA artists' willingness to collaborate with men as well as the content of their artwork suggest that despite the challenges they faced from patriarchy, race was salient. Still, it was exclusionary experiences grounded in sexism that compelled the group to remain exclusively a Black women artists collective.

In social terms, WWA "became a real sisterhood, working together on common aesthetics ideals and developing a professional closeness."[22] In political terms, the collective shaped itself into what is most notable about the founding of Where We At: challenging mainstream art institutions. Just as the Black Panther Party (BPP) created the Ten-Point Program, a list of demands of leaders of American society and an outline of the group's philosophical views, Where We At made a list of demands addressed to the Brooklyn Museum, one of the many mainstream art institutions that denied Black women access to resources and exhibitions and failed to acquire their work. Situated near Bedford-Stuyvesant and Brownsville, neighborhoods that were predominantly Black at the time, the museum's lack of inclusion was especially striking because of its close proximity to a vibrant Black community whose artistic contributions remained largely unrecognized within its walls. In an open hearing, the WWA member Dindga McCannon declared:

We have six demands which we'd like to address to the Brooklyn Museum:

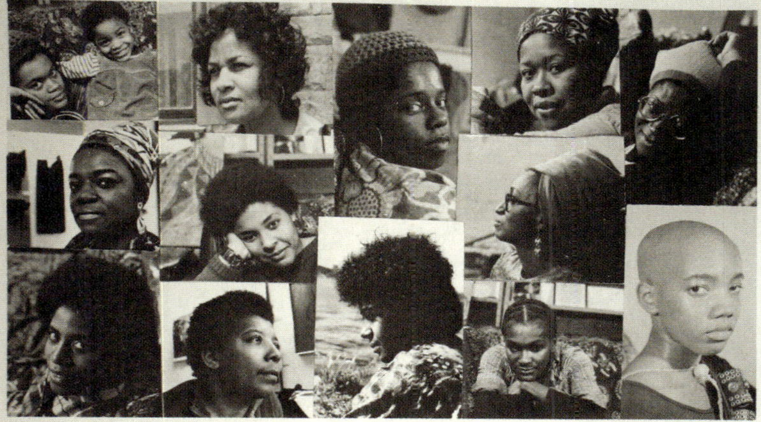

Where We At Collective. *Cookin' & Smokin'*, 1972. Offset printed poster, 14 × 11 in. Collection of David Lusenhop. Photo courtesy of Dindga McCannon Archives, Philadelphia. © Dindga McCannon. (Photo: David Lusenhop)

1. A Black Women's Exhibition

   —Because there never was one
   —So that women should be recognized not only as Black artists, but also as women
   —Because most Black women artists live in Brooklyn.

2. The museums should provide day-care centers or children's workshops so that mothers can attend classes.
3. The museums should underwrite projects and workshops relevant to the community.
4. The museums should provide part-time (as well as full-time) scholarships to women having to work during the day.
5. Any scholarship program should be publicized so that the artists can know about the program.
6. The museum should take an active part in helping the women artists obtain living and working space.[23]

WWA's demands established the philosophical view that mainstream art institutions needed to develop diversity and exhibit art from the community where they were geographically located and from which they accessed city funding. Furthermore, these institutions needed to address the social barriers that prevented them from being accessible to certain populations—barriers such as financial constraints, limited access to childcare, and recognition and equitable representation in relation to race, gender, and class.

Although WWA and many other Black feminist organizations made demands of mainstream American institutions, they were not holding their breath for change. For example, in the fall of 1978, WWA members conducted art workshops for inmates at the Bedford Hills Correctional Facility for Women in upstate New York and the Arthur Kill Correctional Facility for Men on Staten Island; they served youth recruited through Medgar Evers College, where Kay Brown was a professor, under the collective's founding apprenticeship program; and they offered special career-development classes in various art media, including graphic design and illustration.[24] As the WWA collective began to grow, membership was extended to Black women who were musicians, poets, and businesswomen. Dindga McCannon recalls one member in particular, Priscilla Taylor, an "amazing businesswoman" who took over the business operations of WWA. Taylor, along with a strong executive board of directors, secured 501c3 status for the WWA. This allowed the collective to qualify for grants that supported their work in correctional facilities, colleges, and community centers. I asked McCannon to elaborate on the activities that took place in WWA's community-based arts programming. About Bayview Correctional Facilities in Manhattan, where McCannon worked, she noted, "We taught multimedia workshops. We did everything from painting and drawing to quilt making and crochet, to jewelry making."[25] The collective was associated with a program called South Forty.[26] At Bayview specifically, they taught art workshops to women prisoners serving long sentences. The prison administrator at the time, who was very progressive, purchased a kiln for the ceramics program. McCannon recalls that the women prisoners would create ceramic objects and were taught how to make other things that they could sell and put on display in cases that the prison provided. The proceeds of their sales would go to support their families.[27] Documented social initiatives can be found in the Cultural Correspondence Organization's 1984 Directory of Arts Activism.[28] In it, a WWA advertisement reads, "The 'Where We At' Black Women Artists is a sisterhood of professional artists whose commitment is to self-development as well as serving the community at large. . . . We service largely the minority community and have conducted training workshops in prisons, colleges, community centers (youth and senior)."[29] This pithy statement sums up WWA's community-based art initiatives. It also shows the connection between the work that Black women artists create and the cultivation of collective empowerment and wellness for community. Dindga McCannon highlights the fact that most of WWA's members came from the community they served; as a group they were dedicated to giving back and making some sort of impact in the community.[30] WWA members realized the material impact that art could have when community members used the skills they learned, especially craft skills, to supplement their earnings or become

"WHERE WE AT"
BLACK WOMEN
ARTISTS, INC.
154 Crown Street
Brooklyn, NY 11225
(212) 756-1897
Contact: Priscilla Taylor

The "Where We At" Black Women Artists is a sisterhood of professional artists whose commitment is to self-development as well as serving the community at large. Founded in 1971, the members conduct seminars on black women artists, slide/lectures, art exhibits and arts and crafts workshops. We service largely the minority community and have conducted training workshops in prisons, colleges, community centers (youth and senior).
Members are painters, printmakers, weavers, copper repousee designers, photographers, illustrators, authors, gallery owners, sculptors, fibre artists, and musicians.

Where We At Collective. Advertisement in *We Will Not Be Disappeared! A Directory of Arts Activism*. New York: Cultural Correspondence, 1984.

their sole income. McCannon provided more details about how the collective organized community-based arts that focused on social justice issues, including murals and installations that she describes as the forerunners of the popular art installations that we see today. However, what is not often discussed in detail is how WWA artist members created art that improved their individual wellness and contributed to an overall collective empowerment.

By 1986, WWA had grown to thirty members. They had an exhibition at the Brooklyn Museum titled *'Where We At' Black Women Artists: A Tapestry of Many Fine Threads*. In the exhibition brochure, an essay written by Linda Cousins speaks of the WWA artists as individuals:

> As individual artists they have often labored late into the post-midnight hours, working intently on artistic expressions which would not "be still" until they had evolved onto canvas or into other art forms as yet another physical objet d'art was given to the world through themselves by the initial gift, inspiration, and prodding of the greatest Creator of all—the universal Artist.[31]

Cousin's statement primes readers for the brochure images and written narratives that reveal how art played a role in many of the WWA artist members' emotional and creative development. Consider Jennifer Bowden, whose pen-and-ink abstract art is accompanied by her statement:

> Painting has become a form of meditation, a way of knowing myself and growing inwardly. Art is expressing the inexpressible. After the birthing of a work, my concern is that the work will touch others at some unknown core and evoke strong personal emotions. This birth process is for my well-being; the artwork is for the people (the world).[32]

Bowden's statement explicitly connects making art to her own wellness and growth. She uses it as a meditative experience to reach an introspective state, self-knowledge, and reflection. Although Bowden intends her work for a global community, she separates her completed compositions from the art-making process, which she refers to as a birthing process that cultivates a state of well-being. As I combed through the brochure, I came across many works of art that give evidence of the WWA Black women artists connecting their art to health and wellness. The founding WWA member Kay Brown submitted a print, *Sister Alone in a Rented Room*. It shows a Black woman sitting alone in a contemplative state in what appears to be a slum environment. Adjacent to this image is Brown's written reflection:

> I am intrigued by the multifaceted nature of the Black woman artist, who is not only an artist but a wife, mother, and homemaker. I am all of these and as such, almost all my work reflects some aspect of the Black woman—the

daily life that confronts her, her moments of joy, her disappointments, and her struggles.

Although my earlier work focused primarily on this struggle, I have begun to depict a wider range of human emotions, such as cherished moments, dreams and even fantasy. I don't try to interpret my work intellectually. I am directed by a creativity that seems to flow and function independent of intent. It evolves and changes as I grow and as my vision of the world changes.[33]

Here Brown expressed the evolution of her work, which started off addressing Black women's pain and struggle and unfolded to show Black women with a full range of emotion, including joy, and the privilege of fantasizing about alternative experiences. The creativity operating beyond her intent suggests the spiritual realm that developed when Brown created art aided in her own growth and perspective and the evolution of her artwork as well as her emotional evolution; it gave space for wellness.

Another founding WWA artist member, Pat Davis, submitted a collage xerography, *Ritual Series: Suriname*. It shows Black women dressed in indigenous garb in ritual poses on the left and center frame of the collage; others appear to be preparing food on the right side of the composition. Davis's statement is particularly revealing about art and her connection to wellness:

Art is a way in which I can express my inner self and the space around me. My photos express realism by surrealistic means of the camera. I can record history, "the moment." My recent work is a combination of photos, Xerox, collage. I feel a very strong sense of the time, and I try to show all the positive, inner, mental, spiritual and physical energy that we have to call on our inner strengths in these trying times. Art has helped me express this.[34]

At the time this brochure was published, Davis's biography explained that she was "a photographic artist whose goal is to have photography recognized and appreciated as an art form."[35] Davis's use of photography as a tool to artistically capture "the moment" is linked to her goal of showing positive mental, spiritual, and physical energy. This strategy for wellness reflects her sense of empowerment and transparency through the photographic lens. This artistic approach to wellness has proved to be common among contemporary Black women photographers. In later chapters, we will examine how they endeavor to grapple with trying times.

Adding emphasis to why Black women create art for wellness' sake, Rafala Green explains, "The primary motivating force for my work comes from a growing conviction that there is a real need to reexamine, rediscover, and re-experience some qualities and values that have somehow lost their importance in a world dominated by material reality."[36] Green's pursuit of qualities and

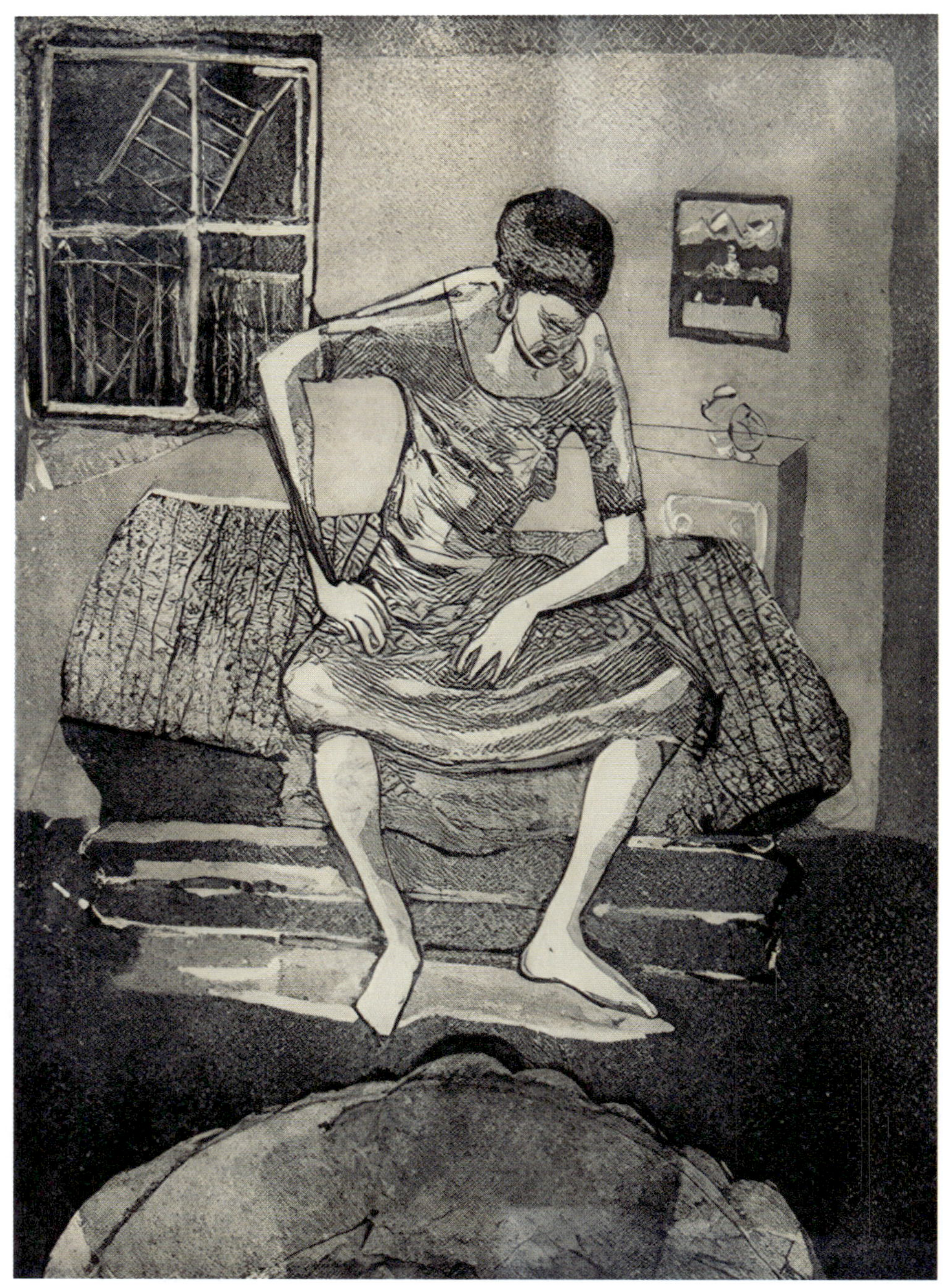

Kay Brown. *Sister Alone in a Rented Room*. 1972. Etching, 16 × 20 in. From the estate of Kay Brown.

values lost to material reality implies that her art-making experience, like that of other artist members of WWA, ushers in a sense of balance between the spiritual and temporal worlds. I find her particularly transparent when she states, "I struggle on a personal level as well as through my work, in order to allow a fuller expression of what is coming from within to diminish the domination of those influences which come from outside myself."[37] Green's words reveal that the internal struggles coincide with the struggles she experiences in the art-making process. Her reflection brings parity to her emotional state and the art-making process. The revealing connection between the WWA members' emotions when making art brings clarity to why the collective would also develop social-justice art and community-based arts programming to foster change in their community. Much of the sociopolitical climate during the group's existence expressed this theme directly and indirectly through a collective identity. The founding WWA member Dindga McCannon's artist statement arguably reveals this sentiment fully when she posits,

> The only degree I have is the degree I decreed on myself for trials, tribulations and a life confined to constant and sudden change. My life is my art. My art is most of my life. It connects me as one African person to all my African brothers and sisters throughout the world, regardless of what language we speak: We all understand visuals.[38]

Here, McCannon establishes a keen awareness of self that is anchored in empowerment and assigns value to Black women's lived experiences. Through art, McCannon navigated the world in such a way that it became a major aspect of her identity and how she conveyed her understanding of a Pan-African Black experience: "My work shows the everyday, the festivals, the arts, and the positiveness of Black people."[39] Creating work that affirms the humanity and positivity of people of African descent is deeply rooted in a Black power paradigm that many, if not all, the members of WWA subscribed to. However, as McCannon continued to explain her positionality in being an artist, she made a compelling argument about the representation of Black women and her need to address this in her artwork:

> A lot of my work focuses on the sister. I feel we are often the victims of so much bad publicity and typecasting that when others discuss us, they make incomplete sentences . . . so I have to let others who ain't hip know that the black woman is and has always been the true queen of the universe.[40]

For some, McCannon may have an essentialist stance concerning Black women's status as queens of the universe. Regardless, her words ring true about the negative representation that has plagued Black women, particularly in Western society. Also, McCannon appropriately includes the metaphor

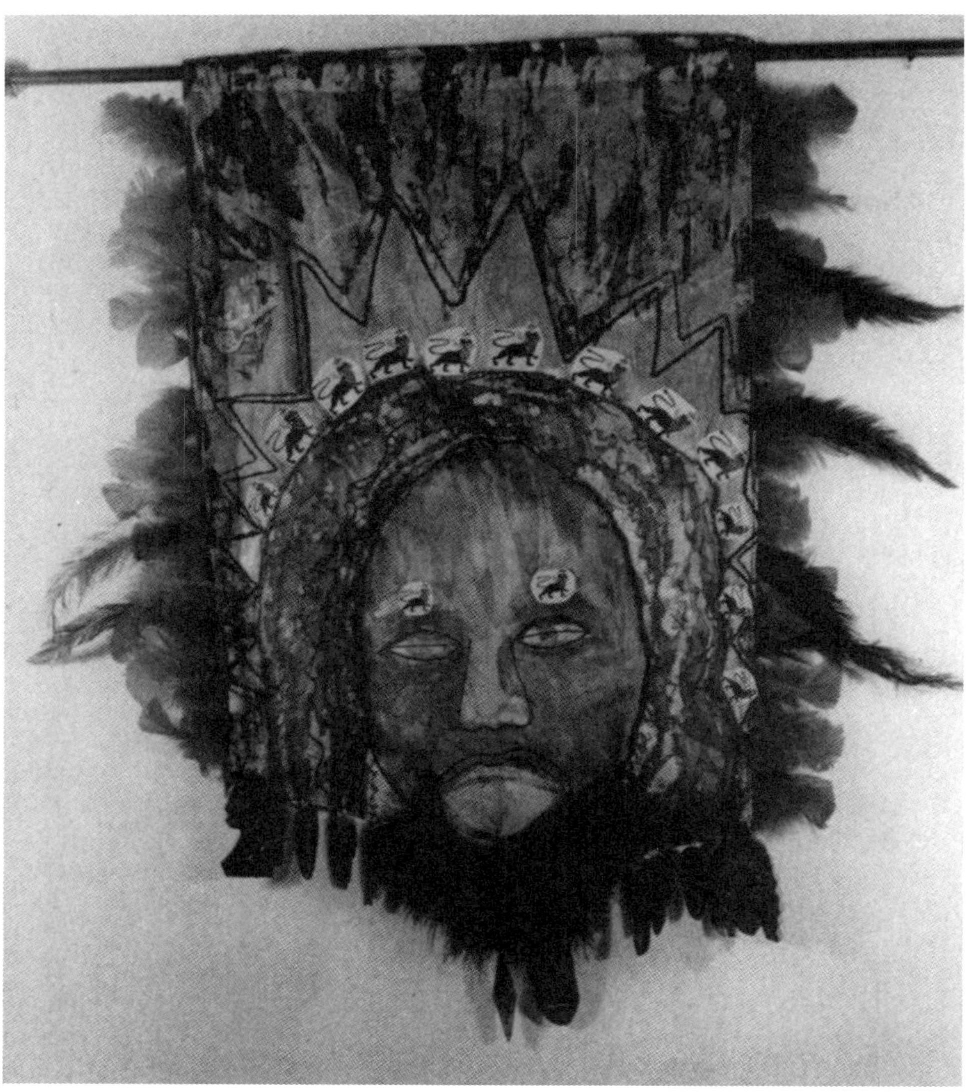

Dindga McCannon. *Memorial to Bob Marley*. Brooklyn Museum exhibition catalogue *"Where We At" Black Women Artists: A Tapestry of Many Fine Threads*. Batik and collage, 18 × 27 in. Photo courtesy of Dindga McCannon Archives, Philadelphia. © Dindga McCannon.

of linking outsiders' discussions of Black women as incomplete sentences: consider the fact that a sentence fragment is missing subject or verb. Within the conversation of non-African-descended people and particularly white people, Black women's true lived experiences of subjecthood are erased. This phenomenon is what compelled McCannon and others to establish and expand

Where We At. She makes this clear in the concluding paragraph of her artist's statement:

> As one of the founders of Where We At, Black Women Artists, I am especially proud of the achievements that we as a collective of artists/women have made and the fact that we have been together for over ten years, still growing with no end in sight. It has always been a source of inspiration seeing the endless, changing creativity and courage of the women as individuals.[41]

So far, this conversation about Where We At has been a launchpad for further discussions about the role Black women artists have played in facilitating individual and collective healing. The significance of sister circles supports the argument that Where We At demonstrates collective empowerment as a source of wellness. As mentioned before, Kay Brown admittedly found the collective's "real sisterhood" and closeness rare among Black women.[42] Her sentiments conflict with the many examples of sisterhood from enslavement to Black club women in the early twentieth century to the present. Still, Brown felt a void in the art world and answered it through her cofounding of Where We At. Through a shared lived experience of being Black and a woman in America, these Black women were able to build a social and professional network that promoted, affirmed, and encouraged wellness through art.

Although "Where We At" Black Women Artists may have been the first of its kind to be documented, Black women's artist collectives certainly do not end with it. The group had a good run well into the 1980s, with over fifty members. It made an indelible mark through its argument for resources and the inclusion of Black women artists within mainstream art society. WWA's work aligned with that of many other Black feminist organizations that "struggled against marginalization or suppression by the larger movements out of which they came."[43] Still, WWA persevered. Since its inception, many formal and informal Black women artists' collectives have developed. One notable group, Women of Visions, Inc. (1981–present), is the longest-running such collective in the United States. Founded in 1981, Women of Visions was established to provide both emotional and professional support for African American women working in the visual arts in Pittsburgh. The organization officially incorporated in 1990 and attained nonprofit status in 1995.[44] Like WWA, this collective has been consistently involved in the professional development and exhibition of Black women artists' work. The journalist Shannon Morris wrote enthusiastically about the group's 1998 exhibition *Apparitions and Destinations*: "What I got out of this virtual collage of Black women's lives, feelings, thoughts and experiences is something almost too powerful to describe. Not only was I thoroughly impressed, I was inspired. These were works that my people had created. I felt proud knowing that the authors of such things of beauty and power were indeed Black and female like me."[45] Morris's excitement was coupled with her discernment that this particular exhibition of "multiple styles" and "personal interpretations" aligned with what Lisa Currin of Highland Park, spokesperson for Women of Visions and a charcoal artist, explained was the show's theme: "[*Apparitions and Destinations*] was the result of one of the group's many brainstorms. We wanted to explore what the title meant to each of us personally. *Apparitions and Destinations* is about where we are personally and artistically at the moment, and each of our perceptions of where we think we are headed. It's about our own personal meaning."[46] Additionally, Women of Visions, Inc. provides community outreach in the city of Pittsburgh and is "dedicated to the transformative change within the African American women's visual arts community."[47] This and other Black women's artist collectives established in the twenty-first century share at least one aspect of their progenitor, Where We At, and all of them exercise the power of association that aids in Black women's collective empowerment and wellness. The continuing significance of Black women artists' collectives is worth exploring more in its contemporary forms, where a mission of social justice and Black women's collective well-being is a common thread holding these groups together.

Ashara Ekundayo Gallery (AEG)

Ashara Ekundayo Gallery (AEG) is an art platform and community venue that was established in 2017 and initially located in the Uptown/KONO Arts District in Oakland, California, before transitioning to an online platform and global pop-up venue. In its physical location, the gallery exclusively showcased contemporary art and new media works of Black womxn of the African diaspora, and artistic creations made in collaboration with Black womxn.[48] Highlighting artistic production across myriad disciplines, AEG specializes in displaying works that investigate and inspire social and spiritual inquiry at the intersection of fact, the Black feminist imagination, and Afrofuturism. I interviewed its founder and director, Ashara Ekundayo, who has been showing up in the world as a curator for more than thirty years. I wanted to learn more about the work she and other Black womxn artists are engaged in through the gallery. Specifically, I investigated the Black womxn artists' collective that spearheaded the House/Full of Black Women project, which developed out of AEG.

To start, the Ashara Ekundayo Gallery was a brick-and-mortar entity for two years and was the only commercial gallery exclusively dedicated to exhibiting Black womxn's art in the United States. While directing it, Ekundayo learned that the community did not necessarily need another gallery. Rather, what they needed was a sacred space where Black womxn could convene, mourn and grieve, to create and laugh, rest, and celebrate themselves and each other through ceremony and healing. This is what made this gallery a space for collective wellness; it was a ritual site. When people walked into that space, Ekundayo learned that many of them had never been in an art gallery. The gallery held space for a range of artists who were either emerging or established in their careers. It also had a space for academics and doctoral students who became artists in residence.

In further trying to create something to heal Black womxn, Ekundayo also established a curatorial residency. This coincided with the vision she had while working on her senior thesis: she decided that she was going to be a curator in the community as a means of healing herself. I asked Ekundayo if her work had evolved since she completed graduate school. She explained:

> It continues to be about that. And it continues to be about, you know, making space, like literally in the magical kind of way in which Black womxn make space, in the magical way that we do. I create a soft place for me to lay my head and for me to like, release. . . . You know, let me go fetch this water, and take a sip and bring us some peace.[49]

Ekundayo's description of her work reveals an enduring commitment and intentional self-care within the context of Black womxnhood. She emphasizes the timeless essence of a particular focus or purpose, stating that "it continues to be about that." This continuity suggests a deep connection to a fundamental principle belief that has stood the test of time. Central to the quote is the art of "making space." However, this isn't a mere physical act; it carries profound symbolic and emotional weight. Ekundayo alludes to a magical quality inherent in the way Black women "make space." This hints at a unique and mystical ability to shape and influence their surroundings, reflecting the resilience, creativity, and transformative power often associated with Black women.

The act of creating a "soft place" emerges as a pivotal theme. It signifies a deliberate effort to craft a nurturing and comfortable environment, extending beyond the physical to embrace emotional and mental spaces. The metaphorical laying down of one's head becomes a moment of rest and rejuvenation, embodying the concept of intentional self-care. This leads to a poignant moment in her reflection when she mentions fetching water. Beyond its literal significance, this act is a symbol of care and sustenance. Ekundayo envisions bringing peace through small, seemingly mundane actions, highlighting the transformative power of everyday rituals.

Ekundayo also weaves together personal and collective elements. The use of pronouns such as "me" and "us" underscores a connection between individual well-being and a broader community context. Her actions are not only for personal benefit but also as contributions to the well-being of a collective, reflecting a communal spirit. Consequently, from the interactions and discussions at AEG, a Black womxn's artist collective called See Black Womxn was formed to continue the work in the San Francisco community.

Ekundayo, a cofounder of the collective See Black Womxn, has seen the initiative expand beyond its initial stages, continuing to develop as a powerful space for showcasing and supporting Black womxn artists. However, the catalyst for the collective was Lava Thomas's sculpture design for a Maya Angelou monument. After approval by the San Francisco Art Commission, the design suddenly was scrapped when "city officials rejected Thomas's design, saying the artist's book-shaped sculpture etched with an image of Angelou's face wasn't what they had in mind: a traditional, figurative statue of the poet."[50] This collective is one of many examples of how Black womxn artists in the Bay Area are organically organizing BWAEs. Ekundayo explains that during one of the last artist's talks at the physical AEG location, featuring the work of Lava Thomas, a conversation ensued on the curatorial work that Ekundayo previously did in East Africa. Ekundayo was part of a curatorial team at Yerba Buena Center for the Arts (YBCA) in San Francisco, earlier in 2020. She had just gotten back from a month in East Africa, working on a census, and was in the middle of installing an exhibition when a shelter-in-place mandate was enacted in response to the rapid spread of COVID-19 in the United States. Part of the exhibition was installed, but other art was still in crates on a dock. Society was at a standstill; institutions like the YBCA had to shut down.

This new reality caused Ekundayo and her curatorial team to develop on-the-spot programming in digital spaces. One of the things that they started to talk about was inviting Black womxn to defend themselves, to be counted, to stand up. And this, according to Ekundayo, is connected to the ongoing problem of Black womxn not being cited, our work not being acknowledged, our labor not being elevated or amplified. She posits, "You know, it's like 'See Black womxn!' Do you, we're telling you, again, you know what we are demanding."[51] Ekundayo's recognition of Black womxn not being cited resonates with the campaign #CiteBlackWomen, founded by Christen A. Smith in 2017. This campaign is "a movement that engages with social media and aesthetic representation (t-shirts) to push people to critically rethink the politics of knowledge production by engaging in a radical praxis of citation that acknowledges and honors Black women's transnational intellectual production."[52] Another campaign, #CiteASista, also advocates for the citation of Black women. It was cofounded in 2016 by Brittany Williams and Joan Collier, and "was launched as a once-monthly Twitter [now X] chat that serves as a space to uplift and center the voices and contributions of Black women in the U.S.A. & abroad."[53] Both initiatives, along with the work occurring at the Ekundayo Gallery, show how Black womxn are committed to centering our knowledge production. Their work also sheds light on how Black womxn artists create ecosystems where we see and cite Black womxn, even if others do not. Ekundayo added that conversation to the census exhibition in the citywide campaign in San Francisco. One goal of the exhibition was to hold two conversations at Yerba Buena Center for the Arts, but in response to the shelter-in-place mandate, they moved the forum online. Ekundayo invited eight Black womxn visual artists into a conversation around visibility. One week featured four womxn artists and the next week the other four. Afterward, the conversations were posted on the YBCA YouTube channel. These conversations evolved into a series called BLATANT that highlights conversations with Black womxn who are creative artists. Not all are visual artists; some are also movement artists and on writers' boards, and new media artists as well.

BLATANT is both a forum and a zine on art, beauty, joy, and rage that developed in response to the current social climate. Ekundayo states,

> What we're looking at is like, you know, blatant joy, blatant rage, blatant outrage, you know. Everything that has been engaged. . . . Everything that we're looking at and exploring and experiencing is so blatant now. There's no under the tongue, there's no, you know, under your breath. It's just like, "Did you just call her. . . . What did you just do?" You know? Everybody's just running up on people, just metaphorically and sometimes physically punching them in the face.[54]

In response to blatant forms of racism, sexism, and other social injustices, artists participating in this series demanded justice. Over time, artists like Shanequa Gay, who is discussed in a subsequent chapter, became part of a BLATANT forum that addressed how her work and imagination give insight on healing. I was already impressed by the work that Ekundayo and other members of See Black Womxn are doing in San Francisco, but the curator wanted to turn my attention to another group of Black women artists creating multi-site-specific art to cultivate wellness and social justice in their environment.

Deep Waters Dance Theater and House/Full of Blackwomen

Before discussing the project House/Full of Blackwomen, it's important to gain insight on one of its founders. amara tabor-smith is a choreographer and performance maker and the artistic director of Deep Waters Dance Theater.[55] I met her for an interview at Stanford University's Institute for Diversity in the Arts (IDA), where she is currently an artist in residence. We began our conversation on a comfortable couch in the IDA living room, a space that felt familiar as I noticed the African diaspora artwork on the walls, decor that emphasized that this was a creative and culturally conducive space for both of us. At that time, we were surrounded by the movements of students, artists getting ready for the Black Star Film Festival, people carrying food to the kitchen, and the DJ setting up his turntables. A growing crowd was assembling on the front lawn of the center. We moved upstairs to a quiet space where we could talk uninterrupted. Since tabor-smith's medium is dance, I asked her to share her journey as an artist. She responded that she has been performing theater professionally since the age of thirteen. She studied under and was greatly influenced by Ed Mock, a queer Black man who was an improvisational dancer, choreographer, and founder of the West Coast Dance Company and Ed Mock Dancers in the Bay Area. She came across Ed Mock serendipitously through a friend who came to visit her for the summer while taking acting classes in San Francisco. The friend encouraged her to take Ed Mock's dance class and compelled tabor-smith to come with her to the class. She recounts, "The memory is so clear in my mind of walking in the studio full of dancers. And then he, as the teacher, walked in the room, and literally his presence had such a deep impact on me. It was like, oh, this is what God feels like. And so, I felt like I was in the presence of God."[56] From there, Mock trained tabor-smith as a dancer and gave her the first experience where she witnessed and felt someone was channeling Spirit through movement. tabor-smith recalls how Mock embodied characters whom he would be dancing and performing. Recognizing that Mock was channeling Spirit, tabor-smith said, "I recognized it then and I still see so clearly. He was the first one to show me what is possible."[57] tabor-smith's first reference to "Spirit" in our conversation was a hint at her belief in the Yoruba religion. Like many other polytheistic traditional African religious beliefs, Yoruba tradition holds that there is a supreme creative force called Spirit, encompassing the universe.[58] Consequently, tabor-smith reveals that at the age of thirteen, "I learned movement is something other than the surface."[59] tabor-smith ended up dancing with Ed Mock until she was twenty-one, when he passed away from complications due to HIV/AIDS. She acknowledges that his spirit and influence are still with her.

tabor-smith had another impactful experience when she joined the Brooklyn-based dance company Urban Bush Women in 1996.[60] She was with them on and off for ten years; in her last two years with the company, she became the associate artistic director. Being a member of Urban Bush Women taught tabor-smith what community-engaged art practices look like through their strategic investment in connecting to the communities where their performances occurred. They offered free workshops to the community to ensure that Black people showed up more often to performances and events. tabor-smith admits, "I am a patchwork quilt of all the people that have influenced me. Just as I am the breathing manifestation of my ancestors' work."[61] Consequently, tabor-smith has integrated community engagement around her dance practice. Her work with Urban Bush Women also led her to realize that she needed to go back home to San Francisco, where her networks of support were, and start making her own work.

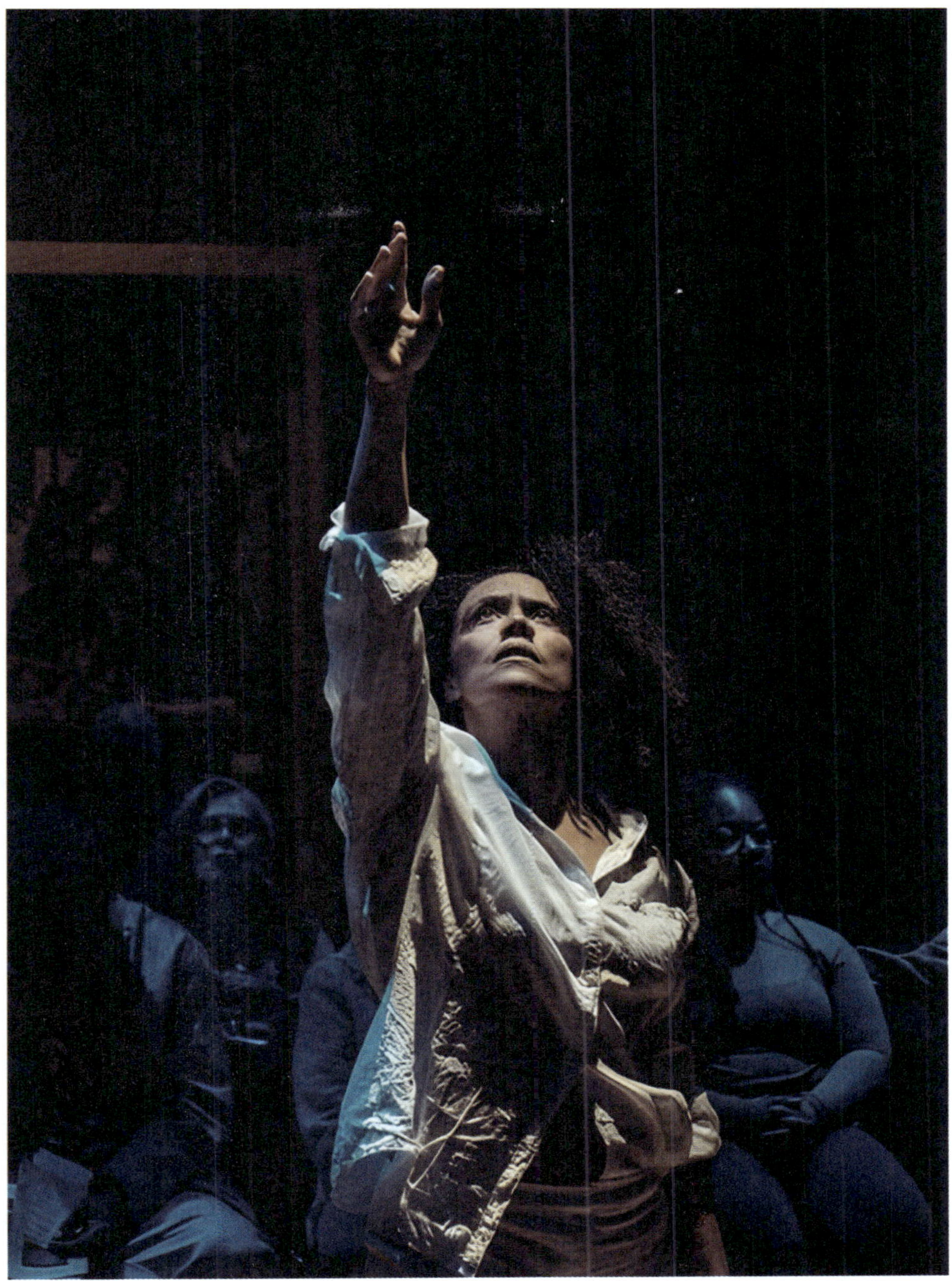

amara tabor-smith in *Passing Through the Great Middle Passage*. HFBW, episode 11, February, 2018. Photo by Robbie Sweeny.

tabor-smith now resides in Oakland. Before her return, she was already initiated as a practitioner in the Yoruba tradition, and it was important for her to be back close to her spiritual family. During our conversation, tabor-smith explained, "My spiritual practice is always the underpinning of what I do, and initially I had questions about what it means to bring one's spirituality to the forefront of their work."[62] Her questioning was based on her own upbringing and what she describes as the dogma of Christianity, which never really resonated with her. Her position is that everyone chooses their spiritual path. When it comes to her artwork, she is not trying to guide anyone in any direction. In fact, for many years she kept her spiritual belief system hidden from others so that they would not feel like she was trying to indoctrinate them. Nevertheless, she used her spiritual beliefs "as the underpinning support for [herself]."[63] At other moments, tabor-smith's spiritual beliefs connected with those of other artists and she felt aligned and accepted. These moments became the building blocks for her to start her own dance company, Deep Waters Dance Theater.

Deep Waters Dance Theater has an intentional focus. All the performers have always been women of color and predominantly African American or of African descent and the diaspora. tabor-smith's main reason for this was that "I felt like for the depth of the work that I wanted to do with people, I wanted to do so with people who understand the issues I want to address based on our shared experience. . . . [T]here's a lot of healing work we need to do with each other."[64] A lot of the healing tabor-smith and other performers address is connected to the impact of racism, inequity, oppression, and internalized inferiority that women of color experience. Performers in Deep Waters Dance Theater are constantly unpacking inequity with an understanding that "if you're not constantly unpacking it, then you're not dealing with the issues" and that "in multicultural settings where there are people who identify as white, their comfort always gets prioritized in the healing experience."[65] These were two important determinants for creating a predominantly Black-woman-centered dance theater company.

I asked tabor-smith what healing and wellness look like. Her answer is that the two are continuous because "healing is a verb. The healing process is a process, it is in action, it is a commitment to dismantling internalized and exteriorized forms of oppression."[66] As tabor-smith and I continued to talk about healing, she used descriptive metaphors that revealed her belief that healing is a journey and a commitment to a deeper level of liberation. Her philosophical understanding of healing and praxis through dance discloses what she and members of her dance company endeavor to do through site-specific work: to find liberation in the moment and to constantly work through oppressive systems that women of color are tethered to and yet must survive within. My conversation with tabor-smith was clarifying for the work I came across on social media platforms when it came to a very specific project, House/Full of Blackwomen.

amara tabor-smith created the House/Full of Blackwomen project in 2015 in collaboration with the director Ellen Sebastian Chang and a collective of Black women artists as a "a multi-site, multi-media, ritual dance theater project addressing the displacement, well-being and sex-trafficking of Black women and girls in Oakland."[67] Participants engaged in social practice and ritual work in a series of episodes over an eight-year period (2015–23). Their public performances demonstrated the effect of community engagement and collective wellness. The collective operated in the dark or underground and presented work that was intense and focused on healing at site-specific locations, according to tabor-smith.[68] Much of the work that occurred in the House/Full of Blackwomen project has been documented via film and archived on YouTube. They have also received national awards and fellowships in recognition of their work. Regarding the wellness of Black women, the collective created an entire series around Black women's rest, called *Black Women Dreaming*. This series involved a several-year invitation for Black women to take naps and rest in a space with other Black women. Rest for Black women is a revolutionary endeavor. This collective insisted that Black women rest when some of its members started searching for images of Black women resting or in forms of leisure throughout history but found very few images in archives or online.

The visual absence of this narrative inspired the collective to create an archive and an opportunity for Black women literally to sleep. Black women in the community would schedule a nap in the middle of the day in a house located in West Oakland. Conceptually, this performance was radical and ceremonial in its call for Black women to rest and to take care of each other— and themselves first. In addition, this community project was an invitation for self-care and wellness that has expanded to other issues that Black women are facing in Oakland.

One of the main House/Full of Blackwomen projects addressed sex trafficking of Black, brown, and Indigenous women and girls in Oakland and San Francisco. This geographical location is listed as number one for sex trafficking in the country. Girls are kidnapped and forced into prostitution. The House/Full of Blackwomen project reframed abolition work. Part of the ritual of this reframing occurred every Thursday when members went out in the community under the leadership of Regina Evans, a sex-trafficking survivor, to create altars along "the track."[69] At these altars the collective left personal protection equipment (PPE), water, and snacks, as well as flowers. They also made art along the sidewalk leading to the Eastside Arts Alliance & Cultural Center.[70] The collective's work is a form of *artivism*, defined as art used to promote "critical consciousness and social change." It aligns with Chela Sandoval and Guisela Latorre's position that "spoken word, street art, indigenous murals, protesting, altar making, and other creative forms are Chicana/Latina examples of artivism."[71] The same artivism activities extend to Black women and Womanist artists who are deeply engaged in connecting these artistic practices to African diasporic cultural overtones. Ekundayo shared with me that the collective's artivism for trafficked sex workers in the Bay Area was its way of saying, "We see you, you are loved, and we are thinking of you."[72] These messages are especially important for these girls because they cannot get out of the sex trafficking rings. A pop-up brothel was located across the street from the Eastside Arts Alliance & Cultural Center, though it is unclear if it is still in operation. Men ran in and out of this storefront building, an inverse to wellness. Sometimes the collective and other participants watched girls walk down the street naked. Sometimes the girls would stop and talk to members of the collective as they built altars along the sidewalk every Thursday. Regina Evans, "a modern day abolitionist in the fight against child sex trafficking," used her skills as a seamstress, actress, and poet to create a space called Regina's Door, an Oakland-based vintage store which operates as a creative arts healing space for young survivors of sex trafficking.[73] She worked alongside amara tabor-smith to create Conjure and Mend, "a sewing salon for young survivors to learn the art of costuming."[74] The name of this space is fitting because both stitching and healing take place within the group's work.

tabor-smith has been the Eastside Arts Alliance's North Star for what collective wellness and site-specific Black women's ritual work looks like through the lens of Afro-Surrealist conjure art, a spiritually grounded practice that merges performance, visual art, and ancestral traditions to invoke healing, transformation, and resistance. Ekundayo explained that the collective exhibited in AEG for seven weeks, transforming it into a ritual space. The last ceremony that AEG had before closing its physical doors was ripping the paint off the walls, a ritual where Black women could wail and grieve. They started pulling paint off the walls as a cathartic experience that was also theatrical and transformative. Ekundayo remembered how people were often transported into a spiritual realm, a religious realm as well, when they participated in the collective's rituals and ceremonies. To gain a greater understanding of the collective's work, the group posted the following statement at the end of each performance that they uploaded to YouTube and its website:

> House/Full of Blackwomen is a site-specific ritual performance project that addresses issues of displacement, well-being, and sex trafficking of Black women and girls in Oakland. Set in various public sites throughout Oakland over a [seven]-year period, this community-engaged project is performed as a series of "episodes" driven by the core question, how can we as Black women and girls find space to breathe and be well within a stable home?[75]

There is a lot to consider in this statement, which lays out the methodologi-cal approach to Black women artists' wellness work through art making and the building of BWAEs. First, the group places significance on its artwork at site-specific locations. The act of creating art reinforces the significance of Black women's ability to cultivate art ecosystems—spaces that not only support their artistic practices but also foster mutual growth and empow-erment within their communities. Furthermore, members engaged in the House/Full of Blackwomen project actively created community-based, ritual performance projects that fostered dialogue around issues of displacement, well-being, and the sex trafficking of Black women and girls in Oakland. Last, their efforts were driven by this pertinent question: "How can we as Black women and girls find space to breathe and be well within a stable home?"[76] This question highlights the connection between wellness and environment because the ability to breathe, literally or metaphorically, is deeply connected to Black women's and girls' wellness. This is especially the case when it comes to mastering breathing within their own homes. For a deeper understanding of how House/Full of Blackwomen employed these practices of wellness, let's consider a few of their episodes.

House/Full of Blackwomen Episodes

In the Arts & Entertainment section of the *Bay City News Foundation*, Amelia Williams explains that House/Full of Blackwomen's politically charged per-formances, "called 'episodes,' in an allusion to stereotypes imposed on Black women about their attitudes—they are site-specific. The collective members dance. They play music. They speak. They hold healing circles. And sometimes, they simply rest."[77] Episodes like "The Meaning of Canaries" drew out the narrative that Black women, like the idiom "canaries in a coal mine," are the first line of sacrifice within a society that is environmentally unsafe and deter-mines humanity's parameters of detriment. The episode "Now You See Me" was a vaudeville-like procession. Group members wore all-white lace clothing, including gloves and full veils, as they walked the streets and held up mirrors and other props in front of onlookers and cars stopped at traffic lights. This performance "was designed to highlight the sex trafficking of Black women and girls within Oakland."[78] Like many of their episodes, "Now You See Me" sparked a dialogue between the performers and onlookers, whose curiosity led them to be participants in the performance. Arguably, such interactions and dialogue about issues harming Black women seldom take place, reflecting the overall invisibility of their experiences in mainstream society. Through art and creativity, Black women artists who participated in House/Full of Blackwomen found the power to create counternarratives that commanded the attention needed to highlight the issues challenging their wellness.

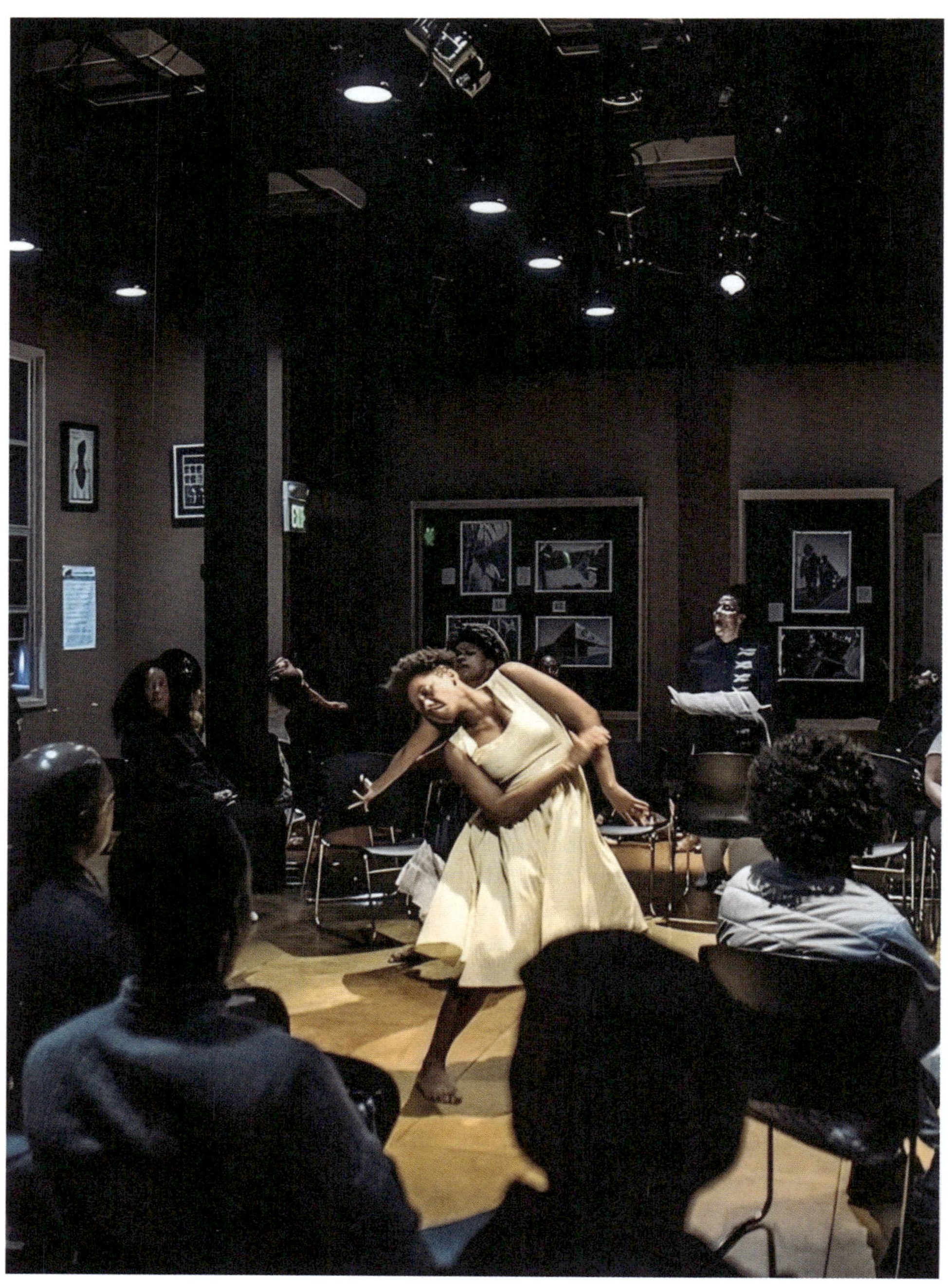

The opening performance of *Meaning of Canaries*, featuring Rayla and Keisha. HFBW episode 5, October 2016. Photo by Robbie Sweeny.

Although many issues harm Black women's wellness, what I find most consistent is Black women's need to rest. House/Full of Blackwomen took on this theme in their eleventh episode, "Black Women Dreaming: A Ritual Rest." This episode was the first one publicly announced. It involved a week-long performance ritual called *The Blessing of the Beds*, which invited Black women throughout the city to engage in a period of ritual rest, sleeping, and dreaming for two-to-ten-hour sessions at an undisclosed location in West Oakland.[79] This calling on Black women to rest is what tabor-smith posits as an attempt to show an absent narrative of Black women. In a 2017 interview with the journalist Sarah Burke for KQED *Culture Cue*, tabor-smith explained, "We know strong Black women, we know fierce, we know sexy, we have all of these images. But we don't see sleeping beauty; we don't see a rested Black woman. This piece is in honor of our right to rest."[80] To facilitate Black women's right to rest, the ritual opened with a recited blessing that asked the women to let themselves rest and be loved. After the resting period, the women left with hugs and pillows that were blessed with sage and essential oils earlier in the night.[81]

The House/Full of Blackwomen project operated over a seven-year period. The lack of permanency of performing art at site-specific locations does not challenge the notion of what a Black art ecosystem is, nor its efficacy. In fact, site-specific art locations and more specifically, the ritualistic healing work conducted in the House/Full of Blackwomen's project, demonstrates Black women artists' ability to transform spaces that give opportunities to create a participatory and collective experience of wellness that is not bound by brick and mortar. When you consider the similarities and differences in how the collectives discussed in this chapter engage Black communities, the ability for wellness to dwell in both transient and more permanent spaces is equally important according to the needs of each respective community.

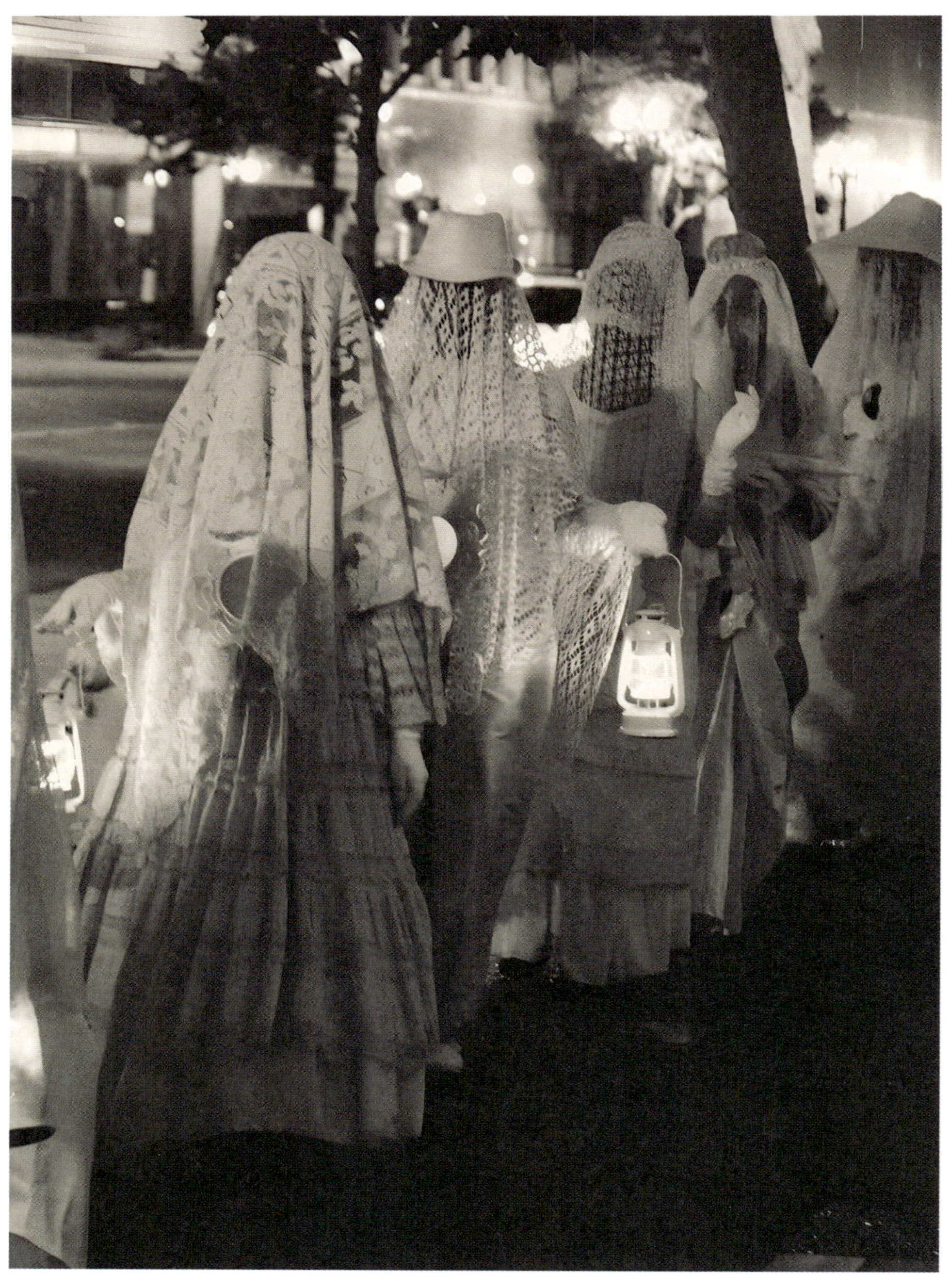

Members of House/Full of Blackwomen. HFBW episode 4, *Now You See Me*. May 2016. Photo by Robbie Sweeny.

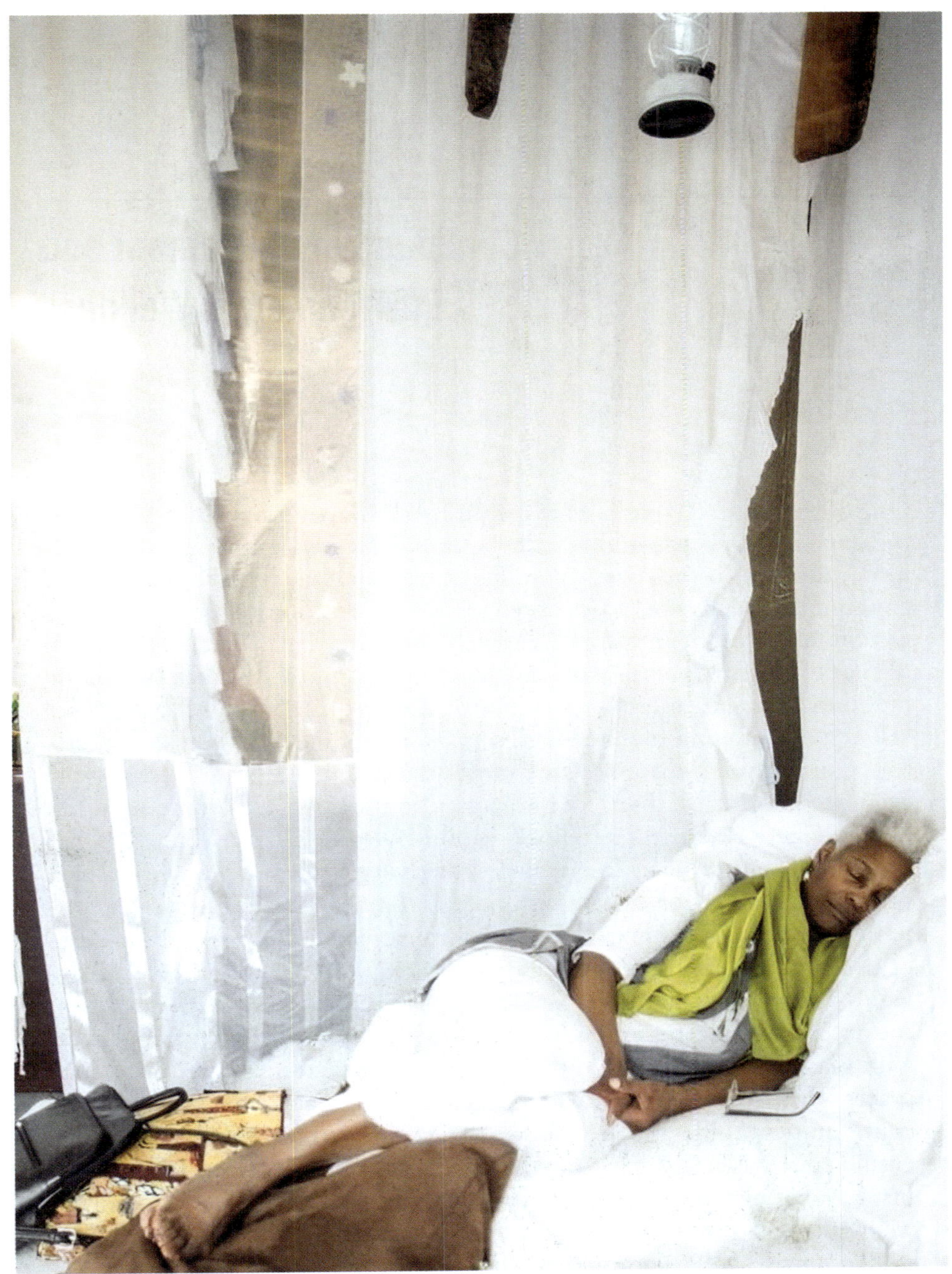

House/Full of Blackwomen participant Karen taking a peaceful nap. HFBW episode 7, *Black Women Dreaming*, March 2017. Photo by Robbie Sweeny.

2

Community Engagement and Environmental Wellness

One of the integral components within Black women's art ecosystems is the presence of Black arts and cultural spaces. These encompass Black museums, galleries, art studios, and community centers, which function as curated environments dedicated to the preservation and exhibition of Black art. In certain instances, these spaces exclusively showcase the artistic contributions of Black women. Typically situated within predominantly Black communities, these arts and cultural spaces play dual roles—supporting Black women artists while offering resources and services to both artists and external visitors. Furthermore, these spaces contribute culturally affirming imagery to their neighborhoods. The activities hosted in these spaces play a crucial role in fostering environmental wellness within BWAEs.

BWAEs' concept of environmental wellness extends beyond its conventional association with natural resources and environmental issues. It also encompasses the creation of environments that nurture and support the well-being of their inhabitants. Within the art spaces explored in this chapter, Black women artists and curators facilitate creative events and dialogue addressing the needs and concerns of the communities they serve. Interviews conducted with Black women artists and their communities identified three distinct art spaces. These spaces are dedicated to social justice initiatives for their respective communities. Some also are hubs for Black women artists' collectives. The ensuing discussion will delve into the positive impact of Black arts and cultural institutions on communities and how they provide a context of environmental wellness.

Black artists are in community with Black art galleries, museums, cultural centers, collectors, curators, historians, and art dealers, to name a few. It is within this ecosystem that many Black artists have built and sustained robust careers. Black museums in particular contrast with conventional mainstream museums, which historically and presently are not equitable in their praxis. LaTanya Autry, an art historian and cofounder of the Museums Are Not Neutral project, has highlighted the lack of equity in mainstream museums by using social networking platforms and T-shirt campaigns. Through these initiatives she argues,

> For the most part, museums are products and projects of colonialism. Because the origins and evolving practices of the construct stem from and perpetuate conquest, they are by nature not "neutral." For decades artists, activists, and scholars in the US and beyond have opposed exclusionary modes of institutions, which include favoring works by White male artists for collections and exhibitions, maintaining predominantly White executive staffs and boards, and other practices.[1]

Historically Black colleges and universities (HBCUs) have played a pivotal role in preserving and promoting Black art through their own museums and galleries. These institutions have provided crucial support and visibility for Black artists, who have often been marginalized by mainstream museums. HBCUs and other Black art museums today continue to be vital spaces for showcasing Black creativity and cultural heritage. They are testaments to the resilience and ingenuity of Black artists, offering a counternarrative to the exclusionary practices of traditional museums. Thus Black art museums and HBCUs contribute significantly to the broader Black art ecosystem, fostering a sense of community and continuity for Black artists.

Museums at HBCUs were some of the first to exhibit the works of Black artists in their collections of African American art. The art historian David Driskell posits, "The HBCUs have not been given the credit they are due. When nobody else was out there championing these [Black] artists, HBCUs were there, claiming them, showcasing them, putting them up on walls, teaching about them."[2] Consequently, HBCUs demonstrated the power and influence Black cultural institutions have had in preserving, documenting, and amplifying Black artwork long before it was popular in mainstream culture.

To be clear, white philanthropists and art patrons were present and involved with HBCUs' patronage of art but took a paternalistic approach. It was the HBCUs' investment in training Black artists, acquiring their work, and providing them professional guidance and support that is the blueprint for how Black art ecosystems operate today to sustain the Black art community.[3] Hampton Normal and Agricultural Institute Museum (now Hampton University Museum) was the first HBCU to collect African American art through acquisition in 1894. Similarly, in 1930, Howard University was the first HBCU to establish an art gallery founded and curated by African Americans. Its collection consists of more than forty-five hundred works. Although there are many other prominent HBCU art museums, galleries, and art depart-ments—including the art program at Atlanta University (now Clark Atlanta University), established by Hale A. Woodruff in 1931—this discussion examines how today's Black art ecosystems have carried on the work of supporting Black artists. One prime example is The Colored Girls Museum.

Vashti DuBois and The Colored Girls Museum

The Philadelphia resident Vashti DuBois is the founder of The Colored Girls Museum (TCGM), located in Germantown, Philadelphia.[4] In 2015 she turned her three-story Victorian house into a memoir museum to make Black women and girls visible and to save her house from being foreclosed on after the passing of her husband. This space and the artwork and artifacts displayed throughout are an example of a site-specific BWAE: it was founded and is led by a Black woman. Its very existence advocates the wellness of Black women on multiple levels, including the curation of visual art and material culture.

DuBois is a trained actress and theater director; her background informs the development of The Colored Girls Museum, as she sees museums as a form of public performance. TCGM's mission is to serve as a public ritual that protects, honors, and uplifts ordinary colored girls, transcending the conventional museum model. Through communal and ritualistic experiences, it seeks to reframe narratives, celebrate dignity, and foster a more inclusive cultural landscape. For visitors, the ritual begins when they book an appointment and continues when they first walk through its door. Each room in TCGM is curated by at least two women and two girls who select a theme and a storyline. Artifacts and artwork that support the intended stories are installed in the space. This method of curation is a strong example of the specialized knowledge created by African American women encompassing theoretical interpretations of Black women's reality by those who live it.[5] Consequently, TCGM's curatorial praxis is purposefully participatory, placing significance on communal memory and storytelling in relation to Black women and girls. When you consider that ethnic minorities and women in general, but especially Black women, have been historically severely underrepresented in mainstream Western art museum exhibitions and acquisitions, TCGM's mission corrects this exclusion. Even now, there is blatant disparity in the diversity of museum staff and administrators who decide what artwork their institutions acquire and display.[6]

I interviewed DuBois to get her perspective on the relationship between museums and the Black community. She admitted that she doesn't really like museums because their exclusionary practices discount Black peoples' artistry and knowledge creation.[7] Yet she embraced the use of the word *museum* in TCGM's name, explaining that "it strategically forces you to engage with [Black women] in a particular way. When we say 'museum' people's backs go up a little bit."[8] The word *museum* implies high culture and sophistication in Western art. DuBois builds on this notion as it pertains to Black women artists and curators. Further confounding the classist and racist notion of museums, TCGM provides a platform for what DuBois describes as the ordinary colored girl, and the exhibitions in this space celebrate her and tell her story the way she wants it told. Here, it is important to acknowledge that when DuBois talks about TCGM, she personifies it as an actual Black girl. The space is very much alive, ideologically and energetically, because of the women who contribute to its development. Some people had a hard time wrapping their minds around this concept when TCGM was first established. Yet it emphasizes the importance of bringing visibility to everyday Black women and girls who are often the visible invisible in society. The museum acts as a force field to protect the experiences and memories of the ordinary colored girl and the things that she values and that are exhibited within its walls. Therein lies the power of BWAEs, because they allow for Black women to be celebrated and to tell their stories the way they want to tell their stories, without restriction or approval from outsiders.

My interview with DuBois piqued my curiosity about the choice of the museum's name. When I questioned her further about her decision to employ the term *girl* instead of *woman*. In response, she said:

> The reason this is The Colored Girls Museum and not the colored woman, or Black woman, is because it is for the big girls and little girls. And it is for the little girl in us big girls. Because what many of us can remember is what was denied to us in terms of protection as girls. For example, how often did we need grace, you know? And nobody gave it to us.[9]

The word *girl* in the title allows Black women to reflect on critical years of development and to revisit those experiences, both positive and negative, that significantly shaped the women they have become. Through its representation of Black girlhood, TCGM opens opportunities for Black women to receive the grace they need to feel safe and to believe that it is all right for them to be themselves and to exist in the world. Grace establishes that whatever happens in life, you are okay, and it is important to extend grace to ourselves and others. Yet this seems to be hard for many Black women, and DuBois contends that "you cannot give what you have not received."[10] Ultimately, TCGM attempts to help Black women recognize what grace is so that we can extend it to ourselves and others.

Regarding the public's reception of the museum, DuBois reveals that TCGM is perceived as a sanctuary that is not exclusively for colored girls but for anyone who is ready for a conscious revolution.[11] That is, when people are engaging with TCGM, they undergo a conscious revolution because they are stepping into a space where the colored girl is the center of the story being told through the eyes of girls who have done so much for so many and for so long. It is very telling that in the twenty-first century, centering Black women and girls is still a revolutionary practice. This is despite the fact that over fifty years ago, the Black women's artist collective Where We At came together to plan the first Black women's art exhibition in known history, "WHERE WE AT," in Greenwich Village. Like the collective whose name implies that Black women artists were establishing positionality in the world, TCGM functions in the same way within its walls. As an act of resistance, DuBois and all those involved in the development of the museum are making the political statement that Black women and girls deserve a space that not only cares for and displays their personal artifacts and art but also allows for a much broader community to locate and access their narratives with permission and in reverence. For this reason, TCGM is an organism having the power of controlling the White heteronormative gaze that has violently subjugated Black women.

TCGM is also an ecosystem that challenges the sustained controlling images of Black women that have proven so adverse to our health and wellness and fostered oppression.[12] DuBois notes that the American history taught in secondary education is problematic. It mainly situates African Americans from a place of enslavement through the Civil War, and as second-class citizens during Jim Crow, the civil rights movement, and the black power movement, while downplaying or erasing the significant cultural and sociopolitical influences and contributions of Black people. Concerning Black women and girls, there is limited acknowledgment or examples of their being fully human. TCGM calls for visitors to understand American history more accurately by acknowledging that ordinary Black women and girls have been at the forefront of America's historical movements. During a time when so many social activists from the Black Lives Matter movement are calling for people to #SayHerName to acknowledge Black women victims of police brutality, TCGM is also working to bring visibility to Black women and girls whose lives are more obscure. DuBois explains that in so many cases, we do not even know our names. We are still discovering who did what in history. One thing is for certain: By establishing a space for ordinary Black women and girls, the message is that their ordinary lives matter.[13] TCGM reminds Black women and girls that you don't have to be a history maker for your life to matter, a message that is cultivating a sense of wellness among its constituents. For the ordinary Black girl, waking up in the morning is an achievement. Going to school every day is an achievement, and our collective work to do all the things that we do makes the world turn and certainly makes America turn. Although the previous statement might be perceived as an essentialist claim, DuBois holds firm to her belief that Black women and girls are the invisible adhesive that holds the country together.

To truly understand how TCGM's existence is situated in community engagement and environmental wellness, DuBois's personal narrative needs to be told. She is a Brooklyn native who was living in New York City with her husband and three children during the September 11, 2001, terrorist attack on the World Trade Center in which the Twin Towers fell.[14] She recalls the anxiety and fear she felt at that time as the nation was under heightened security, with color-coded alerts such as yellow, orange, or red. DuBois describes that event and the days, weeks, and months that followed as traumatizing. She recalls, "One day I said to my husband, 'You know, I do not . . . I cannot . . . I do not think I can do this anymore. Like, I think we need to get out of New York City.'"[15] DuBois had lived in Philadelphia years before. With some convincing, she and her family relocated to Germantown and moved into the house that would later become TCGM. Unfortunately, DuBois experienced more trauma when her husband died in 2014. After that, she faced the threat of losing her home to foreclosure until one day she decided to enact her passion for preserving Black girlhood through the arts and public programming. DuBois had worked in nonprofits for a while, primarily on issues related to Black women and girls, an area that she calls her sweet spot. She admitted in our interview that she was drawn to that type of social service work because of her own girlhood and her desire to "give the thing I wanted that I did not get, and the things that I felt every Black woman and girl should have, which is embedded in The Colored Girl Museum's mission: protection, praise, and grace."[16] In 2015, a year after her husband's death, she opened The Colored Girls Museum.

As much as TCGM is a space that endeavors to cultivate wellness for the ordinary colored girl and all its visitors, the museum's existence is deeply connected to DuBois's attempt to cultivate her own healing and wellness during a time of grief. DuBois recalls that establishing TCGM was driven by the need to do something to focus herself after her husband's death, but it was also because she was mad:

> I was mad because after my husband's death, you know, so many people— actually, mostly Black women—would say things to me like, you know, "You are strong. You have to go on for your children." Like all that shit, and I really just started thinking about how everybody thinks that Black women just have to keep going. Like no matter what.[17]

The "strong Black woman" trope continues to plague and impede the wellness of many Black women. Despite this expectation from others in her community, DuBois had the foresight to honor her grief and acknowledge that Black women should be able to stop and breathe when they "get knocked inside the head" because the appropriate response is to "lay your ass down or go get some help."[18]

The other trope that DuBois contends is the idea of "Black girl magic" when used to describe us. Arguably these terms, often used as labels of empowerment, can cripple Black women by denying us the permission to exercise a full range of emotions and to fully embrace our vulnerability and humanity. This is also why it is so important for Black women to define themselves and to occupy space. The women who contribute to the museum's exhibits through donations of art and artifacts and curating the exhibits are shaping an environment that is suitable for wellness work. They demonstrate how the museum provides key elements of environmental wellness: community, safety, and sanctuary.

During our interview, DuBois explained, "The Colored Girls Museum functions as a public health institution specifically designed to confront a public health crisis affecting Black women."[19] DuBois sees TCGM as a proactive initiative that engages with public health concerns, recognizing the intersectionality of race and gender in health disparities. By focusing on the experiences of Black women, the museum aims to raise awareness about the unique health problems they encounter, challenge existing stereotypes, and contribute to a more comprehensive understanding of public health in marginalized and often environmentally unsafe communities. Her perspective underscores the museum's commitment not only to cultural representation but also to active participation in broader societal conversations. TCGM becomes a platform for advocacy, education, and dialogue, using the lens of public health to address systemic issues affecting Black women and fostering a greater sense of community and understanding. In essence, DuBois envisions TCGM as an integral part of the public health discourse, offering a distinctive and vital contribution to the well-being and visibility of Black women. In many ways TCGM provides what Cheryl L. Woods-Giscombé describes as culturally derived mind/body intervention that emphasizes enhancing awareness of the socially and culturally ingrained role as a strong Black woman and reframing the concept of Black women's strength as inner strength grounded in wellness, wholeness, and self-defined authenticity.[20] Viewing TCGM from this perspective adds a greater understanding to the value of BWAEs as alternative mental health spaces.

Part of DuBois's personal healing of trauma was to get through the process of packing and labeling objects after her husband died. It took a team of Black women from her community to help her. In a similar approach, DuBois invited artists to help curate the first TCGM exhibit, pairing two women to organize each room. She asked them to invite two to five other ordinary colored girls to submit objects related to the theme of the room. From there, the artists curated the space using the donated objects and their artwork. The act of labeling objects and documenting memories reflected DuBois's desire to make sense of the grief and loss she was experiencing. She shared with me her desire to be able to know what and where things were when she came back to herself.

> So, you know, when I woke up from that grieving, I came back to myself and was in a space of understanding. Metaphorically speaking, of course, after that first show, because everything was labeled, and these ordinary colored girls who curated this space took control of the situation through the vein of sisterhood. Those were the sisters who were responsible for helping me do that thing that I knew I needed to do. I needed to know where I was.[21]

TCGM brings clarity to the positionality and location of Black women as well as those who are in relationships with them. The museum's curatorial process demonstrates the significance of sisterhood among Black women and girls and the idea that colored girls should always be in the company of our community. The museum also provides evidence that when our artifacts are gathered with permission, they support us in being able to create sanctuary for Black women who are present and Black women who are not. This is how the curatorial practice began. As it turns out, the *Washerwomen* exhibit is the only one where every object and piece of art in the museum is labeled. It is also the only permanently established exhibit at TCGM. All the other rooms change in theme and content throughout the seasons.

The *Washerwomen* exhibit displays objects that reflect a domestic occupation that many Black women held in the United States. The items in that room once belonged to grandmothers and great-grandmothers. Items like linens, old irons, and church uniforms appear mundane, yet they convey a powerful feeling that the ancestors are also present. DuBois further expounds on what Barbara Neilly, a close friend to TCGM, expressed before she passed away: "There are two sets of women in the Colored Girls Museum. There are the ones who you can see, and then there are the ones you can feel."[22] Neilly's observation suggests that a deep spiritual element in TCGM is connected to its curatorial practice. DuBois compares curating TCGM with how people adorn themselves and dress in preparation to go out into the world. Curating shapes both narrative and experiences for its visitors; part of the experience that DuBois and those involved with TCGM want visitors to have is healing. DuBois's descriptions of the rituals of doing, of making, of arranging objects, create a sanctuary for healing that occurs for many people at a subconscious level when these women respond to the creative praxis of TCGM and other BWAEs.

Building on this theme of healing, the second TCGM exhibition, *Open for Business,* centered on Black women resting and getting a good night's sleep, much like House/Full of Blackwomen's episode *Black Women Dreaming*. The museum was disguised as a bed and breakfast to make TCGM's new presence in the community hospitable to those opposed to its existence. Yet the true purpose of this exhibit was to speak to the need for Black women to connect

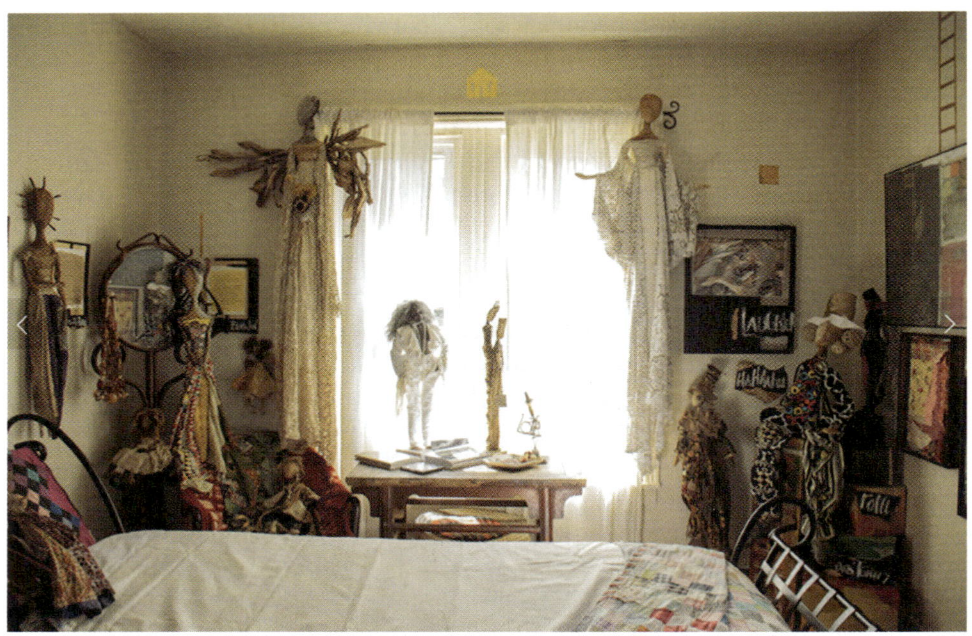

The Colored Girls Museum. A Good Night's Sleep. Photo by Zamani Feelings. Courtesy of The Colored Girls Museum.

with the concept of getting rest. Each room was curated in such a way that when a colored girl came in and out of that space, what she got to take with her were all the remedies for a good night's sleep. Every item in the rooms provided a different cure. Whether it was the scents or specific colors or stones in a room, each room in the museum was designed to connect with a visitor's idea of rest. DuBois explains, "Maybe the first floor was not gonna get you to sleep. Maybe sandalwood was not your thing. Maybe amethyst was not your thing. Perhaps it was the floor that used lavender that put you in a state of rest. And maybe that room would take you out."[23] The room *A Good Night's Sleep* echoed the olfactory stimuli that occurred when essential oils such as sage, jasmine, and sandalwood were used during the *Blessing Bed* ritual at House/ Full of Blackwomen. These commonalities reveal the interconnectedness that Black women artists have in BWAEs. In the context of Black women's well-being, rest creates possibilities for balance and introspection. Although *Open for Business* had an agenda for creating healing and wellness for Black women, its approach was subtle. This was not the case for TCGM's third exhibition, *URGENT CARE.*

The *URGENT CARE* exhibit was TCGM's implementation of a social care experience. It redefined the concept and practice of "urgent care" from triage to aftercare.[24] Every room became a space that you might find in a hospital. Rooms representing triage, pain management, diagnostic imaging, a reflection area, the aftercare suite, a drugstore, and patients' historic records were all part of the exhibit. Artists assigned to these different rooms were asked to think about how they would reflect the theme visually. When visitors came to the museum, they entered the Colored Girl Urgent Care Facility. Each of the curated rooms provided women with something that they would need in life, even if at that moment they might not necessarily have known they needed it. One of the objectives of this exhibition was to give Black women strategies and tools that they could use before they find themselves in deep trouble. *URGENT CARE* also reminded Black women that they already know how to respond in urgent times. And as DuBois says, "It is in us. We just have to remember."[25] Remembrance is a constant motif in TCGM, appropriately applied to the exhibit *In Search of the Colored Girl*.

In Search of the Colored Girl was an exhibition that was inspired by programming directly targeting young Black girls. DuBois was inspired to develop an exhibition that addressed all the ways in which Black women and girls go missing, literally and metaphorically. Seventy-six thousand Black women and girls are currently missing in the United States. Yet this fact has not gained national attention. While in conversation, DuBois asked me, "This number is surprising, but did you know that there are seventy-six thousand Black women and girls missing?"[26] My reply was no, and I suspect that many other people don't know about what should be considered a public health crisis. DuBois assured me that most people are unaware of this problem. *In Search of the Colored Girl* endeavored to call people's attention to the issue of so many disappeared bodies. In 2022, the National Crime Information Center (NCIC) reported that nearly ninety-eight thousand Black women and girls were reported missing. Despite making up only 14 percent of the US female population, they accounted for over 36 percent of missing-person cases, highlighting a significant disparity.[27] Yet to DuBois's point, their stories rarely reach national or local headlines.

Adding to the concept of missing Black women and girls, *In Search of the Colored Girl* at TCGM asked visitors to consider other ways in which Black women and girls vanish. For instance, where in their relationships do Black women and girls disappear, making it so easy for us not to notice when bodies are gone? DuBois's exhibition made visitors ask themselves, "How do we notice where she is?" In one of the curated rooms, several carefully placed photographs highlighted the importance of the archive. The importance of knowing who your people are and where those images come from lends understanding to the positionality of Black women and girls in terms of memories and genealogy. DuBois asserted that at the beginning of the search, "Black women are in the archives; these are our documents and our records. Furthermore, it is

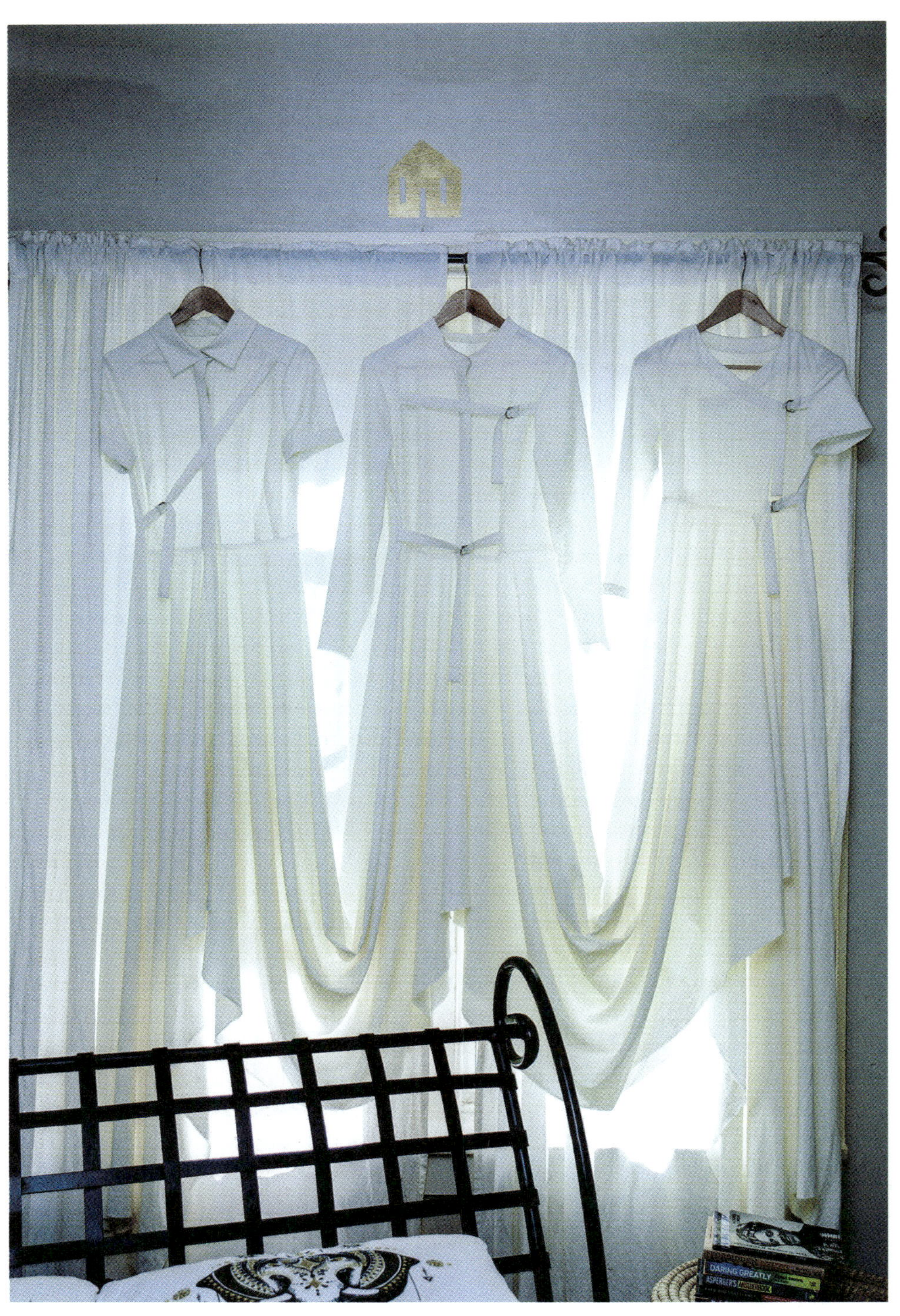

Calli Roche. *Communion*. 2017. Photo by Zamani Feelings. Courtesy of Calli Roche and The Colored Girls Museum.

important to be in control of our own documentation. Because when the community must go looking for a Black woman physically or emotionally, we need to know where to begin."[28]

This exhibit and the others discussed here are all examples of how Black women artists and art practitioners are creating spaces and experiences to facilitate the care of Black women. Although it is a boutique art museum that is unique in its concept and curatorial praxis, TCGM is not the only Black women's art ecosystem addressing the health and wellness of Black women and their respective communities. A similar mission could be found in Love Front Porch and the ArtHouse in Pittsburgh, Pennsylvania.

vanessa german's Love Front Porch and the ArtHouse

Born in Milwaukee, Wisconsin, vanessa german is a multidisciplinary artist who spent her formative years in Los Angeles before she eventually made her way to Pittsburgh, Pennsylvania.[29] german is known for making sculptures out of found materials in the Homewood neighborhood of Pittsburgh where she was a long-time resident. A self-taught artist, german works across sculpture, performance, communal rituals, immersive installation, and photography as a means of repairing and reshaping disrupted systems and spaces.[30] In a later chapter I will discuss in detail the elements of german's work that center on wellness through memorial and communal ritual work. However, the focus of this discussion is the site-specific Black Women's Art Ecosystem Love Front Porch, which german founded in 2011; and the ArtHouse, which she founded in 2014 as part of her role in arts activism and community leadership.

A 2011 MSNBC Rachel Maddow special report labeled Homewood one of America's most dangerous neighborhoods.[31] Since then, efforts have been made to address safety concerns in the community. Data from 2024 indicates a decline in violent crimes across Pittsburgh. However, while homicides were down nearly 20 percent in Pittsburgh, numbers increased elsewhere in the county.[32] Despite the violent description of Homewood, it is crucial to recognize its positive aspects, including a strong sense of community that residents take pride in. Empirically, the neighborhood is "a predominantly African American community that is the poorest, most crime-infested, homicide-infested, and drug-infested area of the city of Pittsburgh, with the lowest economic standards," according to Councilman Ricky Burgess, who attributes much of the violence to gun violence and state legislation that allows for easy, unregulated access to guns, specifically automatic weapons. No one knows this better than german, who has witnessed violence on a regular basis in her community.[33] Yet the artist is quick to acknowledge that this neighborhood has historical roots for Black creatives such as Dinah Washington, who lived there; Lena Horne, who socialized there; and the writer John Edgar Wideman, who also lived in Homewood and wrote a book series called the *Homewood Trilogy*. Despite Homewood's rich legacy of Black creativity, it is often overshadowed by violence.

In her TED Talk: Love Front Porch (2011), german explains how she purchased her first property in Homewood and how in time her front-porch-turned-studio became an informal after-school program where young children in the neighborhood would engage in creating art. Specifically, german began creating large statues she calls "power figures" in her basement. However, when these figures became too large to move out of the basement, she would have to disassemble them and take them out in sections. That's when german decided to make the figures and other art on her front porch, which was situated at a bus stop. Curious and intrigued adults and kids in the neighborhood would come by and watch her make sculptures and say things like, "What is that?" "That's so weird," and "It's actually really weird."[34] german recalls kids asking, "Why are you so dirty?" and "Can I help you?"[35] At first their curiosity was an annoyance, especially when some of the children would strategically swing on the fence and land in her front yard.

Consequently, german found herself turning her yard into an art space for young people. She provided an array of art supplies such as old paints and found objects from abandoned houses in the community. She also gave the kids the instruction that if anyone was there to create art then they had to do so with a purpose. german recalled in her TED talk how some of the children engaged in making art were looking for direction on what to make. german was quick to tell them that this was not an art class but rather she was working, and they must work too. Specifically, she explained, "You have to work. You have to make a decision. You have all these materials in front of you and it's what you want; it's what you threw yourself over my fence for. You've got to make a decision. You need to start with a color and a purpose. You need to start with your favorite color and then you need to decide what you're going to make."[36] Eventually the children internalized her instructions; soon she observed that they were inviting their friends after school. Not only did they get involved in making art but were also teaching their friends the rules on how to get started. While german was in one area of the yard working, kids would repeat what she had told them: "Listen, you need to make a decision. You need to choose a color and a purpose. What do you want to make today?" These instructions seem simple enough on the surface that one might think that they were solely german's strategy for keeping her young apprentices out of her way while she created art. However, on a deeper level, the children were demonstrating that they felt empowered not only to make decisions but to trust themselves enough to do so.

german also shared with her TED talk audience Dr. Martin Luther King Jr's sermon "Loving Your Enemies," that he delivered to an Alabama audience in 1957 and that she often replays. One particular line that she committed to memory states, "Here is a power and love that the world has not discovered. Yet I believe in the power of love. . . . Love is creative, understanding, redemptive, transformative goodwill."[37] This line from King's sermon became a mantra that german would repeat to herself when she was going through her own mental-health battle and multiple attempts at suicide. german explained in her TED talk that it was due to King's message on the transformative power of love and her belief in the power of love through the expression of art that she was able to overcome her mental health challenges. german took a risk—really a leap of faith—and quit her job to become a full-time artist. She endured poverty to commit to what she believed might save her life and provide well-being.

german's personal journey to wellness inadvertently turned into an opportunity to provide environmental wellness for others, particularly young people, in her community when she passed down the lessons that she learned through the vehicle of art and the establishment of a space that she would soon call Love Front Porch. Young people would gather here to create art and "make decisions about their own imagination and creative expressions," which german equates to her notion of love. As she continued her TED talk, german recounted, "I know that it's love because I'm an artist and when I'm making art, I am the very best human that I can be. I'm better in my mind, my body, and my spirit. . . . I am perfected as a human being in these moments, and I recognize that as love."[38] Creating art brings german clarity but also the revelation that when she shares what she loves, which is art, she is sharing something "that would allow these young human beings to expand creativity to be as dimensionally human as they could be in an environment that is so oppressive that it suffers and traumatizes them."[39] And herein lies the impact of this BWAE.

This space created opportunities both for internalizing lessons that facilitate wellness and for creating art that aims to facilitate external environmental wellness and safety for members of its community. Young people learned through internal reflection on what they felt and through creating art that brought a sense of balance to their lived experience of trauma in an often violent community. They also provided validity to their experiences as well as opportunities for healing through some of the themes in their artwork. Furthermore, the young people who were part of Love Front Porch set goals through their art-making process. They often supported each other through the art-making process in ways that taught them to trust themselves and their ability to make decisions. german witnessed kids repeat, "I trust myself," which she interprets as love dwelling inside them as they went through the process of creating a safer community and "[drew] a neighborhood that is organized inherently by love."[40] This opportunity to envision and artistically create a safer neighborhood led to empowering opportunities. The young people who participated in Love Front Porch had agency that allowed them to make better decisions about transforming their environment in a more positive direction.

german recalled one of the first campaigns that sprang from Love Front Porch participants. After hearing fourteen gunshots nearby and during a time when most children were coming home on school buses, german's first thoughts were, *They should do something about that. They should make sure that that never happens again.*[41] Soon she realized that the "they" that she was looking for were herself and members of her community, who could use art as a counternarrative to the violence in their neighborhood. From there, she and others at Love Front Porch began making signs that read "Stop Shooting; We Love You." These signs were placed in peoples' yards throughout the community and have traveled throughout the country in the hope that someone might make a different decision when it came to exercising violence. Although some of the young people were skeptical about making the signs, german challenged them to believe in their ability to have influence. She told them that they had nothing to lose in making these signs if in fact they reminded someone to remember their mothers, sisters, brothers, and so on, whom they would want to be shielded from violence and trauma.

After the inception of Love Front Porch, it evolved into something more formal. In 2014 german purchased two adjacent abandoned houses, each over one hundred years old. One of the houses, called the ArtHouse, was repurposed and for many years provided a community studio, a large garden, an outdoor theater, and an artist residency. german lived next door in the other house, where she also had studio space and where she created most of her visual artwork. It should be noted that she identifies as a citizen artist, to describe how she intended to "inhabit [her] citizenship as your neighbor, as a human, as a gay person, as an American, as much as [she] can."[42] She began calling herself this when she established the ArtHouse. This title provides insight into how german "allows art to guide the way she engages with her community and processes the painful politics of living."[43] This space functioned in what is now a more gentrified Homewood community, open to anyone interested in creating art, but it particularly was a space to address the needs of children and women in the community.

The ArtHouse's external aesthetics distinctly stood out. It was a bright blue house adorned with large stars on its sides and wide vertical black and white stripes around its foundation. People in the community painted and created a mosaic of images like flowers, hearts, hands, eyes, and bright-colored shapes and symbols on the front porch, balcony, and other areas of the house's siding that correlated with textual messages like "We Are All Here Together" across the balcony, and the words "Hope" and "Holy," along with a painted message on the front steps that read, "The Art House Poem: Being at the Art House, where you realize you had wings the whole time." These images, along with the art of children in the community who have made major decisions about the interior décor and paint colors of the house, made this house stand out as a space of hope and healing in a neighborhood that presents a challenge to acquiring them. The aesthetics of the ArtHouse added a dimension of environmental wellness to the neighborhood.

The ArtHouse began as an art space where primarily children and a few curious adults met; over time it also became a space to support an artist in residence. "German [said] that an artist-in-residence left candles burning in the upstairs bathroom on Valentine's Day [2021]. A fire led to serious damage in the ArtHouse."[44] For two years, it remained closed, until german revealed on Instagram that the next incarnation of the ArtHouse would open to the public once renovations are completed. Most revealing is the section where she writes, "My life has been impacted by violence. At the ArtHouse and near my home I witnessed several murders. I have found a total of 5 bodies. I contend with the trauma daily. I hope none of you have to ever endure this."[45] german's trauma speaks to the need of edifices like the ArtHouse that operate as a safe haven and where creative activity can flourish to infuse challenging communities with environmental wellness. This narrative underscores the profound impact of trauma on individuals and the vital role of community art spaces in providing refuge and promoting healing.

The ArtHouse's programming was an example of how Black women artists like vanessa german can assess the social and environmental needs of their communities and organically create an environment for wellness through arts activism and community engagement. Moreover, in the fight against the negative effects of urban renewal and environmental pollution (many of the art resources german used are found objects and litter in the community), this site-specific BWAE was an example of cultural renewal that presented opportunities to preserve and create culture through art. The cultural renewal that the ArtHouse provided expanded community consciousness on multiple issues: celebrating life; reverencing loss through vigils; examining poverty, health disparities, and racial disparities; and much more. Camila Arbelaez contends, "The reimagination of space provoked by vanessa german's art house creates a stronghold against gentrification, giving cultural value to a devalued material space based on the values of the original community rather than those of the occupying force."[46] What's most notable is that the collective work that occurred at the ArtHouse was participatory from the beginning, not a top-down mission of creating a space to "solve" the community's problems. This is significant because community buy-in to participating in activities that cultivate social change also leads to a level of accountability and sustainability.

Consequently, "Ms. german calls the ArtHouse a bit of stability in turbulent Homewood, where she says over 100 people have been evicted as developers buy up property."[47] Gentrification is yet another challenge for Homewood's residents, who are being displaced. According to german, "It means a lot to people that we're able to still be here. The house has been a friend and a neighbor and a constant incarnation for 12 years. . . . There's something about this big, beautiful, glittery blue house. It's a constant presence in the midst of so much change."[48] The ArtHouse exemplified considerable success, with german and others in the community expanding its functionality beyond a space for visual art and cultural production. For example, it included a robust garden that provided food for kids to fight food insecurity and contributed to environmental justice.[49] Furthermore, it became a space where community members could have difficult conversations and commemorate the loss of life of its members through vigils. The planned reopening of the ArtHouse symbolizes resilience and the transformative power of art in fostering recovery and wellness in communities scarred by violence. German's experiences in the Homewood community highlight the essential need for supportive environments that nurture creativity and offer solace in the face of adversity.

In this chapter we have explored the multimedia artist vanessa german's involvement in creating space for wellness and healing through the development of her own BWAEs: Love Front Porch and the ArtHouse. It is safe to say that german facilitates our understanding of how Black women artists continue to organize and provide resources for the communities they live in. They help community members give voice to their experiences and provide resources to create new visual and performative narratives to cultivate awareness and dialog about local issues. In grappling with national issues as a citizen-artist, german has engaged not only with particularly Pittsburgh, Pennsylvania, but also many other communities throughout the nation. Building on this understanding of german's wellness work, the next chapter explores her artistic practice along with that of another artist, Lava Thomas, and their contribution to BWAEs through memorial art.

3

Communal Mourning and Collective Wellness through Memorial Art

When I consider the impact of Black women sculptors in capturing and presenting the Black experience, I immediately think of Augusta Savage and Elizabeth Catlett. According to the art historian Lisa Farrington, Savage "was one of the most politically influential artists of the 1930s."[1] During this time Social Realism was the leading genre of art in the United States. Its characteristics included "illusionary imagery and sociopolitical content."[2] Along with many other artists, Savage was funded by the US government through President Franklin D. Roosevelt's New Deal and the Works Progress Administration (WPA) program. This initiative sought to jump-start the American economy, which was in an unprecedented recession. The Great Depression started with the stock market crash of 1929 and persisted throughout the 1930s and early forties. One of Savage's major accomplishments was a commission by the 1939 New York World's Fair officials. The *New York Amsterdam News* reported, "On December 20, 1937, one of Miss Savage's dreams is to come true. Harlem's new free community center opens at 290 Lenox Avenue and she will be the director. Her second ambition, a commission from the World's Fair Board of Design to sculptor a group which would symbolize the unique contribution of the Negro to American music, was received last Thursday."[3] For this commission Savage produced one of her most renowned sculptures, *The Harp ("Lift Every Voice and Sing")*. Named after the "Black National Anthem" (1899)—written by James Weldon Johnson with music by his brother, John Rosamond Johnson—this sixteen-foot-tall sculpture consisted of a "monumental harp composed of twelve traditionally modeled heads of black choir singers mounted atop fluted columns that stood in for the conventional bodies. These ten bodies formed the strings of the harp, while an elongated arm and an open hand formed the soundboard."[4] *The Harp* received a silver medal, along with significant press attention. Savage exemplified this chapter's conversation on memorializing the Black experience by creating a sculpture, a visual representation of an anthem that we collectively agree expresses our historic and lived experiences as African Americans.

Savage made her own "dream come true," becoming invested in institution building by establishing arts organizations in predominantly Black neighborhoods.[5] She saw an opportunity to build organizations like the Harlem Art Workshop in collaboration with the Harmon Foundation, and eventually the opening of the Harlem Community Art Center. This arts organization gave Black people access to the arts during a time when most arts organizations were in predominantly white neighborhoods, even though New York was the mecca for Black art. Savage is credited with helping train a new generation of artists by providing art instruction to some fifteen hundred students and employing several African Americans at the center.[6] Another part of her effort to develop Black art organizations was the 1939 Harlem-based launch of the first African American commercial gallery in the country. Although its success was brief, this endeavor, and those previously mentioned, are examples of how Black women artists have engaged their communities through art making and by either founding or having an impact on community arts spaces through significant participation.

The artist Elizabeth Catlett's professional work also began during the Social Realism era. She created art in various media over the span of eight decades. She is best known for her political prints and abstract sculptures of women that reflect her involvement in the Black Arts Movement and the women's arts movement, serving as an influential leader for the former. By 1974, when Catlett was well into her sixties, both the art world and Catlett herself recognized that she was experiencing a "lively renaissance" in her career, for which she gave the following explanation: "Part of my acceptance in the art world now is because of my maturity. . . . In the '30s and '40s tokenism was practiced by the exhibitors and only Jacob Lawrence or Horace Pippin would have a show. Now the art world is slightly broader minded. It's both a response to the political demands of the '60s and the economic realities. Black art is marketable."[7] Elizabeth Catlett's reflection on her career renaissance highlights the intersection of personal growth, social and political changes, and economic factors that contributed to her renewed success in the art world. Her experiences underscore the evolving attitudes toward Black artists and the increasing recognition of their contributions to the cultural landscape.

Catlett's sculptures demonstrate how this medium provides a visual language for capturing the dignity of the ordinary, particularly Black women. Catlett explained, "I wanted to show this is a certain kind of beauty. It is not an exotic beauty. It is dignity."[8] The dignity that Catlett has captured in her art can be found in the bronze figure *Pensive Thought* (1968), which portrays a Black woman sitting cross-legged with folded arms, one of which supports the side of her face. The deep cherry-wood sculpture *Mother and Child* (1993) shows a tall woman standing firmly while holding her infant child. These and other sculptures display how Black women sculptors bring depth and subjectivity to their work. Catlett's artwork also celebrates Black leadership in the form of monuments. One of her last works was a thirteen-foot-tall bronze sculpture of the celebrated jazz musician Mahalia Jackson. The statue was installed in 2010 in Louis Armstrong Park in New Orleans, two years prior to Catlett's death. When you consider the rich legacy that both Savage and Catlett have left, it is no surprise that the tradition of using sculpture to create commentary and monuments that commemorate and memorialize Black life continues in the contemporary artworks of vanessa german and Lava Thomas.

vanessa german's *Reckoning of Grief and Light*

In this life I pray for the courage to be my whole entire heart.
—vanessa l. german

As I discussed in the previous chapter, vanessa german is a multidisciplinary artist known for her mixed-media assemblage sculptures. My first encounter with her work was at the Art Dealers Association of America (ADAA) Art

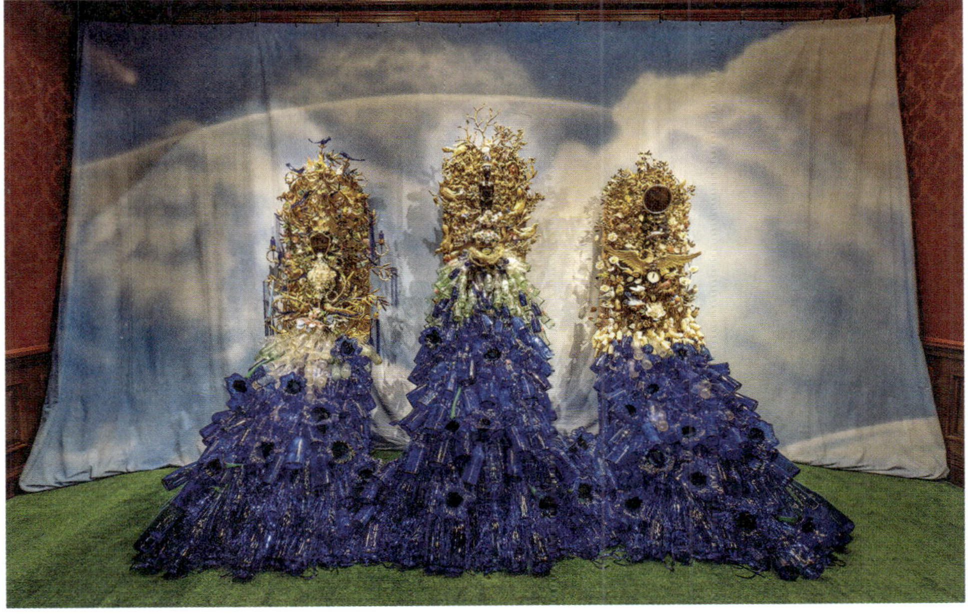

vanessa german. Mixed-media installation of *Reckoning: Grief and Light* at the Frick Art Museum, 2021. Photo by Steve Groves MediaWorks, LLC. Courtesy of vanessa german and the Frick Collection.

Show 2020 in New York City. I just happened to be in the city for another art exhibition that the Community Folk Art Center was sponsoring at the Lubin House when I learned from german's Instagram post that she was exhibiting at the Park Avenue Armory in booth A23. I had been following her for some time on social media; now would be my chance to cross paths with her in person. I immediately went to the Park Avenue Armory in hopes that I could have a conversation with her about her art and art-making process. Unfortunately, I had missed german by about twenty minutes. Her gallery representatives informed me that she had not only left the exhibition space but was leaving the city and heading back to Pittsburgh for another art-related event. Of course, I was disappointed, but I immediately found solace in the small gallery booth, which was tastefully filled with the artist's large-scale installations. Although german was not there, her *Power Figures* were. They commanded the attention and awe of visitors with their scale, colors, and intricate compositions of dense accumulations of found objects affixed to wall-mounted altars.[9] That day I was able to take in the art and comb over visual narratives that presented blackness informed by everyday situations in the Homewood community, where german resided at the time. One important note about german's *Power Figures* is how aesthetically they resemble the power figures from the mid-nineteenth century known as *nkisi nkondi*.[10]

These Central African figures, made of wood, were created by Congolese and Angolan sculptors and ritual specialists who created these figures to host spirits that "generally hunted witches and wrongdoers," to right social wrongs, and to enforce affairs critical within their communities.[11] The *nkisi* statues are often depicted with arms akimbo, a pose of intimidation and power, with nails sticking out of them. These nails "document vows sealed, treaties signed, and efforts to eradicate evil."[12] Additionally, these figures have an empty cavity where medicine powder and other substances were placed to imbue them with specific spiritual and healing powers. vanessa german's sculptures clearly borrow the concept and aesthetics of this African art form to continue the practice of using art to address social injustice and to enable healing. Her *Power Figures* and figurative wall art align with her identity as a citizen artist, as her "enigmatic figures confront gun violence, police brutality, and systemic racism head-on through an accretion of signs and surfaces affirming german's belief in the transformative power of love and art to heal a community."[13] I find german's life work to be consistently healing and unlimited when it comes to spreading awareness of systemic issues that affect human beings in general but Black people specifically. What german demonstrates in her work is how artists on a journey of healing for themselves cannot generate a healing that is isolated from creating opportunities to heal others. Communal healing is perhaps the medicinal ingredient that imbues her artwork with power. german merges sculpture and installation art with performance and art rituals as a

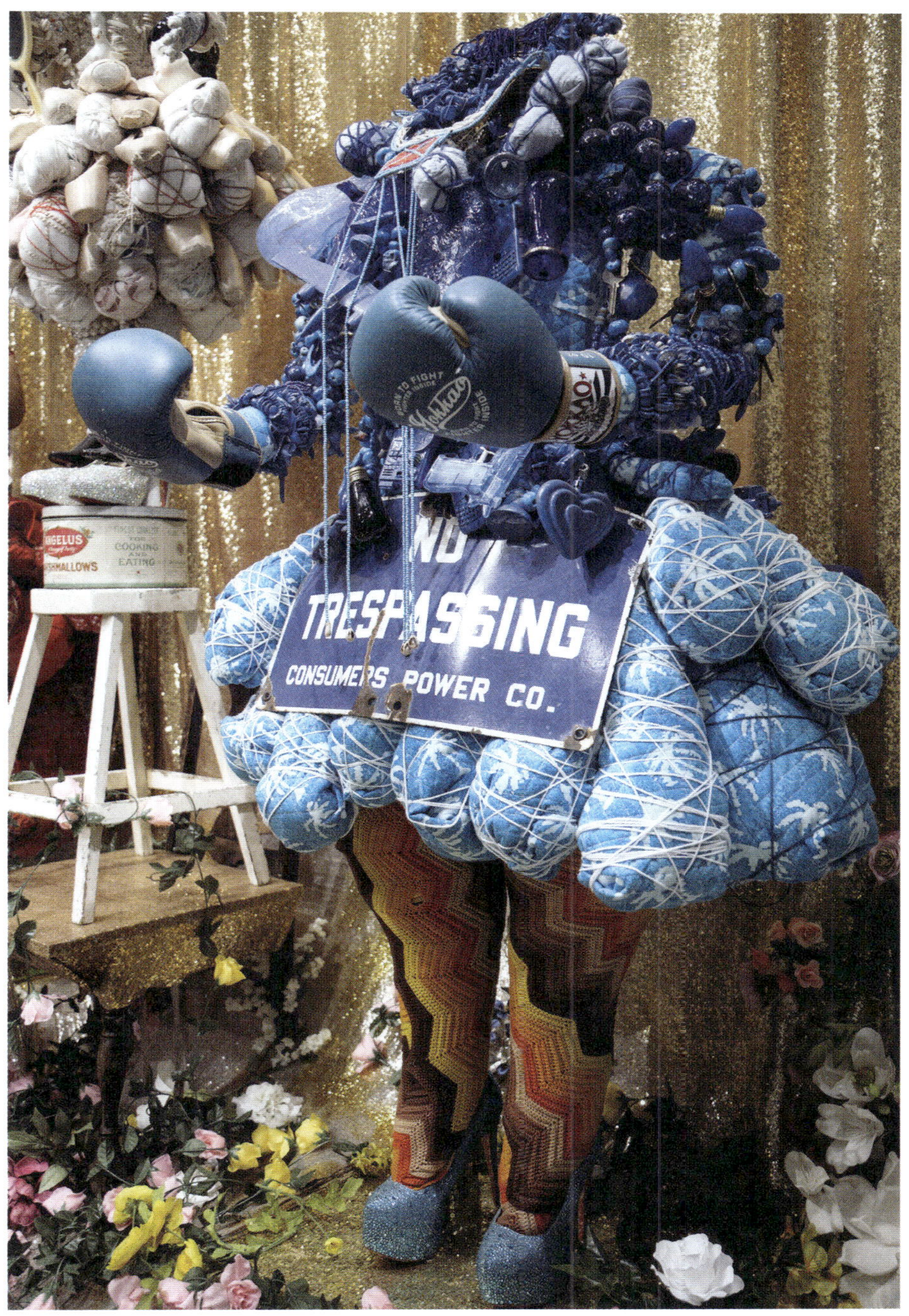

vanessa german. *sometimes.we.cannot.be.with.our.bodies.* 2017. No Trespassing Power Figure. Heather Mull Photography. Courtesy of vanessa german and Kasmin, New York.

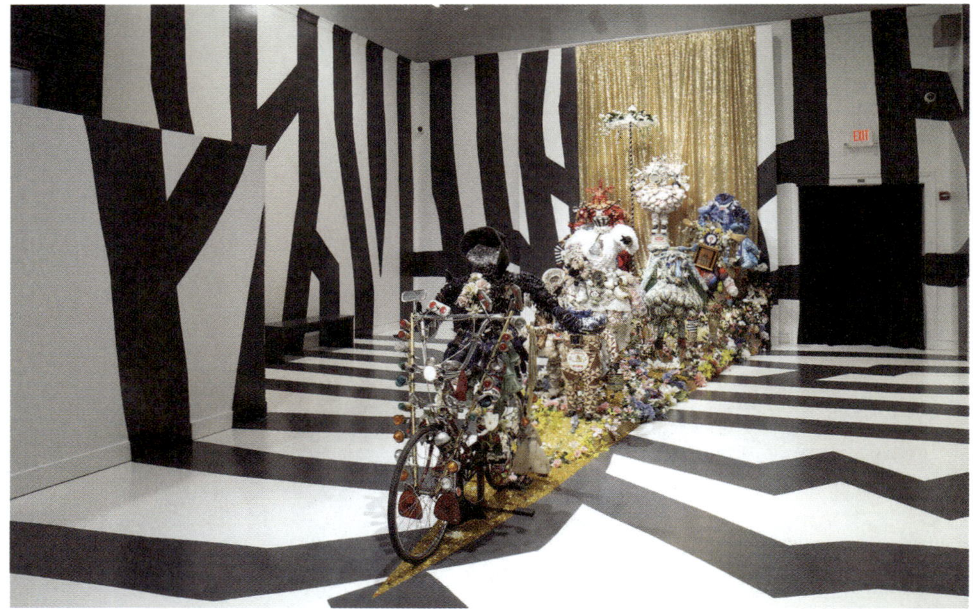

vanessa german. *sometimes.we.cannot.be.with.our.bodies.* 2017. Mixed media installation. Photo by Heather Mull Photography. Courtesy of vanessa german and Kasmin, New York.

kind of arts activism to suture areas disrupted by violence, racism, classism, and sexism as well as other societal ills.

While serving as an artist in residence at the Frick Pittsburgh Museums and Gardens, german created three installation altarpieces for the exhibition *Reckoning: Grief and Light, Nothing Can Separate You from the Language You Cry In* (2021). This exhibition was one of a three-part series that was an elegy for "[George] Floyd, Breonna Taylor, Elijah McClain and other people of color whose lives have been lost to violence."[14] Gold and cobalt blue were the prevalent colors german used in the accompanying installation of the three sculptures (see first figure in this chapter). They are ornamented with hand-crafted glass objects custom made for german by artisans at the Pittsburgh Glass Center, an example of how german's work successfully engaged those outside the Homewood community to contribute to the cultivation of social healing. The sculptures also included symbolic images, for example, "the eagle, a symbol of American liberty, on the Elijah McClain altar is missing his ribbon saying 'E Pluribus Unum.' And the alarm clock, showing 12:05, emphasizes 'it is past time' to resolve the structural issues central to the three Black figures' deaths."[15] Furthermore, the elaborate sculptures effectively "evoke a reimagined wailing wall or weeping river" as a place of reflection.[16] Through her work, german summons the underlying theme of reflection as a tool for creating "meditation on grief, love, and social healing."[17] It puts her work in alignment with how other Black women artists lean on reflection to cultivate wellness.

In her statement, german wrote, "This work is personal. . . . How do I grieve, mourn the losses of so many Black people killed by the police? How do I stay whole and safe and creative in an environment where Black women are shot and killed by the police in their own homes, while playing video games, cooking, or even sleeping?"[18] Making art is deeply personal: for some artists, it is even spiritual. These visual wellness workers create their own healing process. However, as german's questions suggest, creativity can be stifled by trauma or suboptimal environments that are riddled with violence. Still, german has been able to push through and use her creativity to create a dialogue among diverse audiences. What started as personal work for the exhibition *Reckoning: Grief and Light* expanded into a conversation about how mainstream institutions such as museums and other public places can be supportive and agents for change. german asked, "What role can museums play as spaces of intentional social healing?"[19] This is one of many questions that inspired this immersive installation.

Until now, the focus on BWAEs has revolved around Black women founding galleries, boutique museums, community art spaces, and nonprofits, all aimed at cultivating healing environments within their communities. BWAEs can also occur at site-specific locations where art is performed or with pop-up exhibitions. Yet german's access to museum spaces like the Frick Pittsburgh Art Museum as an artist in residence adds another layer of understanding of BWAEs when we consider that the artwork she is creating for social healing is exhibited in mainstream art spaces that create two very important opportunities. The first is to transform public art spaces into a healing space. Because german is a Black woman artist, by design the space of her exhibition becomes a Black woman's art ecosystem. The second opportunity is to hold museums and other public spaces accountable for how they use their resources to address issues in surrounding communities in need. Both opportunities have benefits for these institutions and their patrons. Yet, when I consider the expansive and transformative power of german's art, its power lies in her ability to engage multiple audiences and to bridge the gap between spaces like the Frick Pittsburgh and her Homewood neighborhood. german demonstrated this when, in addition to the *Reckoning: Grief and Light* exhibition, she created several multisensory performances in correlation with her exhibitions, one of which was a 2.5-mile processional called *Blue Walk Pittsburgh*.

Like the San Francisco–based House/Full of Blackwomen, which strategically walked through certain communities to spread awareness of social issues affecting women and communities of color, vanessa german has been creating similar expressive art, starting with her memorial artwork beginning in the 1980s and 1990s, amid the AIDS epidemic in Los Angeles and continuing with her artistic practice to memorialize marginalized people.[20] A precursor to the *Reckoning: Grief and Light* exhibition and *Blue Walk Pittsburgh*, the exhibition *sometimes.we.cannot.be.with.our.bodies* (2017) was held at the Mattress Factory, Pittsburgh, and then reimagined at the Fralin Museum of Art at the University of Virginia in 2019. This immersive installation, which displayed intricately designed figures without heads and heads without bodies, along with a blue colored processional, was an immersive installation of sculpture and sound. german explained, "This work is a dimensional living reckoning. The living reckoning is bold, eruptive, disruptive work against systems & pathologies that oppress & subvert overt & covert violence onto & into the lives & humanity of marginalized people on this land."[21] Following this exhibition, german created a continuum of reckoning work.

The same exhibition was also reimagined a few months later at the Union for Contemporary Art. There, vanessa german led a two-mile "ritual reckoning" procession to honor Will Brown and other people of color lost to violence.[22] Accompanied by seven local performers, she walked silently from the Union for Contemporary Art to the Douglas County District Court, where the group, all dressed in cobalt blue clothing, performed a goodbye ritual song inspired by Mende birth and funeral rites.[23] Including the local performers was consistent with community involvement and support in german's ritual art practice, reflecting collective mourning and solidarity. This was not just an individual act by german but a communal expression of grief and remembrance, enhancing the impact and reach of the ritual.

The performance of a ritual song inspired by Mende birth and funeral rites added a profound cultural layer to the event. The Mende people, an ethnic group from Sierra Leone, have rich traditions that honor life and death.[24] By incorporating these rites, the event connected African cultural heritage with contemporary acts of mourning and remembrance, signified respect for ancestral traditions, and, like german's *Power Figures,* highlighted the continuity of African cultural practices in her work.

For the *Blue Walk Pittsburgh*, german organized another strategic 2.5-mile procession on the one-year anniversary of the death of George Floyd, who was murdered by the former Minneapolis police officer Derek Chauvin. On May 22, 2021, german posted the following caption on Instagram:

THE BLUE WALK is next Thursday evening, MAY 27TH.
This is a reckoning ritual of Love,
Healing, Grief, Grace and Gratitude.
It is a celebration of wholeness.
If you are a Black Person who'd like to
participate in the ritual, DM me. You
will be fitted for your blues and you
learn the movements of the ritual.[25]

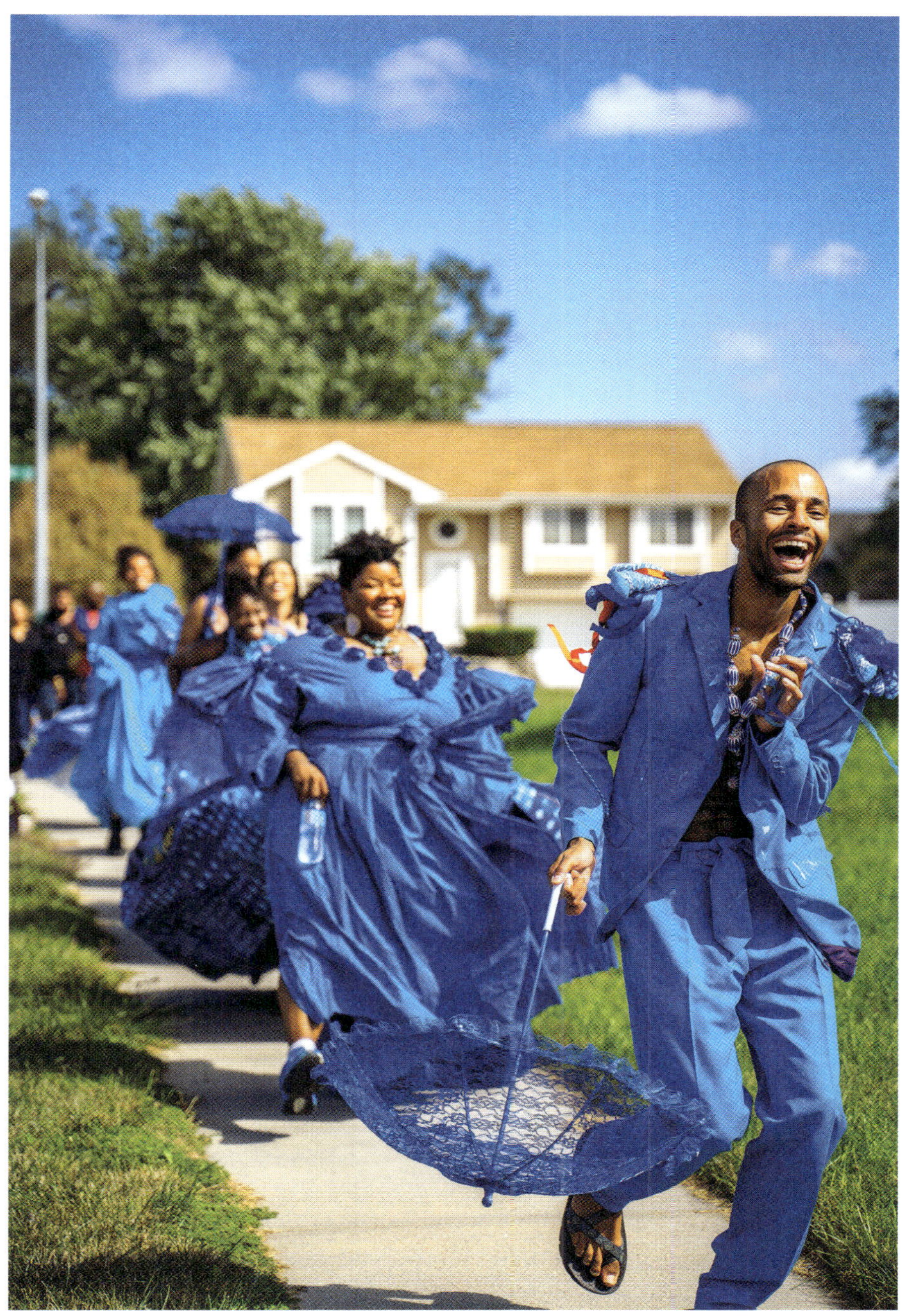

Performers in the *Blue Walk Processional* display happiness as they move through the street outside the Union for Contemporary Art. 2019. Photo by Damion Grace for the Union for Contemporary Art.

Posted with this invitation for community engagement is a photo from the Union Art Center's processional. It shows a Black man in a blue suit with an expression of joy and laughter, holding an open parasol while leading german and others, also dressed in blue clothing and accessories and in mid-laughter. The photo conveys an experience of Black joy that seems inviting and arguably would compel people in the community to participate. However, the advertisement of Black joy is only one component of the range of emotions that german and others cultivated during that experience.

As many Black Lives Matter protests sprang up across the world, german, along with twelve other performing artists, the majority of whom were Black women, dressed in royal blue gowns, tulle, and jewelry prepared for the processional.[26] They met around the front porch of the ArtHouse on a Thursday to lead the *Blue Walk Pittsburgh.* Some of the participants carried parasols and bouquets of flowers that they judiciously gave out to people while walking to the Frick Pittsburgh Art Museum. german and others endeavored to invoke a space for trauma to be fully processed, which german described in an interview with the *Pittsburgh Tribune* as "extended grief and being alive in a Black body, or a transgender body, or a queer body."[27] What began as a gathering at the ArtHouse turned into a journey with audiences standing on the sidewalk as the group walked down the street, engaged in call and response. german could be heard saying, "We love one another, we love this earth. . . . George Floyd—we walk for him."[28] In what was later reported as choreographed movement, the women and a few men in the processional twirled around, lay on the ground and then lined up holding hands after receiving hugs from german. As they made their way through the neighborhoods, at certain locations the group would laugh, wail, and cry out, "Why? I want them back!"[29] This ritual of grief shows continuity in how Black women artists organize with community and use various media, such as performance, fashion, oratory, and dance to cultivate experiences of healings.

The group's commemoration of Black life is an example of Judith Butler's position that "a smaller community still grieves, regardless of the value of the life that has been lost in the eyes of the law or in the dominant racial scheme. But grief becomes grievance, if not a protest and a social movement, when the task of grief is to assert the value of that lost life, to break apart the scheme of valuation that would see it any other way."[30] This act of remembrance not only honors the deceased but also challenges and critiques the systemic devaluation of Black lives. By transforming grief into a form of protest, the group contributes to a broader social movement advocating for justice and equality. Their actions exemplify how mourning can be a powerful catalyst for social change and resistance against oppressive structures.

In addition to the *Blue Walk Pittsburgh*, german has created other social-media content on community-based art experiences surrounding her exhibition. In another demonstration of communal mourning and healing, german explained on her Instagram page that she asked people to send her stories and images of their lost loved ones, which she used as a basis for a live performance that she called *Making/Channeling Poems.* These poems honored the memories of lost loved ones. german also made poems addressing people experiencing grief, sorrow, solitude, and isolation, and poems that addressed the issue of incarcerated community members. She kept her promise to close the event with a "lifting-up song, a song of dedication to the brightness of wonder, and a song of love to the planet earth and the blankets of stars that surround us."[31] Similarly, the Frick Pittsburgh Art Museum posted a video performance on YouTube that shows german dressed in an elaborate cobalt blue period dress. The dress has an attached "grief hoodie," a reference to Treyvon Martin, another victim of white violence. The iconic image of Martin shows him wearing a hoodie that, along with his blackness, became the impetus for his killer, George Zimmerman, to racially profile him.

With her back turned to viewers, german stands in front of the museum. Immediately she begins to walk up the steps and enter one of the open doors. "Interspersed within the recording, german counts the 8 minutes, 46 seconds initially reported as how long Minneapolis police officer Derek Chauvin knelt

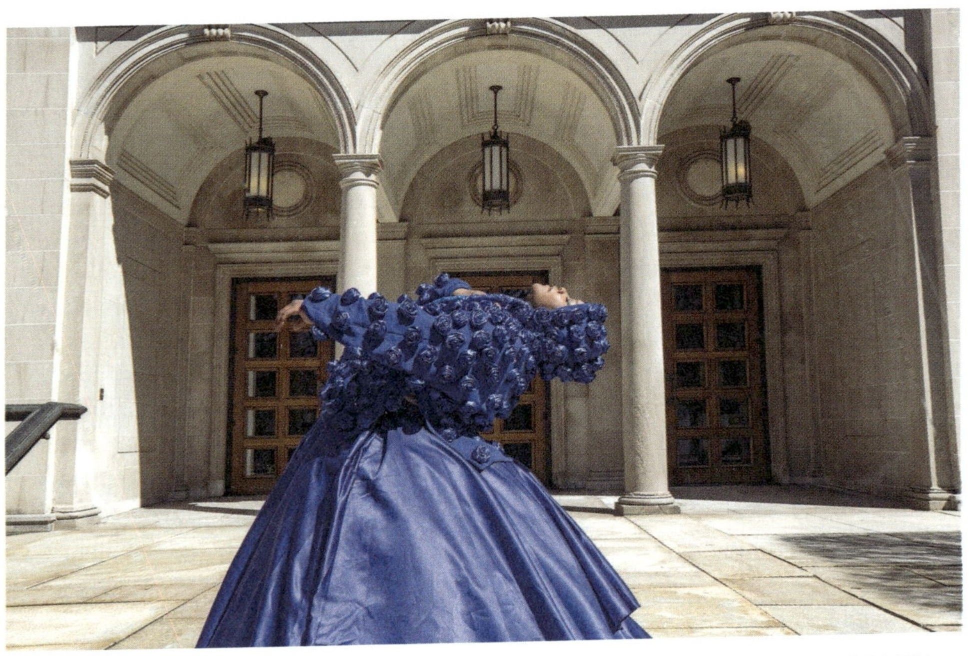

vanessa german leads the *Blue Walk Pittsburgh* as part of *Reckoning: Grief and Light* at the Frick Pittsburgh Museum. May 27, 2021. Photo by Heather Mull Photography. Courtesy of vanessa german and Kasmin, New York.

on Floyd's neck."[32] german's video performance is also set to a soundtrack of *Unburied, Unmourned, Unmarked: Requiem for [Tamir] Rice*, written by the Emmy Award–winning composer Jonathan Wineglass, who was inspired by a libretto by acclaimed historian Dr. Edda Fields-Black.[33] In the rest of the video, german spins with outstretched arms, forcefully bowing and then raising her body up with arms stretched to the ceiling repeatedly in front of the three elegy sculptures in a state of grief before falling to the ground in exhaustion. In one scene, german sits in front of the altar, facing the camera as she grabs a portion of her dress to shield her face. This respite leads into more rapid dance and wailing, accompanied by a woman's voiceover.

What was most compelling about the grief performance and the memorial art installation was its location within the museum. The memorial pieces were installed in proximity to the Italian Renaissance relief paintings of the Frick's Italian Gallery. According to Dawn Reid Brean, the Frick's associate curator of decorative arts, this arrangement facilitates a conversation "between depictions of the Virgin Mary and the infant Jesus from the 14th and 15th centuries and the 21st-century 'martyrs and saint-like figures' of the new installation."[34] Herein lies the power for Black women artists creating BWAEs in mainstream public art spaces. They create not only opportunities for necessary dialogue among people but also between objects through the strategic placement of their art in spaces they don't normally have access to and juxtaposed with Western European art acquisitions.[35] These new conversations call out society's contradictions and hypocrisies on race, class, gender and other identity markers at an institutional level that call for healing and movement toward transformation. The discourse that echoed throughout the halls of the museum through object placement is the result of german's initial response to creating artwork, specifically sculptures, that addresses her personal grief.

On March 31, 2022, less than a year after the *Blue Walk Pittsburgh*, german posted a photo on Instagram from the 2019 Union Art Center's *Blue Walk* procession. It shows a few of the participants, including german, wailing while holding hands and walking in a line. Some of them were bowed over; others stood straight. Their faces express grief and anguish, another characteristic of german's *Blue Walk* processionals. Posted alongside the photo is a caption about a young Black boy who was shot in the head. In her Instagram german recalls her observations of him, as well as fear for his safety prior to his death.

I found out today that someone killed the little boy who sold waters out of a cooler on the street corner a block up from the ArtHouse this little boy with a voice that seemed to stay high-pitched as a little girl i always worried about him for this i worried that the other boys would be cruel to him and that that cruelty would loose him of his own-self. . . .

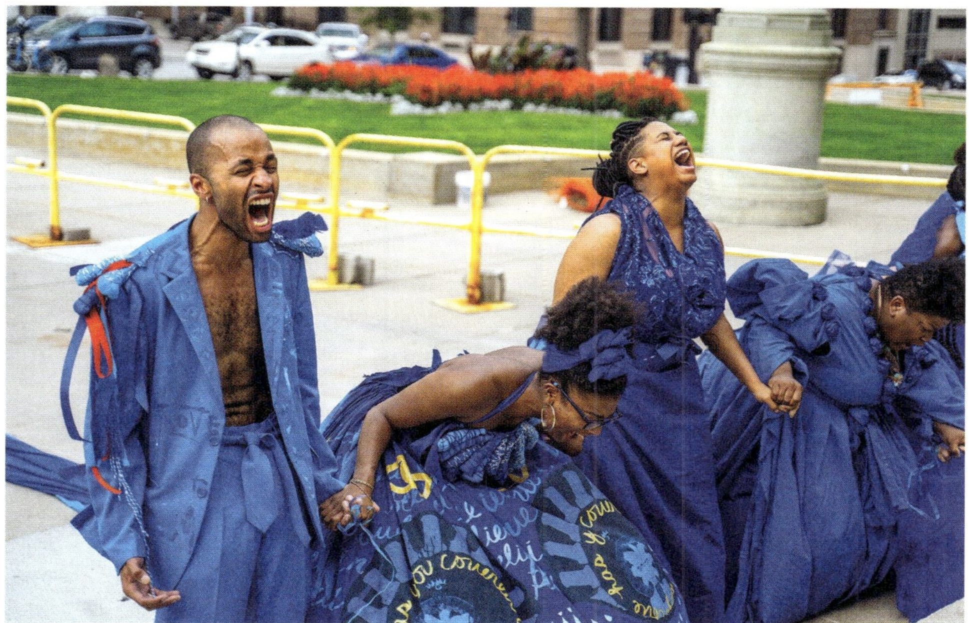

Performers in the *Blue Walk Processional* express grief as they move through the street outside the Union for Contemporary Art. 2019. Photo by Damion Grace for The Union for Contemporary Art.

> I fuckin can't believe that somebody killed him . . . shot him and he was on his bike . . . shot him at 6pm when all the cars were cutting through the neighborhood to bypass the end of rush hour . . . shot him right where everyone knew him . . . knew his face and his voice and his particular way of being a boy.[36]

Although german never gives the name of the boy, Pittsburgh police reported a similar incident around the date of her post, revealing that the victim was fifteen-year-old Dayvon "DayDay" Vickers, a very enterprising and beloved member of the Homewood community who was shot in broad daylight while riding his motorized bike.[37] Through the creation of a memorial power figure that honors the memory of the young boy in her community, german's simultaneous expression of grief and celebration of life also demonstrates how artists shift from strategies for national mourning to mourning local tragedies and social issues. On deducing that the young boy was shot due to his effeminate mannerisms and nonconformity to traditional cisgender heterosexual roles, german created art in his memory. This work exemplifies memorial and grief practices that address not only racial violence by whites but also intraracial violence within the Black community, stemming from toxic masculinity and potential homophobia. The loss of Black life, regardless of the circumstances, is detrimental to the Homewood community, as german exclaims, "None of the corners are ever going to be the same again."[38] The artist rhetorically asks her community, "And of the neighborhood: How do you/we grieve so much? Where does it all go?"[39] These questions, along with the added hashtags "#grief #sorrow #itsallbluenowisntit #itsallbluenow," suggest that grief is both perpetual and ephemeral, a constant emotion that comes and goes. Consequently, how can such a state of grief not be detrimental to the mental health and wellness of the community drowning in it? german was able to channel her grief through creating a sculpture that represented the young Black boy who lost his life on a street corner. She posted the image of the sculpture and recalled in the caption how the boy "would ride up and down the street in that mean little crotch rocket a black boy flying turned himself into a real levitating zoom it seemed like he was on a rocket to the moon."[40]

The imagery of the young boy flying is memorialized in a figurative sculpture of a body with outstretched Black hands running for takeoff from a patch of green grass. From the neck down, the body of the figure is adorned with yellow objects such as yellow roses, buttons, and beaded strings. A round mirror on the figure's chest allows viewers to see their reflections in the figure and consequently feel empathy and closeness to what the figure represents. The head of the sculpture is less figurative and more abstract, composed of blue objects such as butterflies, glass bottles, a bird that symbolizes flying and looks directly out at viewers, flowers, and a subtle placement of a few green leaves. The composition of these objects adds to the narrative of how german remembers the young boy flying through the neighborhood on his bike. The figure anchors the motifs of freedom and exploration. The caption that german wrote on her Instagram post of the image of this sculpture reads, "Hope he iz somewhere flying in a real way a zoom up there in the never-ending cosmos."[41] I liken this sculpture and german's reflection of the young boy to the African American folktale "The People Could Fly."[42] German's awareness of African diaspora narratives surrounding the concept of freedom through flight does not go unaddressed in her artwork. This sculpture memorializing a young Black boy ready to fly expresses a hope that he has flown away to be the boy that he wanted to be, finally escaping the cruelty of the world. As we segue into the next section on Lava Thomas's artistry at the intersection of social justice and memorial expression, german's sculpture becomes a poignant prelude, highlighting the enduring themes of hope, liberation, and the transcendent power of art.

Lava Thomas: Art at the Intersection of Social Justice and Memorial Expression

A press release for the Rena Bransten Gallery's 2019 exhibition *Mugshot Portraits: Women of the Montgomery Bus Boycott* (2018) describes the artist Lava Thomas's solo exhibition as a "series of graphite and conté pencil sketches that transform visual codes of implied criminality into representations of Black women's resistance, emphasizing the initiative, leadership, and sustained labor of women to the boycott's success."[43] Thomas created portraits of women who refused to ride the city's segregated buses during the 1955–56 boycott. In her review of the exhibition, Felicia Feaster points out that the ordinary citizens turned heroines in Thomas's art are a contrast to the "monuments of the Confederate soldiers on horseback, and fire and brimstone segregationists."[44] Thomas created a contemporary take on the civil rights movement after Donald Trump was elected president in 2016. The portraits are Thomas's response to the racist and misogynist rhetoric of Trump's campaign, along with the blatancy of white supremacy. Thomas contends, "Trump is the embodiment of white supremacy, and I was thinking of all the hard-won gains of the civil rights movement, especially in terms of voting and other civil rights legislation, and how women's contributions still to this day have not been

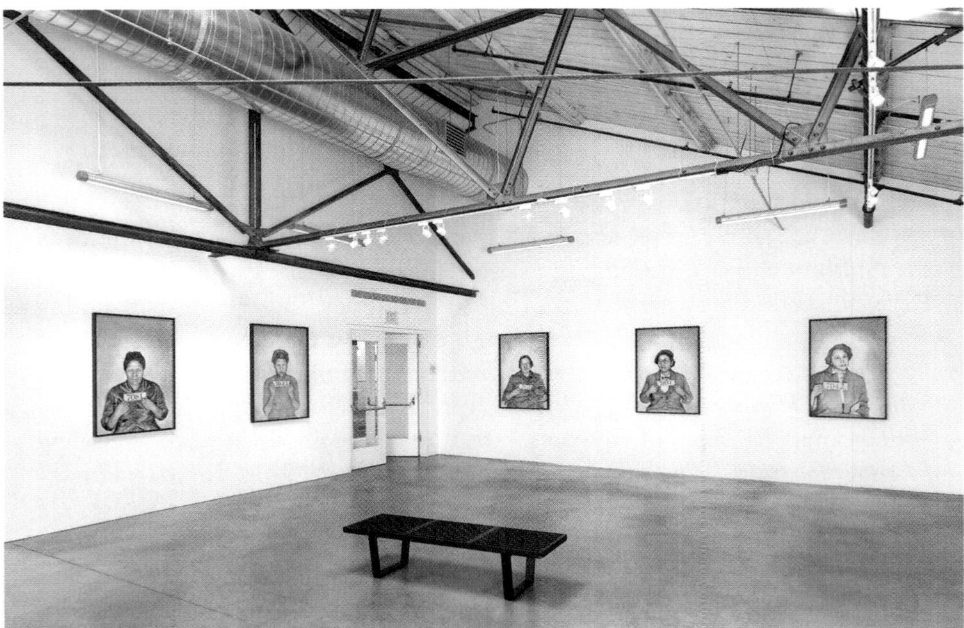

Lava Thomas. *Mugshot Portraits* installation. Rena Bransten Gallery. 2019. Photo by John Janca.

adequately recognized."[45] Thomas was driven to conduct a lot of research, primarily reading books by women who were part of the movement. She, like many other astute scholars, is keenly aware that the taught history of the civil rights movement is very male centered and sometimes erroneously conveys that Reverend Dr. Martin Luther King, Jr. started the movement. Few people know that King was elected to lead the Montgomery bus boycott. However, Thomas's sketches of unsung heroines from the civil rights movement give insight into its grassroots origins and respond to civil rights scholars' concerns about "the superficial presentation of Rosa Parks and of the Montgomery bus boycott, [and] the disregard for the significant contributions of women."[46] The Montgomery bus boycott was organized and strategized by the women portrayed in Thomas's sketches. Thomas describes them as "an army of women foot soldiers and organizers who really led the charge."[47] She endeavored to commemorate their contribution in 2018, during the fiftieth anniversary of Martin Luther King's assassination. Leigh Raiford, a photo historian and professor of African American studies at the University of California, Berkeley, emphasized the importance of Thomas's work in an essay for the accompanying exhibition catalog. She notes:

> We might start with the striking visibility of Thomas' fine line work—intentional, deliberate—which renders these women as highly regarded sitters rather than mechanically reproduced subjects of the state. The purposeful clarity of each hair, each coat thread, each worry line, functions here as a steady etching of history that needs to be carefully attended to. Further exceeding her source material, Thomas has accentuated eyes and hands, underscored a smirk or a side eye. The large-scale portraits, many times the size of a mugshot, are meant to be displayed so that our eyes look directly into theirs, a demand for mutual recognition.[48]

Thomas cultivates mutual recognition by bringing these women's visibility to the forefront and acknowledging the overall legacy of Black women's activism. Regarding her own reclamation of history, Thomas said, "I wasn't thinking about my audience. I was thinking that creating this work was really an act of devotion and I needed to bring their voices to the floor."[49] In 2022, Thomas's exhibition *Homecoming* was on view from April 29 through July 24 at the Montgomery Museum of Fine Arts. It featured three bodies of work, including *Mugshot Portraits*. The director Angie Dodson stated, "Lava Thomas: Homecoming is one of a series of exhibitions presented by the Museum to create a place for individual and collective memory and reckoning. We take to heart our responsibility to be a place where art and artists are recognized for their capacity to transform the thoughts and actions of people and communities."[50] This recognition of Thomas's work is rooted in her ability to "amplify visibility, healing, and empowerment in the face of erasure, trauma, and oppression."[51]

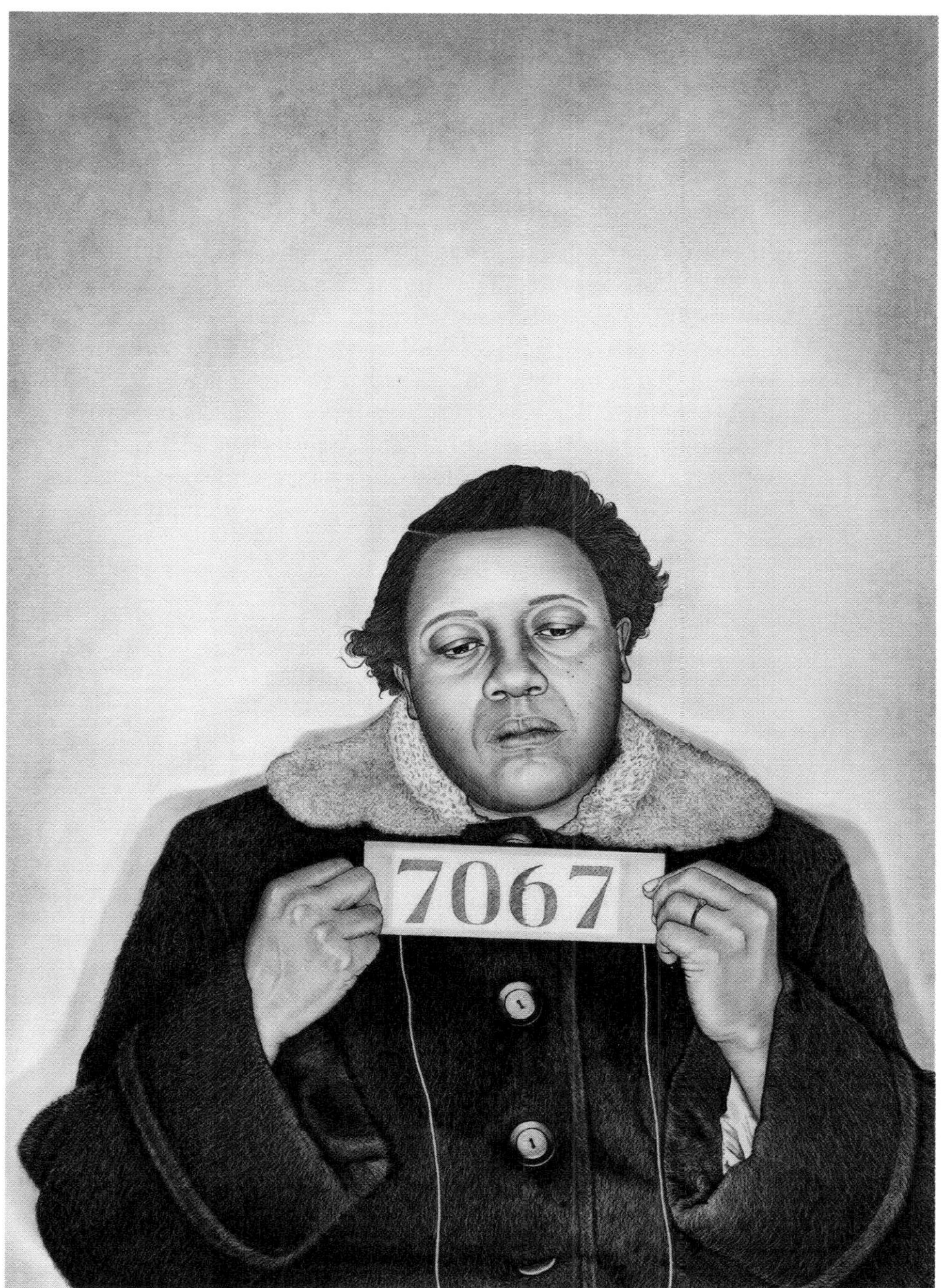

Lava Thomas. *Ida Mae Caldwell*. 2018. Graphite and conte pencil on paper, 47 × 33¼ in. A portrait drawing of Ida Mae Caldwell's mug shot taken after her arrest on February 21, 1956, for her role in the Montgomery bus boycott. Collection of Betsy Blumenthal and Jonathan Root. Photo by Phillip Maisel.

While reflecting on her process, Thomas explained, "It's not my process to think about making work for others or my community. It's something that organically happens."[52] This organic approach emphasizes the authenticity and profound impact of her art, which resonates deeply with those who experience and connect with it. Through her creative process, Thomas effectively bridges personal expression and communal uplift through historical reclamation.

Reclaiming history takes many shapes. Sometimes it involves recentering Black women from the margins of metanarratives that make them invisible. Other times it involves controlling the narrative. Black women artists successfully do this by creating visual counternarratives. Both approaches are practices of wellness. Thomas creates spaces for healing through art for others, but she creates artwork that helps her to process what is happening in the world through the lens of being a Black woman and a Black feminist who is part of a larger human family. Thomas admits that she is transformed by making art, whether by somehow assuaging grief through the process or making visible the legacy of Black women's activism. The result is that her work ends up being seen by its intended audience.

Memorializing Through Alternative Black Aesthetics

I first learned of Lava Thomas and her artwork when I came across a social media post in 2020 on the See Black Womxn Instagram page. The artist was in a public fight with the San Francisco Arts Commission (SFAC), which was spearheaded by the city supervisor, Catherine Stefani. In October 2019, city officials accepted and then rejected Thomas's design for a Maya Angelou monument outside San Francisco's central library. Thomas's design was rejected in October 2019 because Stefani personally did not like Thomas's unconventional design.[53] Thomas's "book-shaped sculpture etched with an image of Angelou's face wasn't what they had in mind: a traditional, figurative statue of the poet."[54] At the base of Thomas's design was a quote from Angelou: "If one has courage, nothing can dim the light which shines from within." This quote would prove to be true as Thomas, along with other artists from the Bay area, successfully challenged, through months of activism and community organizing, the commission's decision to reject her design. In July 2020, Thomas "questioned SFAC's desire to remove symbols of White supremacy while seeking to honor Angelou in the very same visual language."[55] Over the course of a year, it would take many protests from community members, written letters, and meetings with SFAC leadership asking for restorative justice and the halting of a new artist submission process before an apology was issued to Thomas and her design was reinstated. The commission's president, Roberto Ordeañana, acknowledged, "Once we understand the power of restorative justice, and that each of us is uplifted by doing what is

right, the easier it becomes. We thank Ms. Thomas for holding us accountable."[56] Thomas's public fight is a reminder of how institutions have privileged
traditional Western art over nontraditional and non-Western art in acquisitions and exhibitions. The fact that Thomas's design was rejected after being
selected by a jury because SFAC leadership could not accept an alternative
means of commemorating a national icon reflects the cognitive dissonance
among some neoliberal whites and conservatives. After all, the committee
was looking to diversify its collection. They were progressive enough in
initially selecting a nontraditional monument designed by a Black woman
artist. However, when it came to rewarding Thomas for her work, SFAC's
leadership demonstrated inconsistency between their values and behavior.
Thomas reminded the commission of its systemic failures when she held
the floor and read a statement at the July 15 meeting for public comment:

> "The way in which this process was handled is an insult to Dr. Angelou's
> legacy and the principles that she stood for," Thomas said. "Mockery of
> due process, a pattern of disrespect, the erasure of our expertise and intel-
> lectual and creative labor, and the insistence of upholding racist tropes to
> represent one of the most celebrated exceptional Black women of our time
> in the name of honoring her, is beyond outrageous."[57]

The marginalization that Thomas experienced caused trauma for her and
many other Black women artists from her community. It is a reminder
of the challenges these artists have experienced, historically and currently,
because of their race and gender. This incident is also an example of why
Black women artists form collectives for support and why they must employ
wellness and healing. Yet Thomas's experience with the SFAC committee
also demonstrates the value that Black women artists bring to providing an
alternative aesthetic and a Black feminist framework to commemorate and
even memorialize Black bodies. During an interview, Thomas made note
of this when she stated, "Black women should get to decide how we are
going to be represented in the public realm, not politicians."[58] Many of the
SFAC officials wanted a figurative sculpture based on their conventional
understanding of commemorating the dead according to the standards and
expectations of Eurocentric art. However, in a time when many of Western
society's monuments honoring racist figures are being toppled, spray-painted,
or beheaded, Thomas provided a very timely alternative aesthetic that is
worthy of merit. For those who are familiar with Thomas's work, her Maya
Angelou monument design should not be a surprise. The trajectory of her
work demonstrates that her approach to memorializing and honoring the
contributions of US heroes has been innovative, to say the least. One strong
example is the artist's 2016 installation, *Requiem for Charleston.*

Requiem for Charleston

Interlaced throughout Lava Thomas's artwork is a consistent theme of public mourning to address national trauma, such as the June 17, 2015, killings at the country's oldest historically Black church in Charleston, South Carolina, Emanuel African Methodist Episcopal Church. A white gunman, twenty-one-year-old Dylann Roof, joined a prayer meeting and shot nine men and women: Reverend Clementa Pinckney, Cynthia Hurd, Tywanza Sanders, Sharonda Singleton, Rev. DePayne Middleton-Doctor, Rev. Daniel Simmons, Susan Jackson, Ethel Lance, and Myra Thompson.[59] The fact that this heinous act happened in a church, a place many consider to be sacred and a sanctuary from violence, heightened the impact of the news. However, Claudia Rankine notes, "The Charleston murders alerted us to the reality that a system so steeped in antiblack racism means that on any given day it can be open season on any Black person—old or young, man, woman, or child."[60] She argues that furthermore, "a sustained state of national mourning for Black lives is called for in order to point to the undeniability of their devaluation. There exists no equivalent reality for White Americans."[61] This assertion underscores the systemic and pervasive nature of antiblack violence, highlighting the urgent need for national acknowledgment and mourning. Rankine's perspective calls for a societal reckoning that not only recognizes the inherent value of Black lives but also actively works to dismantle the structures that perpetuate their devaluation.

Lava Thomas answered the call and created a wall installation titled *Requiem for Charleston* (2016), which "consisted of 25 tambourines whose drums have been replaced with black lambskin, referring to the quintessential symbol of innocence and sacrifice, inscrib[ing] nine of the tambourines with the names of the murdered men and women; others were left blank in tribute to the many men, women and children who have died in attacks on Black churches."[62] Thomas's choice of the black lambskin is consistent with what the art scholar Kellie Moore recognizes as a feminist mourning aesthetic. Moore explains, "Mourning and its sister terms, grief and grievance, inform techniques of abstraction manifest in feminist artwork from the African diaspora (e.g., the use of black substances—paints, resins, tars, paper, shadow, plastics, inks, and so on)."[63] Thomas's use of this material demonstrates how Black women artists create art for public mourning to foster healing and to memorialize the heroes and sheroes within the Black community. The word *requiem* is defined as "a mass for the dead." It serves as an act of remembrance.[64] As with vanessa german, Thomas's use of the word in the title of her installation reveals what is at the heart of her intention when she creates art. Although not exclusively, Thomas endeavors to memorialize heroes of this nation, many unsung, who have either sacrificed their lives or whose lives have been sacrificed in response to social injustice.

Requiem for Charleston is part of the permanent collection of the Smithsonian American Art Museum (SAAM). It is in *Requiem* and its exhibiting location that Thomas gives space for people to mourn at a national level over a horrific event that captured the nation's attention. When I became aware of this installation, it provoked me to ask, "What does it mean to make art that gives space for public mourning?" Further, "What does it mean to make art that gives space to publicly mourn the loss of Black life at the hands of white violence?" My questions are predicated on the thought that when national tragedies occur, like the shooting at Emanuel African Methodist Episcopal

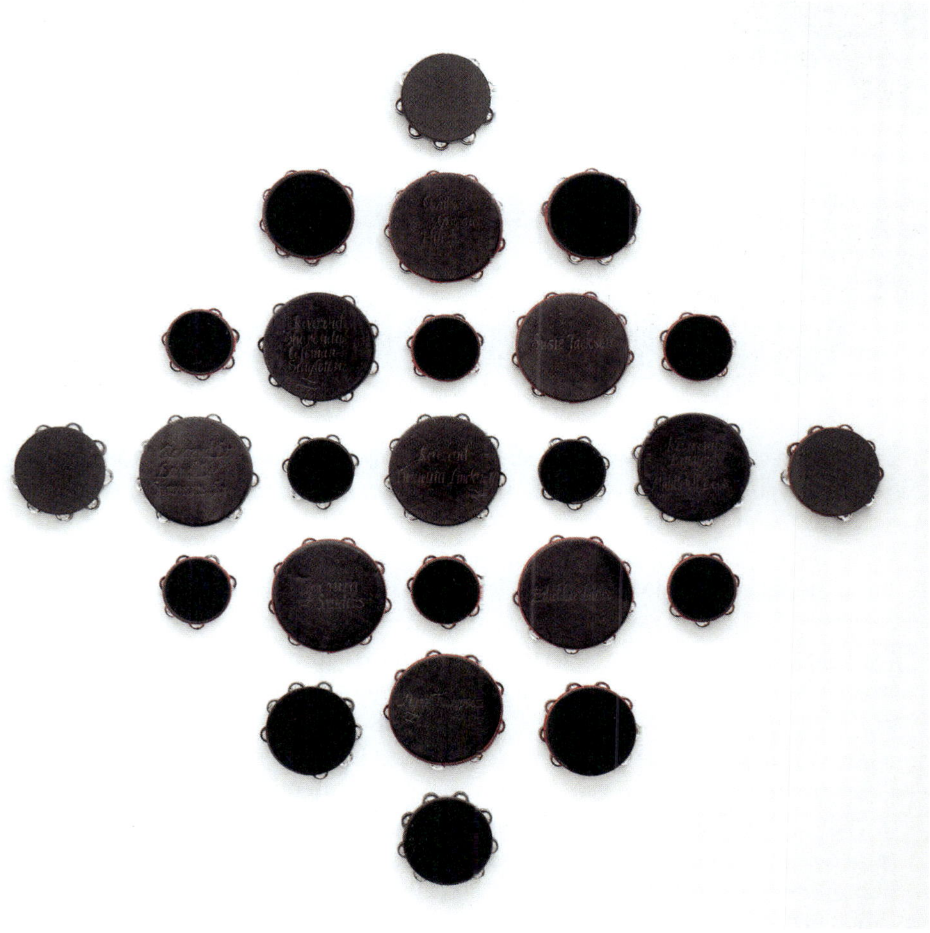

Lava Thomas. *Requiem for Charleston*. 2016. Black tambourines, each inscribed with the name of one of the nine lives lost at Emanuel AME Church. Photo by Kija Lucas. Smithsonian Museum of American Art, Washington, DC.

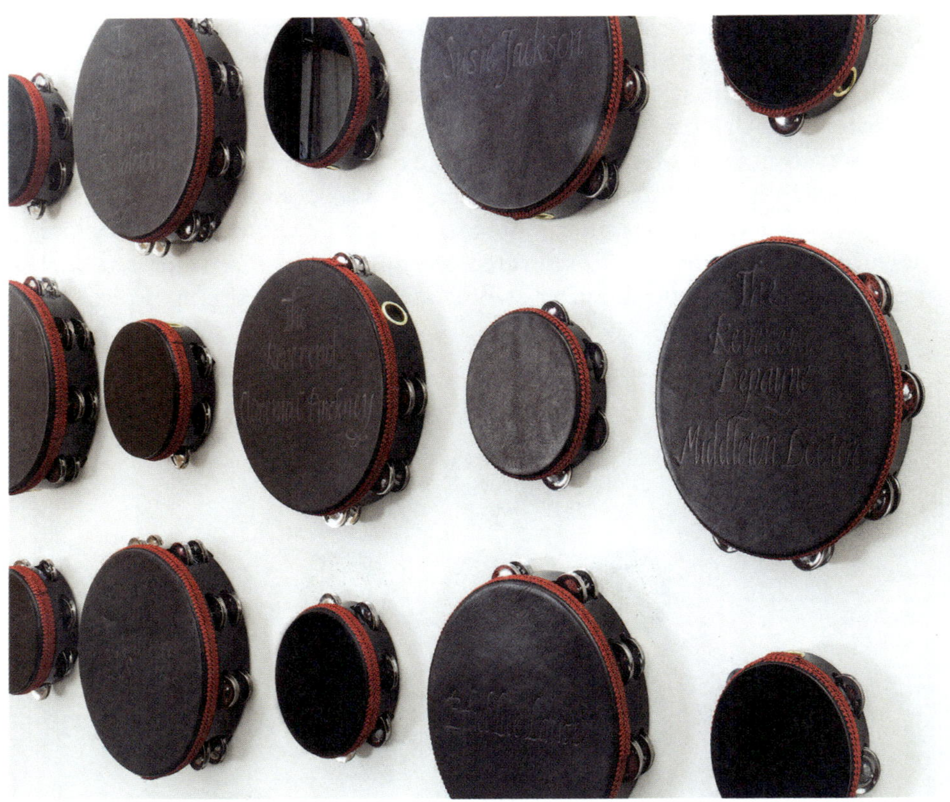

Lava Thomas. *Requiem for Charleston*, detail. 2016. Smithsonian Museum of American Art, Washington, DC. Photo by Kija Lucas.

Church, a collective sense of shock and grief arises as the event is reported in mass media that exposes what I describe as mainstream society's convenient amnesia. In contrast, for Black Americans this tragedy is one of many that has shaped our collective experience of racial violence and domestic terrorism from white people. Although I, along with many others, may see the murders at Emanuel African Methodist Episcopal Church as business as usual in US history, it is still nonetheless shocking and traumatic at a basic human level. Over time, the nation eventually moves on, whereas the families and friends of the victims are left with the long-term residue of trauma connected to the tragedy. When I consider Thomas's artwork and its accessibility at one of the nation's most prestigious museums, her call to remember the lives that were lost shows the power of art and how Black women artists continue to use their art to make people reflect and possibly feel a sense of accountability for the part we as a nation might play in leaving racially motivated violence unchecked within our weak gun-control policies.

Resistance Reverb: Movements 1 & 2

Thomas expanded on the theme of memorialization and the use of tambourines in her body of work for the installation *Resistance Reverb: Movements 1 & 2*. In 2018 Thomas was commissioned to create artwork for the exhibition *Be Not Still: Living in Uncertain Times, Part 2*, at the di Rosa Center for Contemporary Art in Napa, California. She and other participating artists were specifically asked to create art that responded to the evolving sociopolitical climate through a topic of their choice. In her artist statement, Thomas describes *Resistance Reverb* as

> an immersive installation comprised of hundreds of pink tambourines. An instrument of protest, the tambourine has frequently appeared in marches and demonstrations since the mid-twentieth century. Its egalitarian nature speaks to our shared humanity—anyone can play the instrument and its history is tied to cultures around the globe. Many tambourines are suspended from the ceiling in a cloud-like formation while others are mirrored and arranged in a circular configuration on the back wall of the gallery. Their pink surfaces evoke the Women's Marches of January 2017 and moments of feminist activism from the 1980s and 1990s.
>
> Dispersed within the cloud of tambourines are fragments of political speeches excerpted from past and present voices of women's resistance—ranging from Sojourner Truth's 1851 speech, "Ain't I a Woman," to Alicia Garza's powerfully succinct message, "Black Lives Matter."[65]

This tambourine installation, along with fragments of political speeches by women throughout history—dating back to Maria Stewart, the first African American political writer—does not include only Black women but also the Chicana labor leader and civil rights activist Dolores Huerta and the Japanese American civil rights activist Yuri Kochiyama, as well as fragments of speeches by other women activists. *Resistance Reverb: Movements 1 & 2* is an installation that reflects a couple of hundred years of solidarity. Thomas explains,

> I was thinking about feminism and how the history of feminism has always been a fraught one, especially with the relationship between feminists of the 70s and Black feminists. So I created some sort of an imaginary space where all our voices have equal weight, but it is mostly weighted toward Black women's voices. I wanted to create something that had the feeling of being celebratory and something that's hopeful. This installation is something that is aspirational.[66]

What makes this installation aspirational are the kinds of conversations that Thomas had after the killings of Breonna Taylor (March 13, 2020), and George

Floyd (May 25, 2020), which she described as a global reckoning with anti-Black racism. Thomas reflects, "You know what it's like, phone calls and emails, when the truth is that in this history of working together, Black women have not been in a powerful position. So that piece was an aspirational piece; it was a hopeful piece. It was a piece that really spoke to this idea of solidarity, but also very much realizing that it is an aspiration. It is the kind of equitable statement that we have yet to achieve."[67]

Resistance Reverb includes a total of six hundred tambourines. Working with tambourines in her art since 2014, Thomas recalled in our interview that the first tambourine installation she made was a solo exhibition at the Museum of the African Diaspora in San Francisco. For Thomas, the tambourine is a symbol of our shared humanity, because cultures around the globe have this instrument or one like it in their historical and cultural repertoire. It is also an instrument that she grew up seeing played in a Black church. Historically and currently, you can find percussion instruments like tambourines in various European folk traditions, in the Middle East among Jewish and Arab communities, and traditionally among African American cultures. At first the tambourine accompanied spirituals during enslavement and continued through minstrel and vaudeville acts, gospel music, and various forms of popular music that

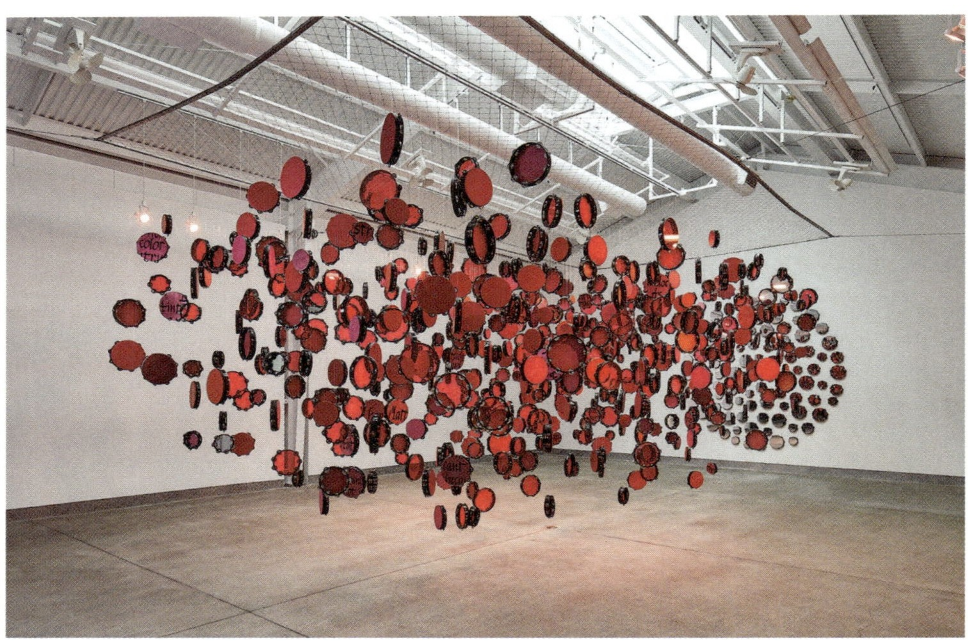

Lava Thomas. *Resistance Reverb: Movements 1 & 2*. 2018. Hall Arts Hotel, Dallas. Photo by Johnna Arnold.

include blues, jazz, and hip hop. There are various iterations of this instrument that everybody can play because it doesn't require any special training. It's one of the first instruments that children have access to. Thomas's use of tambourines in her body of work is multilayered with meaning. Within the context of activism in politics, tambourines reverberate the motif of power being in the hands of the people. This narrative contributes to Black women's understanding and pursuit of wellness as it relates to empowerment.

Curious to know more, I asked Thomas to elaborate further on the symbolism of the tambourine and her personal experience. She said, "I have a very personal connection to the tambourine in a religious and sort of praise context; it is an instrument of joy. And it's an instrument that mostly women play."[68] Like Thomas, I grew up attending a Black church where playing tambourines was a regular part of praise and worship service. On further reflection on my childhood, my first instrument was a small red and silver metal tambourine with a drumhead made of decorated paper. As a child I was excited to have that instrument, which gave me a sense of musicality as I learned to play on beat to music without instruction. My conversation with Thomas triggered several memories of joy. I remember playing my tambourine with such joy and force that one day, I accidentally beat a hole through the paper drumhead, but that did not stop me from still playing along its frame and shaking the zills.

In fact, Thomas and I share very similar experiences, not only associated with tambourines but also early childhood memories connected to art making. I asked Thomas when she first identified as being an artist. She recalls, "I've always known even when I was a child that creating artwork gives me a good feeling, especially because of the way that I work. I was a kid who was always drawing. I was either drawing or reading. Drawing and reading were my two favorite things. . . . Playing the piano, that was something else that I love to do. But my childhood was incredibly difficult and incredibly stressful."[69] So escaping into reading or drawing or playing the piano were all incredibly important to Thomas's survival as well as supporting the argument that art making in itself gives space to healing and wellness. Similarly, Thomas told me, "The search for beauty or the creation of beauty was also essential to my survival and is now the way that I process what's happening in the world around me."[70] When I reflect on my conversation with Thomas, phrases like "essential to my survival," "through escaping," "gives me a good feeling," and "process what's happening" are language that Thomas not only associates with creating art but also express how she has used and continues to use art to heal and/or facilitate wellness for herself.

In navigating the present, Thomas's artwork has turned to processing living in the United States during the Black Lives Matter movement and tragedies like the death of George Floyd, which she describes as "graphically watching a modern-day lynching with George Floyd on video [and] social media."[71] Like many other people, she has been devastated by Black people being killed because of anti-Blackness. She and others who view these deaths in multimedia outlets, like television news and social media, are "bearing witness while Black" and experiencing what Richardson (2020) explains as "gazing into forbidden space—the space of vigilante and state-sponsored violence against Black bodies."[72] Richardson goes on to describe mass media as "a ferocious space that many African Americans always knew existed, even though they never had enough visual evidence to prove that it did."[73] Now, with technology such as camera phones available to the masses, Black people as well as others are not only bearing witness to anti-Black violence but also recording it and sharing it virally on social media. Associated with this phenomenon is the triggering of trauma. Thomas told me that when she heard about the Charleston massacre, she was absolutely devastated to her core. Moreover, she explained, "The only way that I could both process that experience and attempt to heal my own grief was to create a piece about it. And so that piece I did for the Smithsonian American Art Museum now creates a space for national healing. It creates a space for national mourning. It creates a space for national recognition and remembrance."[74]

Thomas has used her personal process of healing her own grief through art to bridge the gap to public healing in ways that are instructive to our understanding about the role artists play in healing communities. Her revelation about her profound devastation and subsequent artistic response unveils a powerful connection between personal grief and collective healing within BWAEs. Her decision to channel that experience into a piece for the Smithsonian Museum of American Art transcends the individual realm, becoming a catalyst for national healing. By creating a space for collective mourning, recognition, and remembrance, Thomas positions her artwork as a crucial contribution to a shared narrative of resilience and remembrance. In this act of translating personal pain into a public medium, Thomas exemplifies the transformative potential of art to facilitate not only personal catharsis but also a broader, national process of reckoning and healing. Artists like Thomas use art to not only memorialize the dead but also to create space for an accessible wake. In her book *In the Wake: On Blackness and Being,* the scholar Christina Sharpe makes the argument for wake work and gives three meanings of *wake*:

> Wakes are processes; through them we think about the dead, and about our relations to them; they are rituals through which to enact grief and memory. . . . But wakes are also the track left on the water's surface by a ship; the disturbance caused by a body swimming or that is moved, in water . . . a region of disturbed flow. . . . [F]inally, wake means being awake and, also, consciousness.[75]

Thomas's *Requiem for Charleston* is an example of "wake work" that causes people to grieve and memorialize the disturbance of Black deaths at the hands of white supremacists. Her art raises awareness of this issue at a national level.

Artists have a long history of commemorating national grief that reflects an even longer history of "Black bodies in pain for public consumption [having] been an American national spectacle for centuries."[76] It is my contention that public consumption of Black bodies in pain is endemic in the United States and deserves critical analysis and commentary enriched with visual counternarratives. In his curatorial statement from the exhibition *Grief and Grievance: Art and Mourning in America*, the late Okwui Enwezor argued that Black Lives Matter identified the condition of Black grief as a national emergency and that artists "have addressed the concept of mourning, commemoration, and loss as a direct response to the national emergency of black grief."[77] These artists' emergency responses call for assessing the role of artists and, as it pertains to the art of wellness, the role of Black women artists who demonstrate a response to "the work of mourning that is both a personal endeavor and a collective ritual."[78]

Thomas's engagement with the public once *Requiem for Charleston* went on view became a conduit for merging personal and collective mourning and healing. For example, she met Reverend Sharon Brisher, whose mother, cousin, and childhood friend were three of the nine who perished in the massacre. Thomas recalls, "She contacted me via email when she heard about the exhibition and the Smithsonian's acquisition. Prior to me appearing on a panel discussion, we were invited to view the piece before the museum opened to the public and Reverend Brisher and her daughter and I had a moment of silence, followed by the two of them searching out the names of the deceased."[79] Thomas's description of silence and the solemn activity of searching for the names of the deceased echoes the experiences of millions of visitors at the Vietnam Veterans Memorial, which honors US service members who fought in the Vietnam War. This national memorial, consisting of two 246-foot-9-inch black granite walls etched with the names of servicemen, is a site of healing for servicemen who, on returning from the war, were not celebrated as heroes because of the war's unpopularity. I find similarities in the lack of regard for slain Black bodies at the hands of racist vigilantes when government policies and the judicial system fail to enact hate-crime laws or hold these vigilantes accountable with convictions.

In comparison, Thomas's *Requiem for Charleston* has the names of the dead burned into the black lambskin tambourine covers, permanently etching them in viewers' memory. Thomas's medium of choice evokes the phrase "like a lamb to the slaughter" as well as Jesus, who is referred to throughout the New Testament as the Lamb of God.[80] Consequently, lambs have become symbolic of the innocent and sacrifice. In addition to these tropes, Thomas's use of tambourines appropriately aligns with what happened the Sunday following the Charleston massacre. Even though tambourines aren't typically used in AME worship, that day, crowds of people took to the streets in support of Emanuel African Methodist Episcopal Church. They rang bells and played tambourines to "make a joyful noise" in support of the church and the victims' families.[81] The tambourine in Thomas's artwork expresses the fact that unlike the tambourines that were played by the church's supporters, the tambourines hung on the wall of *Requiem for Charleston* are permanently silenced. The clear acrylic discs on the faces of some of Thomas's tambourines are strategically placed so that when visitors view the installation closely, they can see their own reflections. As in viewers' experiences with vanessa german's *Power Figures*, the *Requiem* viewers become a part of the artwork, closing the gap between themselves and the human beings who were killed. This powerful lack of distinction removes the sense that terrorism strikes only the "other." It facilitates healing for any viewer, regardless of their race and other factors of identity.

I asked Thomas what feedback or responses to her work she has received, if any. She replied, "The Smithsonian continues to give me updates and they say that *Requiem* is one of the most moving pieces in their collection. It's a quiet piece that requires you to really walk up to it and spend time with it because the names are not immediately visible."[82] The quietness that *Requiem* delivers echoes writer Kevin Everod Quashie's framework of a quiet expressiveness that counters the church supporters' tambourine and bell playing.[83] The meaning of Thomas's art installation unfolds as viewers spend time with it. If viewers are willing to spend that time in a reflective space of quietness, then arguably they can experience moments of quietness that allow for other factors of wellness, such as transparency and healing and even empowerment.

Memorial art created by Black women artists encompasses complexity. On one hand, it makes us painfully aware that lives were lost. This is especially the case for Black lives perpetually taken by violence. On the other hand, their memorial art creates space to celebrate life and to find the beauty and resilience in blackness that allows creativity to flourish despite the insurmountable odds experienced by the Black collective. Before beginning the discussion on vanessa german and Lava Thomas as wellness workers, I pointed out how Black women artists have a long history of doing this kind of wellness work. The artwork and sociopolitical involvement of Augusta Savage and Elizabeth Catlett, along with many others before them, helps to make the case that the trajectory of Black women artist wellness workers has major consequences in reshaping communities and changing minds and, ultimately, the political landscape through visual, written, and performance narratives. In this continuum, vanessa german and Lava Thomas are responding to the movements of their time in ways that are inclusive and effectively galvanize not only members of the Black community but also mainstream public art institutions interested in playing a role in America's reckoning with racism and social injustice at the most or in checking off diversity, equity, and inclusion initiatives at the least. Regardless, there seems to be a consequential transformative justice that comes with german's and Thomas's art that trends in the direction of creative philanthropy.

As we move toward the exploration of Lavett Ballard's impact on individual wellness and artistic flourishing, it is essential to recognize the broader context of Black women artists' function as wellness workers. vanessa german and Lava Thomas exemplify this transformative power through their artistic responses to contemporary movements, resonating with inclusivity and effectively engaging both the Black community and mainstream public art institutions. Their contributions navigate the complex dynamics of America's reckoning with racism and social injustice, encompassing genuine cultural transformation rather than mere compliance with diversity initiatives. In this continuum, Lavett Ballard emerges as an artist poised at the intersection of individual wellness and artistic flourishing, offering a unique perspective that contributes to the evolving narrative of Black women artists as catalysts for transformative justice.

4

Individual Wellness and Artistic Flourishing

When she is quiet, she is ignored.
But the world stands to attention when she roars.
—Lavett Ballard

Art has a unique power to give voice to the voiceless and bring visibility to the unseen. Lavett Ballard's work exemplifies this notion, using her art to make a powerful "roar" that demands attention and recognition.[1] When I first came across Lavett Ballard's artwork, I instantly noticed the materials she uses to center African diaspora experiences, primarily reclaimed wood fences as a canvas for collaging and painting images that reflect Black life in multifaceted ways. Her use of wood is partly an homage to the playwright August Wilson, who so eloquently wrote in his 1985 play *Fences*, "[S]ome people build fences to keep people out, and some people build fences to keep people in."[2] Similarly, Ballard introduces fences in her work to pull her audience into a space of understanding the African diaspora. She mines and repurposes photographs that chronicle her family history and images she draws from historical archives. Then she attaches these photos on the wood canvases to create detailed narrative collages highlighting Black people's collective experiences. These images, adorned with paint and other materials, reflect what Ballard describes as her strong affinity for imagery and history, focusing primarily on creating a visual lexicon of African American female self-identity. Ballard's repurposing of old photographs builds on bell hooks's argument that "access and mass appeal have historically made photography a powerful location for the construction of an oppositional Black aesthetic."[3] The media she uses to create an oppositional Black aesthetic are also the perfect materials for her attempt to reclaim and restore the history and present-day experiences of people whose voices are often stifled, distorted, or pushed to the periphery.

While interviewing Ballard, I came to an understanding that this artist is a Black feminist who subtly presents her sociopolitical stance coupled with stories of her family lineage. Her art-making process first involves selecting photographs of African American women from archival sources and adding gold foil to show their regality and ethnic marks on their faces to connect them to Africa. In counterpoint to showing their beauty, Ballard simultaneously offers some of her subjects' pain and struggles. Her approach to art making often causes her to experience what she calls an asymmetrical emotional balance.[4] The duality of beauty and pain gives more complexity to the figures in Ballard's work and evokes a sense of the roaring and fierceness necessary for Black women to be heard. Further, Ballard's art provides viewers with an understanding that Black women are multifaceted and diverse in their individual experiences of wellness and flourishing. She shows this through personal storytelling and content that reflects everyday life and experiences through an unconventional art medium.

The Significance of Wooden Fences

Sometimes Ballard paints and creates collages on smaller round wood slices. However, her use of wood picket fences as a canvas has brought her the most fame. In 2013 Ballard started painting on wood fences as an undergraduate student studying art. In 2016, near the end of her master of fine arts program, she revisited painting on wood fences with the application of two or three small archival photographs. Ballard found a stockpile of reclaimed wood fences at a fencing company that was more than happy for her to take a few off their hands. In the beginning, her decision to use wood as a canvas was a matter of economics. Ballard needed to work on a cheaper alternative to traditional stretched canvas. As time passed, she found herself drawn to the texture that wood provides to her work. It turned out to be the perfect choice because of the grain within the wood. Old wood has endured over time. It has been through stuff. When Ballard attaches photos and images to its surface, they appear to be painted on the wood. Collage on wood causes a combined effect, making it hard to tell which parts are wood, collage, or paint. This blending of media connects Ballard's visual stories with the wood fences and slices marking time. Metaphorically, Ballard affixes her subjects' experiences to innumerable times.

Furthermore, Ballard's use of wood fences reveals the overall inspiration of her body of work. It connects her art to a larger concept of wellness: family lineage and narratives as a means of engaging and learning about the self. In a moment of deep reflection, Ballard discovered that the real reason she favors wood as a backdrop is part of her childhood experience of traveling from the North to visit her grandmother and the family's legacy house in Virginia.[5] Every summer when Ballard was between the ages of nine and fifteen, her grandmother would travel by Greyhound bus to New Jersey to come and bring her back to Virginia to visit family. She would stay in what they called the "big house." There she would spend the whole summer cleaning the house and visiting with her grandmother. Ballard remembers her grandmother's many stories about their family and other people in their hometown, told while they traveled south. One account is how the "big house" belonged to Ballard's great-great-grandmother, and how in 1910 her sons started building it.[6]

Ballard recalled during our interview, "I'd hear all these stories while staying at this property where I'm seeing beadboard and exposed logs and painted-over logs, with vintage photos of relatives all over the walls. I realized that's where I first fell in love with the idea of wood and photo imagery."[7] The concept of wood, photo imagery, and her family's history essentially converged subliminally for Ballard. While further pondering the connection between her childhood summers in the South and making art, Ballard recognizes why she loves collages and mixing images to tell a story. Acknowledging her talent for storytelling, she affirms, "I could do this forever. I really could. I could just figure out a story I want to tell, the theme, and blend it and do it."[8] Once Ballard figured out how to create visual stories on wood backdrops, she was committed to the process, and it soon became an act of healing and wellness.

Stories My Grandmother Told Me

Inspired by Ballard's visual narratives and body of work centered on Black women, in 2021 I invited her to exhibit at the Community Folk Art Center (CFAC) in Syracuse, New York.[9] Ballard's solo exhibition, *Stories My Grandmother Told Me*, demonstrated a visual inheritance of Black women's stories and a more comprehensive view of how Ballard uses imagery to reflect social issues affecting Black women's stories within a historical context. The exhibition shares its title with Ballard's first-ever intricately collaged fence. In the artwork also called *Stories My Grandmother Told Me* (2017), a group of Black women gather around a "Jim Crow Is Dead!" sign. With gazes directed outward at the viewers, they convey the frustration brought on by voter suppression during the civil rights era. White Americans employed the following tactics to suppress the Black vote: grandfather clauses, all-white primaries, literacy tests, gerrymandering, vote dilution, felony disenfranchisement, and photo identification laws.[10]

Below the sign is an image of a Black woman assisting another Black woman in registering to vote. In another striking image, a Black woman, presumably a suffrage protester, is arrested by three white police officers. As in many of Ballard's collages, another Black woman's face is covered with African-inspired tribal markings as Ballard attempts to "capture the challenges faced by the people she is portraying, connect their stories to their ancestry, and venerate them."[11] The composition and concept of *Stories My Grandmother Told Me* has sparked many other visual narratives about the African American experience

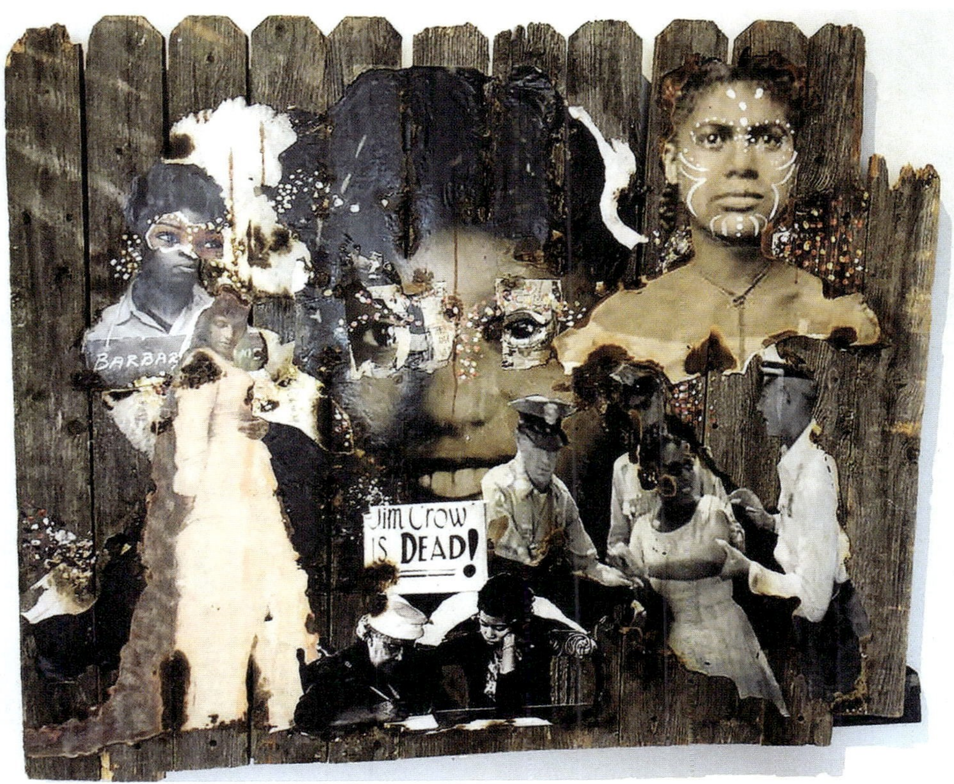

Lavett Ballard. *Stories My Grandmother Told Me*. 2017. Mixed-media collage on reclaimed wood fencing, 36 × 48 in. Courtesy of the artist.

from a Black woman's point of view. For the exhibition at CFAC, Ballard created new pieces of art. She believes that her art-making process, the fusion of wood and archival photography, offers visual narratives directly connected to and inspired by her Southern roots.

I asked Ballard precisely what the title of this show and artwork refers to. She explained that while riding the train down South for the summer, her grandmother would share memorable stories that reflected national historical events of the collective African American experience. In 2021, visitors to CFAC saw *A Dream Deferred* (2020), which pays homage to the Tulsa race massacre of 1921. This fence documents the mobs of white deputized residents who attacked Black residents and businesses in the Greenwood district with guns and explosives.[12] It also amplifies the dignity and beauty of the Tulsa Black community when she surrounds a group photo of Tulsa residents with multicolored orbs and flowers.

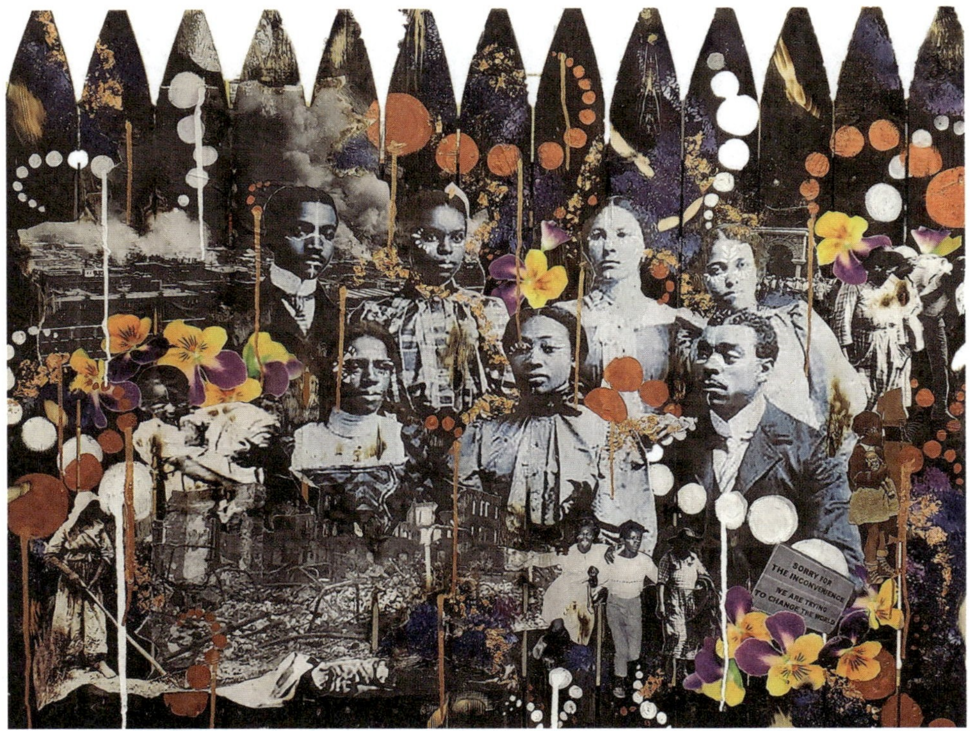

Lavett Ballard. *A Dream Deferred*. 2020. Mixed-media collage on reclaimed wood fencing, 37 × 40 in. Private collection.

Ballard also draws on personal stories of her grandmother, who experienced and protested against discrimination in the Jim Crow South. Her grandmother recalled that she refused to give up her seat while traveling by bus across the Mason-Dixon line. Through the Civil Rights Act of 1964 and the Voting Rights Act of 1965, Congress abolished Jim Crow laws in the southern United States, laws that had enforced racial segregation and curtailed the power of Black voters.[13] However, Jim Crow social codes persist in sustaining segregation between African Americans and white Americans.[14] The resilience and boldness of her grandmother, coupled with her storytelling, influenced Ballard's first wooden fence collage, *Stories My Grandmother Told Me*. Since then, Ballard has continued the tradition of Black women's storytelling in her art by depicting the contemporary narrative of Black women's experiences along with images of her family photos and history.

In addition to her grandmother's stories, Ballard re-created aspects of her childhood home's aesthetics for the CFAC exhibition. In the installation *The Inheritance* (2021), she depicted a room, including faux wooden wall panels

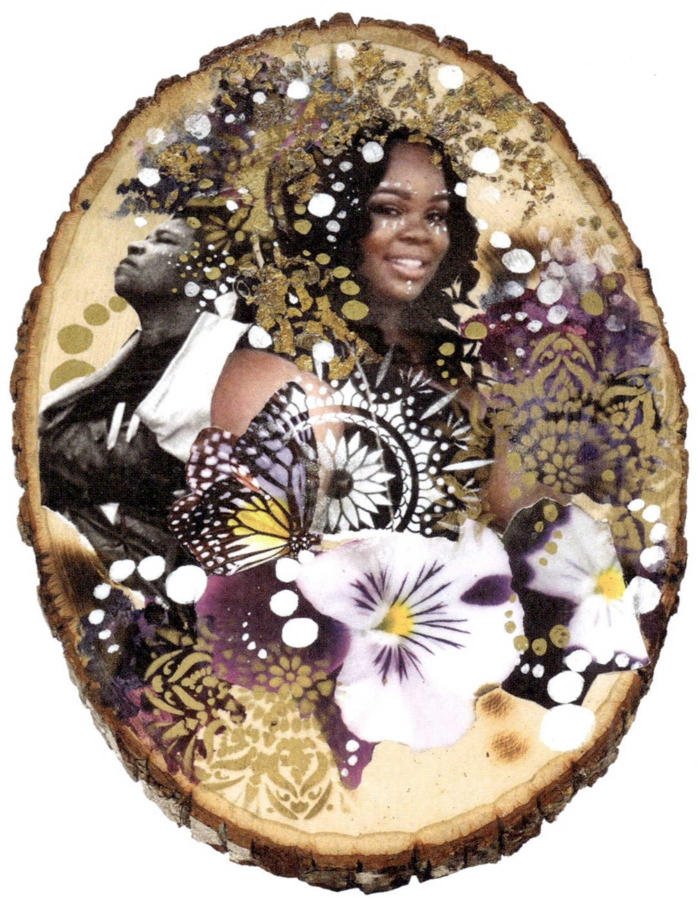

and a vanity dresser, personal artifacts, and mementos from her grandmother, mother, and Ballard herself. A photo of her mother (who passed away from cancer in 2020), pearls, makeup, a purse, an old chamber pot off to the side, and written passages from Ballard's journal were carefully curated on the vanity to tie the three generations of women together and to evoke a sense of legacy.

What is even more nuanced is how Ballard merges her family legacy and inheritance with more contemporary themes instead of only historical references. Hanging on the faux wood panel wall were collaged images on wood slices. Ballard began creating these wood slices, which she called the *Quarantine Chronicles*, during the height of the COVID-19 pandemic (spring and summer 2020) and the Black Lives Matter protests that spread throughout cities in the United States and beyond.[15] Temporarily blocked from entering her studio for months due to the pandemic, Ballard had to work on a smaller scale than usual at her Willingboro, New Jersey, home. in a room the size of a large walk-in closet. The result is wood slices that show images of current social justice issues affecting African Americans. Ballard explained, "I have to be able to create artwork that has a large presence in a small space, like creating the perfect chocolate chip cookie. I only have one bite for people to have before they go to the next thing. It's more of a challenge for me to create artwork that draws people in immediately, that makes them not have to think about what's going on in the news, what's going on in the world."[16] Some notable wood slices pay homage to Black women killed by the police. As an acknowledgment of the campaign "#Say Her Name," Ballard created wood slice collages such as *My Name is Sandra* (2020), *They Call Her Rekia* (2020), *My Name Is Kiyonna* (2020), and *Hear My Call* (2020), a wood slice that honors the memory of Breonna Taylor.[17] Some of these images from the *Quarantine Chronicles* were used to augment the historical images in the social justice film *#SayTheirNames—Women of the Movement*.[18] Other wood slices in the exhibition reflect African cultural iconography by integrating archival images from the African continent, Black girlhood, and themes such as passing, freedom, and resistance, to name a few. *The Inheritance* (2021) ties the present to the past. This installation also had its debut at the Community Folk Art Center's main gallery.

Similarly, *Just Breathe* (2020) depicts Black women who need to exhale while navigating life. Breathing, something everyone alive has in common, is a reminder that we are all still here. Stephanie Evans (2021) argues that as it pertains to Black women's mental health and wellness, breathing is the means and end to stress management as well as the key to living.[19] When Black women engage in more intentional breathing through meditation exercises such as yoga, they open space in their air passages and lung capacity in ways that bring a balance and control necessary for wellness. According to Bylle Avery, we should create space for "breathing life into ourselves," as breathing has a natural healing power.[20] Ballard reminds us of this healing power in both the title and composition of *Just Breathe*, where the central figure in the black-and-white photograph is a young Black woman whose mouth and nose are covered up with gold metallic paint. Ballard surrounds her with beautiful yellow daisies and various blue hues of clouds and white and gold orbs as she gazes off to the right. In the background of the piece is another Black woman with her back turned toward the viewers. She is wearing an African print skirt as she carries a washtub on her head with both hands. In a much smaller foreground image, a little girl mimics the same pose with a small bucket on her head. The whole makes a symbolic connection between Black women's domestic labor and barriers to their wellness. Ballard presents this narrative as historical and multigenerational. From her point of view, this is the reason Black women need to breathe with intention and to implement self-care. The act of breathing may seem like a simple technique, since it is something that

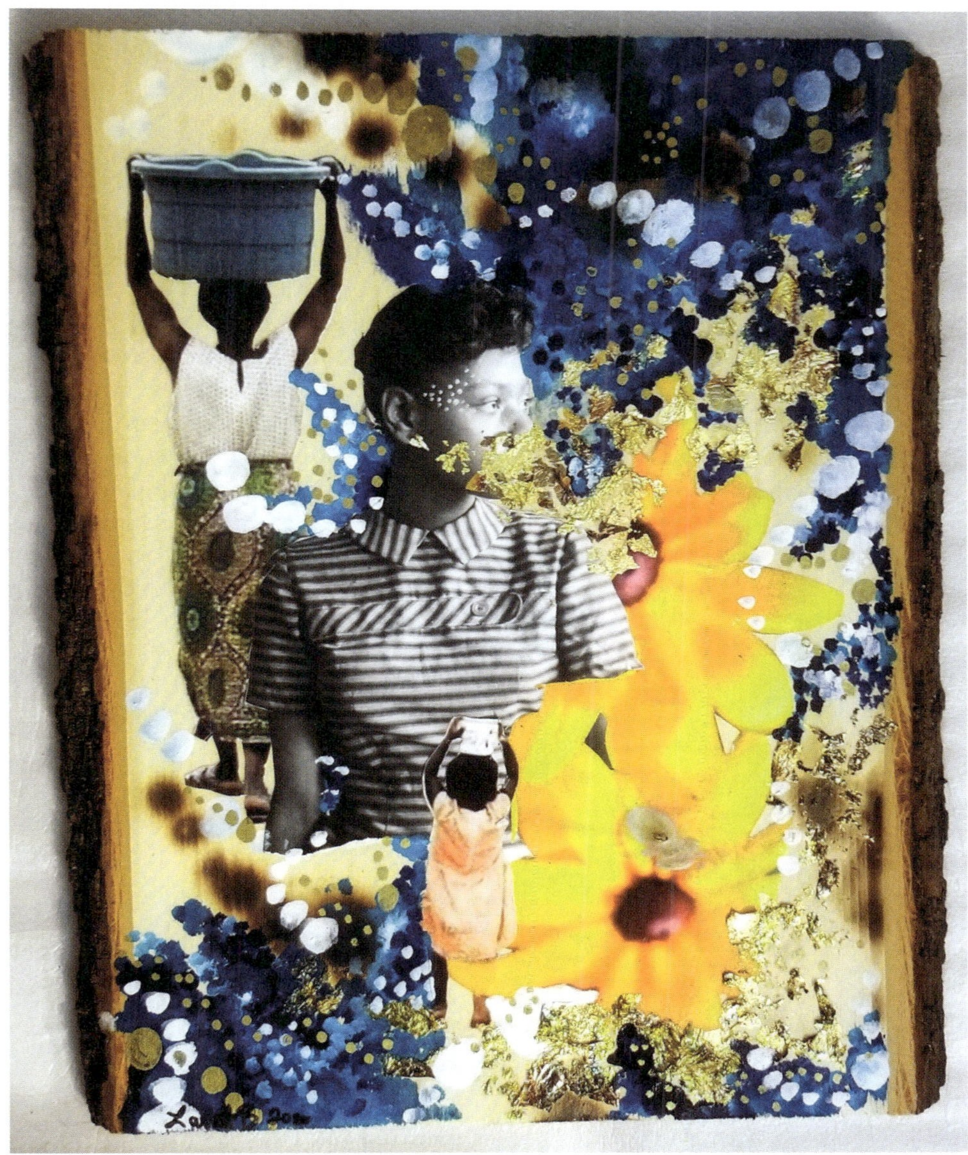

Lavett Ballard. *Just Breathe*. 2020. Mixed-media collage on wood slice, 12 × 11 in. Private collection.

many healthy and able-bodied people do without thinking. However, Evans argues, "Simply saying 'just breathe' is not so simple. Yet breathing is the one thing we cannot do without for any length of time—so, when and however we can, we must persist."[21] Throughout the exhibition *Stories My Grandmother Told Me*, Ballard echoed the persistence of Black women's wellness as it pertains to people of the African diaspora, especially Black women. Her visual reminders fit her purpose as through art she builds a new world that gives Black women space to pursue and actualize aspects of self-care.

Wellness, Art Making, and Meditation

Ballard's process of collage on wooden surfaces is intricately detailed. Some of her art-making processes involve pyrography, burning designs onto wood or paper. She also employs techniques of carving grains in birchwood panels, staining and destructing, deconstructing, and restructuring her work by tearing and shredding materials. Ultimately, Ballard's work involves painting images. While adding gold and metallic foils to her work, she decides where to carve into the wood when it calls for it. Ballard describes the process as a beautiful mess, from which she understands that there is a lot of pretty in something ugly, and there is also a fine line between the two. In her wellness work and art making, Ballard has embraced making mistakes and pushing through to reach the final goal of a completed piece of art. To explore Ballard's wellness and art-making connection, I asked her what the art-making process does for her. Further, how does it connect to her overall being as a person and as an artist? She explained:

> It clears my brain. As a wife and mother to two sons and a new grandchild, I have many responsibilities. So going to my art space, wherever I make my art space, I keep my brain healthy and centered. It's all about me focusing all my creative adrenaline and energy on something that relaxes me.[22]

Ballard's discussion of art making and clarity directly aligns with how Black women artists facilitate wellness. As Ballard explained the state of meditation she experiences while creating art, she showed me artwork she was currently making. I saw a figure of a Black woman whose face she marked with white dots in an intricate pattern she calls mapping. With the focused energy her work brings her, Ballard's art making helps her deal with life's everyday stress. And it was stress from one day that inspired her to map out the figure's face:

> I'm just doing the mapping out and markings on her face. I was a little stressed yesterday because I had schoolwork and a lot of administration work, and I said to myself, "I need to clear my brain." So just the relaxing motion of just picking up my marker and figuring out what pattern I'm going to do and just the repetitiveness of just doing it and doing it and doing it, and not having to think about anything else but this, is so good for my mental health. It just clears everything out. It clarifies the cobwebs, and it allows me to focus on something else, which is beyond healing.[23]

Ballard's process of making dots in her art is akin to attention-based meditation that involves "training attention to focus on an object or a word," such as a mantra or a chant."[24] The moments of clarity Ballard gets from making art occur when she creates a space for emotional balance necessary to rejoin what she calls the real world. After finding time to collect her thoughts, Ballard often becomes clearer on her priorities. She explains, "We all need that. We all need that moment to kind of clear, or as I tell my kids all the time, relax, relate, and release. Relax, relate to the situation, and release. Just let it all go. The moment you do that, you feel so much better."[25]

When Ballard develops moments of clarity and relaxation through art, it reveals how art making connects with self-care. Making art has a direct impact on her emotional and mental well-being. Because she is a wife and a mother, it also affects the well-being of her family, who not only see her modeling self-care but also feel able to have conversations on how to establish it for themselves. While interviewing Ballard, I noticed that she was wearing a black T-shirt emblazoned with the phrase "It's Handled! Black Women Everywhere."[26] Considering that we were meeting to discuss Black women and wellness, I asked Ballard how she interpreted the message on her shirt and how that message connected with her life and being an artist.

Reflecting on the interview question, Ballard explained that she usually ends up wearing her favorite T-shirt when she goes to work in the studio or when she is delivering a piece of artwork. Often when she is putting together an installation, someone in a gallery may ask her, "Did you do this? Or did you do that?" Often Ballard responds with, "Read my T-shirt. I'll literally say, 'Read my T-shirt. What does it say?' 'Oh, okay. You got it.' Read my T-shirt."[27] Ballard believes that Black women often must handle everything in their lives with less help. She describes what are known as the Strong Black Woman (SBW) and Superwoman (SW) tropes. These tropes derived from a well-known intersectional racial and gender stereotype known as the mammy, which traces back to the "mammy" role during slavery in the United States.[28] Carolyn West defines the mammy as a self-sacrificing, mothering woman who cares for her slaveholder's family and household, her own family, and the community without fatigue or being (mentally) affected.[29] An oppressive white society created this narrative to justify the economic exploitation of Black women, who were used as house slaves and to perform other domestic, historically restrictive roles.[30] Over time, Black women have adopted SBW and SW ideologies as contemporary narratives of strength and resilience, despite their consequences of Black women neglecting their physical and emotional health.[31] The "Strong Black Woman" syndrome that many Black women have adopted as part of their coping mechanism makes the burden of their experiences more palatable, connecting back to Ballard's position that "[w]e're built for this. And there is no Black woman that has not had to tell people, 'Listen, relax, chill, we've got this.' If we don't have it, we're going to fake it till we make it, like we do have it. We've got it handled."[32] This "fake it until you make it" ideology is what West describes as *performing strength*.[33]

When Black women perform strength, it involves thinking that they must be strong for loved ones, be survivors, and be hyper-independent despite how they feel. However, this is a superficial strength associated with chronic health issues like anxiety and depression.[34] Black women suffer from the Strong Woman Syndrome, a characteristic seen as honorable. Tamara Beauboeuf-Lafontant points out that the problem lies in the apparent acknowledgment of Black women's work, family responsibilities, and achievements under challenging social conditions as strength. Although it seems to provide a straightforward and honorable recognition, Beauboeuf-Lafontant argues that this commendation is undermined by its actual role: protecting a hierarchical social structure by concealing Black women's experiences of suffering, desperation, and anger.[35] Mental health practitioners have established that it is detrimental to many Black women's psychological and physical health. Thus, as with many other Black women, Ballard's cultural embrace of the mantra "It's handled" challenges her efforts to be in a state of wellness. Also, it suggests, like all the artists explored in this book, she is not absolved from internal factors or from adopting cultural values within the African American community that actually harm Black women's well-being. This example substantiates the established definition of wellness as "an active process through which people become aware of, and make choices toward, a more successful existence."[36] People obtain and sustain good health by actively pursuing wellness. As an artist, Lavett uses the vehicle of art to cultivate emotional wellness. More specifically, she harnesses a sense of wellness for herself and Black women by creating visual narratives that center and empower them, despite their collective experiences of subjugation and marginalization. Siraad Dirshe posits, "White supremacy—which has harmed everyone, including robbing White people of their own humanity—needs anti-blackness to thrive. Centering blackness removes both the fuel and the constraints of White supremacy, allowing everyone to be free of its tyranny."[37]

Ballard's centering of Black women in art did not go unnoticed by *TIME* magazine. In the early spring of 2020, Lavett Ballard and the Black women portrayed in her art were brought front and center when *TIME* commissioned the artist to commemorate the Montgomery bus boycott of 1955–56 in celebration of Women's History Month and the hundredth anniversary of the Nineteenth Amendment. Ballard received an email from D. W. Pine, creative director of *TIME*, who had curated various covers for *TIME*'s 100 Women of the Year. At first, Ballard thought the email was a joke, and she was going to ignore it, but something prompted her to respond. Soon, the trajectory of her art career took an upward turn when Pine asked Ballard to create art highlighting the Black women who had organized the boycott. Ballard created *We Shall Not Be Moved* (2020).[38] In an interview with her alma mater, Rowan College at Burlington County, Ballard described some of the symbolism in the art: "I used Rosa as the centerpiece because she was the one who was able to bring the movement to fruition. I also used images of the buses, of people standing outside waiting, of people walking and yellow roses to represent freedom."[39] The magazine featured her artwork on the cover of the March 5, 2020, issue in select cities. For the February 2023 edition, Ballard was commissioned to create artwork that was included inside the magazine to complement an essay by the Pulitzer Prize–winning author Isabel Wilkerson.[40] This recognition of Ballard's work exemplifies the significant contributions of Black women artists in contemporary discourse.

Ratification of the Nineteenth Amendment took almost a century of activism to succeed. The demand for women's suffrage became a prominent feature in discussing the history of the women's rights movement. The considerable gain realized by that victory involved the collective efforts of many, including Black women, whose contributions have often been ignored by the political silencing that is often predicated on both institutional racism and gender discrimination. Martha Jones argues that notwithstanding the obstacles, over the past two hundred years Black women have developed a vision for American politics and have served in the vanguard, leading and showing the way at the nation's critical turning points.[41]

In *We Shall Not Be Moved* (2020), Ballard highlights Black women's significant contributions by including images of known and unknown Black women who spearheaded the Montgomery bus boycott. A prominent photo of Rosa Parks is juxtaposed with a court document listing other unsung heroines such as Aurelia S. Browder, Susie McDonald, and Claudette Colvin. All of them were instrumental in the success of this historic protest. The presence of these women in both image and text, along with a collage of other archival photos, communicates the collective effect of social protest, beauty, and struggle, as Ballard corrects our understanding of history. Her artistic homage to Black women's participation in securing justice and equality is a visual documentation of their efficacy. Since she was one of a very select cohort of artists for the *TIME* magazine feature, this opportunity significantly elevated her visibility as an artist and lit Ballard's professional path as her prominence grew. Also, the large scale of Ballard's art helps people recognize her work.

Ballard's wooden fence sculptures are particularly notable because of their large size. She uses this large scale as an opportunity to tell Black women's stories from multiple angles. Her most extensive fences are typically seventy-two inches high. She often exhibits them as diptych and triptych installations, surrounded by potting soil at their bases. The mounds of dirt give the

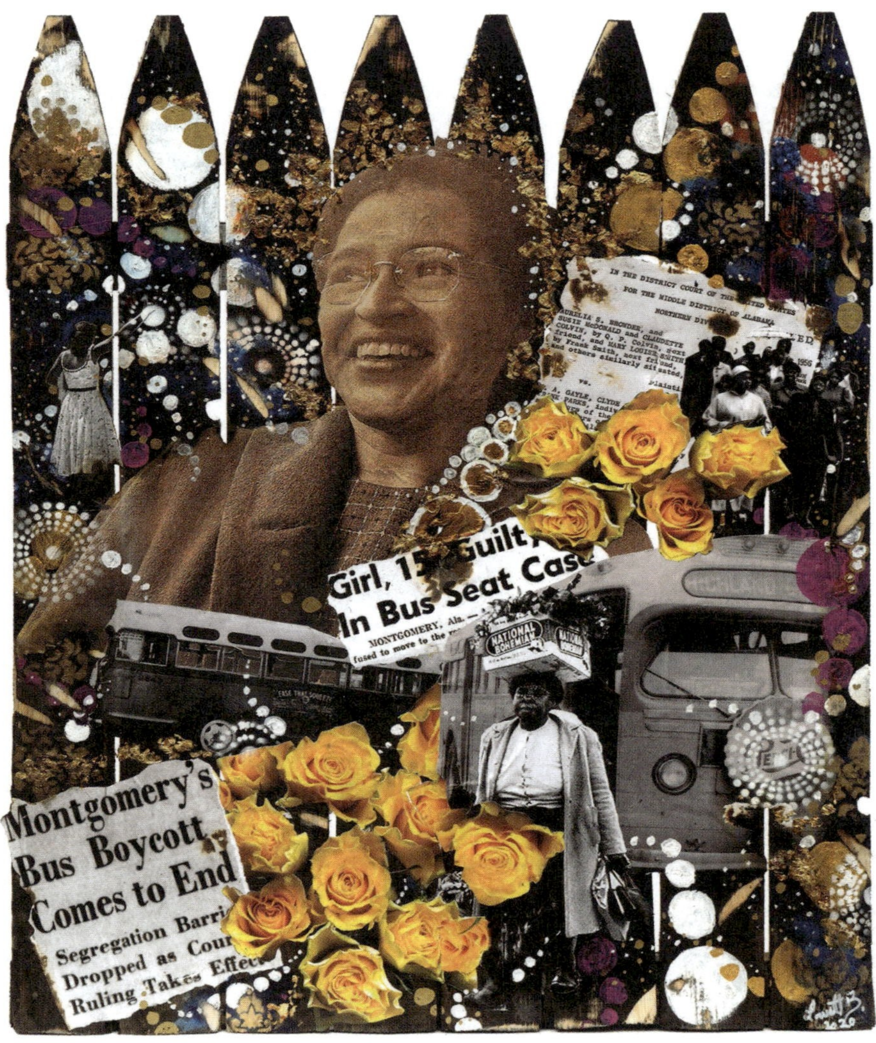

Lavett Ballard. *We Shall Not Be Moved (1955 The Bus Riders)*. 2020. Mixed-media collage on reclaimed wood fencing, commemorating the Montgomery bus boycott, featuring Rosa Parks and other pivotal figures, 36 × 40 in. Courtesy of the artist.

sculptures a more authentic feel, as they imitate outside fences posted in the ground. The large-scale pieces in Ballard's exhibition add a grounding effect that anchors her subjects while getting viewers' attention as a male peacock does when it spreads its tail to display its vibrantly colored feathers. Likewise, Ballard is also trying to get us to pay attention and forces us to engage with her work; we have no way of avoiding these images.

Smaller images layered with just enough pops of color and painted objects temper Ballard's large installations. The small details of Ballard's art and their subtlety prompt viewers to investigate the details, subtly inviting them to explore Black women's collective experiences. I asked Ballard what feedback she receives from people who experience her work. She responded, "Many people are drawn to the intricate details, and often people tell me that each time they look at a particular artwork they find something new they didn't see before."[42]

Ballard's art calls for our attention by making full use of in-the-round sculptures. Ballard sometimes puts a small collage of her family on the back of her art to tie her own history to the visual narrative she is creating. On the back of the sculptures are what she calls "shadow figures" that are sometimes less noticeable but still vibrant. Ballard coined the term "shadow figure" to describe the less vibrant images in her work. The shadow figures complement the narratives conveyed on the artwork's front side. For example, *She Has Risen* (2020) features soft pastel colors on dark wood to tell the story of young girls and women rising and coming into their own within their respective communities. Other imagery reflects Black women's contribution to nationhood, such as an older Black woman sewing an American flag and a younger Black woman holding up her fist as a symbol of Black power. Beautiful flowers, patterns, and white orbs of light guide our eyes and surround these figures.

When visitors enter a gallery and approach the back side of *She Has Risen*, they see a shadow figure. For example, the silhouette of a Black woman holding up gold, bronze, and copper lights that symbolize planets. Ballard subtly gives the figure hair using burnt and smudged wood, and orbs of light adorn the figure as a headdress and necklace that drizzle down her body. Like the images on the front side of this sculpture, the shadow figure has risen and controls the light. Like all the shadow figures in Ballard's work, this figure pulls viewers closer in by making them work to see its composition. Shadow figures also add continuity to Ballard's exhibitions so that, regardless of the side from which you approach her sculptures, you get the same floating narrative.

A shadow is a dark area or shape produced when a body comes between light rays and a surface.[43] Often shadows are symbolically connected to something ominous. Yet in Ballard's work, shadow figures are counterparts to the self that encompass a bit of mysticism with newfound visibility. They also facilitate Black women's wellness by shaping the unmanifested and unheard lessons, dreams, and characteristics of Black women that often get buried or marginalized. Ballard offers visual space to the unknown parts of Black women that reflect their complexity and vulnerability. Black women are not afforded this opportunity in mainstream societies that subjugate them and discredit their lived experiences.[44] Lavett Ballard also wants humanity to hear Black women's voices along with the symbolic shadowing of Black women's wellness.

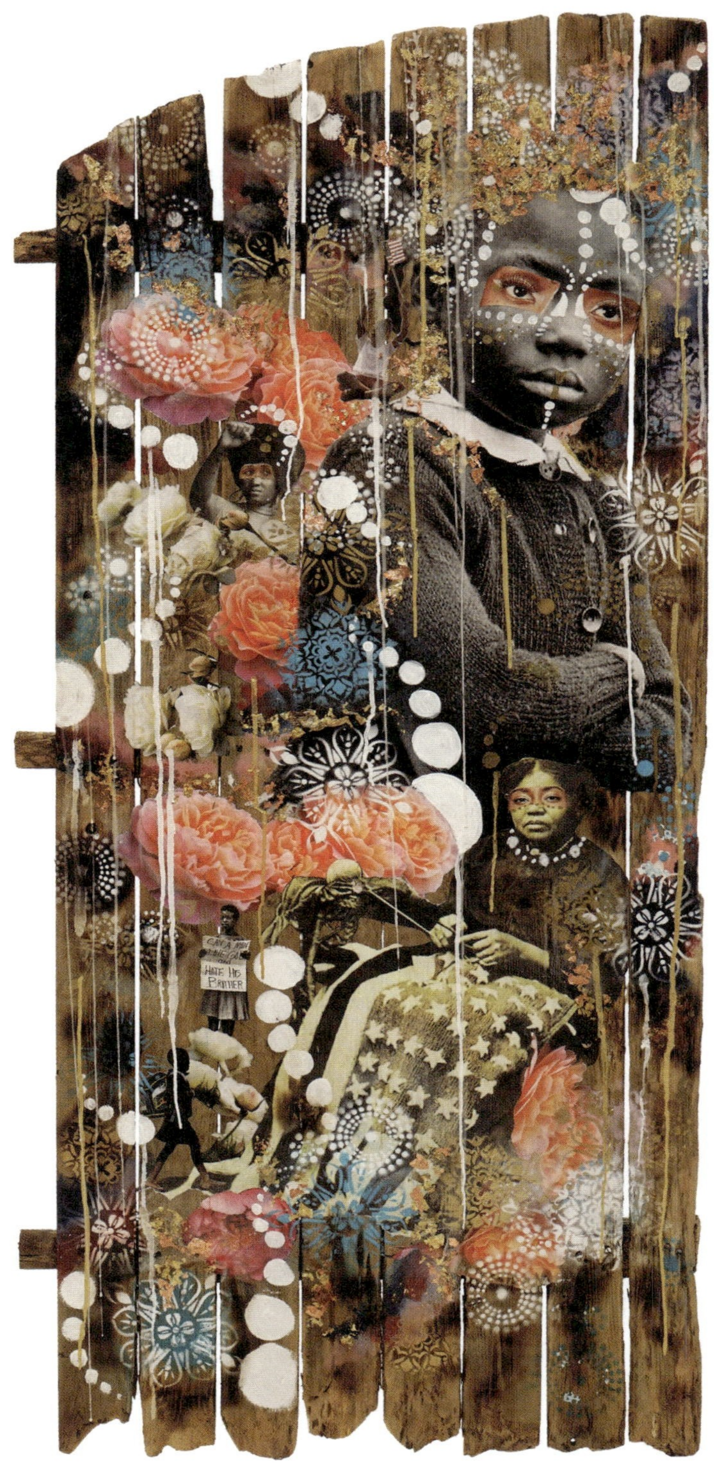

Lavett Ballard. *She Has Risen.* 2020. Mixed-media collage on reclaimed wood fencing, 68½ × 31 in. Private collection.

In the fall of 2020, Ballard's collaged fences were exhibited online by the Long-Sharp Gallery.[45] The title of the exhibition, *When She Roars* (2017), is also the title of Ballard's very first large-scale fence panel piece. Ballard explained the significance of this piece in a recorded account for the online exhibition. Before she created this large panel, she struggled to identify where to place the collage images of African American women's stories that she had been working on for some time.[46] Then, in what Ballard describes as a serendipitous moment, a storm destroyed her neighbor's wooden fence, causing it to fall from its posts. In the destruction, Ballard saw the symbolism of the wood and decided that it made the perfect substrate. Months would go by before Ballard applied the collage images to the wood. During that time, she perfected her collaging process by figuring out the most sustainable adhesive to use. With more clarity about her art-making process, Ballard chose one large panel from the neighbor's fence as her landscape. Ballard describes the panel she chose as being more worn than the others. It had very rough edges and was chipped and broken in places, much like the women she would portray on it. This story links Ballard's material choices to the heightened emotional experiences of Black women.

When She Roars (2017) features the photo of a girl holding a sign with the word "JUSTICE" on it. The last three letters of the word, "ICE," are blocked with a raised fist from another collaged Black female figure. Other Black women have their fists raised as they gaze at viewers defiantly, daring them to fight them or argue with them. An image of a woman from Africa with transposed collaged lips is off to the left-hand side of the panel, and at the bottom of the canvas is the striking image of Mattie Howard Harris. Howard was a high school student protester arrested during the Children's Crusade

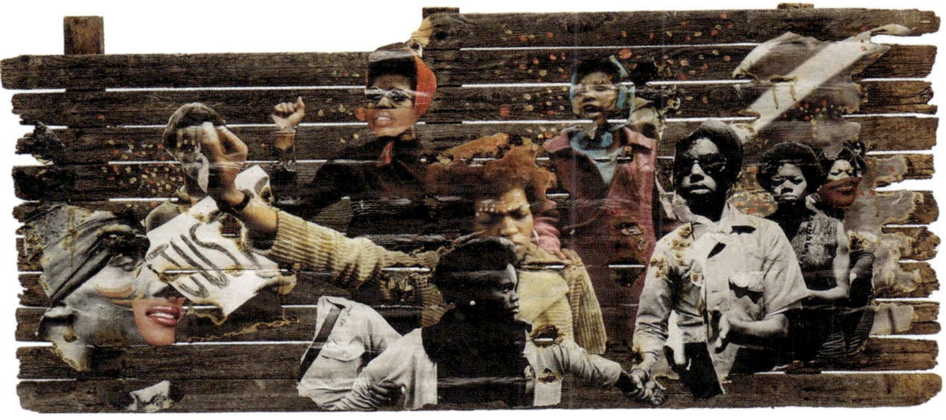

Lavett Ballard. *When She Roars*. 2017. Mixed-media collage on reclaimed wood fencing, 63 × 30 in. Courtesy of the artist.

in 1963.[47] Rather than showing the arresting officer handcuffing Howard, Ballard's collage shows Howard clasping the hand of a young Black woman initiate from the 1970s Black Panther Party. Ballard explains that the gesture communicates, "I've got you, sis." Ballard wants viewers to know that all the figures in this piece interact as though they are in the same space, even though they come from different times and places. Accordingly, we should not ignore the narratives and experiences of these women. By creating this visual narrative, Ballard is "asking the viewers to hear and see them roar."[48] The artist's endeavor to give Black women visibility and voice provides a pathway for wellness while creating the context of the work and the images.

Ballard accomplishes this through a process of transparency and sharing Black women's stories in a way that extracts truth and vulnerability from their experiences.[49] When creating art, Ballard fosters a dialogue with viewers via images she carefully excavates and researches. Consequently, she brings Black women the visibility they so often have been denied but rightfully deserve. Most important, Ballard challenges emerging generations of scholars and collectors to raise questions about how more space can be given to artists like her to provide a complete picture of the American experience.

In the summer of 2020, Ballard was doing a lot more work at a time when it was challenging to find a focal point. This challenge led her to a space of more profound reflection on what visual narratives she should create. When asked to describe her experience of creating art during the global pandemic and a long period of social isolation, she explained, "Right now, a lot of us are kind of lost in this environment around us. While creating art, I had to ask myself, what information do I filter for my health and body? What information do I want to let go?"[50] Ballard's questions reveal that the narratives she tells in her art can affect her health and wellness. This is so true that she must be intentional in exploring or not exploring certain content as a means of wellness. Much of her process involves going back and forth on what to include or omit in her work. Ballard describes her art-making process in the following way: "Sometimes I say to myself, 'It looks really messy. Do I like it looking messy?' or 'Should I just texture the hell out of this piece? Do I like it that way?'"[51] Ballard's conversations with her artwork reveal that much of what she's experiencing and observing in the world is reflected in her art. Included is what she filters in and excluded is what she filters out as a means of securing wellness. Her careful choice of images and narratives involves a lot of internal negotiation. While making art, Ballard will often look at the wooden canvas she is working on to assess what she likes about it or if the artwork needs something else. Sometimes she'll add material, only to take it away. It's apparent in Ballard's description that she is in constant dialogue with her art. I asked her if the art speaks to her. On reflection, Ballard explained, "Oh yeah, oh yeah. All the time. My kids will tell you that while I'm working in my studio space, they'll think I'm on a Zoom call or phone call because they hear me saying, 'Why are you giving me this trouble? Why are you doing this to me?' And they ask, 'Are you okay, Mom?' And I tell them, 'I'm just talking.' And they say, 'Okay, okay. You sure you're fine?' I tell them, 'I'm just trying to work something out.'"[52]

Two things stand out from Ballard's dialogue. First, not only is she speaking to her pieces of art but they also are speaking to her on an emotional level. Through this process of negotiation, agreements develop about what types of stories about the Black community and specifically about Black women get told. The personified artwork gives Ballard space to expand her visual representation of a particular story or figure and connect it to a broader narrative or to other figures in that artwork. In its totality, the piece of art soon becomes a more comprehensive and more communal narrative. Ballard's process of "trying to work something out" echoes the birthing process that Where We At member Jennifer Bowden described in chapter 1. I interpret Ballard's process of conversing with her artwork and allowing the artwork to respond as a dynamic and intimate engagement with the creative process. Ballard communicates this symbiotic relationship through her craft, expressing thoughts, emotions, and ideas. Simultaneously, the artwork "talks back" by revealing unexpected nuances, insights, and forms that emerge during the art-making process. This reciprocal dialogue is a reflective and iterative practice. Ballard's vision evolves in tandem with the evolving expression of the artwork, fostering a space for her personal wellness through a unique and organic creative exchange.

Many artists who attend graduate school for visual art will share their experiences of being brutally criticized at every turn. Sometimes instructors critique their concepts, artistic forms, or basic techniques—for example, how they hold their paintbrushes while painting or why they choose a particular palette of colors. Often, the experience of matriculating through an MFA program can leave the student-artist second-guessing whether they are good enough to be an artist—in addition to the racial and gender bias reported by many Black women who have attended art school. Yet Ballard explains that at this point in her career, she is no longer bothered by outside critiques. Instead, she lets the work critique itself.[53] Part of the negotiation between Ballard and her artwork involves a process of applying images to and ripping them off her wood canvas and then later asking, "Why did I do that?" only to come back to a piece and come to an agreement. "Oh, that's why I needed to rip it off. It needs something else here."[54] Therefore, some of Ballard's latest work is messier, more complex and, in her opinion, more intriguing visually.

Many of Ballard's collectors who are familiar with her previous work are accustomed to those simpler compositions. However, Ballard's current artworks involve many images in a single piece. The scavenger hunt that she invites viewers on is similar to finding a person's soul. She gave this analogy:

"A person you meet can look attractive from the outside; however, it is only when you have conversations with that person that you actually begin to know whether she is also attractive on the inside. The same can be said about Black women, who are layered beings, yet are denied space or permission to be fully human because of antagonistic public scrutiny or criticism."[55] In this way, Ballard's art becomes a powerful medium for exploring and celebrating the complexity of Black women's identities. Through her intricate compositions, she challenges viewers to look beyond surface appearances and engage with the deeper, multifaceted realities of her subjects. Her work not only offers a visual feast but also invites meaningful reflection and dialogue about healing.

Women Heal through Rite and Ritual: Ballard

In Ballard's work, there is a direct connection between wellness and Black women serving as community healers. I first recognized this in Ballard's artwork in *Women Heal through Rite and Ritual* (2020). Ballard submitted five collages on wooden fences that present visual narratives of Black women as healers within their communities. Initially, when the gallerist and curator Myrtis Bedolla extended an invitation for Ballard to exhibit, the artist did not think she had a catalog of work that fitted the show's theme. However, once she read Bedolla's short description of the idea of the gallery show, she recognized that at least one piece of art in her portfolio fitted the exhibition theme perfectly. From there, Ballard decided to create four new works of art to exhibit. She is the first artist listed in the exhibition's online catalog, with the presentation of *Kindred* (2018), the initial artwork that she recognized as having a theme of healing and wellness.

When asked what inspired her to create *Kindred*, Ballard shared that literature she reads often inspires her ideas for her artwork. So her love for the author Octavia Butler's catalog of work, specifically the book *Kindred* (1979), connected with Ballard's desire to create a piece of art that examines the idea of women traversing time and space to preserve their family lineage. As it relates to the group exhibition at Galerie Myrtis, Ballard explained:

> I felt that *Kindred* was the piece that was most about rites because it is this idea of women and how we control the family and how we pass down from generation to generation this idea of how things should be done, how we are the nursemaids, we are the teachers, we are the educators, we are the cooks, we are the chauffeurs, we are the everything in the family. Most importantly, we're the historians. We're the ones who pass down the knowledge from one generation to another.[56]

Expounding on the idea of Black women as historians, the vanguards of community, and the keepers of generational knowledge means that we are

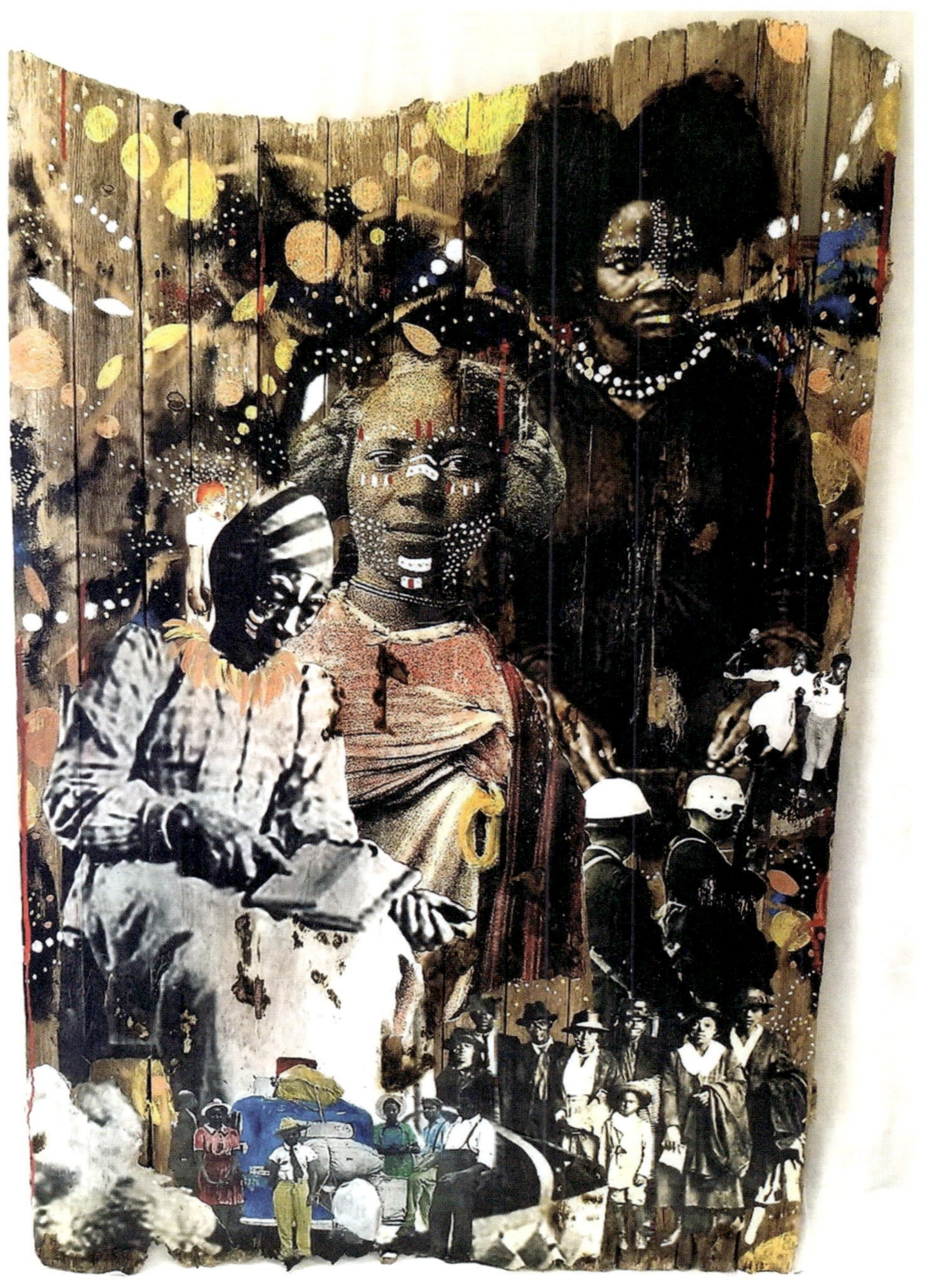

Lavett Ballard. *Kindred.* 2020. Mixed-media collage on reclaimed wood fencing, 72 × 48 in. Private collection

empowered to shape how we see ourselves and how other people in the Black community see and internalize a knowledge of self as individuals and a collective. Ballard's thinking and art making echo Butler, who wrote, "Sometimes I wrote things because I couldn't say them, couldn't sort out my feelings about them, couldn't keep them bottled inside me."[57]

Through the composition of *Kindred* (2018), Ballard builds on Butler's ideas about Black women needing to save themselves and their lineage. At first glance, viewers can see three prominent and centralized collaged Black female figures on a backdrop of orange, white, and yellow orbs, placed diagonally to suggest a family lineage. In conversation, Ballard explained that these women represent three different generations. Placed in the forefront, they connect to a larger story of the Great Migration and the movement of African Americans from the South to northern US cities such as Chicago, New York, and Detroit.[58] Juxtaposed to these women in the lower frame of the wooden fence canvas is a collaged black and white historical photo of an African American family from the rural South arriving in Chicago in 1920.[59] Men, women, and children are holding their coats and are surrounded by luggage while they gaze at viewers of Ballard's artwork. Ballard added a painted blue car packed with suitcases and large tied-up bundles of personal belongings on the roof and the back end of the vehicle that will accompany them. She also includes other archival images of African Americans and applies painted splashes of color to their clothes that make them stand out.

In contrast, and with their backs turned toward viewers, in a black and white photo two White male figures with shotguns in hand represent law enforcement and face two Black women who are running almost off the right-side margins of the wood canvas. *Kindred* consists of many historical images of the Great Migration, which Ballard believes "was spurred by Black women saying this is not working for us, and we need a new opportunity."[60] *Kindred* is also a visual concept that Ballard connects to the themes in Bedolla's exhibition. In her art many Black women advance social norms and practices, conventional acts, and solemn ceremonies. As a Black woman, Ballard is primarily invested in highlighting Black women's experiences in her work. Some of these Black women are family members. In *Women Heal through Rite and Ritual*, all the main subjects in her work are Black women.

While discussing another piece in the exhibition, *A Song Flung Up to Heaven* (2020), Ballard addressed how that large, in-the-round wood sculpture presents themes of healing in the Christian church, with the majority of the figures being Black women facilitating healing through song and prayer. Colorful orbs surround the Black women in this work; some have tribal markings on their faces, connecting African American women with their African ancestry. Also included in the artwork are Ballard's favorite flowers, sunflowers. It is no coincidence that Ballard includes them. Sunflowers are associated with worship and adoration because they always face the sun; they symbolize unwavering faith and unconditional love.[61] Furthermore, this sculpture depicts Black women singing, praying, and worshiping, posed with their arms outstretched. Some women appear to be older and would be considered the mothers of the church: "The congregation looks at them as very godly ladies serving as examples to the people and ensuring stability to the church."[62] The women wear their Sunday-best white dresses, which identify them as missionaries or ministers in the church. What is particularly noticeable about this sculpture is that one of its pickets is damaged. Ballard intentionally chose a broken fence for her piece to represent the brokenness that she says many people hope to heal through Christianity.[63] I asked Ballard why she chose only to depict Black women in this artwork. She explained, "I am a Black woman, and I think I would be doing a dishonor to my ancestors. I think they would roll up from the great beyond and say, 'We gave you all this talent, not to be drawing a whole bunch of other people.' Not only that, but I think in the art world, there are so many people appropriating our image of who we are, and they don't know anything about who we are."[64] What Ballard is describing is the prevalent patriarchy that exists in the art world. An introductory essay on women in the visual arts notes, "From ancient times to the present, women throughout the world [have participated] in the arts in diverse and stimulating ways but, instead of recognizing the social barriers to entry [that] women faced when trying to engage with the art world, the discipline has generally deemed women's contributions as non-existent or inferior to those of men."[65] Unfortunately, leadership in the art world amplifies Black and white men's voices more than women's.

Ballard has observed that this is especially the case when men paint and draw Black women. However, she questions if artists who do not identify as Black women but who paint them as subjects can fully capture the essence of their experiences. She asks, "Do you know us? Do you really know our struggles unless you are us?"[66] Ballard feels compelled to make art that is centered on Black women in ways that align with Patricia Hill Collins's stance that "Black women have insisted on our right to define our own reality, establish our own identities, and name our history."[67] Supporting Hill Collins's position, Ballard finds it refreshing and authentic when she comes across artwork by other Black women artists whose work provides imagery and commentary on Black womanhood. As a practicing Black woman artist, Ballard contends, "I have some authority on what I'm putting out there. I'm putting out images of my mother, aunts, cousins, sisters, and friends. The people in my work are also people I come across in everyday life. I also add historical figures from archives; I have to research and learn their histories. I'm allowing them to kind of embrace their history. I'm giving them that power to do it in my work."[68] Here Ballard gives further insight into how creating art is a form of

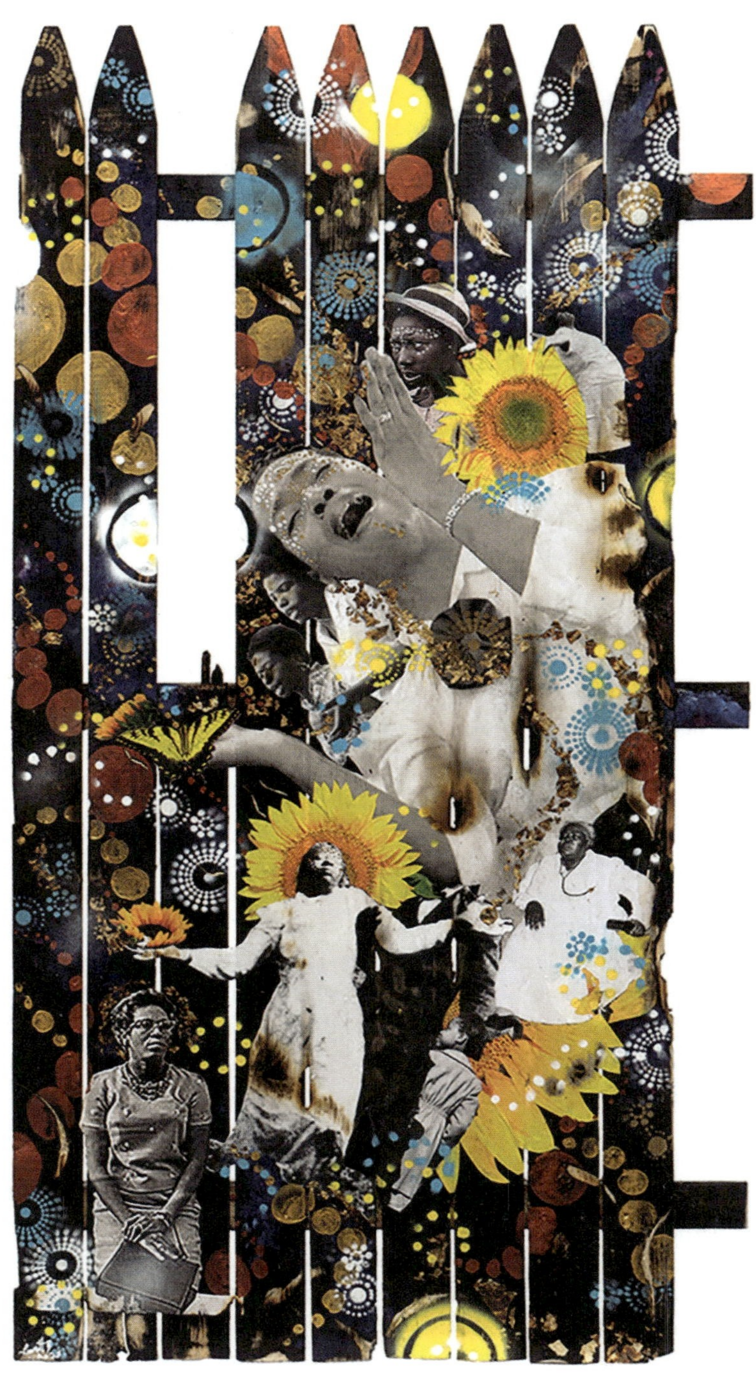

Lavett Ballard. *A Song Flung Up to Heaven*. 2020. Mixed-media collage on reclaimed wood fencing, 71 × 37 in. Private collection.

creating wellness for herself and other Black women. As an empowered artist, she centers on Black women's experiences and family stories that anchor her understanding of Black womanhood within her own identity.

Bringing stronger emphasis to the much larger overarching theme of family lineage and the creation of Black women's wellness are two Ballard collaged fences, *She Is Immortal* (2020) and *Healing Rituals* (2020), both in the *Women Heal through Rite and Ritual* exhibition. They address different types of healing provided by Black women. The composition of *She Is Immortal* has an archival photo of Henrietta Lacks surrounded by pink flowers, various colored orbs, and collaged photos of other Black women, including a young Black girl. Ballard named the artwork after Lacks (1920–1951), a Black woman from Roanoke, Virginia, who provided medical research with the HeLa cell, a sample tissue taken from her body without her consent. Lacks was a wife and mother of seven children. Like many people from her hometown of Roanoke, Virginia, she worked as a tobacco farmer until she and her family relocated to Dundalk, Maryland, in 1941. Almost a decade later, Henrietta Lacks was diagnosed with cervical cancer and went to Johns Hopkins Medical Center for treatment.

While she was under medical care, her physician, George Otto Gey, took two samples from her cervix, one each of healthy and cancerous tissue. Gey discovered that the cancerous cells from the biopsy demonstrated a rare characteristic of duplicating themselves at a high rate and could be kept alive long enough to allow more in-depth examination.[69] During her two-month hospitalization, Lacks's cancer metastasized, and she died on October 4, 1951. Medical researchers continued taking samples of Lacks's living cells while her body lay in Johns Hopkins's autopsy facility. Since then, her cells have continued to live and have been mass produced all over the world.[70] Controversy arose regarding the use of Lacks's cells because neither Henrietta Lacks nor her family ever gave consent or received compensation for the contributions derived from the HeLa cell. Yet her family medical history and private information have been published and commodified for medical research and commercial purposes. Lacks's story is part of a long history of African Americans' contributions to medical research and clinical practice without consent and often through unethical approaches. The story of Henrietta Lacks became mainstream news when the researcher and author Rebecca Skloot published *The Immortal Life of Henrietta Lacks* in 2010.[71] Henrietta Lacks and her memory have an important presence in the medical field as well as in popular culture. Her story has been told in plays, poems, thematic exhibitions, and a movie produced by Oprah Winfrey.[72] In 2018, a painted portrait of Lacks by Kadir Nelson was donated for joint ownership to the National Portrait Gallery and the National Museum of African American History and Culture.[73] The immortality of Henrietta Lacks extends beyond her HeLa cells to her personal

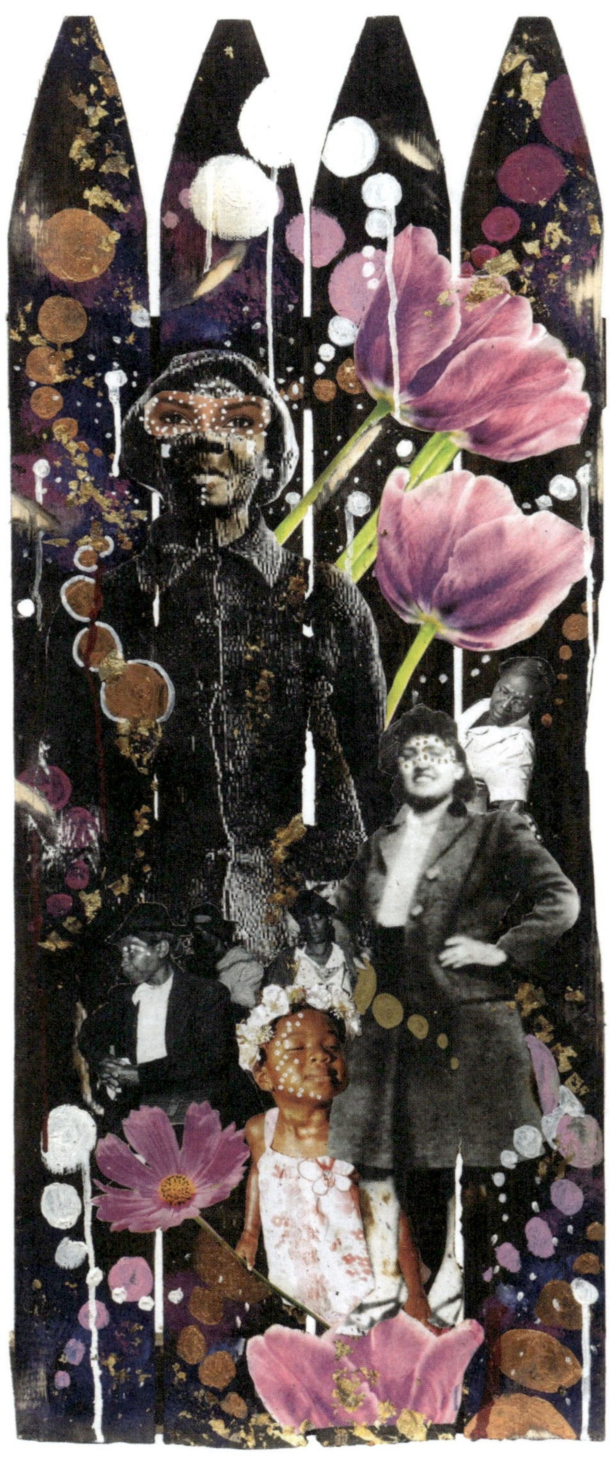

Lavett Ballard. *She Is Immortal.* 2020. Mixed-media collage on reclaimed wood fencing, 28 × 18 in. Private collection.

story, which includes her family lineage. Adding to it is the artwork of Lavett Ballard, who has placed Lacks within the narrative of Black women as healers.

To start, Ballard tries to capture the characteristics of Henrietta Lacks, who was known for being ultrafeminine and who wore many pink, fuchsia, and purple clothes. In her painting, Ballard adds historical photos of women sharecroppers to represent the tobacco-farming Lacks family. Ballard includes the figure of another Black woman whose hand is resting on Lacks's left shoulder. The woman is a midwife, a vital inclusion because Lacks gave birth to her seventh child four months before being diagnosed with cancer. Also, as Ballard explains, "Midwives during Henrietta's era weren't just taking care of the children, but also of the mothers."[74] Sheena M. Morrison and Elizabeth Fee assert that by the 1920s, midwives were primarily displaced by physicians in Northeastern cities because it was more modern to give birth in a hospital. However, in the South, "African American mothers preferred home births to hospital deliveries because they could avoid the prejudice and discrimination they often experienced in White society."[75] Physicians, both Black and white, argue that there was a correlation between the unsanitary practices of midwifery and high infant mortality rates for women. Still, their position did not eradicate the role of Black midwives, whom Black women deemed more trustworthy and empathetic to their needs.

Symbolically, Black midwives as represented in this artwork are directly connected to health care and are healers in their communities. "The midwife laying hands on Henrietta might have been her first introduction to personal medical care."[76] As Ballard continued to discuss the composition of *She Is Immortal*, she soon expanded her healing narrative to the spiritual realm. In her portrait of Lacks, who was extremely religious, Ballard adds images of two women sitting to her left in a church setting. All the imagery in this artwork reflects Lacks's sense of community and her legacy, giving her a place of immortality in the art world. As mentioned before, Ballard does not confine her archival figures to their historical period. She employs another characteristic in her artwork: she ties the past to the present by adding a little girl's photograph at the bottom frame. This girl is the daughter of one of Ballard's friends who has been diagnosed with sickle cell disease. The image of the young girl is significant because researchers have connected a cure for sickle cell diseases to HeLa cells. It is most likely that whatever treatment this young girl is currently receiving is connected to Henrietta Lacks's immortal cell line and thus her healing. When Ballard explains the symbolism in *She Is Immortal*, it is clear that her work has layers of detail. Keeping her audience in mind, when Ballard creates art, she aims to have people look at the work closely and slowly to see all the images she has added, large and small. Convinced by one of her former art professors that a great piece of art is something that you may not fully get, but you can't stop thinking about it, and it compels you to go back to look at it further, Ballard explains, "That's always my aim with my work. I want it to draw you in immediately, but you want to sit there and just kind of look at it and find all the nooks and crannies and stories within."[77]

As mentioned earlier, Ballard includes shadow images on the back of some of her two-dimensional artworks. Ballard imagines some of them to be images of women raised in Africa before colonialism with the freedom to be who they wanted to be, whether a cook, a shaman, a griot princess, or a mother. When describing them, Ballard explains that she creates shadow creatures only in black. They have no distinctive features but rather remain outlines or silhouettes. On the back of *She Is Immortal* there is a shadow creature. Lavett states, "This piece, I felt, called for a shadow piece because it is a narrower fence panel. It just screamed that she had something else to say." Images added to the back of Ballard's work are comparable to the B-side of a record that few people are aware of until they flip it over and play it, only to discover that there are great songs on the B-side too. So, like Ballard's earlier claim that she wants the audience to look for the details in her work, her shadow creatures allow curators and viewers who are privy to the backside of the art to explore the piece more.

Ballard recognizes that early archives such as the Library of Congress or The Library Company of Philadelphia did not record the names of many African Americans. She pays homage to those Black people whose names we don't know but whose images enrich her visual narratives by literally giving them space on her wooden canvases. She tries to tie these unknown figures back to their African ancestry by using certain cultural symbols. Ballard also provides these figures with purposes and identities that establish a collective story about the African American experience. As it relates to healing and wellness, Ballard's incorporation of shadow creatures symbolically restores their history, as she celebrates unsung heroes from the African diaspora. Both healing and wellness are connected to the collective survival of Black people's ancestors, who faced insurmountable odds.

Healing Rituals

Playing off the Pietà or Madonna and Child trope, the central figure in *Healing Rituals* (2020) is a grayscale image of a Black woman praying over a child. The woman's head is bowed. She is shrouded with a white draping hijab, her eyes closed, her lips slightly parted. Even more noticeable is that her hand is covering most of the upper part of the child's face except for one wide open eye. Ballard transposed the child's open eye from another image with a brown flesh tone. She explained that the actual photos of the two figures came from an archive titled *healing ritual* and that "the reconfigured image of the child who should be closing her eyes and waiting for the healing wants to see the

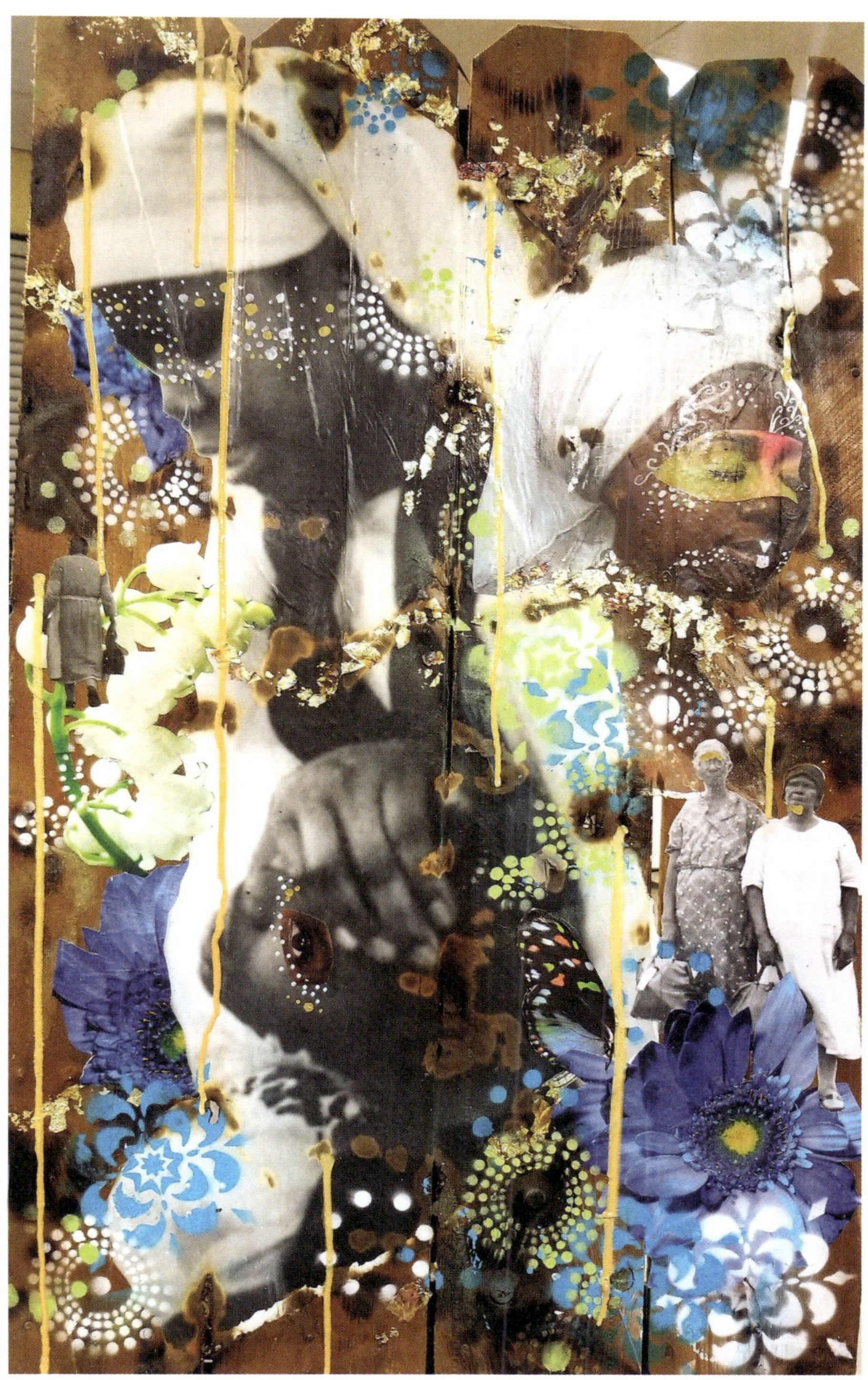

Lavett Ballard. *Healing Rituals*. 2020. Mixed-media collage on reclaimed wood fencing, 36 × 27 in. Private collection.

healing."[78] The "laying on of hands" in this composition portrays what Ballard describes as "having faith in a higher power."[79] Expounding on this display of faith, Ballard, explained, "There has always been a strong presence of older Black women leading prayer bands and rituals that call for the healing and deliverance of family members and community members"; this also informs the composition of *Healing Rituals* (2020).[80] Toni Morrison highlighted the tradition of Black women as spiritual healers in their community in her 1987 novel *Beloved*. Led by the character Baby Suggs, a respected elder in the Black community, Black men, women, and children would often meet in the Clearing—a wide-open place cut deep in the woods—to hear her preach. "After situating herself on a huge flat-sided rock, Baby Suggs bowed her head and prayed silently. The company watched her from the trees. They knew she was ready when she put her stick down."[81] After her silent prayer, Suggs calls for community members to come from the trees and into the Clearing.

Shouting, praise, and worship along with messages to love your flesh—"Love it hard"—resonated within a community of people who were often in need of support and relief from racial subjugation.[82] In *Healing Rituals* (2020), Ballard, the wife of a minister and a church member, highlights the traditional role of healer that Black women play in informal spaces and religious spaces. Also included in this piece are other archival images of Black women. Another Black woman in grayscale is juxtaposed to the right of the central figure. Ballard strategically positions this figure so that her head also blends into the woman's shoulder in grayscale. She explains, "This was purposely done to kind of trick your eye and fit her into the whole composition. The first-mentioned healer is now on the shoulder of another healer and suggests a community of support and prayer partners that exists among healers."[83] She includes a historical image of two Black "Granny" midwives from Florida carrying their medical bags to represent medical healers. A few other smaller figures of Black women in the background play a supporting role in this piece's overall narrative, all surrounded by blue gerbera daisies, stenciled patterns, and dripped paint. In her interview, Ballard articulated a vision of creating a visual galaxy that goes beyond mere artistic expression. She intertwines individual wellness and artistic flourishing, as she envisions her artwork as a conduit for diverse forms of healing, instilling a profound sense of grace and peacefulness in viewers. Ballard's creative process thus becomes an immersive journey, where the symbiosis between individual well-being and the flourishing of artistic expression converges to construct a celestial realm of visual serenity and therapeutic resonance. Two other artists whose work also extends BWAEs into the celestial and more spiritual world are Delita Martin and Shanequa Gay, discussed in the next chapter.

5

Nurturing Cultural and Spiritual Wellness

When I think about art it changes minds and hearts,
and minds change systems, and systems can
change life—and I get to be a part of it.
—Delita Martin

This chapter delves into the work of two influential Black women artists, Delita Martin and Shanequa Gay, examining how they cultivate spiritual wellness both individually and communally. Although neither operates within traditional art institutions, their creative practices reflect a deep commitment to healing and empowerment. They are diverse in their approaches, media, and art-making processes, yet both use their work to explore and critique personal and collective experiences. Through their unique perspectives, Martin and Gay are shaping a powerful understanding of the Black community, offering insightful contributions from a Black feminist standpoint.

Delita Martin is a formally trained printmaker from Conroe, Texas. Now based in Houston, she has turned her focus to changing minds, hearts, and systems through arts activism.[1] She primarily creates portraits of African Americans, especially Black women, using paint, fabric, and paper. Throughout her work, she consistently documents Black women in her community. They are not well known to many, but they are the foundation of many others' success. On an even deeper level, Martin conveys what she feels is not present enough in contemporary art, the spirituality of Black artists' work, particularly that of Black women artists. Although Martin works to center spirituality in art, her endeavor is part of a cultural legacy. Within African diaspora art, identifiable African spiritual philosophies from ancient civilizations are present in the aesthetics of Black people in the United States, the Caribbean, and other parts of the world.[2] However, Martin believes that exhibitions highlighting Black spirituality do not readily sell on the market because that art is not popular. Still, she doesn't adhere to popular culture; instead, she creates work connecting to what she deems essential. Speaking further on the overall theme of her art in our one-on-one interview, Martin affirms, "My work and its very core is about identity and reconstructing the identity of Black women."[3] Through portraiture, Martin engages in various conversations regarding identity, addressing the construction of spiritual, physical, and emotional identity through an Afrocentric lens.

Martin's work explores how Black people wear these different identities in the temporal and spiritual realms. To understand her visual mapping of Black women's identities and spirituality, we must consider the artistic and cultural influences that shaped her as an artist. Martin grew up in a house full of creativity. At the age of five, she declared that she wanted to be an artist. Her earliest memory of creating art was on the back of a portrait of Jesus that her father painted. He was a trained artist who had studied under the renowned Professor John Biggers of Texas Southern University. Martin's father also made furniture and quilts and was a writer. Martin recalls, "We created all the time. It was just natural to create."[4] Her parents nurtured her creative activities and encouraged her ambitions. She aspired to walk in her father's footsteps by attending Texas Southern University (TSU) and studying under John Biggers to become an artist, although by the time she matriculated at TSU, Biggers was no longer teaching at the institution. Still, Martin majored in art with a concentration in drawing, earning an undergraduate degree. One of the classes that she was required to take was printmaking, where her classmates worked on scratchboards and drawings, yet never touched a press. It wasn't until Martin was thirty years old and in graduate school that she decided to be a printmaker. Again, she was inspired by Biggers's work in printing and also by her professor, Harvey Johnson. The lithograph prints of both artists fascinated her. She remembers thinking as a student, "I am going to learn that later. You know, I just put it in the back of my mind like, okay, that is on my list of things to do. I am going to learn that, and so I did."[5]

Martin became a trained printmaker. She moved around to many parts of the country with her husband because of his career in human resources. Her experience of meeting diverse people is something she credits with strengthening her creativity. For four years, she served as an adjunct professor at the University of Arkansas, where she taught printmaking, drawing classes, art history classes, and a capstone (final project) class. However, teaching and printmaking disappointed Martin, as she did not feel like an artist in these roles. While reflecting on this experience, Martin recalled, "I wanted to get into the studio and really discover myself as an artist."[6] Pushing past the limitations that she felt came with her training, Martin believed it was important to get in the studio to become a creator. Making the distinction between printmaking and being an artist, Martin explains, "It was the most freeing thing I have ever done but the most difficult thing I have ever done."[7] I asked Martin to elaborate on the difference between her working as a printmaker and being an artist. She responded, "My philosophy that I developed over that time was if I cannot draw it, then I will paint it. If I cannot paint it, I will print it. If I cannot print it, I will collage it. I will do whatever is needed to convey a story."[8] This philosophy sets the foundation for how Martin approaches art making now. She marries the different processes and media of art to create narratives about Black people that cultivate wellness through the realms of Afrocentricity, spirituality, and empowered identities.

Delita Martin's Blueprint for Holistic Well-Being

During our interview, I asked Martin to define wellness. Martin interprets wellness as an experience that people have when they connect with themselves. She explains, "I feel like we have this inner . . . this inner thing that tells us what we need and what we need to happen. So I always tell people you have to teach people how to treat you, and you have to learn how to treat yourself."[9] Martin explains that it is an individual's responsibility to be "okay" and centered regarding one's understanding of wellness. She describes this as being balanced and at peace. Peace often comes with setting boundaries and with the word "no." Martin explains, "'No' is a magical word in the art world. There seems to be no way to say it without seeming rude or without malice, but you have to take care of yourself."[10] With boundaries in place, Martin starts her day with meditation. By 5:30 a.m. she is in her studio, and with a cup of coffee or tea in hand, she soon gets to work. In the evening, when she arrives home, she makes time to lie in her bed, close her eyes to think, and become self-aware in her surroundings. While meditating, she may ask herself, "What are the sounds that I am hearing? What do I feel? Can I feel the pain on my skin? What does it feel like? You know, if someone sits, if my husband sits on the bed, how does that change what I am feeling? You know, just really connecting with the space that is around me."[11] Martin's intentional self-centering through meditation and reflection is similar to Mindfulness-Based Stress Reduction (MSBR). The practice of MSBR includes four tenets: Be present, on purpose, in the moment, without judgment.[12] Through meditation, Martin set out on a spiritual path that changed the trajectory of her work for the better.

Through more self-awareness and self-centering, Martin escapes the limitations of what people think about her or the art that she makes. She discovered that she became free through self-centering. When she works in the studio, she disconnects from the world. I asked Martin what disconnecting from the world looks like, and she explained:

> I think for me, what stands out the most is centering myself. Because I feel
> like sometimes I get caught up or can easily get caught up in this whirl-

wind of everything that is going on. So when I come into the studio and sit down, I just disconnect from the Internet. Disconnect with the phone calls. Disconnect with the list of things that other people have for me to do. I have to do that. I cannot do them. I, at some point in time during the day, have to do that. And um, I think that is like the top of my list.[13]

Disconnecting from the world as a means of self-care provides space for Martin to reflect on the visual narratives she wants to tell in her art. One memory that she became keenly aware of through reflection is going to church with her grandmother. Raised in a Southern Black church, Martin recalls how many of the church members were over sixty years old; as a result, it was a dying church with around ten members left. When Martin attended church, she was fascinated with what she observed: the practice of prayer, the laying on of hands, the playing of tambourines and drums, singing, dancing, speaking in tongues, and many other outward expressions of praise. One practice that particularly caught her attention was when members of the congregation would get in a circle and sing songs that involved a call and response. Martin states that as a child, "I did not realize that they were doing a ring shout, a very African-based cultural activity."[14] A ring shout is an ecstatic, transcendent religious ritual, first practiced by enslaved Africans in the West Indies and the southern United States. Worshipers move in a circle while shuffling and stomping their feet and clapping their hands. This form of worship became a Christianized practice in some African American churches in the twentieth century and is still a common practice among the Gullah people of the Georgia Sea Islands, Black churches, and non-Black Pentecostal churches to the present day.[15] According to Anne Harris, worshipers believe that its presence in worship services is a unique way to hear God's voice. She writes, "A ring shout is a ritual where people come together and hold hands in a circle and ring praises to the Creator. All hearts and minds are focused on the mission at hand, for the blessings that are needed; and for a community of worshipers to see and feel the power of God."[16] Years later, through research, Martin found a commonality between the church activities she had observed as a child and Conjure and other African-based religions.[17] The shared aspects spurred her interest in making them a topic in her art. Martin started looking at different experiences with family members that linked back to African cultures and religions while questioning the contradictions between acceptable church worship practices and African religious traditions that the church determined were heathenistic. For example, Martin states, "You are taught, as a Baptist, you do not commune with spirits, but it's acceptable to commune with the Holy Ghost. That is all okay. But I question what the difference is."[18]

Not only does Martin see aspects of African spirituality in the Black church but also observed it within her family and their daily activities. Martin recalls that her grandmother kept a Mason jar on her dresser, filled with items and mementos of family members. Martin remembers, "Every so often she would pour them out on her bed and she would go through it. Oh, this ring belonged to this person, or you know, this is a button off your grandfather's uniform that he is wearing. She would have all these memories and all these stories captured in this jar."[19] For Martin, her grandmother's Mason jars are reminiscent of Conjure jars.[20] Although her grandmother was not collecting items to cast spells, Martin believes that in some way, such as the transference of African culture, her grandmother, along with most African Americans, continues to do things embedded in our ancestral memory.[21] Through cultural nuances, Martin intends to recover and restore history and cultural practices in the African American experience.

Black Moon

Black Moon (2019) is a mixed-media portrait employing relief printing, charcoal, fabric, paint, and decorative paper that has been hand stitched onto a gelatin print. Viewers see a Black woman with short-cropped hair holding a translucent globe with a blackbird inside it. Her gaze is fixed leftward on the blackbird. Its head is turned away from her as it looks backward in a way that echoes the Sankofa bird symbol. *Sankofa* is an Akan word meaning "to return and recover it."[22] The Sankofa bird "symbolizes the quest for knowledge and the return to the source."[23] The portrait's background is dark orange, a color representing vitality for Martin, with opaque yellow circles that resemble sliced pineapples and other circles containing blue-hued objects. Some of the yellow circles are translucent and cover parts of the woman's face and body. When discussing the symbolism in *Black Moon*, Martin revealed that the patterned background that we see is what she calls the "veil scape," that is, a space between the waking world and the spiritual world through which people make a transition.

The patterns move in and out of the figure with varying degrees of opacity. According to Martin, "they are symbolic of how we marry into the spaces we occupy. So when figures are in a spiritual space, that is how I present them. And that varies from person to person."[24] Martin uses many circular patterns in her work, even when the figure is male, because she always wants to represent a female presence. She associates circles with the moon, which, in many cultures, symbolizes femininity and women.[25] The blackbird in this portrait, as well as in Martin's other works, represents the human spirit. Blackbirds are also part of the memory of her grandmother, who kept a lot of birds as pets. The curator Kheli Willetts wrote an essay on Martin's earlier portraits and the symbolism in her work: "Sometimes the birds are dead and their feet are bound, indicating spiritual death; others fly freely."[26] The significance of the

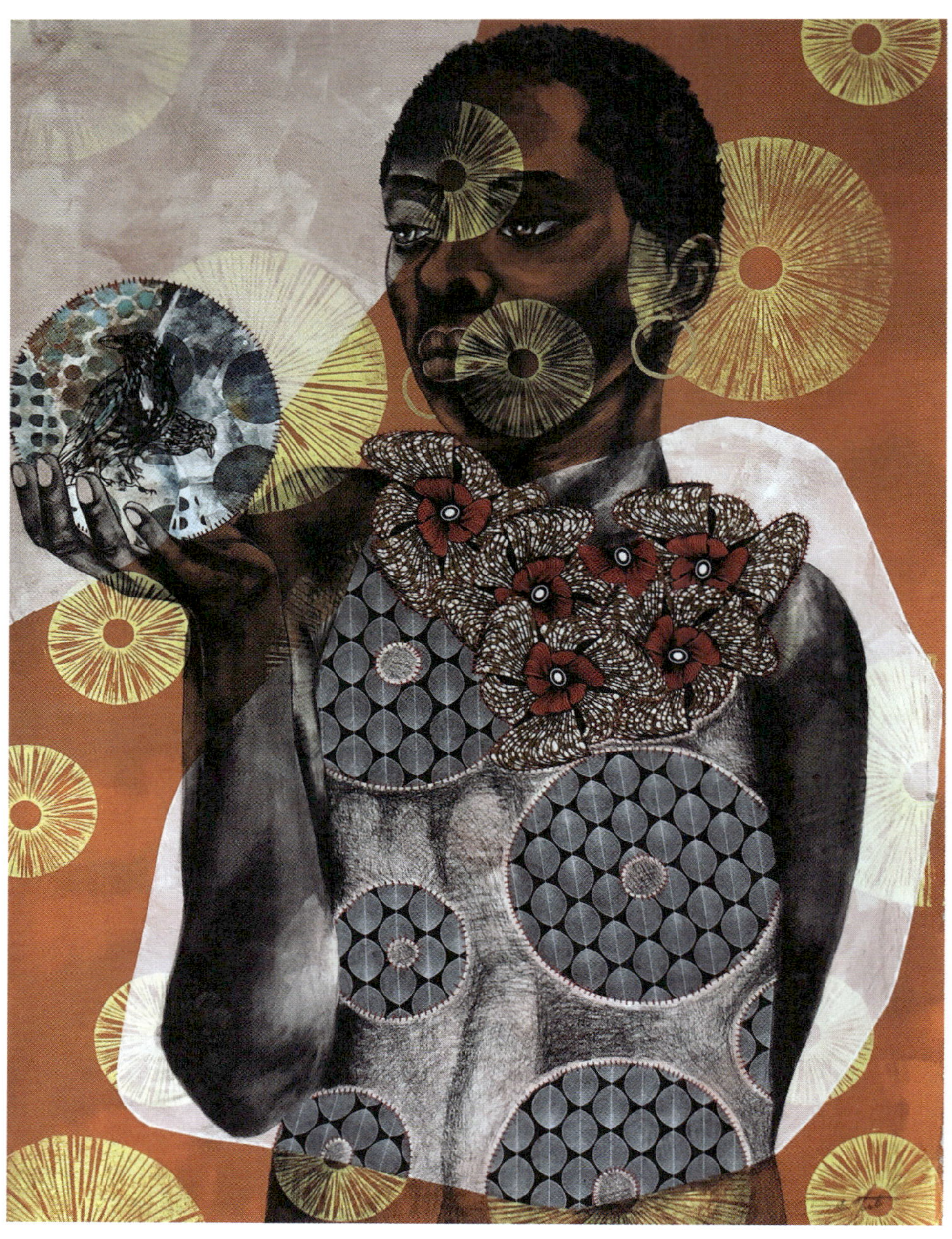

Delita Martin. *Black Moon*. 2019. Acrylic, charcoal, decorative papers, fabric, gelatin, hand stitching, relief printing, 72 × 51½ in. Courtesy of the artist.

title is that a black moon is the second new moon in a calendar month. This rare lunar event has spiritual and astrological significance, often associated with new beginnings, introspection, and setting intentions. Martin creates a visual narrative of a Black woman becoming or transforming into her spiritual self when she connects the moon's symbolism with the blackbird's symbolism. Her gaze at the blackbird is an act of self-reflection that gives space for her spiritual transition. Through her contemplative gaze at the self and her powerful posture, this woman can facilitate a spiritual and cognitive audit of the self. Martin emphasizes this transition to wellness via Afrocentric spirituality through the African-influenced patterns of the clothing the woman is wearing.

Star Children

Martin uses the same color scheme of orange, red, and blue and West African iconography in *Star Children* (2019) to convey the power of sisterhood in the Black community. In this portrait, Martin depicted subjects who were not her family members. Martin's previous subjects were all family members—her grandmother, mother, and other close kin—whom she revered as spirit women conveying the essence of Black essence. Martin divulged that in the last few years, "I have drawn inspiration and intentional inspiration from women around me. So it was not that I was not doing that before; it just became intentional and more directed."[27] Martin started taking digital photos of family members who posed for her in her studio. Then she took her work a step further by inviting other women not related to her to pose for pictures. In *Star Children*, the models are biological sisters. Martin met one of them, Neifei, a recent high school graduate, at an art exhibition. She had a presence about her that Martin wanted to capture. After getting permission from Neifei and her mother, Martin drew several images of her; she is the figure wearing orange in the portrait. Staying connected through social media, Martin used photos that Neifei sent her and others that Neifei posted. At one point, Martin discovered that some of the images that she had downloaded were not Neifei but her sister. Although two years apart, the two young women looked almost identical. Inspired by their resemblance, Martin had the sisters come to her studio to pose for her. She observed in their interaction with each other that they spiritually and emotionally completed each other—so much so that they reminded Martin of "these Celestial children that would always be together. So I titled this piece *Star Children*."[28] Aside from the visual narrative of sisterhood in this artwork, it is important to note how Martin engages other people in her art-making process. Her process is participatory and communal to the point that she makes the art for herself and others, resulting in a spiritual exchange. When asked about her role as an artist, Martin explains, "I don't think I'm in charge. I'm a conduit for things to work through me, and I'm totally okay

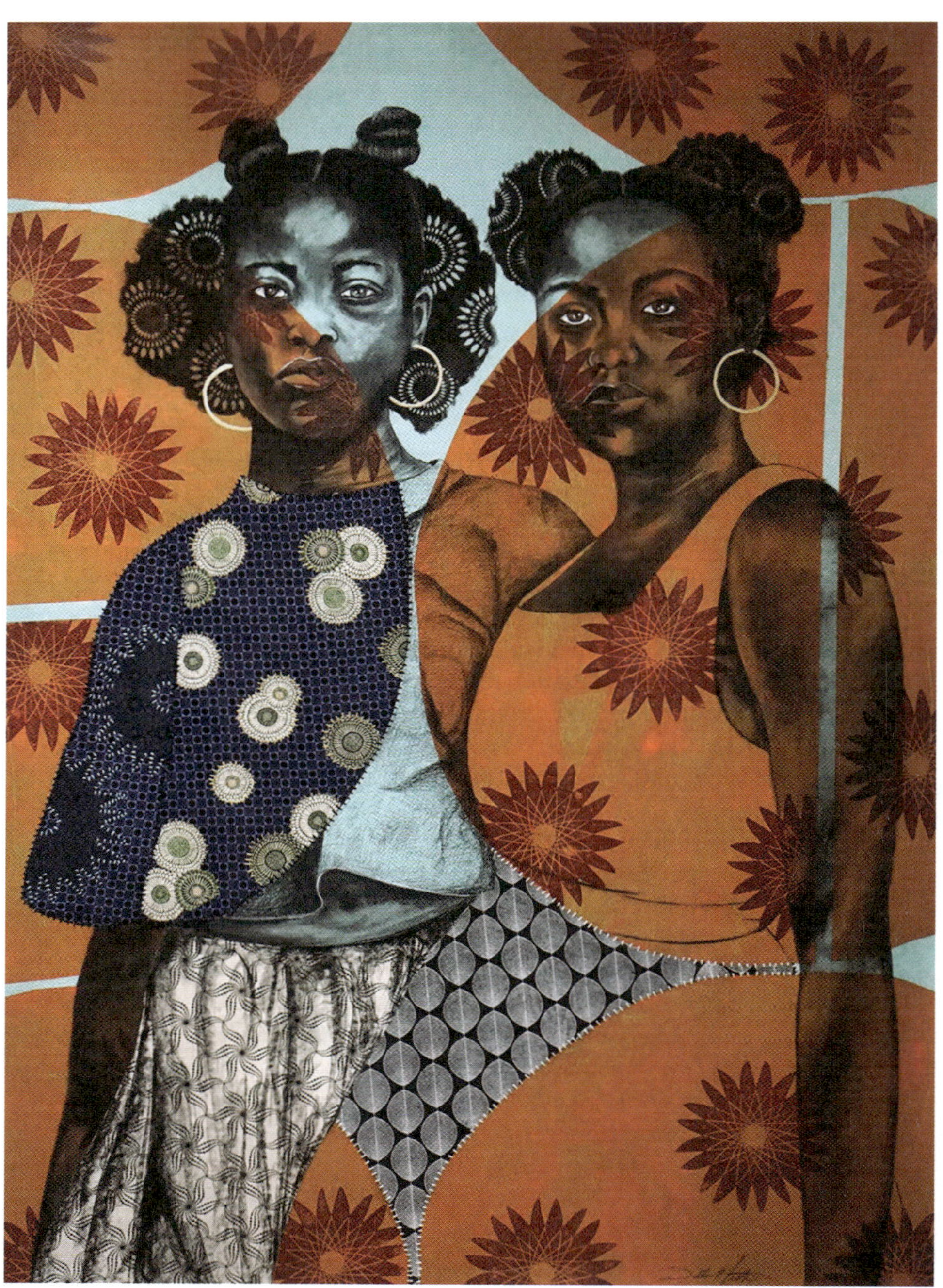

Delita Martin. *Star Children*. 2019. Acrylic, charcoal, decorative papers, fabric, hand stitching, liquid gold leaf, 72 × 52 in. Courtesy of the artist.

with that."[29] Recognizing that she is an instrument of creativity through whom other people tell their stories, Martin asked herself the question, How do I create something larger than myself? This inquiry translated into the series *I See God in Us*, which includes *Black Moon* (2019), *Star Children* (2019), and *Six Persimmons* (2019). On further reflecting on what it means to create something larger than herself, Martin felt part of that answer was bringing other women she feels connected with into the work. From these connections among kindred spirits come portraits that are not overtly descriptive in their story but are a record of remembrance rather than making any explicit statement about life as an African American woman.[30] Martin's connection with her subjects is an essential part of her art-making process. In turn, she facilitates opportunities for Black women to gather and share their experiences.

Martin is also part of an artists' collective called ROUX. Based in Houston, it includes three other Black women artists: Rabea Ballin, Ann "Sole Sister" Johnson, and Lovie Olivia, whose "works navigate between styles of the past and the proposed future and address experiences unique to Women of Color residing in the American South."[31] As a member of a Black women's artist collective and an artist on assignment to center the essence and experiences of Black womanhood, Martin stays consistent with her goal. Yet, if we were to sum up the totality of her work in one phrase, it would be "capturing the spirit."

Thinking back on her work with Dr. John Biggers, Martin shared a short story about her visit to a fellow artist, Gene Lacey. While there, she saw a portrait of Lacey created by Biggers. The portrait looked nothing like Lacey, but according to Martin, "when you looked at it, you instantly knew who it was. He had figured it out; he had mastered how to capture her spirit. That is what I am interested in."[32] When a person becomes the subject of her work, Martin—not interested in creating hyperrealistic art—strives to capture the one thing that makes that person who they are. Any factor might capture a person in portraiture, "even down to the slightest tilt of [their] head."[33] The essence of Black women—their natural hairstyles, posture, clothing, and even how they emote with their eyes absent a smile—allows viewers to experience their beauty.[34] The essence of Martin's subjects is the rudimentary aspects of their identities and life experiences. Martin builds complexity with textures, shapes, colors, symbols, and the positioning of the subjects' bodies. Martin also creates artwork on a vast scale to bring hypervisibility to Black women in art.

Six Persimmons

In the 72-by-51.5-inch work *Six Persimmons* (2019), Martin presents a self-portrait that embodies the elements that she employs in her work. In her essay

"Beyond the Tangible," Khelli Willetts identifies five specific characteristics that are consistently present in Martin's body of work: symbols, color, expression, pattern, and spirit.[35] Like the moon representing women and the birds representing the human spirit, many other symbols have a special meaning in Martin's visual language.[36] Many of the symbols that Martin incorporates are domestic objects. In *Six Persimmons,* you see two figures facing each other and floating in the air. The figure on the right is Martin herself, holding a bowl with a bird perched on its edge. Martin and the blackbird, with its head turned backward, appear to be gazing at the other female figure floating on the left side of the canvas. This figure is also Martin but in silhouette. It has no detailed features but is a black-shadow image of her body. I asked Martin to divulge the meaning of this self-portrait. Here I learned that bowls in her artwork represent a woman's womb. When a young girl is shown carrying a bowl, it means she is carrying on a lineage and the birthing of future generations. With regard to color, Martin will tell you that she struggled with color theory in her early years as an art student. Her instructors told her that she misused color. Rather than following the rules, Martin uses colors that reflect certain feelings and experiences, calling her choice of color palette the Delita theory. Blue hues are present in all of her work, because it is a very spiritual color that centers her. It also represents significant memories in her life, including her father's funeral, where every member wore blue and his funeral floral spray included blue flowers. Ironically, Martin's family never planned on a blue-themed funeral. Adding further clarity, Martin states, "When I look back on certain periods in my life that were emotional or transitional, blue has always played a part in that, a part in working through it, getting over it, processing it, whatever, I see blue."[37] Martin's blue palette along with her use of birds, symbolic of the spirit, and bowls as symbols of the womb, align with indigo dyeing and orisha iconography in the Yoruba religion. Stephen Hamilton notes that indigo and the women responsible for its manufacture play a unique role in Yoruba society. In many parts of Yorubaland, indigo dyeing and other female coded artforms are associated with Iya Mapo, the primordial artisan who taught the art of dyeing and many other crafts to humankind. He further explains, "The worship of the orishas Osun and Yemoja is strongly connected to the cities of Osogbo, Ibadan, and Abeokuta, which were three very prosperous centers for indigo dyeing industries during the pre-colonial, colonial and post-colonial eras. These female deities are the owners of the rivers (the Osun and Ogun rivers, respectively) that run through these towns. They are both associated with divine coolness, healing, fecundity, and the womb."[38] Although Martin never has offered a direct connection to the orishas in Yoruba religion, the similarities between Martin's art and Yoruba traditions underscores the cultural depth and historical significance embedded in her work.

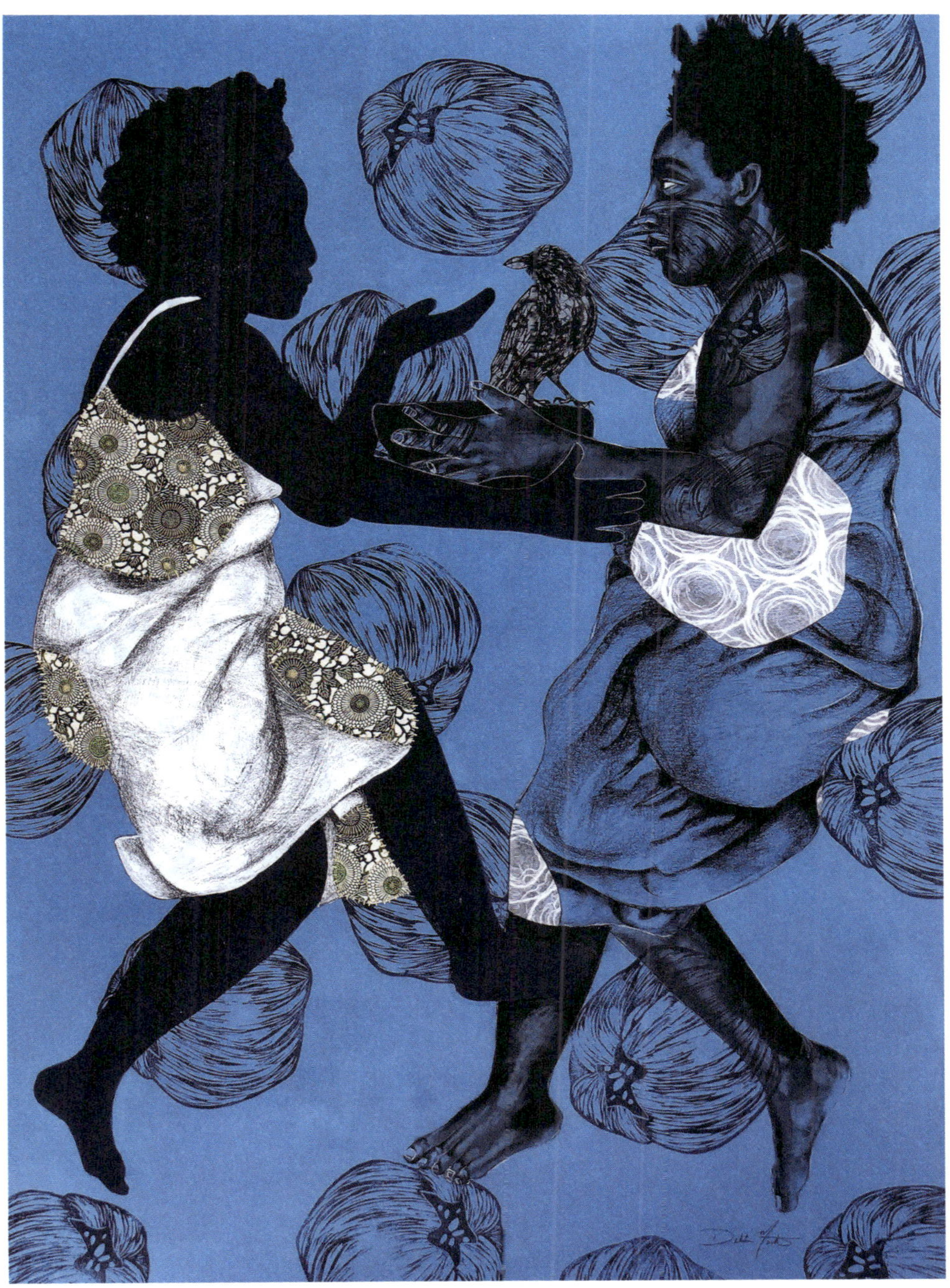

Delita Martin. *Six Persimmons*. 2019. Acrylic, charcoal, decorative papers, hand stitching, relief printing, 71½ × 51½ in. Courtesy of the artist.

The literary scholar Georgene Bess Montgomery explains that Ifa, a creationist religion, encapsulates African life, thought, and cosmology. This profound spirituality underscores the inherent and intimate connections among all living and nonliving entities.[39] The presence of African spiritual iconography in Martin's work highlights a continuity of cultural memory and the resilience of African spiritual practices, illustrating how these elements survive and adapt within the African diaspora. Martin's art is a visual testament to the enduring influence of African spiritual beliefs and their profound impact on Black American cultural expressions.

The images in Martin's art also have East Asian cultural references. *Six Persimmons* is a self-portrait of Martin floating in and out of the spiritual world. Martin's choice of title is an homage to the thirteenth-century Chinese monk Muqi Fachang who, using ink on paper, drew six persimmon fruits. Martin explains, "There had been artists throughout art history who have done images that reference *Six Persimmons*. And in Buddhism I believe *Six Persimmons* is symbolic of the highest state of enlightenment, and persimmons themselves were considered the fruit of the gods in Greek mythology."[40] Martin's understanding of the symbolic meaning of persimmons in art history and particularly in East Asian cultures provides significant insight into her self-portrait. Martin also grew up with a persimmon tree in her backyard and ate the fruit all the time. She incorporated it as a way to talk about a state of being. In *Six Persimmons* she goes on the spiritual journey through time and connects with a higher part of her identity. "I am floating in a state in which there are two of me. There is a physical me, and there is a spiritual me, and we are connecting [with] and offering to each other. And we are in conversation with each other."[41] Martin's conversation in the portrait represents the meditative reflection she described earlier, where she finds balance and a center of self. The visual elements in *Six Persimmons* and their connoted meaning are a solid and layered example of how Martin is a wellness worker for herself through her art. Both her art-making process and her artwork exemplify her interest in symbolically connecting the physical world and the spiritual world, reflecting the presence of spiritual wellness in BWAEs. Martin shares interest in addressing spirituality in art with the artist Shanequa Gay, who was also part of the group exhibition *Women Heal through Rite and Ritual* at Galerie Myrtis.

Shanequa Gay: Black Women Healing through the Devout

If I were not here, I would have to be invented.
—Shanequa Gay

To fully understand and embrace the narratives of the Atlanta-based artist Shanequa Gay, viewers must be willing to traverse both the physical and spiritual world in her art. Gay raises public consciousness about the devaluation of those she calls "African ascended" women.[42] The composition of her art involves the reconfiguration of the Black female body through photography, performance art, paintings, and mixed-media sculptures. Her quote suggests that Black women and girls play a critical role within their respective communities in helping other peoples' realities make sense. However, this translates as a marginalized and subjugating experience for them. Through art, Gay works to push back against the margins and expand the space wide enough that Black women are now at the center. The curator Karen Comer Lowe noted, "She's presenting Black women in these unique ways, but they are the main characters of the work; they're the protagonists."[43] The artist does this most effectively by creating visual narratives that explore a new Afrocentric and Black feminist mythology.

During our interview, Gay rhetorically asked, "What does African American or African ascended mythology look like when it visually comes from Black imagination? What does our own Willie Wonka factory, or *Where the Wild Things Are*, look like when Black people have the freedom and resources to create what they imagine?"[44] Her questions alone suggest that living in a creative space where one can conceive a mythical world and existence is not an opportunity often afforded to Black people in the United States. Gay argues that, collectively, Black people are too occupied with trying to survive systemic racism. However, as an artist, Gay explains, "I'm creating those worlds for African 'ascended' women. I am responsible for those stories because they are a language of resistance that says I matter. I matter as a woman. I matter as a person of color. I matter as a human being."[45] So in a broader conversation, Gay connects creating art with her purpose. Operating with purpose is a core value for this artist. She communicated this a few years back as an inspirational message to other creatives in her city on the local TV show *Creative Mornings Atlanta*. When asked to select a topic to discuss, Gay chose purpose. "I am definitely one who believes that my gifting shows through art that creates what I call 'a destiny language'."[46] Gay contends that her purpose on earth is to be creative. For the Creative Mornings Atlanta show, she tapped into her other area of creativity, spoken word, to deliver the following poem inspired by the jingles she grew up listening to in the 1980s:

> We got a purpose, but you've got to keep an open eye. I have got a purpose just for you and I. We've got a purpose, but you have to keep an open mind. God has a purpose just for you and I. We've got a purpose, but you have to keep an open mind. The universal purpose made for you and I.[47]

Continuing this train of thought, I asked Gay, "What is the purpose of your making art, and what are you trying to say through it?" Gay revealed that she is trying to expand herself as far as possible as an artist through her art.

Her creative endeavors come with a responsibility connected to making art to build up her community and develop a language for the world to understand how important Black people are and to recognize and acknowledge our contribution to society. Gay sees herself as a keeper of Black people's narratives: "Whatever way I am expressing—whether that is through painting, visual arts, or speaking, lecturing, teaching, design—in all of those things, I am responsible for my creative gifts."[48] Gay is an accomplished artist who exhibits work in various galleries, museums, and public murals. In 2013, the Congressional Club commissioned Gay to make an illustration of the White House for then First Lady Michelle Obama.[49]

Yet there was a short period, four years to be exact, when she walked away from making art. Her brother's death in 2008 proved to be a pivotal experience that Gay had to heal from before resuming her calling to be an artist. I asked Gay to describe her career trajectory to date, and she revealed that the journey has not always been easy. Still, at an early age she recognized her gift and hustle. While in elementary school, she would often paint on friends' pants and help them create their book report posters—and get paid for her services. Gay possessed a natural business acumen for art and also drew inspiration from popular culture. While growing up, she, like millions of people, watched *The Cosby Show*, and it wasn't long before Gay became acutely aware of the art displayed throughout the Huxtables' living room.[50] Specifically, artwork by Varnette P. Honeywood permeated the TV show. Her socially conscious, brilliantly colored collages and paintings depicted African American life in familiar and positive settings and were seen by millions of viewers on mainstream television.[51] Gay remembers asking herself as a child, "How do I get my art on TV? How does that happen?"[52] Soon her parents were paying for private art lessons from her first mentor, Brent.

Brent, an openly gay white man, was a choir member at the church that Gay attended. Along with teaching her art skills, he was the first person to take her to the High Museum in Atlanta. Gay told me, "Brent was the first person to introduce me to the possibilities of my art."[53] Through his mentorship, Brent encouraged Gay to enroll at the Art Institute of Atlanta, where she eventually earned degrees in graphic design and fashion marketing. From there, Gay worked for a little while as a freelance graphic designer. However, the work was not as fulfilling as the little figurines she created during her free time, giving them names and developing storylines for them. Soon, through more mentorship from a man named Doyle and the encouragement of a friend who asked, "About how long is it that we gonna keep coming to your house and seeing paintings on your wall but them never leaving your household?" she began exhibiting her work.[54] Early in her career, Gay started to show her work on what is known as the "Chitlin' Circuit" of the art world, which includes a wide range of venues in which Black artists are predominantly exhibited.[55] At the time, she was known for depicting Southern life and Black women in church hats. She also had a solid collectors' base, although Gay is not a traditional artist. She recalls that in 2008, she was "having all these dreams about Black men running, shape-shifting into deer."[56] Those dreams would change the trajectory of her career.

Fair Game

When Gay started to paint hybrid images, they consisted solely of Black male bodies with the heads of deer and other animals. Gay explains that the dreams she began having in 2008 were a response to pervasive police brutality against Black men in the United States and her concern about what might happen when her Black son went out into the world. As a result, her series *The Fair Game Project* was born. While it was on view at the Hammonds House Museum, the *Atlanta Journal-Constitution* described the series as "likening arrests, murders, lack of justice and socioeconomic disparities of African-American males to hunted game," and as "part thought provoking, controversial, conversational and personal . . . [delving] into issues affecting the black community and beyond."[57] The artist began creating work that addressed the unyielding violence and injustices committed against the Black body by showing police and other men with shotguns chasing the hybrid beings as if they were wild animals. I asked Gay to elaborate more on what she felt when she created the *Fair Game Project*. She candidly shared her memories: "I was looking for ways to speak about what was going on in the world. Initially, I was protesting, right? I was going to these marches and getting upset and looking for ways to take action. But I recognized that for me, I needed a different form of protesting because 'This footwork is not enough for me.'"[58] During that time, Gay was in graduate school, with a platform and a diverse audience among her cohort. She found satisfaction in showing her artwork and fostering critical dialogue with various groups of people who entered her studio space.

In *Open Season* (2015), viewers see "black silhouettes against yellow and blue chromatic backgrounds chasing deer-men. The deer-men are running for their lives and trying to escape the distant figures of men pointing shotguns at them, only to face the obstacle of barbed-wire fences that they must leap over to escape. The scene in this acrylic-on-wood painting reflects frustration, fear, and societal constraints that Gay felt whenever she heard of a report of police shooting an unarmed Black man, whether in her community or elsewhere. In an interview with *Burnaway* magazine, Gay attested, "[My] goal is to develop a visual language that might make people uncomfortable, but that helps us articulate how police brutality is affecting Black men and the greater popula-

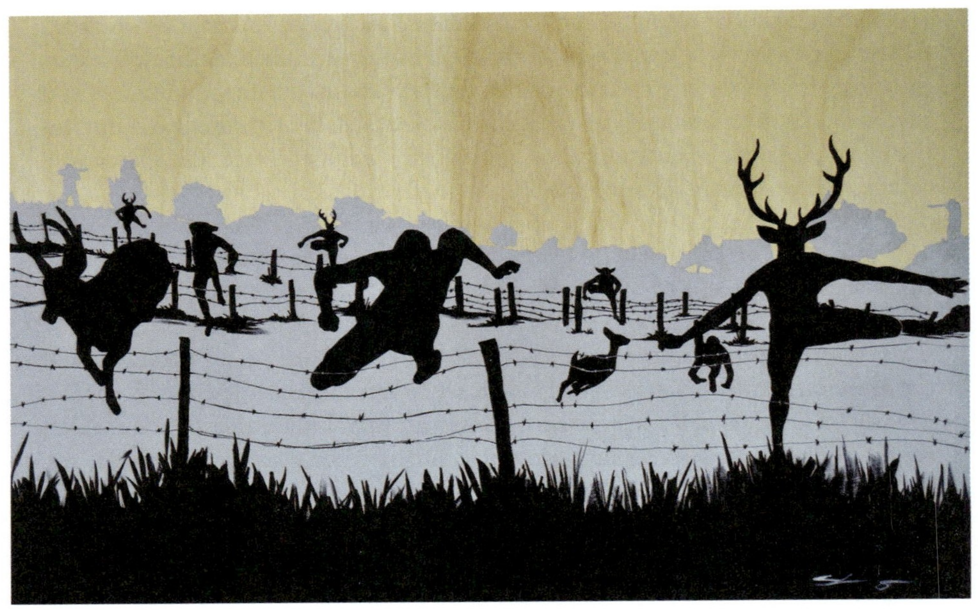

Shanequa Gay. *The Fair Game Project: Open Season.* 2015. Acrylic on wood panel, 24 × 48 in. Collection of Dr. Tony Burks.

tion."[59] Creating a body of artwork for the *Fair Game Project* gave Gay a new visual language and a focus on arts advocacy. She currently and almost exclusively portrays Black women subjects and current events affecting our lives.

The Birth of the Devout

By 2018, Gay had been in conversation with Galerie Myrtis's founder Myrtis Bedolla. Bedolla invited her to participate in the group exhibition *Women Heal through Rite and Ritual.* At the same time, Gay was still a student finishing up her Master of Fine Arts thesis at Georgia State University. She was also flying back and forth to Miami, Florida, to paint a mural for the Super Bowl, painting murals in Atlanta, and preparing to go to Art Basel.[60] She started moving away from the *Fair Game Project*, which focused solely on Black men, to a body of work focused on Black women as mythical, godlike figures. As with the *Fair Game Project*, Gay felt that her work was risky. The provocative theme of creating a hybrid Black female body and associating Black women with the divine sometimes provoked criticism that she was creating blasphemous images. However, as Gay notes, "I was tired, and I was weary from creating the work for the *Fair Game Project*. I needed, you know, a new narrative for myself that I found in creating this language of these kinds of devout figures, these godlike women, this mythos."[61]

Gay is often inspired by reading and listening to the works of thought leaders. While conceptualizing new themes for her artwork, she drew inspiration from the YouTube video series *The New School* that featured a conversation between scholar and Black feminist bell hooks and the American feminist, journalist, and sociopolitical activist Gloria Steinem. In the interview, the two women discuss three thousand years of erasure of divinity among women and animals as the nineteenth-century Egyptologist James H. Breasted recorded it. What became revelatory for Gay was when bell hooks asked, "How can Black people ever truly decolonize their minds? How can we ever indeed be free if we cannot imagine God-forms, God-figures with ourselves?"[62] Inspired by this line of questioning, Gay picked up the mantle to create Black women as mythological beings known as the "devout."[63] Using the visual language of hybridity, the devout come directly from what Gay describes as the Black imagination and an effort to create fantasy and new mythology, grounded in a culturally inflected spiritual wellness.

She often depicts the devout with girth to reflect the women in her family. Gay also creates visual narratives associated with nature and beauty. Most important, these women can intercede on behalf of Black people who have been shot and killed by police officers. Often, Gay layers her artwork with symbolism. For example, many images show the devout offering up watermelons or fried chicken as a sacrifice. I asked Gay why she chose those two foods as sacrificial items. "I take the things that are supposed to degrade us and turn them into something beautiful."[64] Thus she creates a counternarrative to the denigrating stereotypes of Black people always eating watermelon and fried chicken by depicting them as sacred within the mythological world she is creating.[65]

As they relate to Black women's spiritual wellness, I interpret Gay's efforts as a form of empowerment and an attempt to challenge the controlling images that have historically plagued and presently plague Black women. Gay confirmed this in our interview when she explained that despite reverently depicting the women in her family in her early artwork, she felt challenged by her observations of men disempowering the same mighty women in her family and society.[66] This was a stark contrast to the men in her family, who often supported and uplifted women in the family and community. For this reason, "Gay's work serves to restore and reclaim power, and central to that effort is the Black female."[67] Her earlier attempt to create agency and visibility for Black women by painting them in beautiful church hats eventually evolved into a focus on the devout, for whom creating a language of agency and empowerment that accurately conveys their divinity.

In Gay's spiritual symbolism, the devout represent three-fifths beings, both human and godlike. This counters the three-fifths clause in Article I, Section 2, of the US Constitution. It declares that enslaved Blacks would count as three-fifths of that state's number of white inhabitants for representation in Congress.[68] Building on this narrative and on interpretations that African Americans as individuals were considered three-fifths of a person, the hybridity of Black people in Gay's artwork inverts them into godlike beings. She states, "And so, for me, you know, while they feel like they are chasing game, for me, they are chasing God, and the chasers fear the chased; they fear Black people's divinity."[69] Consistently, Gay incorporates four animal masks in her work: a deer-head mask that symbolizes youth and innocence; a bull's-head mask that associates Black women with strength, boldness, and courage to bear the responsibilities that Black women often have when they are the heads of households without men; and masks of vultures and ravens, scavenger animals representing cleansing and cleaning up, as Black women are often thought of as the cleanup women physically, emotionally, and spiritually.[70]

While Gay was in graduate school, the spiritual themes in her work were not well received initially. She often felt misunderstood and discouraged from exploring the mythological world she was creating. Her professors regarded her ideas as nonacademic or unscholarly. In defiance, Gay consistently seeks to articulate a spiritual language through art that centers on Black women. Her understanding is that spirituality is inseparable from the identity development and experiences of Black womanhood. Consequently, the photograph *acceptance* (2019) demonstrates how Gay creates a pathway from which these conversations can ensue.

An *ini-she-ation* in Wellness

In 2019, with her shows *ini-she-ation* at Chastain Arts Center and *The Devout Griot, Emotional Keeper* at Anne O Art (both in Atlanta), Gay challenged the church's support of male power.[71] *acceptance* (2019) is a black-and-white photo printed on Somerset Velvet Paper. Like many other photos in this series, it shows how African American girls make the transition into womanhood through initiation rituals. In the photo, a young Black girl is dressed in white patterned pants and a tank top and wearing a deer-head mask on top of her head like a helmet. She faces her mother, a Black woman in a white sleeveless sundress and wearing a bull-head mask. As the two gaze into each other's eyes, what is most noticeable about this photo is how the child's right-hand rests on the woman's breastbone, while the woman has both of her arms resting at her sides.

I asked Gay to provide the context for this photo, and she explained that it was similar to many others that she used as references for painting. Like

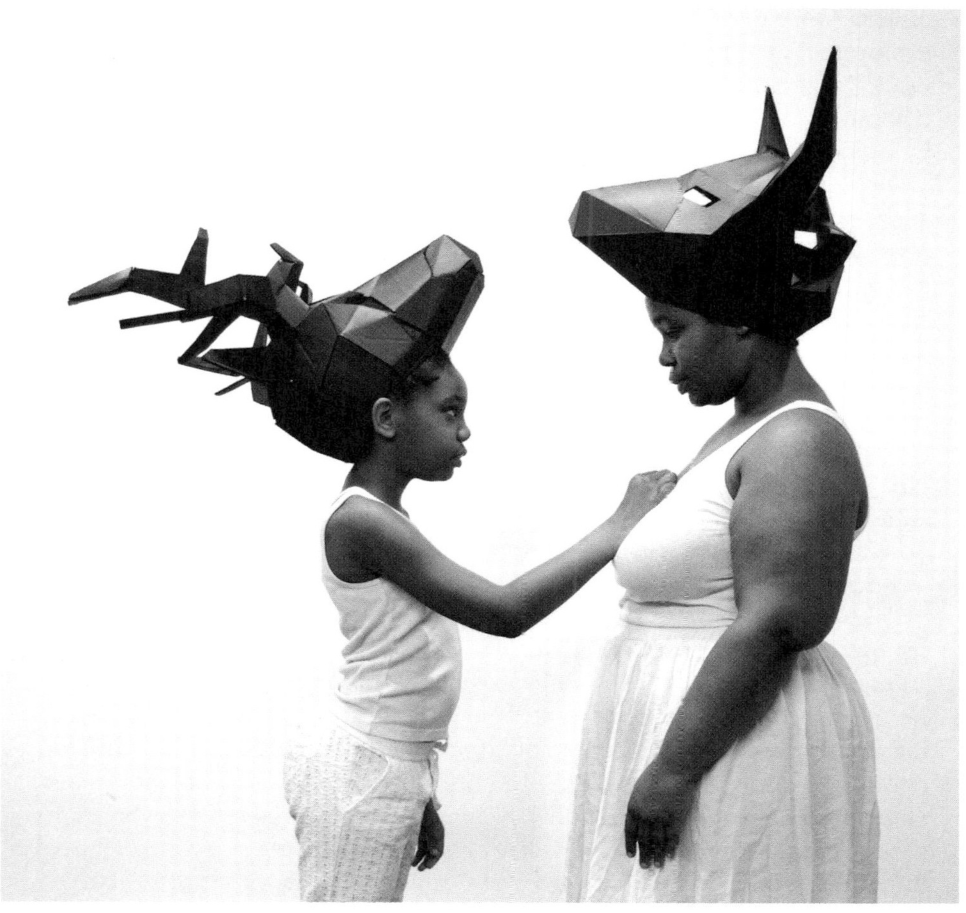

Shanequa Gay. *acceptance*. 2019. Limited-edition black-and-white photograph on Somerset Velvet paper, 34¾ × 35¼ in. Courtesy of the artist.

Delita Martin, Gay would sometimes invite people to her studio to pose for pictures that she would later use to create art in other media. When people visited her studio, they were equally drawn to the photos and the paintings. Gay soon realized "the photographs were just as much a part of the language of my paintings and drawings."[72] She began looking at her photos in new ways. Without saying a word, the subjects in *acceptance* communicate the virtue of accepting each other through their gaze. Specifically, the mother looks at her daughter, whose hand is over her mother's heart, conveying the importance of mother-daughter relationships. Originally, Gay created this image for a previous exhibition titled *Initiated*. Yet she found that the idea was powerfully relevant to the show *Women Heal through Rite and Ritual,* since the photo reflects how young Black girls move into the world of womanhood. When exploring Black girls' rites of passage, Gay asks, "What does that look like for us?"[73] Cognizant that many other cultures outside of the African American community have recognizable, ceremonial rites of passage, Gay was challenged by her lack of knowledge about rituals for young African American girls.

Yet "rites of passage programs can be traced back to Kemet as part of the African initiation rites that were used to provide a clear definition of roles, responsibilities, and expectations in the transition from youth to adult and promote a healthy self-image and self-esteem."[74] Through art, Gay builds on rite-of-passage praxes that often focus on transitions in life and the mastery of emotional, spiritual, and physical tests and tasks involving family and friends' active engagement and involvement.[75] Gay's perspective on Black girls' rites of passage aligns with the spiritual world she creates in her artwork. In *acceptance*, we see the realm of the devout, who initiate and accept the young girl. Through acceptance, the devout practice spiritual wellness within their community. The mother in this photo imparts a sense of agency and internal power ensuring that, in time, her daughter can take ownership of her own wellness when necessary.

The photos *in praise* (2019) and *in unison* (2019) are similar black-and-white compositions depicting Black women wearing long white sundresses with animal masks over their faces while holding up small watermelons as sacrifices. *in praise* shows two devout figures facing torward the viewers. In *in unison*, the devout face each other while offering watermelons as a sacrifice. In both photos, Gay connects attributes of holiness and the sacred with the devout. As mentioned before, her use of watermelons as sacrificial offerings attempts to reverse their negative connotations for Black people. Gay also learned through research that watermelon was a fruit associated with the new harvest in ancient Egypt. Like modern-day canisters, travelers ate watermelons for nourishment, particularly during the dry season.[76] Consider the iconography in Gay's photographs. The devout engage in spiritual systems that connect them directly to the African continent. Consequently, what Gay has created from a Black imagination is anchored in an Afrocentric worldview that makes way for Black women in her artwork to access wellness more readily than in a Eurocentric worldview.

In Gay's paintings, the themes and images are consistent with the photos. In *heaven's gate*, there are similarities within Gay's work to the works of both Lavett Ballard and Delita Martin. In *heaven's gate* a devout figure wears a white dress and black-and-white-striped socks over hooved feet. The history of stripes in fashion has evolved. During the Middle Ages, people involuntarily wore striped clothing by official orders to mark their outcast status. The pattern was linked to people who did not play by society's rules. By the twentieth century, many people wore stripes, including prisoners, whose striped clothing was a

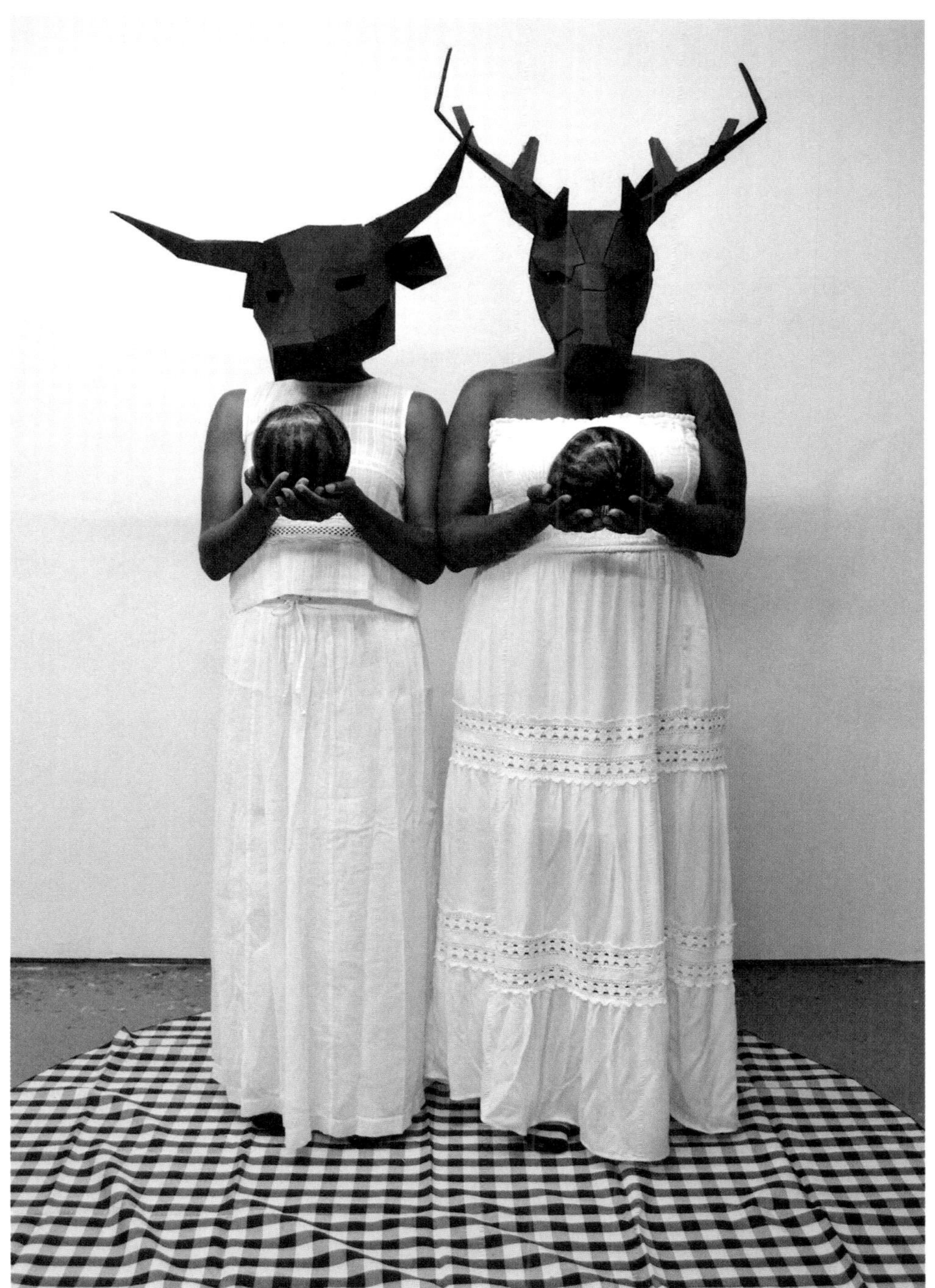

Shanequa Gay. *in praise*. 2019. Limited-edition black-and-white photograph on Somerset Velvet paper, 44 × 30 in. Courtesy of the artist.

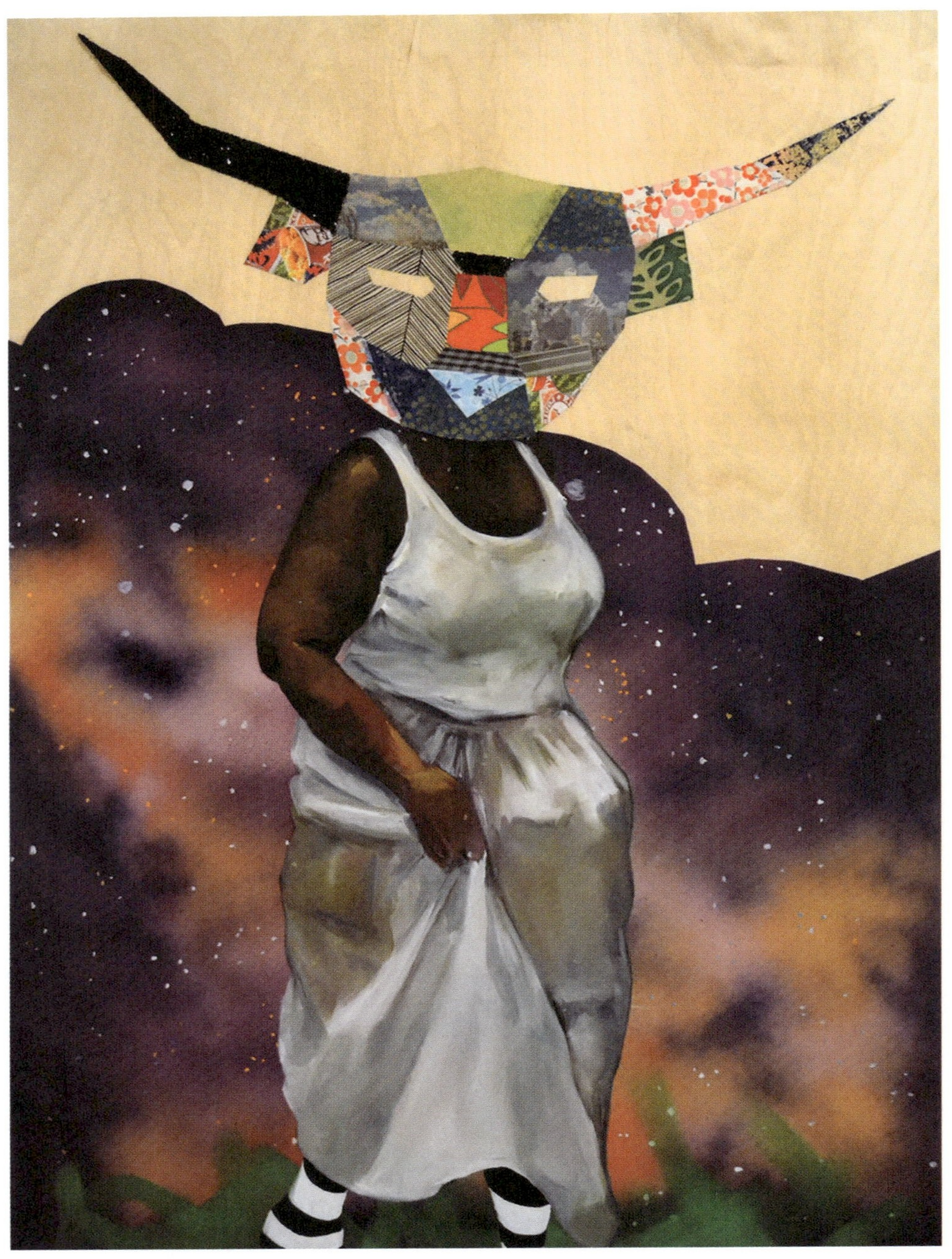

Shanequa Gay. *heaven's gate*. 2019. Acrylic, aerosol, oil, Flashe paint, collage, black glitter on wood panel, 40 × 30 in. Courtesy of the artist.

marker of incarceration.[77] The devout in Gay's art wear black and white striped socks to symbolize the entrapment and subjugation of Black women by societal norms. Gay argues that Black women experience a polarizing existence within the temporal world, represented by the black-and-white stripes.

As a more personal layer to the symbolism in her work, the figure in *heaven's gate* wears a bull-head mask created out of patchwork-quilt-looking paper. As in the works of Ballard and Martin, the bull-head, quilted mask in Gay's work represents the activities of her family members. Specifically, Gay's great-grandmother and great-aunt made quilts from scraps of family members' clothing and other personal belongings. Gay confirms, "When you think about the language of the quilt, the quilt is a narrative. It is a storytelling of who we are."[78] Gay's symbolic value of quilting is twofold. First, it is part of a tradition that involves bringing Black women together in community. Second, through quilting and quilting circles, Gay has access to stories about her family and community that she integrates in her artwork.

Additionally, the devout in this painting is standing in the cosmos, which Gay refers to as heaven's gate. The significance of this piece is that it shows that the devout can navigate the spiritual world as well as the temporal world. When an artwork depicts the cosmos, we see clouds. In contrast, when they are depicted in the earthly world, we often see green grass in the background to signify the difference. When the devout navigate other planets, it builds up to social justice themes in Gay's artwork where the devout are protectors and guards of the Black community.

The visual imagery of the devout and the correlating titles convey that the devout are often busy cultivating spiritual wellness. Here are a few titles to

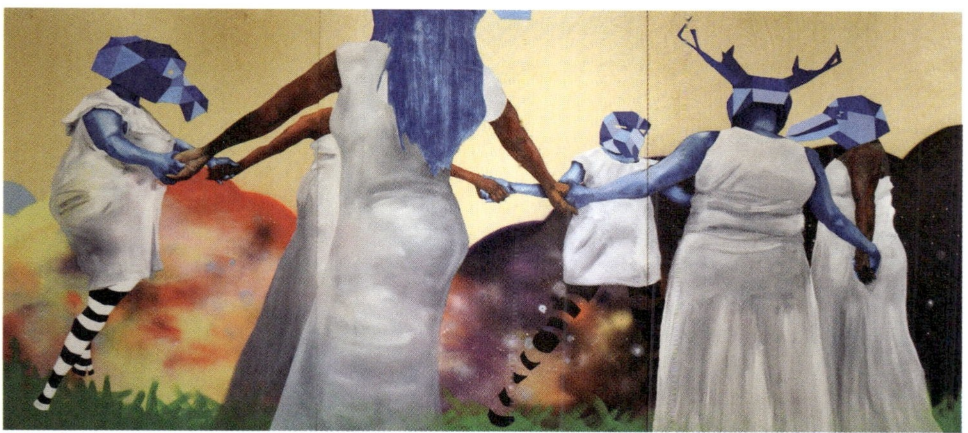

Shanequa Gay. *healing circle*. 2019. Triptych, mixed media on wood panel, 108 × 49 in. Courtesy of the artist.

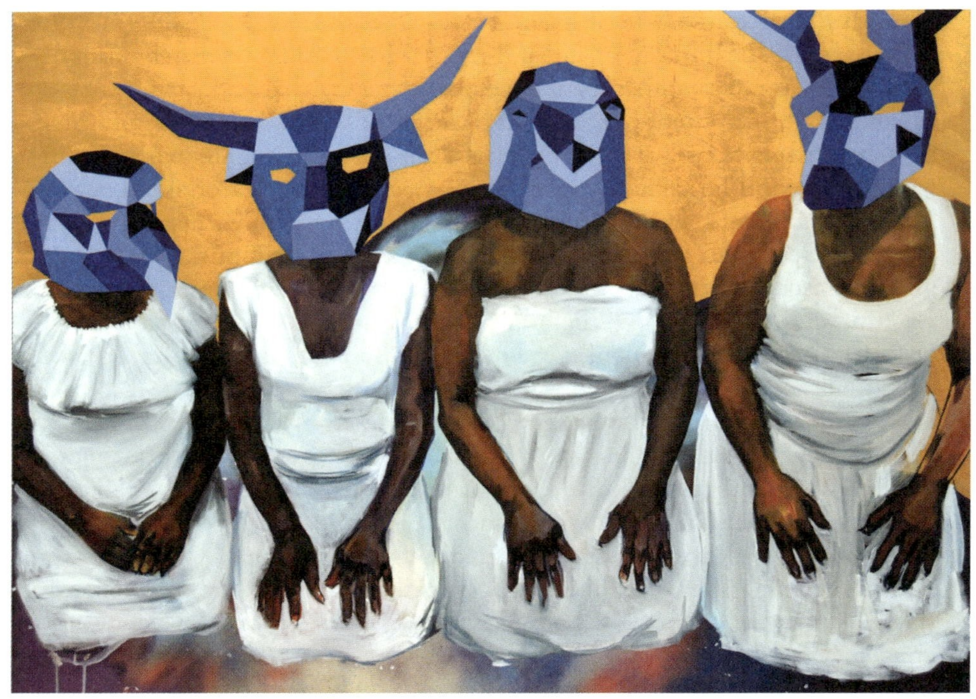

Shanequa Gay. *summoning*. 2020. Acrylic, aerosol, Flashe paint on wood panel, 36 × 48 in. Courtesy of the artist.

consider: *holy offering* (2020); *healing circle* (2021), which shows a group of the devout holding hands while standing in a circle; *intercessory deities* (2018); *covering* (2021); *ini-she-ation* (2019), a play on the word *initiation*; and the *unnameable, unspeakable divine ascension* (2019). All these titles convey that the devout are in a perpetual state of healing and wellness. They often are presented in groups that reflect the power of Black women's association. In *summoning* (2020), Gay presents all four devout archetypes in blue geometric masks and white dresses. She strategically painted the devout in blue lapis-colored masks to represent their divinity, calmness, and revolutionary peace.[79] In *summoning*, the devout also kneel in prayer while in a spiritual realm.

Gay expounds on the power of Black women gathering: "We have to be in a place of healing, especially in the midst of each other. In this position, we impart self-care; there is self-care and praying together and having oneness."[80] Gay also sees a connection between community and divine healing. On the rare occasion that a devout is depicted alone, she is in an emotional state of dominance. However, Gay is more invested in the devout working together as a collective and states, "I see empowerment and being in a trifold or being in a group of more than one where two and three are gathered."[81] By gathering, the devout are unified, meaning Black women are on the same page in the most powerful way imaginable. Except in artwork like *ascension* and *healing circle*, many devout are stoic and still. Their stillness reminds Black women to be present and not get caught up in what Gay describes as "this notion that busyness is freedom." Gay herself must create balance in her life because she has so many projects and responsibilities. In more recent times, she has been committed to cultivating a space of acceptance for creatives and particularly Black women artists who, through transparency and group settings, share that there have been times when they were looking for "their tribe," only to feel rejected. Acknowledging that creatives are often not given to joining groups but rather challenging group identity, Gay believes Black women creatives must create safe spaces for each other.[82] This idea is also a theme in her artwork that shows up when she creates sculptures of the devout.

i come as us

In 2018 at the Sumter County Art Gallery, Shanequa Gay returned to her initial inspiration for creating hybrid beings in *i come as us* (2018). The installation included four devout figures as monumental sculptures in response to continuous violence against Black women's bodies. The sculptures are ten feet high. All wear distinct colors and patterned dresses, with black masks representing the four archetypes in Gay's work: the bull, the deer, the raven, and the vulture. These sculptures stand in front of a ten-foot-high by fifty-four-foot-wide black and gold mural. At first glance, the mural looks like a design of flowers. Gay revealed that she wanted to lure viewers to the installation with a visual language of seduction, beauty, familiarity, and the large scale of her work.

A closer look at the installation reveals that the stemmed flowers in the mural design are the faces of women, specifically four victims of violence: Renisha McBride, Sandra Bland, Korryn Gaines, and Erica Garner. Except for Garner, the other three women represented in the motif were unarmed and died at the hands of the police. Garner, an American activist and advocate for police reform, was affected by police violence when her father, Eric Garner, an unarmed Black man, died when a New York City police officer held him in a lethal chokehold during an arrest.[83] It is significant to note that Black women experience trauma directly and indirectly because of violence in their community. Gay positions the devout in front of the mural as guardians who convey a level of fear. Concerning the masks in Gay's work, the artist wants you to consider the following: "When masks cover entire faces of the devout, they are looking, they are looking at you, but you ain't necessarily looking at them. They have power over the gaze."[84] Their empowerment counters the

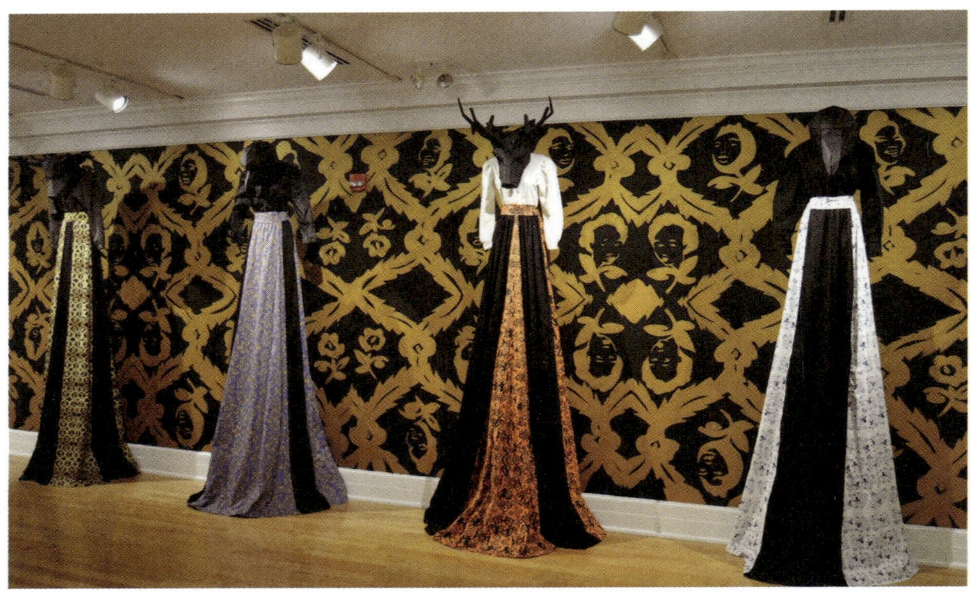

Shanequa Gay. *i come as us*. 2018. Four dresses, acrylic, and paper sculpture, 10 × 54 ft. Installation, Sumter County Art Gallery. Courtesy of the artist.

experience of how others in society view Black women. Black women have not often had power over the gaze. Yet the devout in Gay's artwork have this power, and behind their masks, they are staring back at you, the viewer. As Gay explains, "You do not necessarily have that power over them because of the masks that hide their eyes."[85]

Along with the masks in Gay's sculpture, the extremely tall stature of the devout figures also conveys a sense of empowerment. They guard the mural while looking down on viewers who approach them. Their stature expresses their divinity. Gay revels in adding layered meanings to her work and her conversation. She revealed that the devout in this installation also represent the four women they are guarding. With a tone of clarity and conviction, Gay stated, "I conceived of seeing Korryn, Erica, Renisha, and Sandra transitioning into these new beings, these new creatures."[86] The four women represented in *i come as us* have the space to make the transition out of victimhood; through the realm and sisterhood of the devout, they become ancestors, they become intercessors, they become something godlike. The divine beings move beyond the status of victimization here on earth and transition into something new. Within BWAEs, their transition symbolizes a spiritual act of wellness necessary for Black women. However, the goal is for Black women to reach this state without having to die through violence and trauma.

When Shanequa Gay takes viewers on a visual journey through the devout, we can piece together her idea of what wellness looks like for Black women. In response to some specific interview questions about wellness, Gay revealed that for her, wellness is a sense of belonging. She creates space where the Black women in her work have balance and are empowered by gathering. After deep reflection, Gay described wellness as "moving beyond where I have been to where I desire to be."[87] Thus wellness is the goal, but it is also constant in ways that feel circular to Gay. As a result, the artist wants "to be in the consistency and continuity of wellness."[88] Her desire gives meaning to the iconography of her work, which often depicts Black women in prayer circles, communal circles rather than a linear arrangement. "Linear" implies hierarchies, and that is not wellness, according to Gay. Wellness needs to be circular. It needs to be complete. It needs to be womblike for Gay, who states, "You always want to be in a position of giving birth and giving birth does not always mean a human is coming out of your body."[89] Shanequa Gay's art reminds us that we all can give birth daily to wellness through creativity, new ideas, and new ideologies and theories. As the progenitors of humankind, Black women can and must assume this right in terms of giving birth to wellness and experiencing what Gay calls "womb living."[90]

Crooked Images: The Visual Perceptual Field of Black Women

Some of Shanequa Gay's most provocative and layered works are her film shorts. The artist uses film to layer sound with still images and moving images of the devout. In the video *the crooked room* (2018), Shanequa pairs the video and images of the devout with an audio recording of Dr. Melissa Harris-Perry discussing how the visual perceptual field of Black women is distorted or crooked.[91] In the voiceover, Harris-Perry explains that the framework of cognitive psychology is about how what we see influences how we figure out where we are in space. Further, it is the responsibility of the person to determine what is straight up and down in a space or a world that is off kilter. Navigating a world that is off kilter has become the lived experience for many Black women throughout the African diaspora. When we look deeper into cognitive psychology, we understand that some people are field independent and can find the straight up and down despite the crooked angles around them. However, the vast majority of people are field dependent. In response to crooked and distorted spaces, these people can adjust themselves as much as forty-five degrees but perceive themselves as straight up and down because they are aligned with the crooked images. In her book *Sister Citizen: Shame, Stereotypes, and Black Women in America* (2011), Harris-Perry likens the experience of field-dependent people adjusting themselves to crooked spaces to experience normality or a world that makes sense and that has order to the experiences of Black women, particularly in America.[92] She describes Black women's experiences of walking in a room where everything is off kilter and the world that they expect to meet at ninety degrees is actually at about sixty-two degrees. It's a world where pictures and mirrors look upright but Black women must fix and adjust the pictures or mirrors in order to see themselves in them. According to Harris-Perry, the implication is that the perceptual field for African American women is imbalanced. Thus the real political and healing work is for Black women to find their own authentic sense of self in a social, political, and historical environment that will keep giving them back negative and crooked images and reflections.

Gay uses Harris-Perry's audio recording as a voiceover for a film that shows both still images of her artwork and a dance by Black women wearing masks and performing as the devout. Harris-Perry's voiceover in the video is enlightening to those who may not understand what it is like to be a Black woman in America. It also validates Black women's experiences in a world that invalidates and distorts our very experiences. Harris-Perry's stance that Black women's real political work is just to try to find a sense of their authentic selves in crooked spaces is the work that Black women artists have been doing for years. Like the women in Gay's painting *healing circle*, the women in *the crooked room* are wearing white sundresses, animal-head masks and black-and-white-striped knee socks. While holding hands, they shift and move in a circle, sometimes changing directions. In an interview with the gallerist Myrtis Bedolla, Gay explained that the dance performance was a "kind of witchery" that she drew from the three witches in Shakespeare's play *Macbeth*. Gay explains, "The witches in the play didn't really have power other than their words and language," a realm of power that reminds Gay of old-school Black women in the American South.[93] Through experimentation and film, Gay was looking for ways to depict the power of shifting between worlds while creating the sense of cognitive dissonance described in Harris-Perry's voiceover. The artist provides the images with three-dimensional form by changes in color, camera framings, and flickering lighting techniques. Images of the women dancing sometimes fade and are replaced by photo images and paintings from Gay's previous work. When brought together, the entire film creates what Gay calls a "cosmic galaxy and spiritual world where the devout are empowered in the space that they are in."[94] The empowerment of Black women is a consistent thread in Gay's art. As with most superheroes, the devout's masks are a source of power. According to Gay, Harris-Perry's argument that Black women adjust their perceptions in crooked spaces helps to relay the tilt, bend, and symmetry that happen when they wear their masks. Masks allow for the Black women in Gay's artwork to protect what they know to be true and to create a safe space for themselves and their families while navigating crooked spaces. Gay's use of masks in her artwork echoes Paul Laurence Dunbar's poem "We Wear the Mask" (1895), in which he writes, "Why should the world be over-wise, in counting all our tears and sighs? Nay, let them only see us, while We wear the mask."[95] In a variety of art media, Gay presents the society of Black women saving themselves and others through rites and rituals that cultivate a process of healing and strategies for wellness. As much as Gay is attempting to create this in new worlds and mythical spaces, her artwork has real implications in the temporal world and for Gay personally.

Shanequa's Blueprint for Holistic Well-Being

Gay's art and her wellness are tightly interwoven. As she states, "My art is my wellness, and I was looking to create a safe place for me."[96] At the early age of four, Gay created a safe space in her room by drawing on her walls. Since that time, she has consistently drawn on walls by creating murals that provide a language of healing through art. She found that "through coloring, drawing, writing, singing, dancing, and poetry, all those things have freed me."[97] The inarguable continuity in her work extends beyond the devout series. Gay also paints murals that commemorate people slain in her community, like the mural for Alexis Crawford, a Clark Atlanta student killed by her roommate.[98] That narrative was one of betrayal, explains Gay.[99] These murals are not only a personal catharsis but also offer a communal space for healing and remembrance. By addressing both personal and collective trauma, Gay's art becomes a powerful tool for societal reflection and emotional restoration.

Similarly, a recorded video performance, *ode to kathryn johnston* (2016), brings attention to the murder of Johnston, a ninety-two-year-old African American woman living in the Bluff district of Atlanta, Georgia, who was shot and killed by two police officers in 2006. The officers entered her home with a no-knock warrant under the pretense of a "botched drug raid" that they falsified.[100] In both examples, Gay is consistent in giving space to both memory and healing. She describes her work as communal healing. She uses it not only for her own recovery but for others who need a space to heal and sometimes grieve at the monuments and proverbial altars she creates.[101] The space for healing that Gay provides in her work is transactional between herself and the community, and she gives back through the vehicle of art.

Delita Martin's and Shanequa Gay's artwork have thematic similarities. On several occasions their work has been juxtaposed in group exhibitions. Both artists create work that provides sociopolitical commentary on the African American community's experience: historically, currently, and in the future. They also demonstrate the impact that Black women artists have through their art.

Delita Martin and Shanequa Gay converge at the intersection of artistic prowess and a profound commitment to nurturing cultural and spiritual wellness through their distinctive styles. With an unwavering dedication to the transformative power of art, these visionaries embark on journeys that extend beyond mere visual expression. Delita Martin, with her masterful use of portraiture, and Shanequa Gay, through her dynamic multimedia art, weave narratives that transcend the canvas, fostering a dialogue that transcends cultural boundaries and embraces spiritual nourishment. In their artistic endeavors, both Martin and Gay offer more than mere visual aesthetics; they present a captivating exploration of identity, heritage, and spirituality, creating spaces where viewers can engage in a shared experience that contributes to the cultural and spiritual well-being of individuals and communities alike.

6

Ancestral Memory and Generational Wellness through Photography

For those who encounter my work, I want them
to stop, I want them to pay attention, I want
them to not be able to look away.
—Tawny Chatmon

The representation of Black children in photography can be used to establish a link to ancestral memory, creating a visual continuum of Black experiences. This connection to the past contributes to generational wellness, providing a sense of continuity and shared history. It reinforces the importance of preserving and passing down cultural narratives for the well-being of present and future generations. I explore these themes in Tawny Chatmon's artwork and her 2021 exhibition *If I'm No Longer Here, I Wanted You to Know. . . .* Through the lens of photography and the layering of mixed media materials, the Maryland-based artist Tawny Chatmon has captured the regality of Black youth. In a biography statement, Chatmon explained how she became a professional artist: "My work and life have gone through many phases that have led me to create the work I do today. I attribute this evolution to three major shifts: the decision to no longer pursue a career in dramatic arts, the birth of my first child, and the death of my father."[1]

Tawny turned to photography as a medium for expression and as part of her journey of self-discovery. It was also a means of earning an income. At nineteen, she received her first camera. For the next five years, through self-teaching, she learned the mechanics and various genres of photography. Chatmon also developed skills in Photoshop and took jobs in graphic and web design. When Chatmon became a first-time mother, she found a new subject—her son—and a passion for documenting his life through the camera lens. This led her to photograph other family members and their special moments. Chatmon's documentation of her family, then and now, has been a consistent means of sharing what is most important to her—her role as a mother. Further, her work shares a perspective of "a Black woman and mother of three Black children [who] is motivated by 'leaving something important behind'."[2] Within the larger meta narrative of Western society, the celebrations of Black childhood and familial bonds are few and far between. Black children are often mistreated and denied childhood by being considered adults at an early age. Supporting evidence can be found in the Georgetown Law Center on Poverty and Inequality, which released a quantitative study titled *Girlhood Interrupted: The Erasure of Black Girls' Childhood*. This research utilized an online questionnaire to assess whether adults perceive Black girls as more mature and adultlike than white girls. The data showed that adults view Black girls as less innocent and more adultlike than their white peers, especially in the age range of 5 to 14, and linked these perceptions to disparities in punishment in the realms of education and law enforcement.[3]

Through her opulent aesthetic—inspired by the Austrian painter Gustav Klimt's Gold Period—Chatmon creates visual counternarratives that center Black childhood. She often depicts her subjects in regal clothing. Her work is best described as crisp pictures of cherished people adorned with loosely painted jewels and flowers with ornaments, rendered with pigment and gold leaf and sometimes three-dimensional, complementing lustrous shades of Black skin and hair.[4] To add a spiritual presence to her subjects, Chatmon employs the Byzantine art aesthetic of elongating their bodies and clothes, so that these figures overwhelm the space. Yet they also embody a stillness that echoes what Kevin Quashie describes as the sovereignty of quiet, in which quiet "is a metaphor for the full range of one's inner life—one's desires, ambitions, hunger, vulnerabilities [and] fears."[5] As in Lava Thomas's art, the grandeur and the stillness of Chatmon's figures add to the complexity of her photographs and the conversation she is having in *If I'm No Longer Here, I Wanted You to Know. . . .* This series is a visual love letter to her children as told from the point of view of a mother who hopes for a better world in the present and future, not only for her children but for all children. Consequently, "each picture is an affirmation, and a hope for a golden life to come."[6] As an artist and a mother, Chatmon posits, "I am speaking from the standpoint that I have this feeling or this realization that I won't be here forever. So I think of my children and what I want for them, the world I want for them, and how I can make better use of myself to contribute to that before I go."[7] Chatmon's work primarily focuses on creating a safe and healing space in Western society for Black childhood, which is feared and often indistinguishable from Black adulthood.

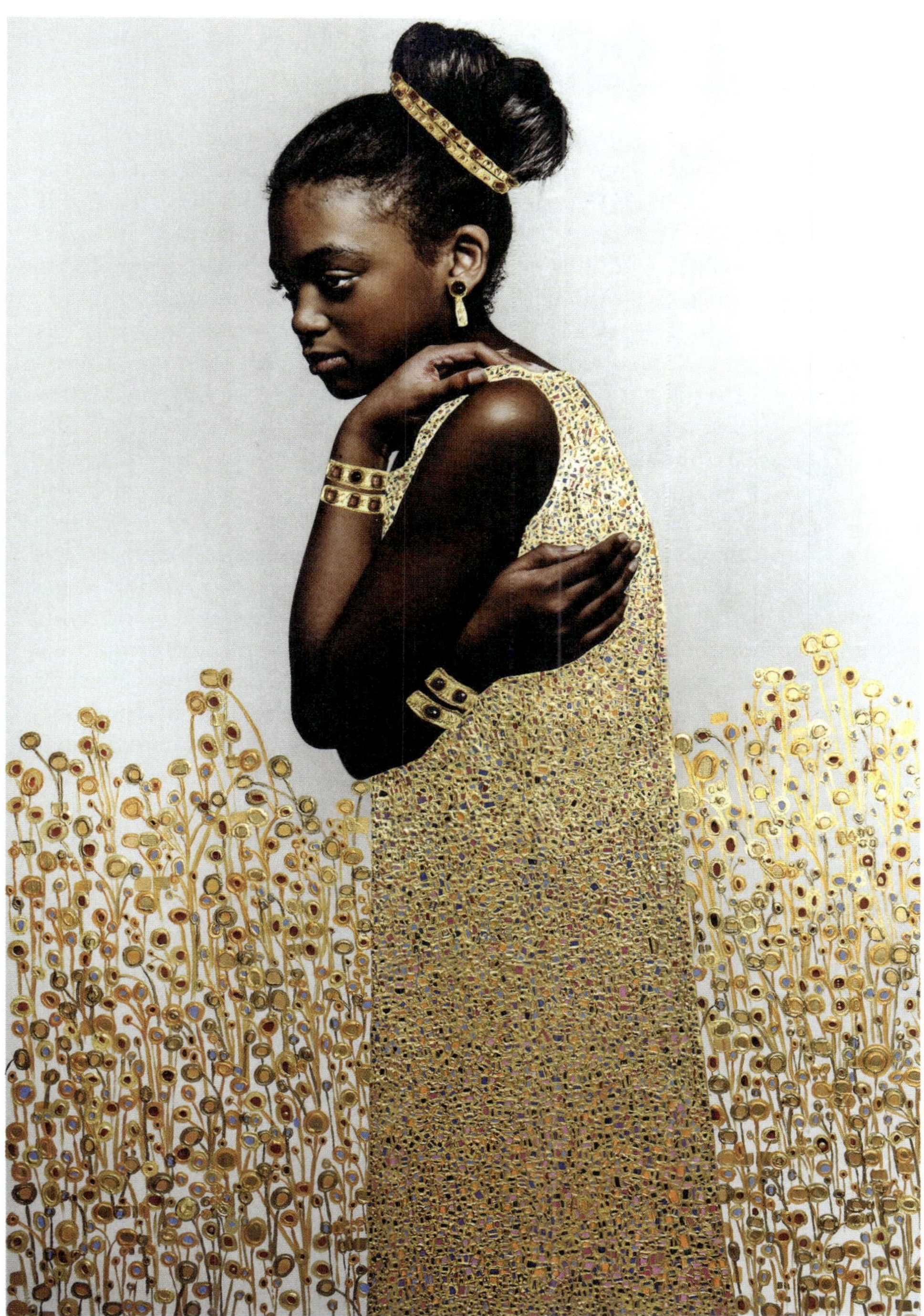

Tawny Chatmon. *But She Already Knew They Were More Precious Than All the Jewels and Gold in the World*. 2020–21. 24-karat gold leaf, acrylic, ink, precious and semiprecious stones (Mohave copper turquoise, emerald, amethyst, ruby), on archival pigment print, 30 × 45 in. Courtesy of Tawny Chatmon and Galerie Myrtis. © Tawny Chatmon.

Illuminating the Power of Sisterhood
and Community Among Black Girls

While I was interviewing Chatmon, she explained that in the United States, innocence is a privilege not afforded to some Black children. Victims inform her sentiments of police violence, such as twelve-year-old Tamir Rice and eighteen-year-old Michael Brown, both of whom were unarmed and who were shot and killed in 2014 by police who feared they were dangerous. Those two and the many killings of unarmed Black people have sparked movements such as Black Lives Matter and a new Black art renaissance that has added artistic commentary to the current social fabric, both within the United States and abroad. After the shooting of seventeen-year-old Trayvon Martin in 2012, Chatmon recalled, "All of these things started to weigh on me."[8] She found herself responding to violence against Black youth by capturing their innocence and natural beauty through photography.[9] Chatmon explains that although Black childhood is not protected and valued, society does value gold and precious stones. This message is distinctly present in the image *But She Already Knew They Were More Precious Than All the Jewels and Gold in the World* (2020–21). Thus, when Chatmon adorns the figures in her work with both elements, she is symbolically covering them with protective armor.

In her work *Best* (2020), the image of two girls facing each other while engaged in a hand-clapping game evokes the early development of sisterhood among Black women through play. Chatmon explains that she photographed several girls separately in the same pose before selecting the two subjects for the final composition. In addition to the theme of sisterhood, Chatmon made a conscious decision to have a dark-skinned girl and a light-skinned girl come together to address and counter practices of colorism. In *Best*, viewers see the possibilities of these young girls overcoming this history: not only are they best friends but they bring out the best in each other. Chatmon wants viewers to know that Black girls and women can bring out the best in each other and can look out for each other with the same concentration and dedication that it takes to engage in the game of handclapping.

Similarly, works such as *Joy* (2020) and *Created in Her Image* (2020) pair two Black girls in the frame. In *Joy*, the two girls are physically connected by holding hands and touching foreheads as Chatmon captures them in mid-giggle. We see their innocence on display as they mirror each other's joy. In *Created in Her Image*, two young Black girls evoke a sense of reflection. The subjects in this are identical twins whose faces and upper bodies merge to emphasize their connection. I asked Chatmon to elaborate more on this photograph, whose title is a biblical reference to being created in the image of God. She explains that the title is a play on words and the notion that God could be a Black woman. Further, this work emphasizes Chatmon's desire for viewers

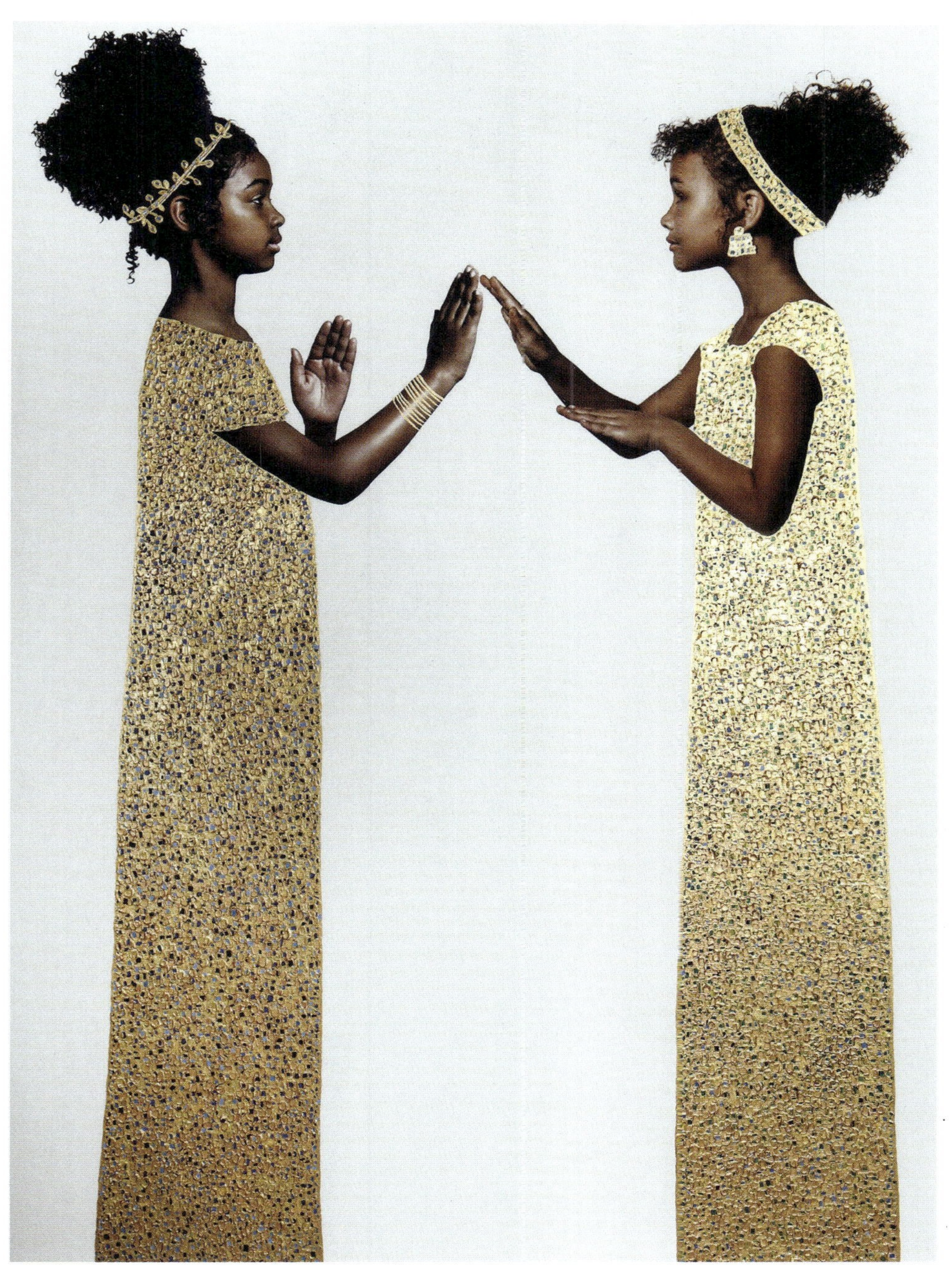

Tawny Chatmon. *Best*. 2020. 24-karat gold leaf, acrylic or archival pigment print, 30 × 40 in. Courtesy of Tawny Chatmon and Galerie Myrtis. © Tawny Chatmon.

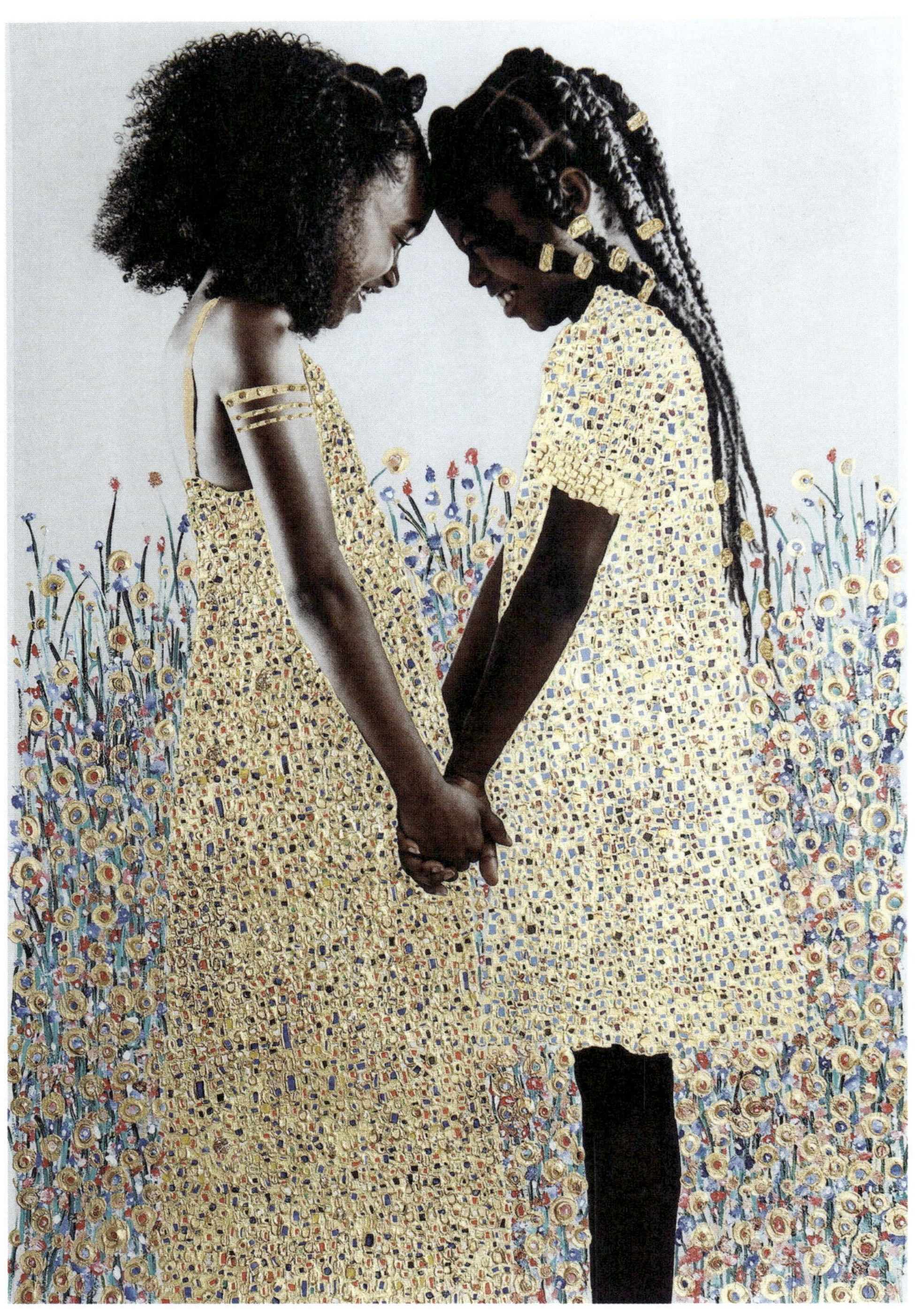

Tawny Chatmon. *Joy.* 2020. 24-karat gold leaf, acrylic on archival pigment print, 20 × 30 in. Courtesy of Tawny Chatmon and Galerie Myrtis. © Tawny Chatmon.

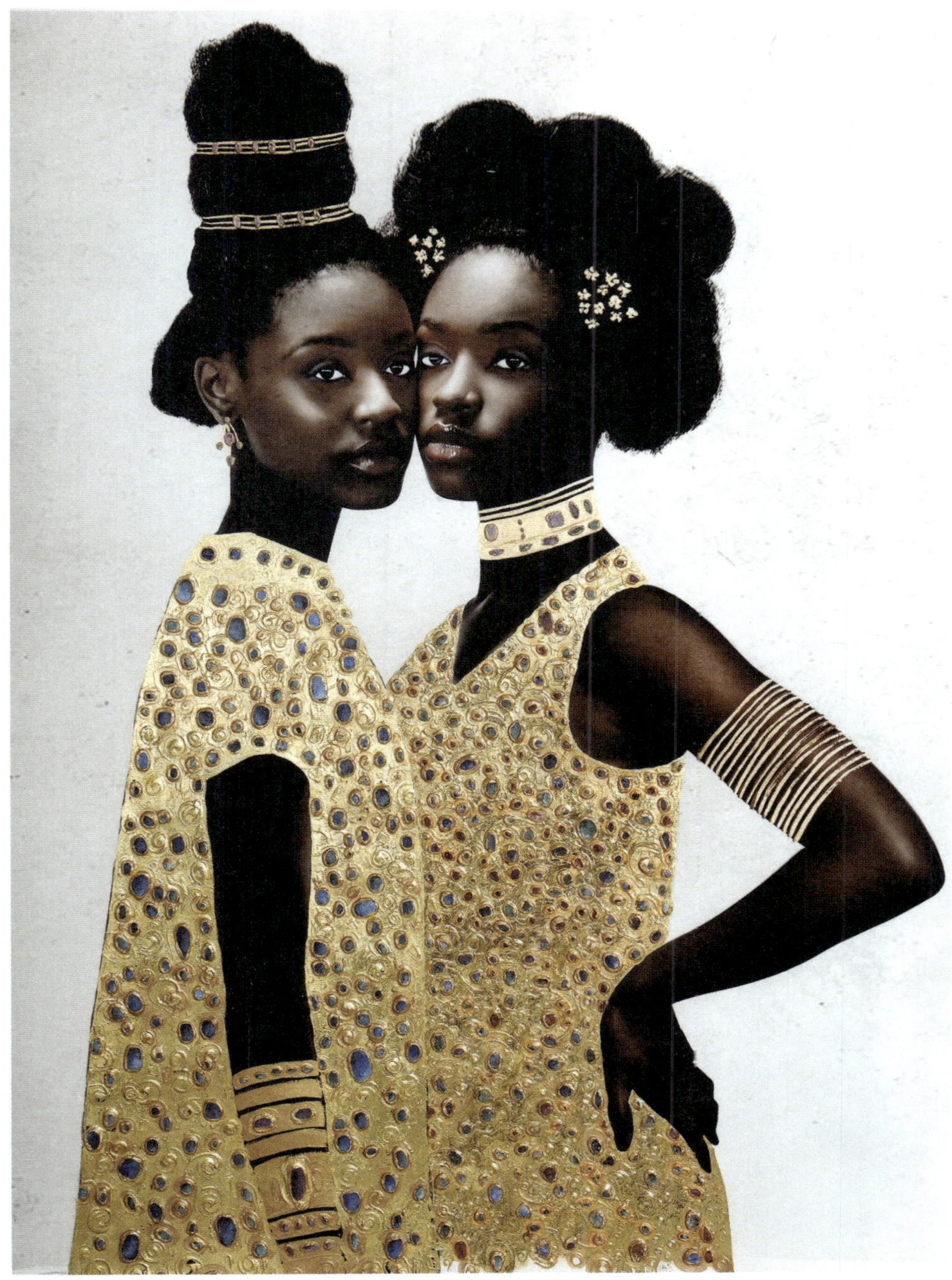

Tawny Chatmon. *Created in Her Image.* 2020. 24-karat gold leaf, acrylic, mixed media on archival pigment print, 30 × 40 in. Courtesy of Tawny Chatmon and Galerie Myrtis. © Tawny Chatmon.

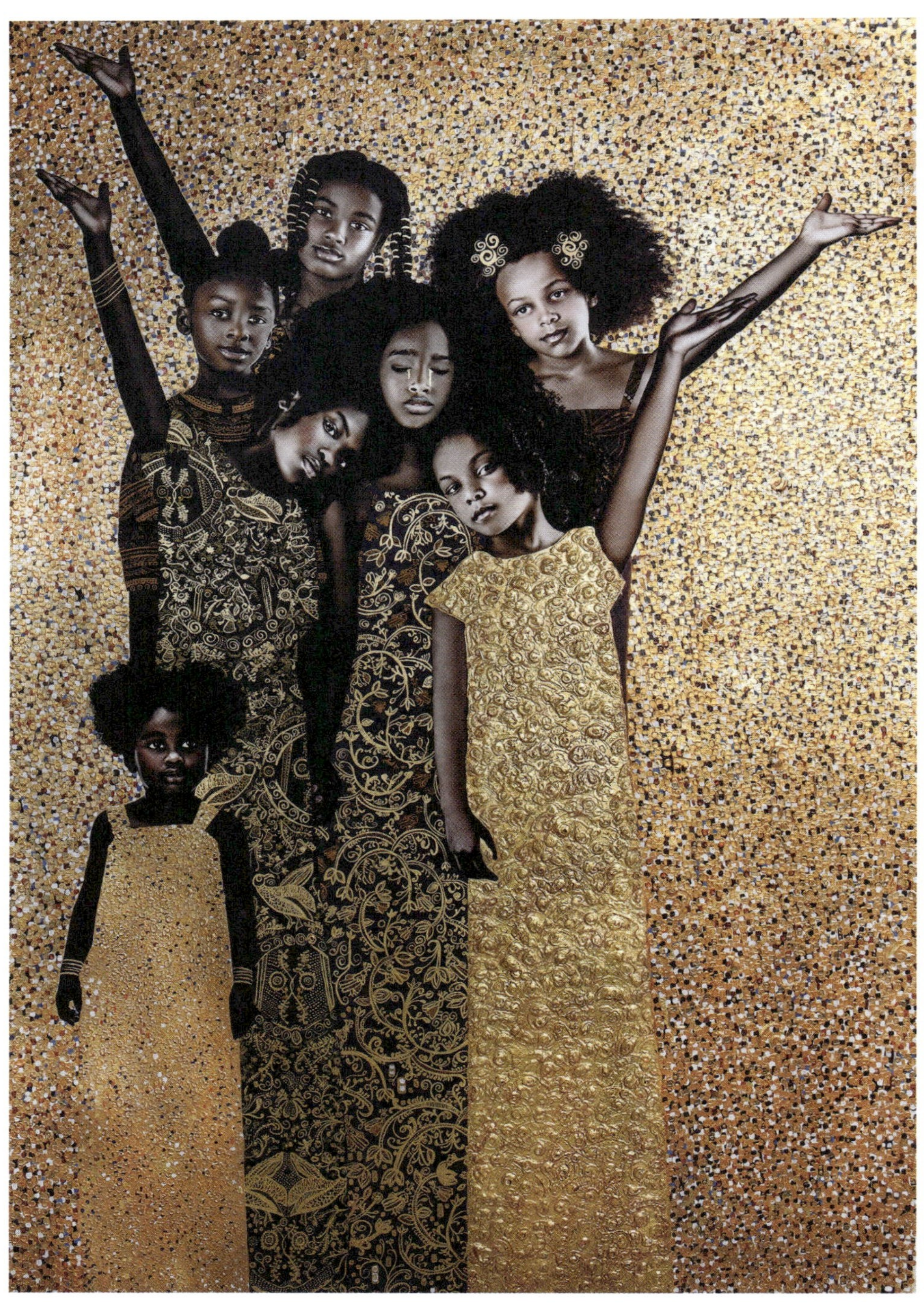

Tawny Chatmon. *It Was Never Your Burden to Carry*. 2020. 24-karat gold leaf, 12-karat gold leaf, acrylic on archival pigment print, 28 × 46 in. Courtesy of Tawny Chatmon and Galerie Myrtis. © Tawny Chatmon.

to see themselves in her art and to look inward, not outward, for approval. Both images add breadth to Chatmon's conversation about the importance of Black girlhood and the solidarity fostered in these relationships. This message is intensified in *It Was Never Your Burden to Carry* (2020), where viewers see a group of seven Black girls huddled together with arms outstretched.

The central figure in *It Was Never Your Burden to Carry* (2020) is a girl whose eyes are closed as streams of gold tears run down her face. The remaining girls appear to hold her up, with the weight of their bodies shoring up hers. Two of their heads are also resting on her shoulders, supporting her head. In conversation with Chatmon, she explained that "this artwork serves as a reminder that although children are the future leaders, it is not their burden to fix past generations' mistakes."[10] Altogether, this composition resembles a tree rooted and anchored by jewels, textured gold dresses, and intricately designed fabric with images of birds and flowers. I asked Chatmon about the relevance of the birds in her work. As with many other details in her artwork, there is a personal story connected to the images of birds, which she relates to the passing of her father, with whom she shared a close relationship. Like the birds in Delita Martin's art, the birds in Chatmon's art have a spiritual connotation. They specifically symbolize spiritual ancestors who follow and guide people in life. Thus vital elements of the past, present, and future in this exhibition coalesce to shape what Chatmon wants us, the viewers, to know.

Black Children Leading the Way in Forward-Looking Portraits

In many ways, Chatmon works on the margins of Black futurism. Her subjects live both in the present and in an ideal world that she wants to be better for them, a world that protects Black joy, a world that they deserve. Consequently, Chatmon communicates opportunities for an optimistic future by having some of her subjects look off to one side. In both *Ahead* (2020) and *Look Forward, Beloved* (2020) the subjects are Black children whose gaze is directed outward and away from viewers toward a positive future that may counter some of the negative experiences of Black children. In contrast, the girl in *Destined to Lead the Way* (2021) gazes directly at viewers to anchor Chatmon's message that the children in her work are our future leaders.[11] When Chatmon's subjects are not looking to the future, they are sometimes in pensive thought, as portrayed by Chatmon's oldest daughter, Kailynn-James, in *But She Already Knew They Were More Precious Than All the Jewels and Gold in the World* (2020–21). Or they stand resolute like the young woman in *And Then She Said, "I Never Asked You To Worship Me."* Both photographs communicate youth's wisdom to viewers. These are turning points in Chatmon's work because her most important endeavor is to impart knowledge to her children, who are often her subjects, like her daughter in *But She Already Knew* (2020–21).

As we see in *But She Already Knew* and *And Then She Said*, Chatmon is quick to remind us that children can teach adults lessons, too. This message becomes more apparent in *The Children, Too, Helped Us Grow* (2020). Kaicie-October, Chatmon's youngest daughter, stands with clasped hands in a field of purple, gold, and blue-stemmed elongated flowers, suggesting the notion of play and growth. Reappearing in this work are the ancestral birds that seem to guide in her growth. Her daughter's outward gaze toward viewers pulls us into the experience.

Capturing the Strength, Joy, and Promise of Young Black Men

Many of Chatmon's subjects are young Black girls. However, being the mother of a son, Chatmon feels she would be remiss if she did not create a visual love letter that included Black male subjects. Recall that Chatmon presents a young boy in *Look Forward, Beloved* (2020) to facilitate the conversation about an optimistic future and, in many ways, self-determination. Chatmon's work also addresses the traumatic present, where police officers and civilians have killed many unarmed young Black boys and men in America. In some circumstances, it is vigilantes such as those who in 2020 pursued and fatally shot the twenty-five-year-old jogger Ahmaud Arbery because they wrongly suspected him of burglary.

Chatmon's son Kardan, the oldest of her three children, is the subject in *In Your Hoodie or Your White Tee* (2021), a response to these tragic events. Chatmon offers his portrait as a confirmation that young Black boys are not a threat in general or in particular because they might be wearing a hoodie or other clothing that mainstream society associates with criminality. He is featured wearing gold pants and a white hoodie embroidered with the same embellished gold leaf and floral patterns found elsewhere in the exhibition. The history of hoodies and racial profiling has spurred various forms of activism, including the Humanize My Hoodie Movement, which seeks to promote racial equity by displaying powerful statements on hoodies to counteract the myth of Black criminality.[12] The historian Tanisha Ford asserts that "throughout the global Black Freedom Struggle, Black women have incorporated beauty and fashion into their activism."[13] Chatmon's portrait of Kardan in a gold-embroidered hoodie conveys respectability and worthiness of admiration and acceptance, exemplifying the ongoing tradition of Black women using fashion as a form of activism. This representation challenges prevailing narratives and offers a counternarrative to the often negative stereotypes associated with hoodies. By blending fashion with activism in art, Black women artists like Chatmon continue to redefine and assert their agency in public discourse, advocating for a more inclusive and equitable society.

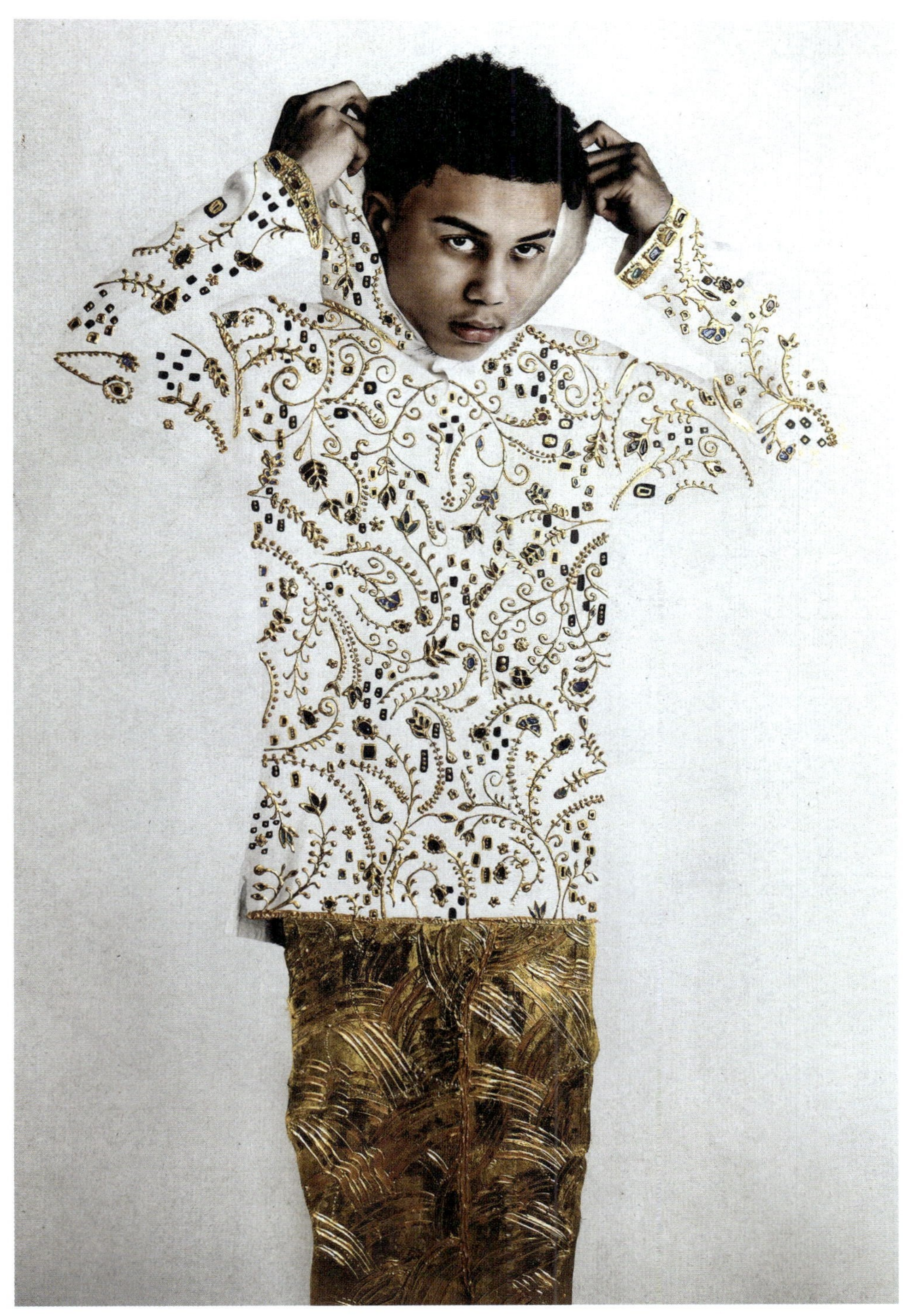

Tawny Chatmon. *In Your Hoodie or Your White Tee*. 2021. 24-karat gold, acrylic on archival pigment print, 20 × 30 in. Courtesy of Tawny Chatmon and Galerie Myrtis. © Tawny Chatmon.

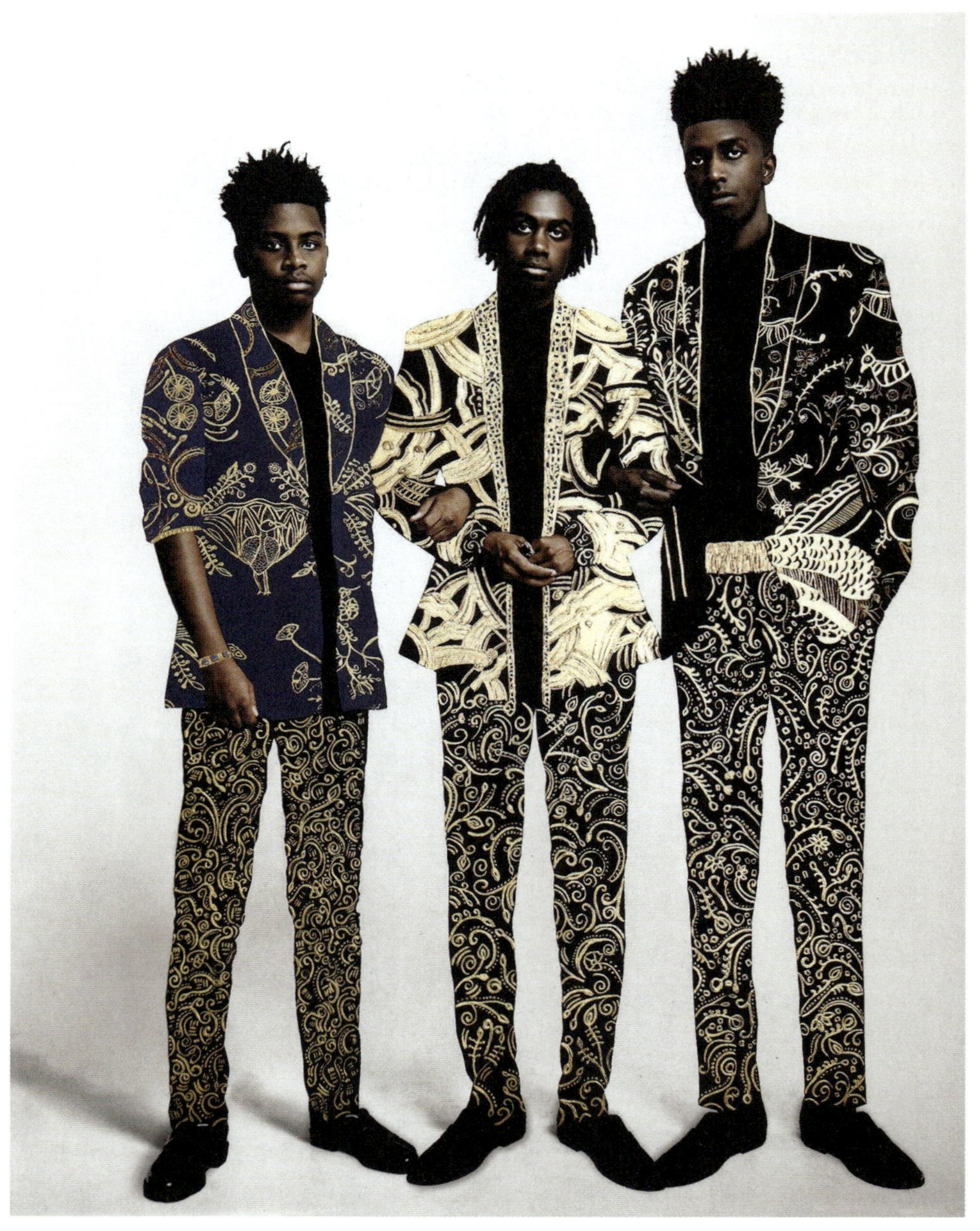

Tawny Chatmon. *Bridgetower Frieze*. 2018–21. 24-karat gold leaf, acrylic on archival pigment print, 30 × 40 in. Courtesy of Tawny Chatmon and Galerie Myrtis. © Tawny Chatmon.

Chatmon builds on her celebration of Black boyhood in *Bridgetower Frieze* (2021), where three brothers are standing side by side with arms linked together. Along with tapered and twist-locked hair, the brothers are wearing elaborate black, gold, and midnight blue clothes with detailed patterns that resemble West African textile aesthetics. The title of this work is a tribute to Gustav Klimt's *Beethoven Frieze* (1901), whose iconography addresses the yearning and struggle for happiness driven by motives of compassion and ambition. Chatmon named her artwork after the eighteenth-century violinist and composer George Bridgetower, of Polish and West Indian parentage. Beethoven was deeply impressed with Bridgetower's virtuosic violin playing. Chatmon brings diversity to aesthetics both in title and composition. The three brothers form a frieze or wall of support, holding each other up in the spirit of brotherhood. The hope is that these young Black boys will grow to be like the adult Black man in *He's Got the Whole World in His Hands* (2020).

In *He's Got the Whole World in His Hands* (2021), we see a Black family unit that includes a father embracing his wife, who holds their two children, an infant and a toddler. The father's posture implies protection and love as he envelops his family with his arms. They are his world and connected to a greater purpose in life. The family's portrayal cements Chatmon's love letter to Black children and sums up the exhibition *If I'm No Longer Here, I Wanted You to Know. . . .* The portrait communicates that many Black children are built from a foundation of love as the parents in this portrait affectionately look downward at the toddler on the right side. She gazes up at them, in a position to receive the assurance of their presence. The infant's subtle gaze toward the viewers pulls us into their space of intimacy and into the conversation of how we must protect, adore, and love Black children; a better future depends on it.[14]

Tokie Rome-Taylor: Reclaiming African Diaspora History through Photography

Whereas Tawny Chatmon uses photography to help shape a more optimal future for Black children, the mixed-media and photo-based artist Tokie Rome-Taylor photographs Black children in period clothing to reclaim African diaspora history and counterimages that "only resign them to distorted histories of subjugation, suffering, and second-class humanity."[15] Rome-Taylor employs photography as a "memory tool," encapsulating the creolization and hybridity of African American culture.[16] She integrates African and Western symbols alongside found objects, which she transforms into artifacts. She positions these elements strategically in her photos to act as conduits of personal and cultural memory that give space to subversive rebellion and cultural autonomy. In her artist's statement she explains, "Children are the subjects I

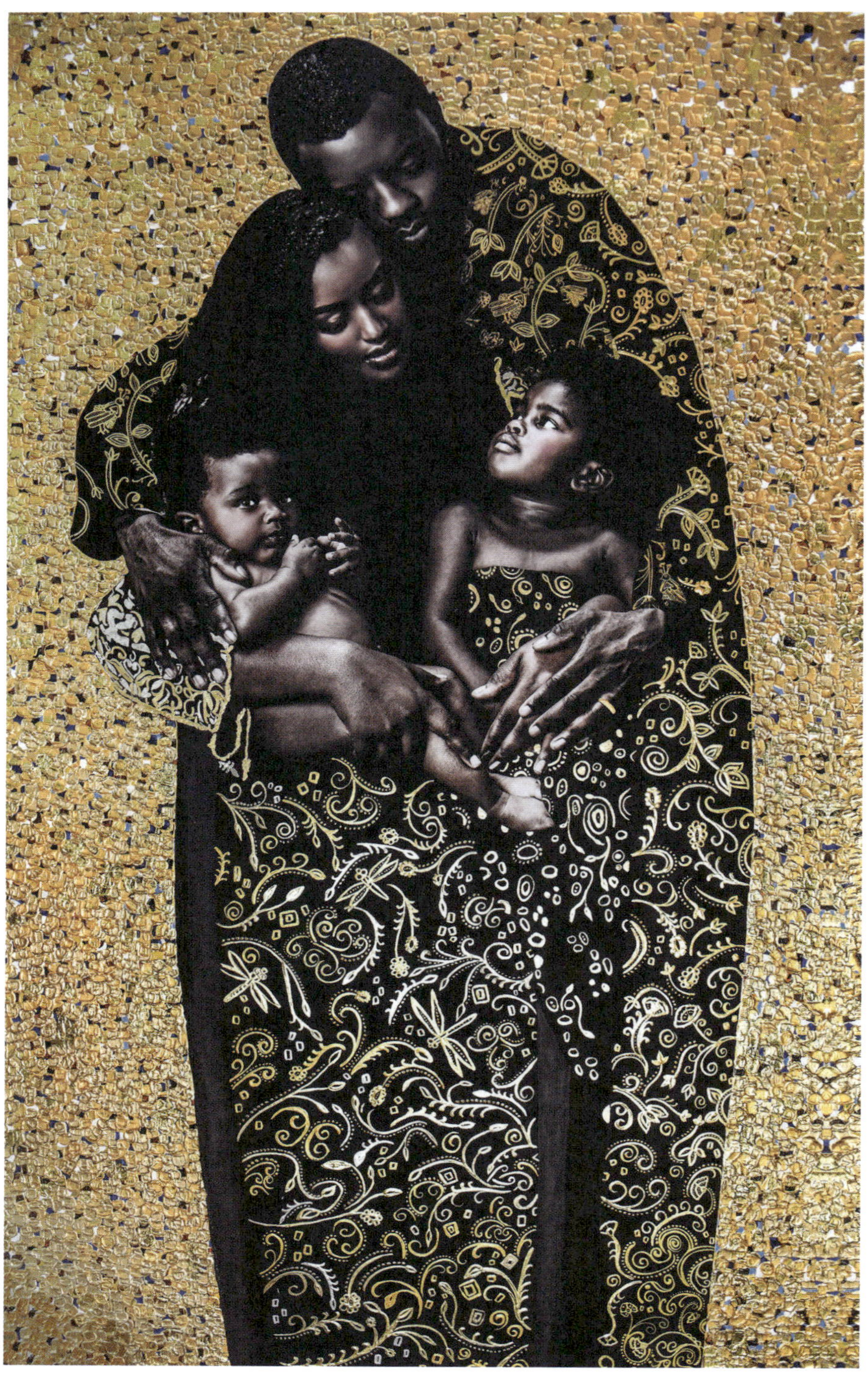

Tawny Chatmon. *He's Got the Whole World in His Hands.* 2021. 24-karat gold leaf, 12-karat gold leaf, acrylic on archival pigment print, 28 × 46 in. Courtesy of Tawny Chatmon and Galerie Myrtis. © Tawny Chatmon.

use to speak of a sense of belonging. These images of Black and brown children re-examine history and tradition, through photographic portraits that counter the propaganda of inaccurate stereotypical, subjugated, and inferior historical depictions of people of color. They represent a visual elevation that has been omitted from mainstream Western history."[17] Reclamation is the central theme in Rome-Taylor's work, and just as Delita Martin uses Sankofa, Rome-Taylor seeks to express reclamation in her portraits.[18]

Rome-Taylor's use of children as subjects is connected to being the mother of five children and working as a secondary art teacher for over twenty years. Both roles revealed that Black and brown children are bombarded with negativity by the media. Furthermore, Rome-Taylor believes that the media instill in children's minds the notion that they are inferior and less valuable and that they don't belong, making them feel like outsiders in their own communities. Rome-Taylor's artistic mission is to counteract these harmful narratives by reclaiming the representation of Black and brown children. Her portraits are a powerful corrective to the skewed images in the media; they present these children in a light that affirms their worth and belonging. Thus Rome-Taylor not only restores their dignity but also instills a sense of pride and identity in her young subjects and her viewers. Her work is a testament to the transformative power of art in reshaping perceptions and fostering a more inclusive and affirming cultural narrative.

When reflecting on her own experience growing up, Rome-Taylor shared, "I'm from Atlanta, born and raised. My sister and I were a rarity, in a city that is this Black Mecca, where all these illustrious Black people have created amazing businesses. We have Black leaders. We have Black intellectuals. We have all these Black college institutions. But growing up here, I did not feel the impact of being surrounded by Black excellence."[19] Rome-Taylor grew up in the poverty-stricken neighborhood of Parkwood and Long, also known as Memorial Drive. This community is one of many that experienced economic depression due to white flight in the 1970s. The economic collapse of her community resulted in concentrated poverty, where institutions such as public libraries were shut down to save the city money. The memory of not having access to a library while in elementary school made her aware of the poverty surrounding her, an awareness that was compounded by not having a sense of community or a sense of belonging. Furthermore, when Rome-Taylor would visit institutions such as the High Museum during school field trips, she recalls not seeing any representations of herself or people in her community. She explains, "The presence of Blackness did not exist in this institution that when you think about it, it is the repository of a community's cultural values."[20] The lack of Black representation in museums and galleries piqued Rome-Taylor's curiosity. She began to ask critical questions like, "What does a culture value? Why do institutions hold onto and collect certain types of art and not others?

Why is the Western gaze of artwork centered?" Her queries also made her critical of the art education she received in school and its limitations.

Unlike her white classmates who went on to study art in higher education with the message in mind that they could be professional artists, Rome-Taylor laments that she did not receive the same message even though she attended the same school as they did. She was conditioned to go to college to be an art teacher, and that is exactly what she did. Her mission was to change the narrative by creating curricula that were diverse and that would combat negative messages about Black boys being threatening and Black girls being hypersexual. She also wanted to reclaim African American history by establishing that its starting point was not American slavery but rather the continent of Africa, where African scholars have established a baseline for a discussion of the continent and the beginning of civilization.[21] Rome-Taylor's pedagogical approach to art education is to decolonize young people's minds, and this is also reflected in her art. It is the reason most of her subjects are Black children, through whom she is creating a spiritual theme of survival and strength.

Self-Care and Artistic Growth: Rome-Taylor's Personal Journey

I asked Rome-Taylor if her notion of self-care is reflected in her artwork and art-making process. Thinking of her artistic messages and visual imagery, Rome-Taylor is reminded of the journey that got her to this point in her career. She recalls,

> I worked at least fourteen years as a high school art teacher prior to me working literally for myself. And then before that, I taught elementary for nine years. I also had been coaching other artists all this time, and they ignored me sometimes. So in connecting back to myself, it was an opportunity to get in the game because my sister, who knows me about as well as anybody beyond my husband, knew what I was capable of, and she kept encouraging me, 'Get in the game. Come on, Tokie. Get in the game.' With all the mental creativity and planning and plotting that I have been doing, when I started making for myself, my journey was not about figuring out what I was going to say, or what I was going to do. It wasn't any of that. With crystal-clear clarity, I knew photography was going to be the medium. I knew children were going to be the subject. I knew objects were extremely important to the message that I was creating because that was what I was drawn to.[22]

It is important to note the encouragement of Rome-Taylor's sister, Sachi Rome, who is also a visual artist. Both Rome-Taylor and Rome are members of a small and informal Black women artists' collective that call themselves the

Cast Iron Collective. That name is a nod to the traditional Southern family artifact: real cooking, such as frying chicken or making biscuits, cannot be done except in a cast-iron skillet, suggesting that the collective is putting in real work. Rome-Taylor's level of support in the Cast Iron Collective is "about finding your tribe of folks whom you can trust, who are not backbiting, tearing you down or competing with you."[23] The collective's support is augmented by the support of her husband and children, whom she credits with being her major champions. Yet the collective provides professional and emotional support in ways that demonstrate that when Black women support each other, they create opportunities for healing and wellness that lead to professional and personal thriving.

Like the other contemporary Black women artists discussed in this book, Rome-Taylor demonstrates that she has found wellness in the work she is passionate about. She posits, "When I started working for myself—and by that I mean creating for myself—I carved myself from the surface of 'I am Zoey, Reginald, Grayson, Ziggy, Rome-Taylor's mom, and Reginald Rome-Taylor's wife and sister to Sachi.' That was how I carved Tokie back out."[24] Thus Rome-Taylor's portraits not only focus on a reclamation of African Diaspora history and Black childhood but also on a reclamation of self and Black womanhood that is defined and shaped by these factors.

Blending Ancestral and Western Iconography through Photography

When I look at Rome-Taylor's portraits, I am reminded of a line from Dr. Maya Angelou's poem "Our Grandmothers": "I go forth alone, and stand as ten thousand."[25] Much of the iconography of Rome-Taylor's work denotes the presence of African ancestors. Rome-Taylor explains that her visual references to ancestors convey a sense of "strength" necessary for Black people's survival. Specifically, "In the strength that we have ancestors behind us pushing us forward, if we hold still and learn to listen, not for the purpose of practicing religion but as a means of spirituality, we understand that there is so much we can achieve as individuals, and as a collective. The way for me to do that is through artwork."[26] As much as Black children are the impetus for Rome-Taylor's photography, their subjecthood is developed by a collective ancestral past. Rome-Taylor's work underscores the vital connection between ancestral memory and the wellness of future generations. By visually embedding the strength and presence of ancestors in her portraits, Rome-Taylor provides a source of empowerment and continuity for Black women and children. Her art ecosystem fosters a sense of identity and resilience that transcends individual experiences, creating a shared space for collective healing and growth. Through her evocative imagery, Rome-Taylor not only honors the past but also lays a foundation for generational wellness, where the wisdom and strength of ancestors are harnessed to nurture and uplift present and future generations of the Black community.

In trying to understand Rome-Taylor's process for beginning a photo session, I asked her to explain how she connected the ancestral and present worlds. Rome-Taylor explained, "I begin with children as subjects because they are like blank slates, embodying the tabula rasa theory, which posits that children arrive without preconceived notions. The experiences they encounter—what they see, hear, and do—inscribe the narrative of who they become and where they feel they belong in society."[27] Incorporating ancestral knowledge helps Rome-Taylor's models develop a more affirmative sense of identity.

Rome-Taylor is also informed by reading and researching that is focused on three tenets: material culture, spiritual practice, and the Black culture of the American South. Part of her research is to look at ethnography and archaeology to learn how people existed day to day and how they survived. Through her reading, she gets ideas for objects that inform the composition of her artwork. For example, Rome-Taylor's research on African American slavery and material culture revealed that when archaeologists dug at sites that were presumed to be slave quarters and where enslaved Black people lived day to day, they discovered storage pits in the corners of these homes. They found spaces for tools such as hoes and trowels and for personal items such as buttons, coins, musical instruments, and cutlery.[28] For this reason, viewers will discover scraps of iron nails, bone, blue buttons, and shells as part of the mise-en-scène of her portraits. Speculation has arisen from these archaeological discoveries that the practice of burying personal items was a remnant of spiritual practice more than likely carried over from West Africa, as a great many enslaved Africans were brought to America from that region.[29] Rome-Taylor's research informs what we see in her work to date. She draws on the tradition of using objects in ritual, making offerings to ancestors, using adornment in ritual practice and celebration, and in living and moving day to day life.

Some of Rome-Taylor's photographed portraits depict children making offerings, but you won't see food or gold or African beads. Rather, you'll see jewelry, such as pearls, in the offering bowl, mixed in with cowrie shells and buttons. The mixing of mother-of-pearl and pearl jewelry and cowrie shells symbolizes the blending of Western African cultures and Black Southern culture that has developed over time. Cowrie shells symbolize wealth, fertility, prosperity and protection in certain African societies and Southern Black culture. Some scholars speculate that the mother-of-pearl buttons found buried in slave quarters were actually the property of enslavers. African Americans would take their enslavers' personal possessions in order to assert a certain level of spiritual control over their oppressors.[30] Moreover, trying to assert this type of spiritual control was perhaps an attempt not to lose a child or to avoid being abused, raped, or sold away from loved ones. Adding jewelry is one of the many examples of how Rome-Taylor integrates an ancestral presence into her work. She explains, "It's a deliberate lean back in time. Not a specific time but a lean back in time to what I envisioned as an alternative past. A past where these individuals were viewed as equal. The individuals in my portraits were loved, and they were never under threats of harm or abuse."[31] Take into consideration how Rome-Taylor uses her materials to reclaim history and their symbolic meanings. Her work facilitates healing and wellness for herself, her subjects, and her viewers.

Rome-Taylor creates visual counternarratives through photography that center African iconography and history. She creates an alternative reality for her subjects and viewers that separates them from the denigrating experiences and narratives that have shaped African diasporic history by invoking a positive connection to this history in the portraits. For viewers, "These Western symbols of wealth are used to cause a psychological shift within the viewer and revisit cultural and ancestral traditions of adornment."[32] Reclamation and restoration of African diaspora history is a process of healing for anyone affected by the negative distortions of history that give space to racism and Black subjugation.

Viewers will also find gold-stitched thread in Rome-Taylor's portraits, which turns her work into mixed media. The threads symbolically connect history with the present and future. Rome-Taylor pulls those threads together for herself and for those who view the portraits, and for those who will engage with her work in the future to facilitate meaningful discussions. Similarly, her incorporation of halos represents the presence of Judeo-Christianity in the American South.[33] Rome-Taylor grapples with the historical tension of white enslavers using Christianity as a tool of control to create subservient Africans who were more amenable to slavery. However, she works to reconcile this history with the cultural development of the Black church, which retains significant elements of African spiritual practices. Like Delita Martin, Rome-Taylor has also closely observed African ring shouts, foot stomping, and other African ceremonial practices found in Black churches. By adorning her subjects with halos, she adds to her visual composition a subtle discourse that intertwines Christianity and African spirituality but with a greater emphasis on spirituality than on religion. Rome-Taylor acknowledges in her work that the Black church as an institution has been a site of spiritual healing, political mobilization, and cultural preservation in ways that inform African Americans' collective experiences today, regardless of their participation or not within the church.

Let's turn our attention to the portrait *An Offering* (2020). The subject, Rome-Taylor's youngest child Zöe, is a young girl who holds out an offering bowl to viewers. The bowl is filled with pearls and jewels and sits atop a woven gold halo in between the figure's legs. Rome-Taylor argued, "Many people from the West associate halos with religion and exclusively Christianity. Yet the depiction of halos shows up in other religious art."[34] Rome-Taylor explained, "I want the conversation to be about connecting to spirituality more, so that Christianity, which is what I feel like is more central in the African-American church—there church members are more connected to the spirit and to spirituality than to a particular religious practice."[35] Like the other contemporary Black women artists discussed in this book, Rome-Taylor sees the importance of portraying what Robert Farris Thompson calls "the flash of the spirit," which he explains "is of a certain people specifically armed with improvisatory drive and brilliance."[36] The preservation and centering of African spirituality in Rome-Taylor's work leads viewers to understand that its presence in the collective lives of Black people has led to our survival and well-being.

Just as Chatmon pays homage to Klimt's Gold Period, Rome-Taylor appropriates aesthetics from European art. In our conversation, Rome-Taylor revealed that before she takes photos with her digital camera, she carefully stages her studio with heavy velvets and lace. This is a nod to Dutch Renaissance masters and chiaroscuro, a use of strong contrasts between dark areas and one source of light. Rome-Taylor's staging of objects also recalls Renaissance paintings. She explains,

> Sometimes I'll have a piece that has a little table, and on the table, there'll be binoculars or a magnifying glass or a vessel with the cowrie shells and the buttons, and that is also a nod to how artists prepared for paintings in Renaissance times. When they were commissioned to paint those pieces, they would have these specific exotic fruits on the table, or vegetables. There was Venetian glass and sometimes a figure of an African serving in the background and then you might have the sitter spaced just so for the painter to capture all these buffs. The objects that are there, including figures in servitude, are representative of the value and status and accumulated wealth of the sitter.[37]

Rome-Taylor's intention is to subvert these Renaissance visual narratives by repositioning Black people as the wealthy sitters rather than objects or commodities. However, P. A. Mullins notes, "What is interesting is that early encounters with Black African people [in] imagery in Europe were not examples of 'primitive' savages, but the Virgin Mary, Saints, and Black African royalty. The depiction of Black Africans in artworks suggests that at the start of the enslavement of Black Africans, there was not a uniform depiction of frightening or backward humanoids with Black skin in Europe."[38] These early representations of Black people in nonsubjugated roles add another layer of interpretation to Rome-Taylor's portraiture as restorative. By reclaiming these historical portrayals and positioning Black people in roles of dignity and

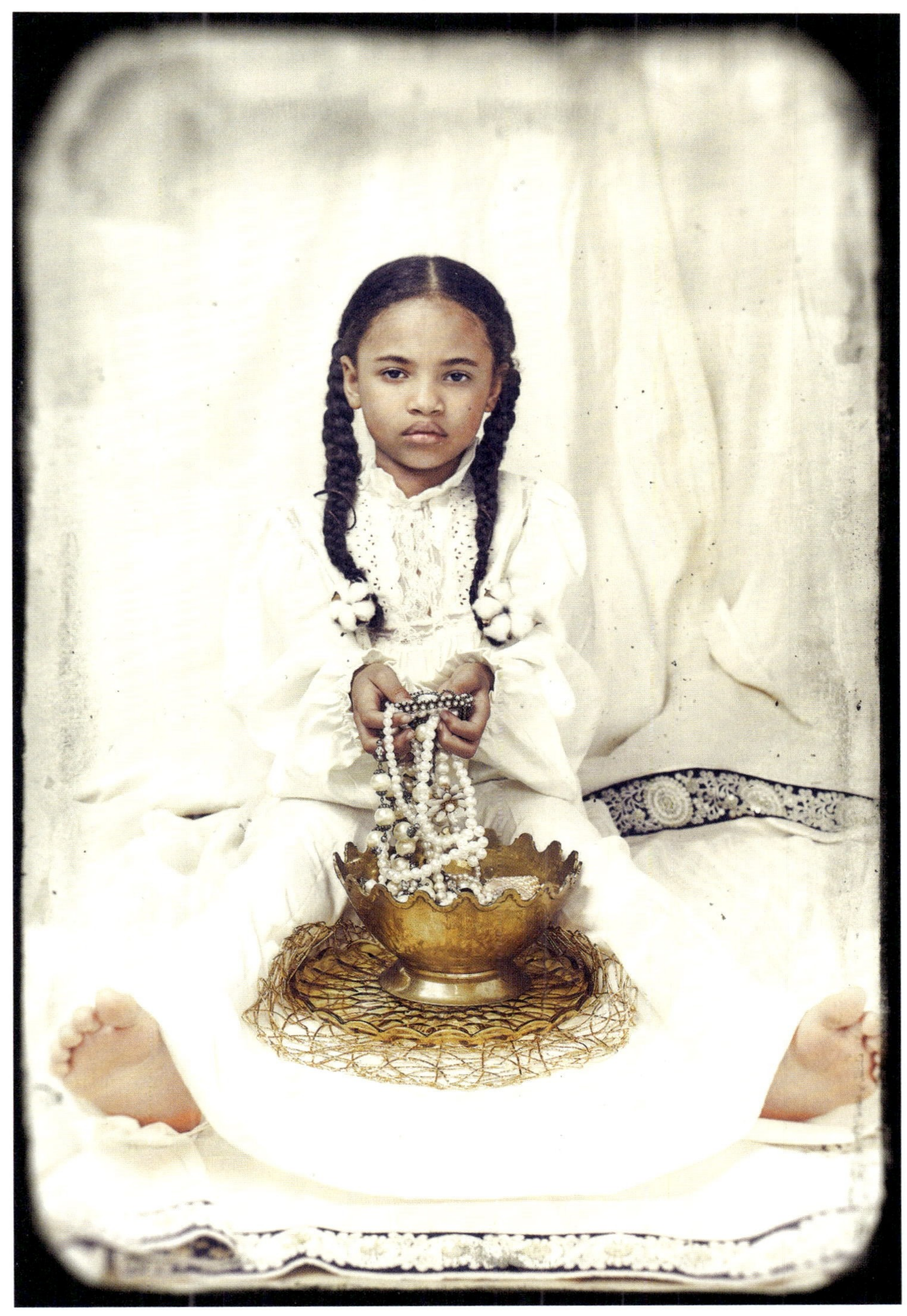

Tokie Rome-Taylor. *An Offering*. 2020. Archival pigment photograph on cotton rag, 36 × 24 in. Courtesy of the artist.

affluence, Rome-Taylor challenges contemporary viewers to rethink ingrained stereotypes and to acknowledge the long-standing presence and significance of Black individuals in history. Her work not only corrects the erasure and misrepresentation of Black people but also emphasizes the continuity of Black excellence and humanity. This reclamation and repositioning are a powerful form of visual activism, aiming to heal the wounds of historical marginalization and foster a more inclusive understanding of cultural heritage. In doing so, Rome-Taylor contributes to the ongoing dialogue about race, identity, and representation in both historical and modern contexts.

Legacy Through Objects: The Role of Heirlooms in Rome-Taylor's Portraiture

A significant part of Rome-Taylor's art-making practices is participatory. The objects she stages in her portraits are often personal items that reflect the identity and heritage of the model.

Her methods currently include having her models bring in family heirlooms to stage in either the background or the foreground of the portrait. Over time, Rome-Taylor noticed that often "so many of them would say, 'No, Tokie, we don't have anything like that.'"[39] In working in communities of color where the tradition of passing down heirlooms is considered a practice connected to generational wealth, the initial thought of many of Rome-Taylor's models was that they didn't have heirlooms. However, Rome-Taylor's requests for objects caused many of her models and their families, who didn't come from generational wealth, to reflect on items that their elders and ancestors were known for possessing. Rome-Taylor recalls how some of her conversations with participants from her community led to the discovery of family history: "'Well, Tokie, my grandfather had this item. My grandmother has this item. Would this be appropriate?' And then they would share their family history in connection to the object."[40] Rome-Taylor's query about family heirlooms sparks conversations within participants' families. The objects they lend her to integrate into her portraits extend beyond the narrative that she is trying to tell; rather, she personalizes their history into the narrative.

Rome-Taylor's art-making method and community engagement facilitate transparency and healing when participants come to terms with parts of their family histories that are painful, or difficult at best. In a recent project where Rome-Taylor was putting together materials for her first authored art book, she worked with nineteen families to collect materials and shoot photo portraits. Understanding the power of query, Rome-Taylor conducted soft interviews and asked the prospective models to look for certain family objects. About half of the families had heirlooms, and all of them had stories to share. For participants who didn't have physical objects to bring to the studio, that

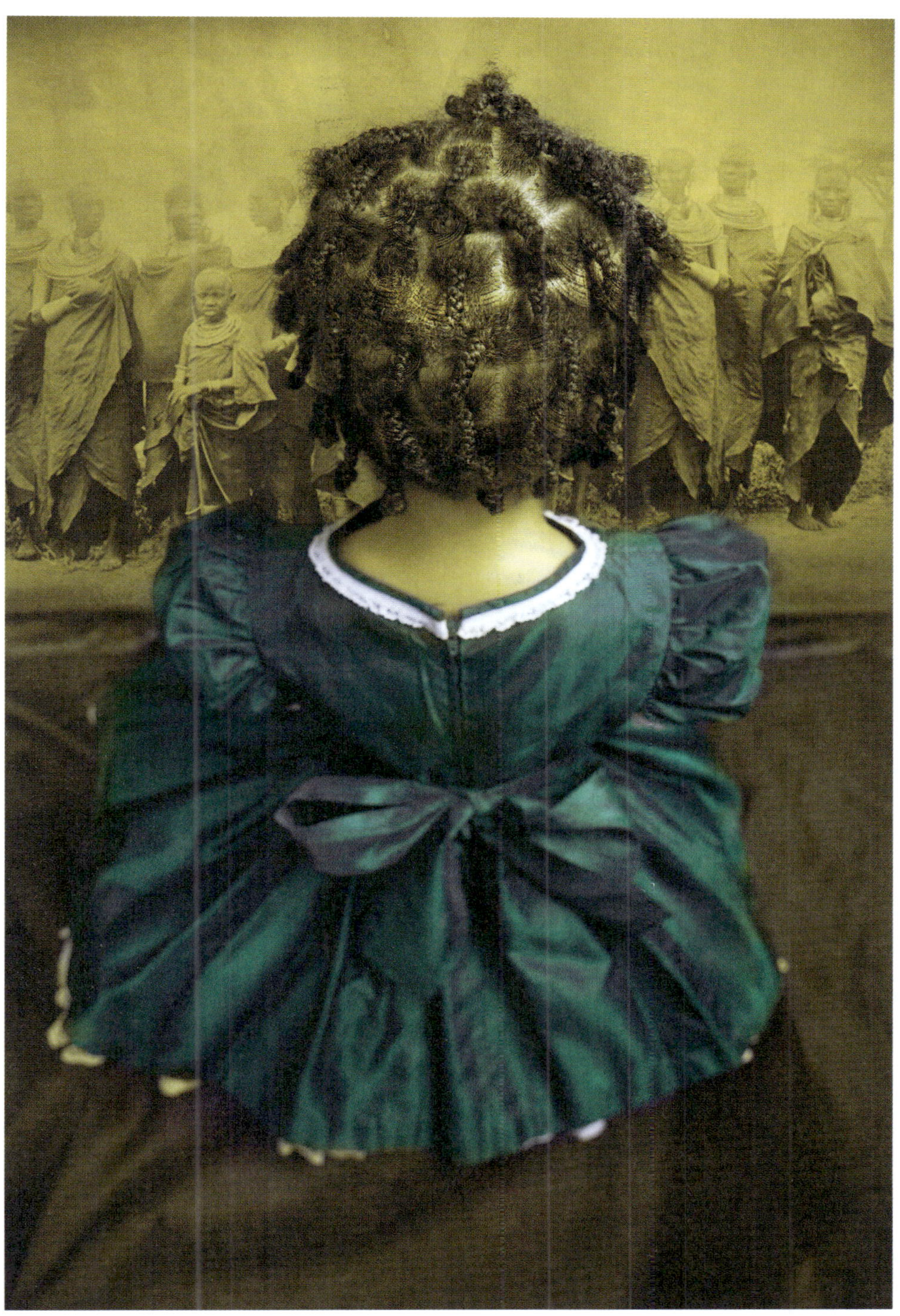

Tokie Rome-Taylor. *In Conversation*. 2021. Archival pigment photograph, digitally collaged vintage image on cotton rag, 36 × 24 in. Courtesy of the artist.

revelation was sometimes painful, heightening the awareness of lost history, at least in material terms. Yet even these participants came up with objects that helped represent the family stories they had knowledge of and that they wanted to share in their portraits. This process is part of Rome-Taylor's overall goal of reclaiming history through photography and for her models; their participation becomes a reclamation of lost history, family tradition, and culture. Another component of Rome-Taylor's method is the conversation regarding ancestral traditions and how people pass on stories and memories. Rome-Taylor posits that the way to do this is by designating objects in your family to be the repositories of the stories you want to tell.[41] Thus, although certain families that Rome-Taylor interviewed felt they didn't have heirlooms to share, they did say they were going to designate something that they would pass down to their children with a story and history behind it. This alternative practice gave the families space for empowerment and agency to create heirlooms for the next generation.

Looking Back and Seeing Forward

As mentioned, Rome-Taylor uses her own children as subjects in her photography. The subject of *In Conversation* (2021) is her daughter Paige, then four years old. The young girl is wearing an emerald-green dress with a white lace collar and box braids. She sits with her back to the viewers while looking at a sepia-toned archival image of African children and women. While researching online, Rome-Taylor discovered this image. By incorporating it into her portrait, she enables some of the figures in the photo, especially a young child, to engage directly with viewers, thereby reclaiming control over the Western gaze likely present in taking the original photograph. I asked Rome-Taylor to expound on the meaning of the portrait and its title and she explained, "The young girl in the portrait is in conversation with the past and she is on this journey to connect back to the freedom of knowing her history."[42] *In Conversation* conveys the Sankofa motif that is woven throughout Rome-Taylor's work. Her suggestion that young Black children practice this principle emphasizes the need to deprogram and counter harmful messages about blackness as early as possible in the lives of Black people.

Rome-Taylor depicts the power of looking and redirecting the gaze through both her subjects and their use of objects. She uses objects such as mirrors and binoculars to reinforce these themes.

Rome-Taylor's son Reginald is the model in *Scout* (2020). He is dressed in an elaborate gold and purple jeweled shirt. Like many of her subjects, he also has a gold, woven halo behind his head. However, what stands out the most is that this young boy is peering through binoculars that look directly out at the viewer. Compare this image with the portrait *See Me* (2018), which depicts

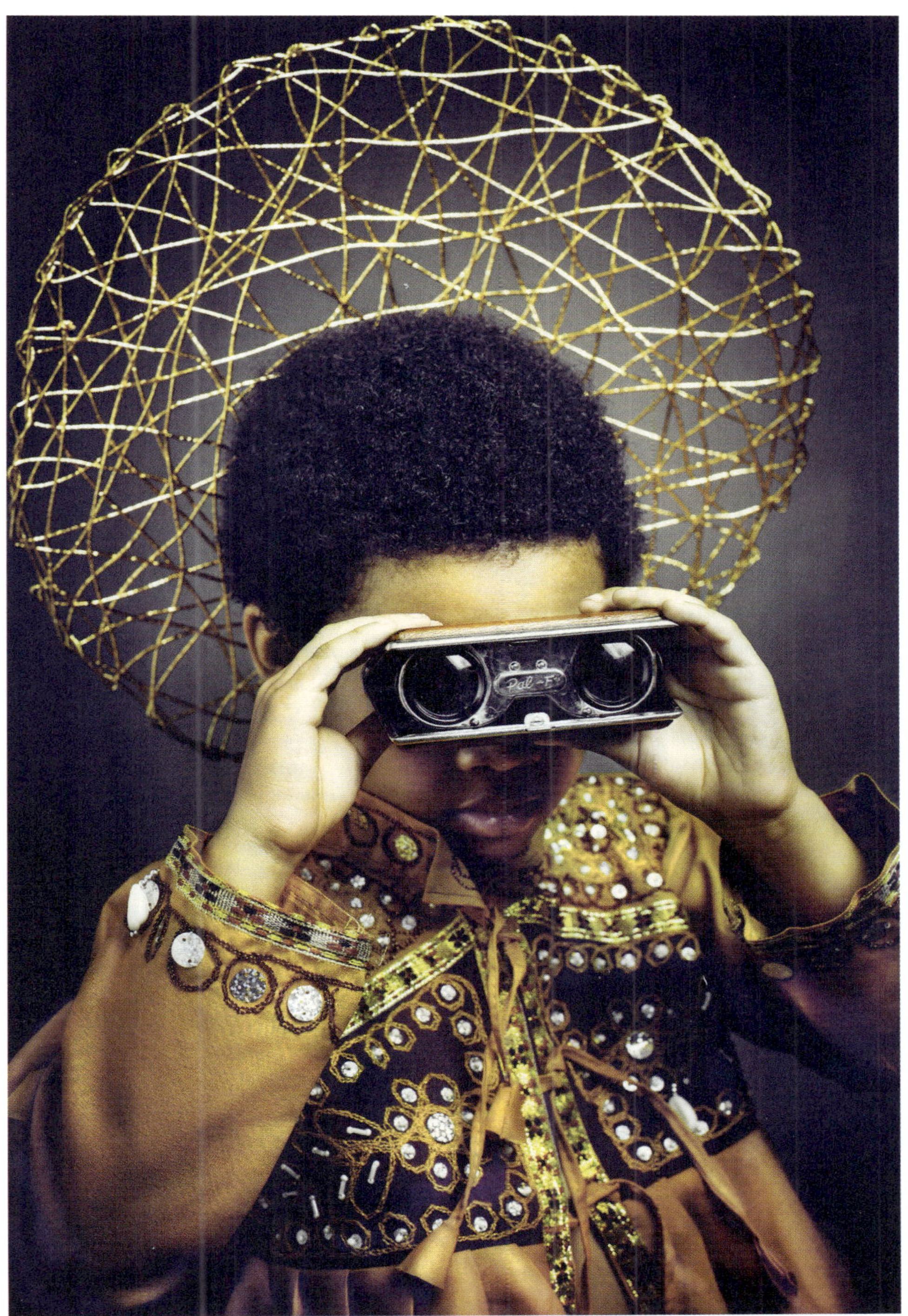

Tokie Rome-Taylor. *Scout*. 2019. Archival pigment photograph on cotton rag, 24 × 18 in. Courtesy of the artist.

a young Black girl sitting sideways from viewers while holding up a mirror that shows her face looking out through its reflection instead of directly. The barefoot model in the portrait has two small pieces of raw cotton in her natural coiffure for decoration as a symbol of the American South, and she is dressed in a champagne-colored period dress with lace trim and with layered pearl bracelets on both arms. Both *Scout* and *See Me* give space for the visibility of Black children who are dressed like the wealthy and surrounded by Renaissance decor. What is most notable about these portraits and others similar in composition are the reflective objects. Rome-Taylor states, "Binoculars and mirrors serve as tools for simultaneously looking back and seeing forward. A mirror, when you consider it, acts as a means of time travel. Nobody thinks about it like that because they're so common. Consider what a mirror is really doing: When the light hits it, light has gone into the past and it's bouncing back to your retina so what you're seeing is something that has existed in the past."[43] For Rome-Taylor, the mirrors are all about seeing back into the past while also seeing the present and future. Similarly, the binoculars in her work symbolize searching forward and searching into the past.

Rome-Taylor's use of mirrors parallels vanessa german's use of mirrors and other reflective objects in her power figures and wall art. Both artists employ these elements to evoke a sense of time travel and self-reflection, connecting their subjects to a broader historical and cultural narrative. Rome-Taylor's reflective objects are powerful metaphors for the interconnectedness of time and memory, emphasizing the importance of understanding historical context and its impact on the present and future. This duality of vision allows the subjects of her portraits to reclaim their narrative, highlighting the resilience and continuity of Black heritage. The presence of these objects in her artwork invites viewers to reflect on their own histories and the ongoing influence of the past, fostering a deeper appreciation for the rich tapestry of Black cultural identity.

Rome-Taylor regularly reclaims African diaspora history and opportunities for healing through references to literature and literacy in her work. She promotes the aphorism "Knowledge is power."[44] *The Prince of Knowledge* (2018) depicts a young Black boy standing on a stack of literary classics. Her triptych photos are an homage to the literary works of Toni Morrison. Both are examples of how Rome-Taylor reclaims and counters her experience of growing up without access to a public library and lacking affirming experiences while in public high school in Atlanta. Rome-Taylor uses photography to call out the importance of not only reading and writing literacy but also cultural literacy, the ability to understand all the subtle nuances that come with living or working in a particular society.[45] For example, cultural literacies shaped by the African oral tradition and ancient African art add to the aesthetic of Rome-Taylor's work. Her portrait *My People Could Fly* (2018) is a reference

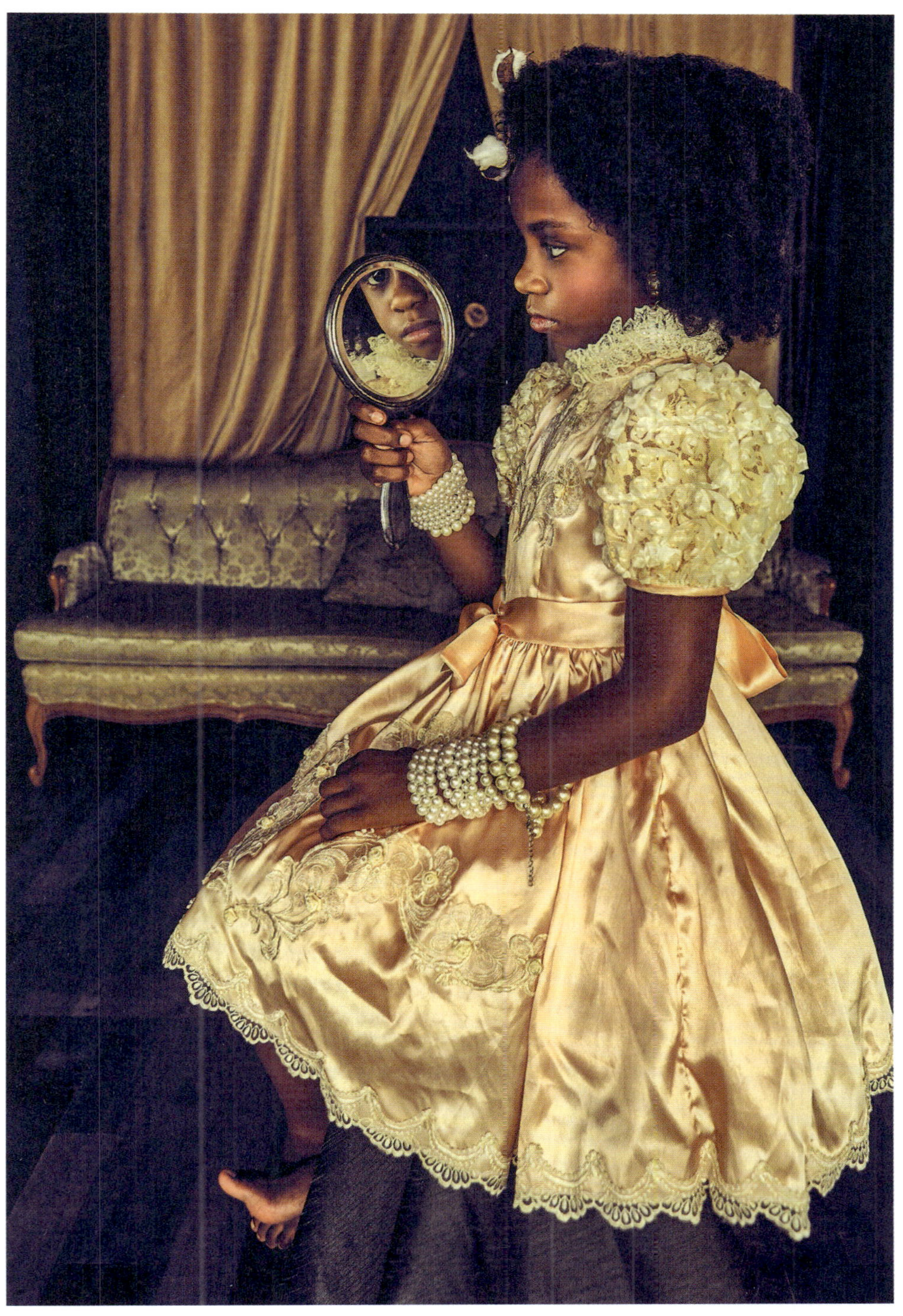

Tokie Rome-Taylor. *See Me*. 2018. Archival pigment photograph on cotton rag, 30 × 20 in. Courtesy of the artist.

to the book *The People Could Fly: American Black Folktales*, Virginia Hamilton's retellings of African American folktales encompassing African-influenced stories about wisdom, spirituality, and empowerment for African-descended people. Rome-Taylor's visual reference to the "preserved memory of the flying Ibo people on St. Simons Island" depicts a Black girl wearing a white ruffled lace dress with a matching lace collar necklace.[46] Emerging from the backs of her shoulders are white feathers like wings. A warm glow of light glistens on a pearl crown around her naturally coiffed hair. The portrait's soft brown velvet backdrop blends with the girl's skin tone. She sits poised and stoic, looking directly out at audiences with her hands crossed and resting on her lap. Her serious yet regal gaze can also be read as an act of resistance.

My People Could Fly (2018) echoes the regality of Ejagham girls from the extreme south of Nigeria and eastward into the southwest region of Cameroon. Robert Farris Thompson writes that young girls entered the prestigious Nnimm Society before marriage. Partaking of powers mystic and political, they became leaders among women. In full regalia, the ritual dress consisted of body paint, myriad shells, a crown of feathers adorned with monkey bones, and concentric necklaces, bound in leather about the neck and shoulders of the Nnimm woman.[47] There are similarities between Thompson's description and the visual composition in *My People Could Fly* (2018). Still, what is most similar is not only the dress of the figure in Rome-Taylor's work but also her demeanor, which mirrors Thompson's explanation of how a single feather identifies a Nnimm woman, marking her as different from ordinary persons. Rome-Taylor's subject in *My People Could Fly* (2018) does not wear the Nnimm feather, traditionally worn trailing down the back of an initiate's head. However, the girl's feathery wings mirror the regality and extraordinary essence of young girls in the Nnimm society. This portrait also supports how Rome-Taylor wants young Black girls and all African-descended people to see themselves, empowered and limitless because of their ancestral past.

In the photographic realms of Tawny Chatmon and Tokie Rome-Taylor, a profound connection to generational wellness and ancestral memory materializes through the artists' discerning lenses. Chatmon, in her intricate embellishments of portraits, orchestrates a visual symphony that transcends mere representation. Through the amalgamation of symbols drawn from personal and shared histories, she not only preserves but also renews the essence of ancestral memory, creating a resonant bridge between the past and present. On the other hand, Rome-Taylor's deliberate interplay of materials and meticulous research reconstructs narratives of historical resilience and spiritual fortitude. Her photographic compositions, laden with cultural symbolism and ritualistic motifs, are an ode to the collective memory of African diaspora history. Together, these artists utilize the photographic medium not merely as a means

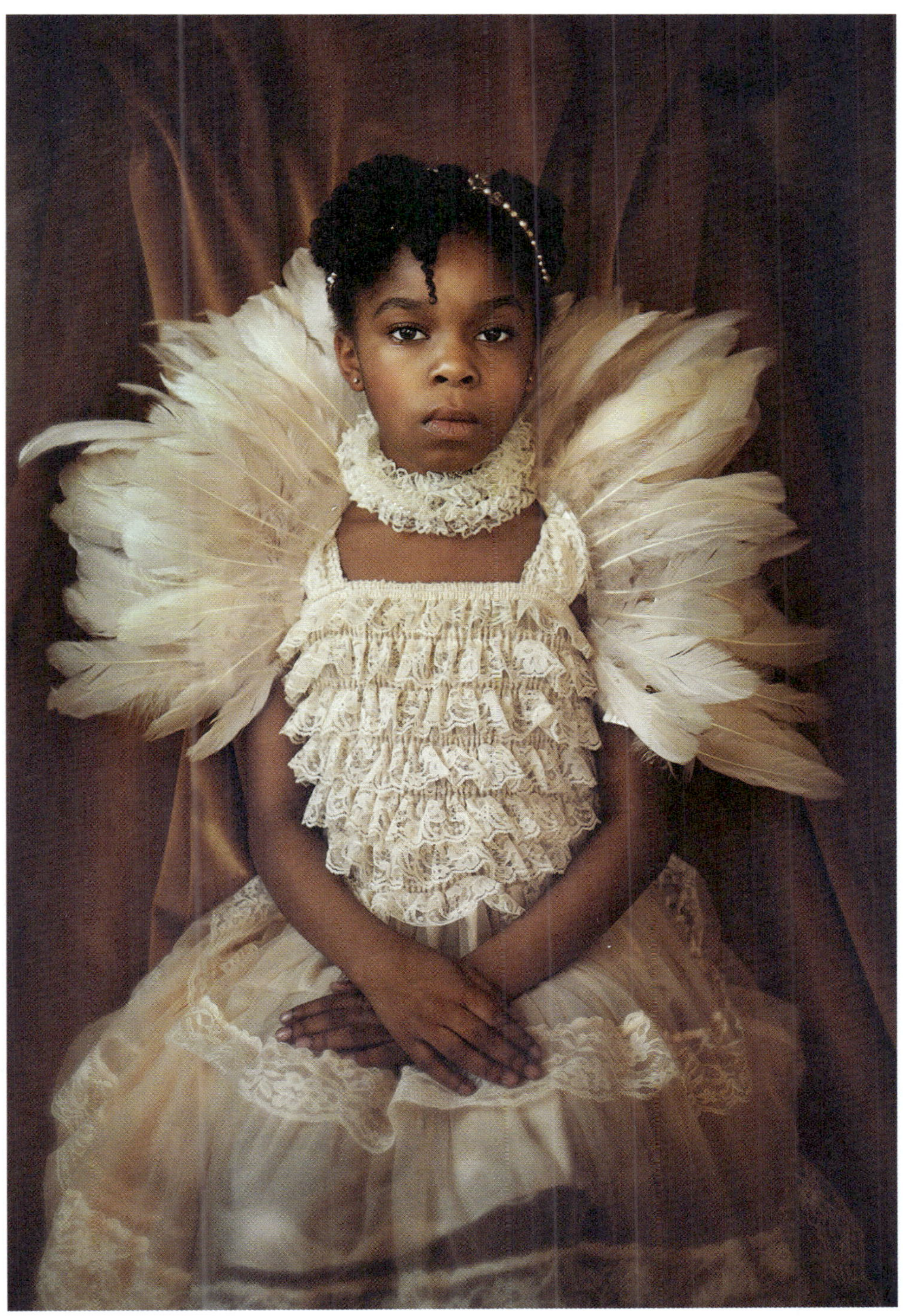

Tokie Rome-Taylor. *My People Could Fly*. 2019. Archival pigment photograph cn cotton rag, 36 × 24 in. Private collection.

of capturing moments but as a conduit for the preservation, reclamation, and celebration of ancestral legacies. Both artists demonstrate the art scholar and photographer Deborah Willis's position that "what we imagine and know about beauty through the visual image is mediated by photographers and framed from their experience of photography."[48] Through their lenses, they offer not only a visual feast but also a timeless testament to the enduring vitality of generational wellness and the enduring power of ancestral memory.

Chatmon and Rome-Taylor's interweaving of ancestral memory and generational wellness becomes a poignant testimony to the resilience of cultural heritage. Their photographic narratives extend beyond individual stories, creating a collective tapestry that resonates with the enduring strength of generations past. As the next chapter delves into the realm of Black women artists cultivating wellness through abstract art and cognitive wellness, Chatmon and Rome-Taylor's works serve as luminous beacons, guiding us to a deeper understanding of the healing potential embedded in artistic expressions that honor our shared ancestry.

7

Abstract Art and Cognitive Wellness

Through color, I have sought to concentrate on beauty and
happiness, rather than on man's inhumanity to man.
—Alma Woodsey Thomas

Alma Woodsey Thomas's emphasis on color in the quote above is instructive about how abstract artists can build visual narratives using primary elements of art—color, line, and so on—without depicting objects in the physical world.[1] Abstract art can be defined as comprising nonfigurative art elements, such as action painting, color field composition, or hard-edged geometric shapes. Abstract art ranges from slight or partial abstraction to total abstraction, which shuns realistic depiction. Abstract art includes many subgenres, such as abstract expressionism, conceptualism, and minimalism, that "extend the abstract idea that art should have its own reality and not be an imitation of some other thing."[2] Thomas, an abstract expressionist painter and art educator, is one of the more recognizable Black women artists in United States history, as many of her professional accomplishments made history.

 In 1924, Thomas became the first graduate of Howard University's newly founded Art Department. At the age of sixty-nine, this modernist painter became the first African American woman to receive national critical acclaim as a nonfigurative painter. In 1972, the Whitney Museum of American Art in New York and the Corcoran Gallery in Washington, DC, honored Thomas with a solo exhibition.[3] A trailblazer, Thomas was also the first Black woman to have work acquired by the White House.[4] These achievements, along with favorable reviews from art critics, document the rare success that Black women artists have achieved in the genre of abstraction. Thomas, whose work was influenced by the Washington Color School and the techniques of French impressionism, created a body of work that is colorful yet "entirely dependent on strokes: small, rough patches laid down in dense, eccentric patterns on painted canvas grounds whose colors show through, providing subtle, rhythmic counterpoint."[5] Painting by brush was a departure from the staining techniques developed by other Washington Color painters. Yet her technique expressed how she was "inspired by the shifting light filtering between the leaves of trees in her garden."[6] These formalistic characteristics included what Thomas described as "geometric abstractions."[7] At the time of her death, the *Washington Post* reported that despite her seeing "a world of things in many hues with no ethnic twist," she was repeatedly included in shows of exclusively African American artists.[8] This tension highlights a broader, long-standing issue within the art world regarding the categorization and visibility of Black artists. This limited classification not only undermines her contributions to abstraction but also reflects a pervasive tendency to define artists through a narrow lens based on ethnicity rather than their artistic merit. Ultimately, Thomas's legacy challenges us to reconsider how we categorize artistic expression and recognize the diverse influences that shape an artist's work, transcending simplistic racial narratives. By examining Thomas's work through a more inclusive lens, we can appreciate not only her individual artistry but also the broader narrative of Black women in abstraction who have historically been marginalized. Furthermore, Thomas's story deepens our understanding of BWAEs by highlighting the interconnectedness of individual artists' experiences and their collective struggle for recognition and validation. In addition to Thomas, other Black women have made significant contributions as abstract artists despite historically being underrecognized.

Black artists who create abstract art depart from a long tradition of artists creating representational art that seeks to counter denigrating and anti-Black visual narratives in the Western canon of art and visual culture. Leigh Raiford notes that abstract works made by Black artists pressure and destabilize Black art as a category and their works "destabilize the notion of certitude attached to visualizing racial Blackness."[9] With their nonfigurative works, these Black artists have committed to a formalistic expression that is connected to conceptualism and internal feelings more than to the verisimilitude of Blackness. Barbara Chase-Riboud's sculptural abstractions, Alma Woodsey Thomas's color field abstract paintings, and Howardena Pindell's mixed-media abstract art have given Black women artists visibility in a canon whose Black artists are overlooked and/or excluded.[10]

Addressing this erasure, the National Museum of Women in the Arts (NMWA) 2017 exhibition *Magnetic Fields: Expanding American Abstraction, 1960s to Today* presented the work of twenty-one intergenerational Black women abstract artists to underscore the diversity of abstract art and to "testify to the enduring ability of abstraction to convey both personal iconography and universal themes."[11] This recognition of Black women artists' abstract art is important to our overall understanding of how they cultivate wellness through art making when we consider the idea that "abstract art, since it does not represent the material world, can be seen to represent the spiritual."[12] Including Black women's abstract artwork as artifacts of wellness deepens our understanding of how Black women artists engage as wellness workers through making art that is connected to their deeply personal spiritual and sociopolitical life experiences. More recently, I have met contemporary Black women artists who have embraced abstract expressionism. Two contemporary artists, Amber Robles-Gordon and Dianne Smith, have opted to move away from traditional representational art, instead crafting works that embody a more abstract relationship between materials and both individual and collective well-being.

Amber Robles-Gordon: Self-Healing through Abstract Visual Language

I first met Amber Robles-Gordon during an exhibition at Miami Art Week in 2021. She and I struck up a conversation about each other's work in the art world. It was there that I learned of Robles-Gordon's project involving art quilts and social justice. She is an Afro-Latina woman originally from San Juan, Puerto Rico, with family members also from St. Thomas, US Virgin Islands. Robles-Gordon told me in an interview that she is of mixed African, Taino, and Spanish heritage, a blending that is common in the Caribbean and that her heritage informs the art that she creates.[13]

Like many of the artists discussed earlier, Robles-Gordon has an early memory of her five-year-old self that was a major turning point in her life. At the age of three, in the early 1980s, she and her family moved to Arlington, Virginia, a predominantly white community. People there were less familiar with someone who looked like her, a deep-brown-skinned girl speaking Spanish. The artist recalled being relentlessly teased by her kindergarten classmates when her mother would pick her up from school and the two would begin speaking in Spanish. To stop the teasing, Robles-Gordon told her mother that she no longer wanted to speak Spanish, a language that is a mark of colonialism in the Western Hemisphere. Frantz Fanon argues that "to speak a language is to participate in a world, to adopt a civilization."[14] Spanish-speaking countries, where nationality and language are more salient than other identity markers, have distinctive cultural differences from Anglophone territories. These distinctions imbue language, food, and the arts. Consequently, when Robles-Gordon recalled no longer wanting to speak her native language, she shared, "In some ways it became a precedent for how I was to tuck away that aspect of my heritage."[15] The linguistic aspect of her identity diminished, and her Blackness became more salient while she was living on the US mainland, along with a feeling that the other aspects of her identity did not matter.

Amber Robles-Gordon's loss of her native tongue eventually led her on a journey to heal her five-year-old self through what she calls a "visual language." Fortunately, not all her cultural heritage was lost in her formative years.

Robles-Gordon credits her mother with exposing her to Afro-Latino visual and performing arts. This exposure included other Afro-Latina women in her community who would gather during cultural and art events where performing and dancing sometimes would ensue. The experiences that Robles-Gordon shared with her mother and other women in her community fostered feelings of joy and the desire to create her own art. When visiting art museums at an early age, she was drawn to impressionism and abstraction, along with bright colors. Exposure to the arts led her to resolve "years ago not to wait until she was 45 or 50 years old to determine what to do with her life."[16] Years later, when Robles-Gordon enrolled in the master of fine arts program at Howard University, her employment of abstraction in her work was a continuum of interests. She was also inspired by the work of Alma Woodsey Thomas. When Robles-Gordon came across Thomas's work, her use of colors, concentric circles, and nonfigurative expression resonated with how she wanted to express her experiences in life and begin her process of healing.

In contrast to Alma Woodsey Thomas, Robles-Gordon is more of a multi-disciplinary artist who has used diverse media of art to create visual narratives about social and environmental justice, relationships, and personal and communal healing. What has been most consistent is her use of textiles and found objects to create colorful mixed-media compositions. I asked Robles-Gordon what relationship wellness has with her work. She explained, "I learned early that creating art was me conveying what I am feeling through art. I am connecting with my feelings, and this is foundational for my emotional well-being. I am also connecting with a higher source, and the process is a cycle."[17] This cycle connects to her notion of healing, which she explains is "an ongoing state." For her mixed-media series *Heal Thyself* (2006–08), the artist created three works on canvas to explore the complex social constructs of femininity and womanhood. In her artist's statement, Robles-Gordon wrote:

> In *Glass, Bra, Purse and Belt Traps*, *Metaphysical Planes of Life*, and *My Elements*, I focus on objects that I associate with femininity and womanhood, such as underwear, belt buckles, and memorabilia that women collect. These objects are depicted as having two aspects. One aspect refers to their feminine assignment, while the other alludes to the phenomena by which the objects/tools we use become "traps" that can inhibit one's full development and expression.[18]

The traps Robles-Gordon refers to are the material possessions and markers of femininity such as clothes, jewelry, and other accessories that bind women and cause us to focus more on outward appearance than on developing an authentic self. One thing that I appreciate about Robles-Gordon's work is her acknowledgment of the complexity of challenging these gender signifiers and societal norms. Regarding the burden of material entrap-

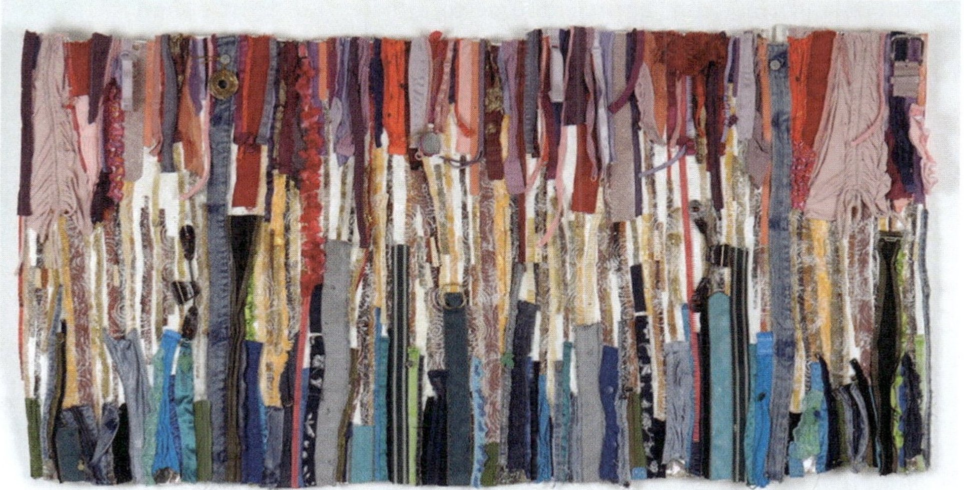

Amber Robles-Gordon. *Metaphysical Planes of Life*. Mixed media on canvas, 36 × 60 in. Courtesy of the artist.

ments, she explains, "Some days, I relish the privilege of being a woman: shapes, curves, emotions, accessories, etc. On other days, managing all the details of being a woman feels like a huge chore."[19] The issue of confinement is not so black and white when one considers how some women are complicit in their own confinement. However, this also means that women can also be complicit in their own healing.

Robles-Gordon's advocacy for self-healing is predominantly centered on people and particularly on women becoming their authentic selves despite the restrictions imposed on them. Furthermore, it is through abstraction that she creates conceptual art that relies on viewers understanding the symbolism behind objects that women use to hold, tame, and express the very femininity that entraps us. Robles-Gordon explains, "Due to varying gender-based norms within society, cloth or fabric is often associated with women and our roles. Through my artwork I explore these relationships and cause viewers to questions their own cultural and ethnic heritage, their relationship with energy both within themselves and their environments as well as their awareness of color and light and its impact in their daily lives."[20] Furthermore, Robles-Gordon's use of a multicolored palette symbolizes the diversity of women and their common experience with sexism and patriarchal oppression. The use of a rainbow motif to represent the diversity of women's experiences from a Black feminist perspective is not new in the arts. For example, the 1976 premiere of Ntozake Shange's first theater piece, *For Colored Girls Who Have Considered Suicide / When the Rainbow Is Enuf,* addressed the issues of Black women suffering from oppression due to a racist and sexist society.[21] These twenty poetic monologues, or choreopoems, are meant to be performed to dance and music by a cast of seven nameless African American women who are identified only by specifically assigned colors. In 2014, Robles-Gordon's sculpture *My Rainbow Is Enuf* was commissioned by the Schomburg Center for Research in Black Culture as part of the group exhibition *i found god in myself*, curated by Peter "Souleo" Wright that celebrated the fortieth anniversary of Ntozake Shange's choreopoem. Robles-Gordon was asked to create art that would represent the last poem in Shange's work, "A laying on of hands."[22] In this poem, all seven characters, and consequently colors, deliver parts of the poem. As a collective they reveal that despite the touch from a lover, a mother, and other external sources of comfort, that feeling of "missing something" is "a laying on of hands" that can deliver "something promised, something free," "making [them] whole."[23] The expression "laying on of hands" is an allusion to various accounts in the New Testament where the laying on of hands was an act to either heal the sick, as in faith healing, or to confer the anointing and receiving of the Holy Spirit after Jesus Christ's ascension to heaven.[24] When creating the commissioned art, Robles-Gordon decided to focus on the end of the poem. She explains, "Now instead of a 'single' color she was fully integrated, and this spiritual awakening revealed that she was always enuf."[25] Also, the more integrated woman in the poem comes to the realization that she has the power to lay hands on herself and to heal by actuating self-love, and the poem ends with the declaration, "I found god in myself & I loved her/I loved her fiercely."[26]

Building on a body of artwork that reflects self-healing, Robles-Gordon's multicolored installation sculpture *My Rainbow Is Enuf* consists of mixed media on chicken wire shaped in the form of expanded wings. The artist explains that it is "a testament to the cycle of life, a woman's will to grow, to create, and her inner drive to continue to love others, but more importantly her ability to love herself."[27] Robles-Gordon admits that the artwork is a manifestation of her internal color spectrum that she identifies as her spirit.[28] As is the case with many artists discussed in this book, Robles-Gordon's work is auto-ethnographic and reveals her intention to center women like herself as part of her journey to healing. She explains, "Overall I believe artwork should represent one's life. . . . I don't have a solid definition of what art is to others. However, for me art is language—a method of communication. It is an extension of my relationship to the universe."[29] Arguably her work in abstraction is a longing to recover those aspects of her cultural identity that she lost at the age of five, which has become more evident in her current work.

In more recent years, Robles-Gordon has been creating mixed-media installation art with a multicolored motif. Very little figuration occurs in her work, but occasionally the artist surprises viewers with its presence.

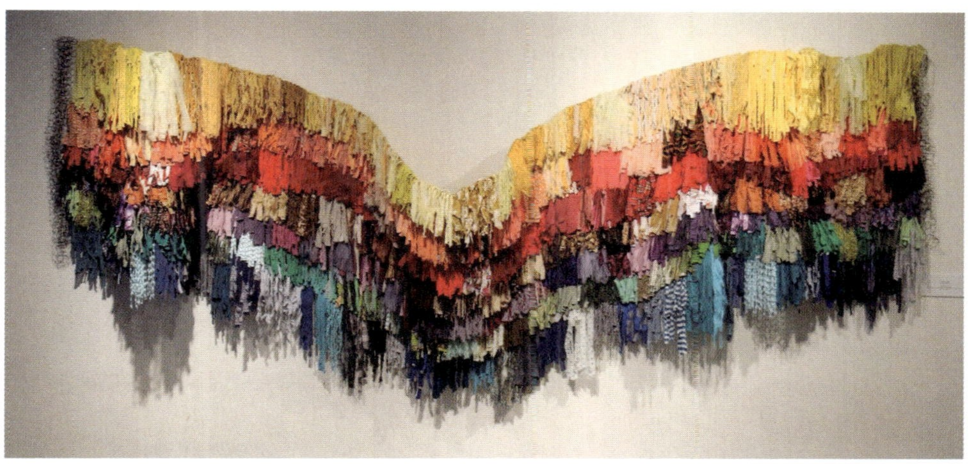

Amber Robles-Gordon. *My Rainbow Is Enuf.* 2014. Mixed media on chicken wire, 4 × 24 ft. Philadelphia Museum of African Art. Courtesy of the artist.

In 2019, Robles-Gordon created the series *Remembering Who I Am*, which consists of "a personal collage quilt, a compilation of constructed images and concepts regarding self-love, relishing life and romantic love."[30] The quilt is imbued with cultural references to her Caribbean heritage and influenced by the works of the Gee's Bend Quilting Collective, the artwork of Alma Woodsey Thomas, and *Love Duality* by the artist Mark Walker.[31] This work is also inspired by a romantic breakup, and the artist describes this art-making experience as "awaken[ing] a pressing desire to visually organize what is important to me and what feeds my spirit."[32] I find that Robles-Gordon's admission reveals how she is self-healing and creating a sense of order and balance through reflection. Building on this narrative, the artist said, "In some sense, I wanted to visually represent the ecosystem of my wholeness and life."[33] This reflection connects back to the overarching theme of BWAEs, of which Robles-Gordon's life and sense of wholeness is a microcosm. Her implementation of self-care through art making is the driving force of her overall body of work. Her cultivation of wellness is both physically and cognitively rooted in deep introspection, part of a larger context of what many Black women are doing as a whole.

In 2019, Robles-Gordon created a series, *The Temples of My Familiars*. Seven collages on canvas conveyed what the artist described as "abstracted concepts" and "visual language." The title of this series is a nod to Alice Walker's novel *The Temple of My Familiar*, in which "each of the characters in the novel is either an artist from the beginning or becomes one in their process of spiritual development."[34] It is fitting that Robles-Gordon would

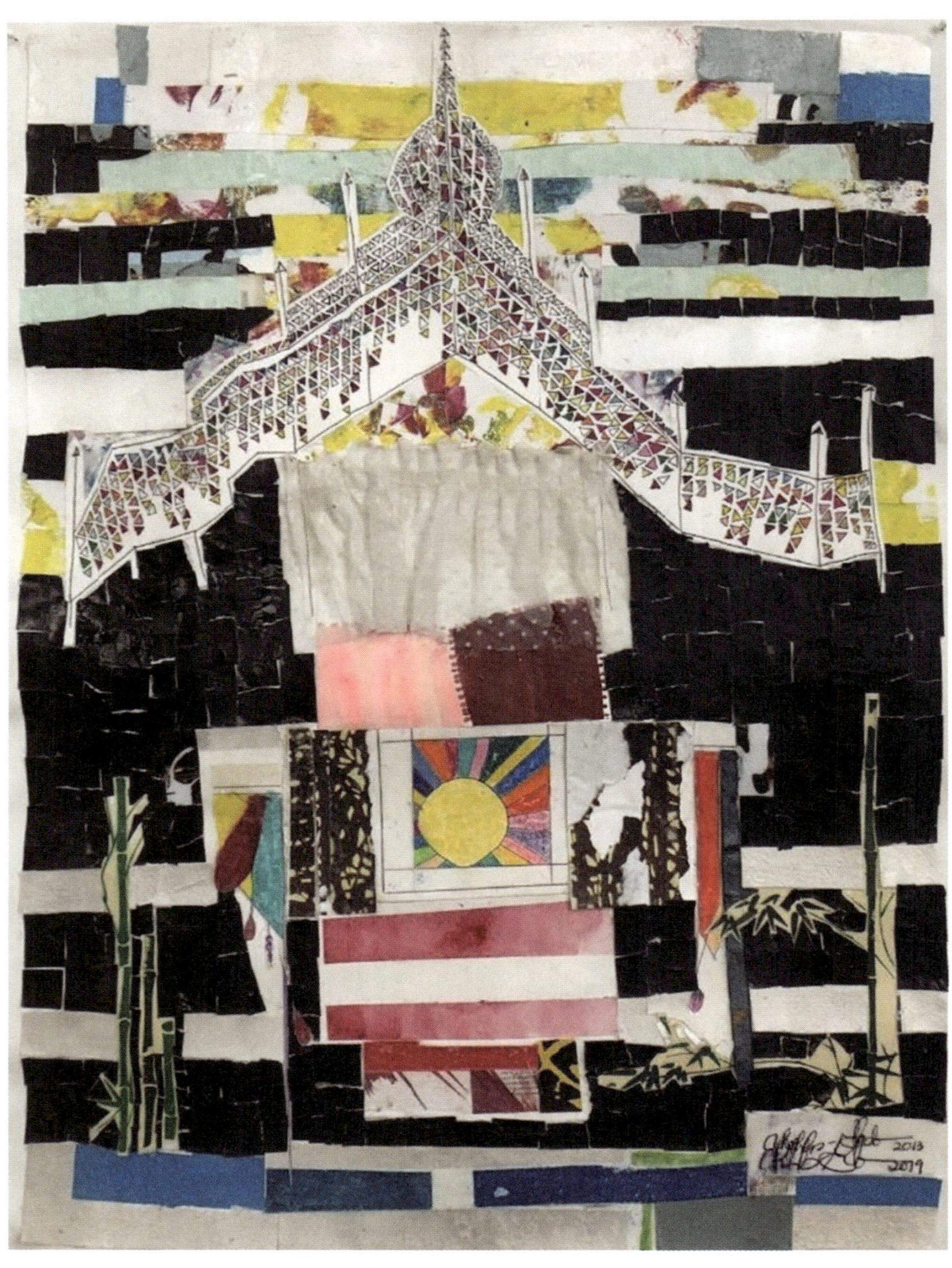

Amber Robles-Gordon. *The Temples of My Familiars: Anointed and Deserving*. 2019. Mixed-media collage and found objects on canvas, 23 × 17 in. Courtesy of the artist.

create a body of work based on Walker's novel, since she also connects her spiritual development to being an artist and developing art through a process of reflection and transparency.

The title of each work in this series begins with *The Temples of My Familiars,* followed by a distinct subtitle that provides viewers with context regarding what the artist is addressing in that work. For example, *The Temples of My Familiars: Anointed and Deserving* is a compilation of geometric shapes and colors that convey the artist's self-expression and self-affirmation. In her artist's statement, Robles-Gordon clarifies how the art relates to her feelings about herself: "During a recent journey through past work, contemplations, beginnings and endings, I enccuntered fragments of myself. These fragments vibrated silently, yet continuously, like piercing questions waiting to be answered. The various languages beckoned and moaned to be unified."[35] When one considers that much of the composition of this series consists of fragmented shapes combined to make a whole, it reflects Robles-Gordon's process of obtaining unification or wholeness through the making of art. What becomes more evident is that each collage has an overall sculptural geometric shape made from the compilation of many smaller shapes. Robles-Gordon describes each as a temple, "a place of spiritual practice and sacrifice in which I could place my familiars—my visual languages. A place where they could be re-rooted, re-formulated, and take on a new life."[36]

Robles-Gordon's creation of temples allows a more abstract and conceptual understanding of Black women's art spaces and the larger contribution Black women artists are making to the wellness ecosystem. Through abstraction she is building a conceptual space that allows for spiritual energy and healing to flow. Although deeply personal, her abstract art is accessible to viewers who connect with it and accept her invitation to reflect and heal, as it leaves space for interpretation. Robles-Gordon's making the personal accessible goes beyond content or the visual narrative she creates. Rather, through public art and installation pieces, she opens her visual narrative of healing to the masses. I find a similar invitation of healing through other abstract artists such as Dianne Smith, whose body of work is mostly large installations and performance based.

Dianne Smith: Creating Wellness through Newly Assigned Value

One of the most resourceful artists I have come across while exploring BWAEs is Dianne Smith. Like Robles-Gordon and german, she is a master of turning "stuff" into intriguing art. A multidisciplinary artist, she works in the abstract with roots in Afro-Belizean culture; she demonstrates the continuity and sustainability of the African diaspora through artistic cultural practice. I met

Smith at Art Miami a few years ago through Lavett Ballard. As the three of us sat down to have lunch, I quickly learned about the significant impact Smith is making within BWAEs. Smith grew up in the South Bronx of New York in the 1970s. Her parents were immigrants from Belize who didn't really understand the school system in the United States. Consequently, Smith navigated her community as a highly independent child. When she entered middle school, she spent a lot of time in art class. She was also strongly influenced by an art teacher who encouraged her to apply to specialized art high schools such as the Fiorello H. LaGuardia High School of Music & Art and Performing Arts. Smith passed the entrance exam and enrolled at the school, where her creativity was nurtured amid like-minded students, teachers, and administrators. From there, she applied to only one college, Otis Art Institute of Parsons School of Design, which is now Otis College of Art and Design in Los Angeles, and was admitted.

Smith recalls having a difficult time finding her footing in college, and she left before completing her foundation year. She returned to New York and ended up modeling and traveling. She even moved to Europe for fashion modeling and got married before resettling in Los Angeles. While recovering from a miscarriage, she turned on the television and came across a PBS special about the Harlem Renaissance. Her high school education exposed her to many predominantly white museums and art institutions, where she took several after-school art history classes. Yet she recalled, "no one ever mentioned the Harlem Renaissance."[37] She was fascinated by a history that she never was taught in all her years as an art student at LaGuardia Music and Art. Ironically, the school was in Harlem at the time, down the street from the Studio Museum of Harlem. When Smith came across the PBS documentary, she was in her twenties and in a failing marriage. She decided to leave her husband and move back to New York—specifically to move to Harlem—and be an artist. Smith had no money and moved around, living with friends before eventually settling into a small studio apartment in Harlem in the 1990s to "figure this art thing out."[38] Her journey is another reminder of how becoming a professional artist is a calling for many. Smith made the most of being in a community with rich historical roots for African diaspora people. She also became more connected with her Caribbean roots once she embraced the technique of knotting and weaving material to create sculptural art and installation art that is often site-specific.

Prior to embracing abstract art as her genre, Smith did go back to school. She attended Plymouth University in the United Kingdom, eventually earning a master of fine arts degree from the Transart Institute for Creative Research in Liverpool. Building on her formal education, Smith also credits her current trajectory of art making to critical conversations she had with her friend Danny Simmons. Simmons is a Neo-African abstract expressionist painter and the cofounder and chairman of the Rush Philanthropic Arts Foundation, which provides disadvantaged urban youth with arts access and education. Smith met Danny Simmons in the early 2000s, while she was a figurative painter creating figurative work that reflected the Black community. One night, she and Simmons were in conversation, and he asked her, "Well, how long does it take you to finish a piece?" She responded, "Two weeks." Simmons hadn't seen her work but asked, "What the hell are you doing?" He went on to say, "Well, I wanna see the work." When he visited Smith's studio and saw her figurative paintings his reaction was, "It's clear you can paint. And you're probably a much better painter than I am. . . . I just don't know why you're painting this shit."[39]

Smith recalls that the little Bronx girl inside her took offense and wanted to dismiss Simmons's critique. After going through a series of emotions and tears in private, she reflected more about what he said, which was, "Figure out who you are as an artist. Find your voice and free up."[40] Danny Simmons was right. Smith was creating work based on what she thought was expected of her, which was representational art, including African-style sculptures and motifs that she eventually transformed into two-dimensional works. Smith describes her early work as "beautiful and ornate and really good."[41] Despite the quality of her work, she remembers saying to herself, "Oh my God, but that's not the kind of artist I am."[42] And after embracing this revealing truth and the words of her friend, she ended up painting a piece that was the opposite of figurative work. When Simmons came over to see the piece, he said, "By far, this is the best shit you've ever painted."[43]

Smith's story about how she evolved into being an abstract artist is instructive in how BWAEs are not siloed or exclusively influenced by Black women. Sometimes inspiration and encouragement come from other outside groups or individuals invested in seeing Black women win. It also demonstrates how a journey of wellness through art is connected to artists' clarity and authenticity in the art they create. Many artists besides Smith evolve and grow in their approach to art making. This is borne out by their skills and techniques as well as in the overall cohesion of their body of work and the stories they tell. Smith's professional trajectory has taught her to take risks and to not be an absentee artist but rather an artist who goes out and engages the art world by attending exhibitions, traveling, and expanding her work and learning beyond her community. Smith has also built a cadre of other artist friends and comrades along the way. Yet what I find most influential to the work she produces is the cultural knowledge of art that she learned as a child.

Smith's creative praxis is informed by a rich Afro-Belizean culture. Much of her artwork consists of knotting butcher paper into large sculptural installation art. The way she knots the butcher paper is carefully planned, and the type of butcher paper she uses affects how the installation art will look.

This knotting of paper is similar to the basket weaving that she learned from women basket weavers in Belize. When I asked Smith to elaborate further, she explained, "Like many women in Belize, my mother and her five sisters were basket weavers because the family was not very well off; they were poor. They would weave intricate baskets and that's how they would make an income."[44] Traditionally, basket weaving in Belize has been connected to a certain socioeconomic class and more specifically to women. While Smith's father spent a lot of time working away from the home, the women and the young girls of the family would make baskets as a collective. Smith remembers going to Belize as a kid during the summer until she was about twelve years old and having to learn how to weave baskets. At the time it wasn't something she embraced. In fact, she resented having to weave baskets and preferred running around the yard and getting dirty. Basket weaving felt like punishment, and Smith would get in trouble if she did not sit down and participate. Despite her resistance, this was the expectation of girls from her community and a form of cultural preservation. Smith recalls that one of her aunts, Louise, was the only one attempting to hand down the tradition to her and others. Louise was a stylish woman educated in the United Kingdom and "had a very colonized way of being that came out in her diction and overall performance."[45] Yet she understood the value of passing down this cultural knowledge.

The Reconstitution of Things: Newly Assigned Value

For many summers in Belize during her formative years, Smith stayed at her family's home, weaving baskets. It wasn't until she started investigating three-dimensional art making as a graduate student that she realized that she was very good at doing it. As she started thinking about material and working with clothing and other kinds of fiber, linen, ropes, and strings, her memory of basket weaving came back to her. Her reflection led her to call her mother to ask about the tradition, but her mother said she did not remember. Smith also called her aunts, but they essentially said, "I don't want to revisit that."[46] Perhaps it was the association of basket weaving with poverty that caused many of the elders of Smith's family not to want to remember or revisit the task of basket weaving. However, as an adult and professional artist, Smith started knotting and weaving on her own, relying on muscle memory and what felt right to her. After not getting specific guidance or techniques from family members, she decided not to look up any specific weaves or knots. Instead, she wants her technique to be an inherent experience, which she describes as the "familiarity of the unfamiliar." This approach to art making has since become a throughline in all her art making that she calls "newly assigned value."[47] And although she has not retained specific details of knotting and weaving, it is still familiar and connected to her Afro-Belizean heritage and culture and lived experiences. Smith explained, "My hyphenated identity—female, Black, American of Belizean descent—along with my Harlem community and my experiences studying, working, living, and traveling throughout Europe and Africa, has given me a broader perspective of the world. Just as paragraphs, pages, chapters, and volumes delineate a book, my work encompasses all that I encounter."[48] The concept of newly assigned value stems from two sources: Smith's upbringing in the South Bronx and her Belizean heritage, where traditions are passed down.

The custom of table setting and preparing certain foods is another cultural memory that demonstrates the idea of newly assigned value. Smith describes how in Belize everyone comes home for lunch, and her grandmother would cook and set the table. Family members would eat a full meal in the middle of the day, and then go back to school or work. In the evening, whatever protein was left from that meal got reconstituted into supper, or tea. The ideas of not wasting things and taking a little and turning it into a lot, was very familiar to Smith. They registered with her because of how she grew up in both spaces, the Bronx and Belize. While she was growing up in the Bronx, Smith's family was the only Caribbean one in her building. Still, the neighborhood was diverse, with Black people from other parts of the world and other American regions, like the South. Even in the Bronx, among diverse groups of Black and brown people, Smith remembers a sort of communal living. When she outgrew clothing, it was given to younger kids in her building. This sharing of resources was common. It taught her to be able to take something and turn it into something else, or to think about a thing beyond its intended use. Smith's memories and her process of assigning a new value to materials are evidence that making abstract art is intentional and resourceful. When Smith decided that she was going to build a career creating minimalist-abstract art, she felt more aligned with her authentic self. Her art-making practice is connected to an ancestral memory that holds cultural pride and value. As an artist, Smith is adding to the sustainability of her cultural and artistic heritage.

Smith's cultural memory has also become a reclamation of abstract arts and the African diaspora. Smith, who spent years studying art history, also studied abstract artists such as Willem de Kooning, Jackson Pollock, Clyfford Still, and the other predominant white abstract male artists whose work did not resonate with her but was centered in the curriculum. Now, she regards the African diaspora as the center of abstraction in light of ancient African art and the materials used to create concepts and ideas in abstract ways. Later, she became aware of the abstract artist Norman Lewis, whose work had been present in her community for many years. Smith saw his works in person for the first time when she walked into the Studio Museum of Harlem and immediately found them arresting. This started her on a search for more Black abstract artists, such as Richard Mayhew, Frank Bowling, Joe Overstreet, and Alma Woodsey Thomas.

Smith's first art exhibition was at Skylight Gallery in Brooklyn, New York. At that time, she was in her twenties, exhibiting with older, more established abstract artists with whom she would eventually be compared. There weren't a lot of young abstract artists at that time, as the trend for her peers was to create figurative work. Smith decided to stay the course, continuing to develop her wrist and hand techniques for knotting and weaving materials. She stated, "I would tell myself oh, I do this now, and I just really stayed true and committed to my voice."[49] Smith could hear her friend Danny Simmons' call to figure out who she was as an artist echo in the back of her mind. When she was in her thirties, her view of the world began to change. She began taking notice of what was happening in her immediate surroundings, which also informed her creative practice and consequently her development of wellness. By the mid-2000s, Smith hit a wall creatively. She was suffering from imposter syndrome and wasn't active in the art community. Recognizing that she was in a slump, she applied for a residency in Berlin, Germany; she needed the synergy and fellowship that comes with being around other artists. While in Berlin, she started making three-dimensional pieces, which eventually led to her earning her MFA.

Abstract Sculptures: The Art of Knotted and Twisted Butcher Paper

Dianne Smith's use of butcher paper to create installations was birthed while she was in graduate school. When she was asked to create artwork for a show on Governors Island about the history of African Americans in New York, she thought long and hard about what materials she should use. One day while walking in the Wall Street area, she looked down at the pavement. She recalled, "It hit me that I could not talk about the history of African Americans in New York without talking about the Middle Passage, because at one point the island of Manhattan had more enslaved Black people on it than white people." New York was a major port for the slave trade; Smith wanted to have a succinct conversation that encompassed this history and its effects. The cracks in the sidewalk that she saw that day were significant because they led her to think about mark making and imprints. They tell stories connected to hidden histories, such as the 1991 discovery of a burial ground for enslaved Africans in Manhattan that a group of construction workers inadvertently dug up while working on a new construction site.[50] Smith explains, "Those cracks were holding our ancestors."[51] While exploring this historical narrative, she connected the idea of butcher paper and its use for wrapping meat to cargo and shipments. When thinking about enslaved Africans who were human cargo in the Middle Passage, she thought they were like meat being shipped, and the symbolism of the butcher paper led her to begin working with the paper and crinkling it. The crinkled paper led her to think about how elders in a family develop wrinkles in their skin, much like the cracks she saw in the Manhattan sidewalk. For Smith, those wrinkles hold memories and a diasporic history. Some of these histories we know; some of them we may never know but are passed down through the descendants of enslaved Africans.

Smith builds on her belief in the inherent or ancestral memory that shows up in people's movements and ways of being in the world. She captures movement in her twisting of specific types of butcher paper. This medium has become her way of marking, storytelling, and creating a language of multiple histories. Her technique has also become very familiar as she notices the hand motions that she uses to create. Making this type of art is a healing process that connects her to her grandmother, who wove baskets, scrubbed clothes on a washboard in her backyard, and made bread or johnnycake, a staple in Caribbean communities. Smith also remembered how the women in her neighborhood would braid hair, which called for certain hand and wrist movements. When going through her creative process of knotting and weaving art materials, Smith asserts, "I am recalling those same movements."[52] It is strongly evident that Smith's art-making practice is rooted in cultural practices of Black women's labor. Through knotting butcher paper and other materials, she is centering the laborious experiences that many Black women have endured. This is another point of wellness as Smith creates beauty from the pain, exhaustion, and sometimes socioeconomic trauma associated with certain types of labor. The visual narratives in Smith's work are intentionally African diasporic, yet she has built a body of work that engages audiences from diverse ethnic groups, as many people have found themselves and their own stories in her knotted and woven sculptures.

Afro Syllogism is a series of installations that exemplifies the outcome of Smith's ritual of knotting and weaving. Using a large roll of brown butcher paper, nails and staples, Smith walked into a gallery space, Atelierhof Kreuzberg in Berlin, and began an organized process of wrinkling the paper on site. Her process included different kinds of turning and twisting that caused different effects as well as the effect of being present. *Webster's Dictionary* defines a syllogism as "a kind of logical argument that applies deductive reasoning to arrive at a conclusion based on two propositions that are asserted or assumed to be true." Sometimes the conclusion from this type of deductive reasoning is not true. This was something that Dianne Smith wanted to highlight—that is, the faultiness of conclusions—after an encounter with a racist taxi driver in Berlin.

Smith was trying to catch a taxi along with two girlfriends who were also Black when they noticed that taxis would approach them and then drive off

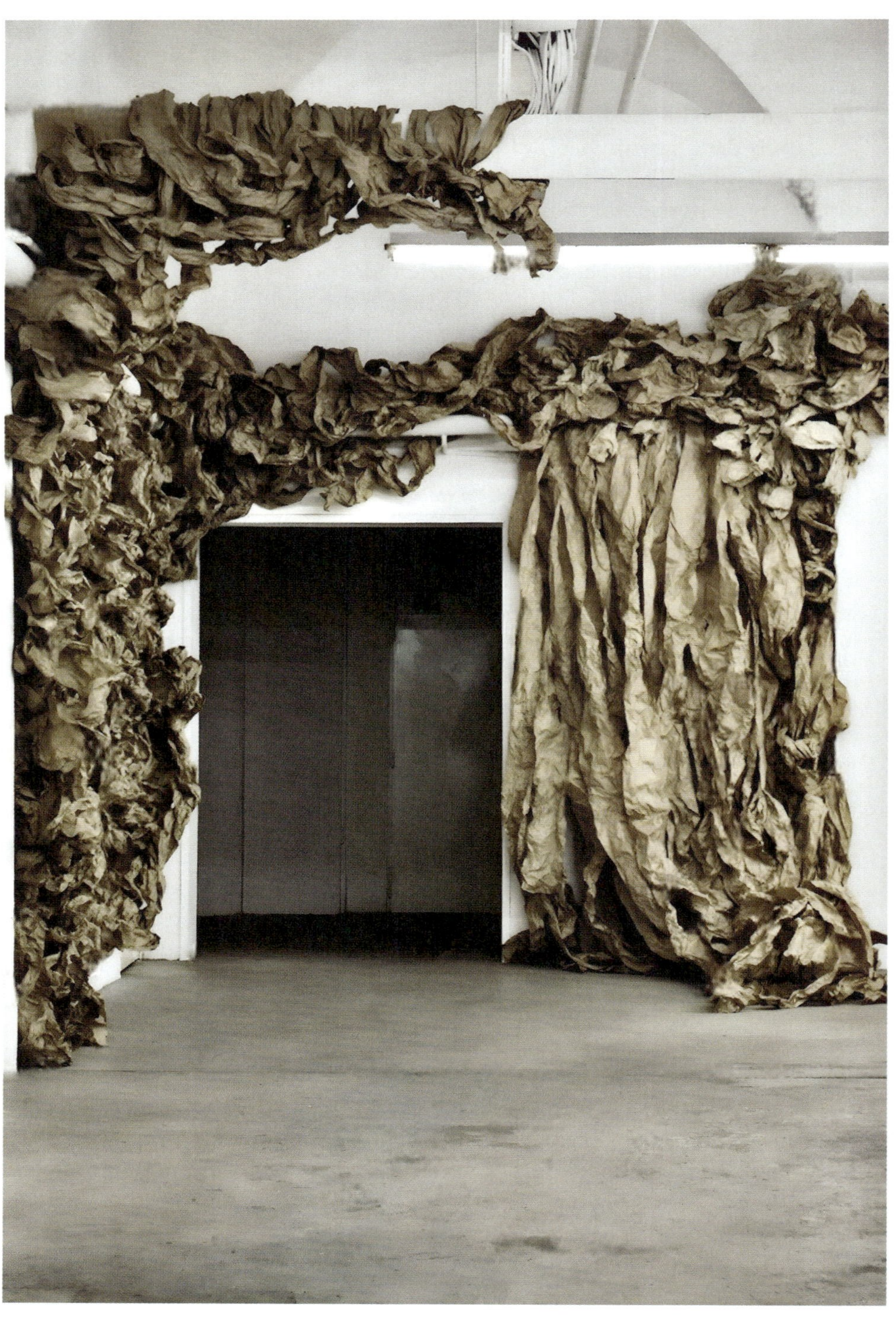

Dianne Smith. *Afro Syllogism*. 2012. Brown butcher paper, nails, and staples. Atelierhof Kreuzberg, Berlin, Germany.

or bypass them entirely. Believing this was racial discrimination, Smith put her assumption to the test by having one of her fairer-skinned girlfriends with long hair stand farther down the street to catch a cab. From a distance, this friend looked more phenotypically white, and she was able to catch the next cab. Smith and the other friend rushed into the cab as well and soon discovered that the driver, who was from India, was in fact anti-Black. He immediately told them to get out of the taxi. That was when Smith took control of the situation and uncharacteristically told the taxi driver, "You're going to shut the fuck up and take us every place we need to go," all while giving him a lesson on racism.[53] The taxi driver initially made assumptions about Smith and her friends, but during the car ride he became privy to conversations about Carnegie Hall, concert pianists, celebrity hair stylists, law and politics, and other topics that suggested that Smith and her friends were well educated and of a particular socioeconomic class. Later this incident made Smith think about assumptions and how people draw conclusions about blackness and Black people. This became the inspiration for the installation.

The first *Afro Syllogism* exhibit focused on the trauma that Black people constantly live with. In trauma there is pain, but Smith also wanted to uplift the elegance, beauty, and strength she finds in Black people. The syllogism installations are meant to convey diasporically all the complexities and identities among Black people as we navigate the world and experiences like the one Smith and her friends had with the taxi driver. Creating the installation was a form of wellness as Smith processed her experience of discrimination. Her work extends beyond portraying the taxi driver incident. The context of this work also reflects her perspective that "we're living in perpetual trauma and today we're living in a space of trauma porn. . . . I have a responsibility as a maker to talk about these things in terms of how I'm concerned about the diaspora, but also to take care of all of us."[54] Part of Smith's caretaking of Black people is leading with the beauty that she recognizes in the collective diasporic experience. This approach to wellness and healing addresses the collective trauma that has been highlighted in the media. Smith posits that Black people feel trauma both directly and indirectly. She explains, "We feel it when we watch the death of George Floyd, and when we hear about the death of Breonna Taylor; we feel it so deeply." Smith feels that it is her responsibility as an artist to be able to have conversations about trauma while at the same time ensuring that she is not traumatizing her community even more by perpetuating trauma through art and contributing to trauma porn. Working in abstraction helps her to achieve this delicate balance, since it does not render literal and figurative representations of trauma.

Smith's process and reasons for making art are extremely rooted in healing and cultivating continual wellness. When George Floyd was murdered and the video was televised, it affected Smith deeply. In response, she created an audio/video of the incident, which consisted only of text and sound embedded in butcher paper sculptural walls. She made the decision not to include the original video or images of the incident to avoid perpetuating trauma triggers. Her argument is that "people become so immune to what they are seeing, but they are not listening."[55] Smith's audio with text forces audiences to be present at what was happening to George Floyd at that moment. The video, *George Floyd: Seven Minutes*, opens with the text: "7 Minutes," "George Floyd," "Look How They Doing People Out Here," "Please," and "Please, I Can't Breathe." These quotes are from Floyd, and Smith incorporates quoted text from bystanders as well as the officers, all while we hear seven minutes of the audio recording of the incident. The captioned audio compels viewers to slow down their reading and to really extract all the voices present in the last seven minutes of George Floyd's life. As much as the creation of this video helped Smith to process what millions of people witnessed, her artwork is an outlet for others who might feel anger and frustration at first but who also might be open to engage in the critical dialogue that is needed for healing and wellness.

Navigating Wellness through Abstraction

When I asked Smith how she defines wellness and to explain its connection with her artwork, she replied, "I define wellness with happiness, truly living in a happy place and being happy with self."[56] Her take on wellness does not mean that people who are well do not experience unhappiness but rather that "no matter what is going on in the world, you can be upset about something but the core of who you are is a happy person." When people master being upset about something without that situation changing how they feel about themselves, that is wellness for Smith. She creates space for wellness by giving what she calls "visual voice" to her feelings and thoughts. In an interview with *Morning Call*, Smith shared the following: "As a multidisciplinary artist, I think about what it is I want to say and find the best way or medium to say it. . . . Whether it's painting, sculpture, installation, video or photography, I can bring visual voice to my thoughts and experiences."[57] The things that Smith cannot always articulate verbally but are important to be addressed come through her art. This approach to wellness has been crucial because as Smith said, "The last five years have been nothing but trauma in my life. I lost a very close friend in 2017, my mother and father in 2018, and my brother in 2019 at the onset of COVID-19."[58] Smith disclosed that she also caught the coronavirus very early on. Her physical illness was exacerbated by two other autoimmune diseases that she manages daily and that have taught her to be an active participant in her own care. She has already had experience being a caretaker to both of her parents, who lived in different states and who were

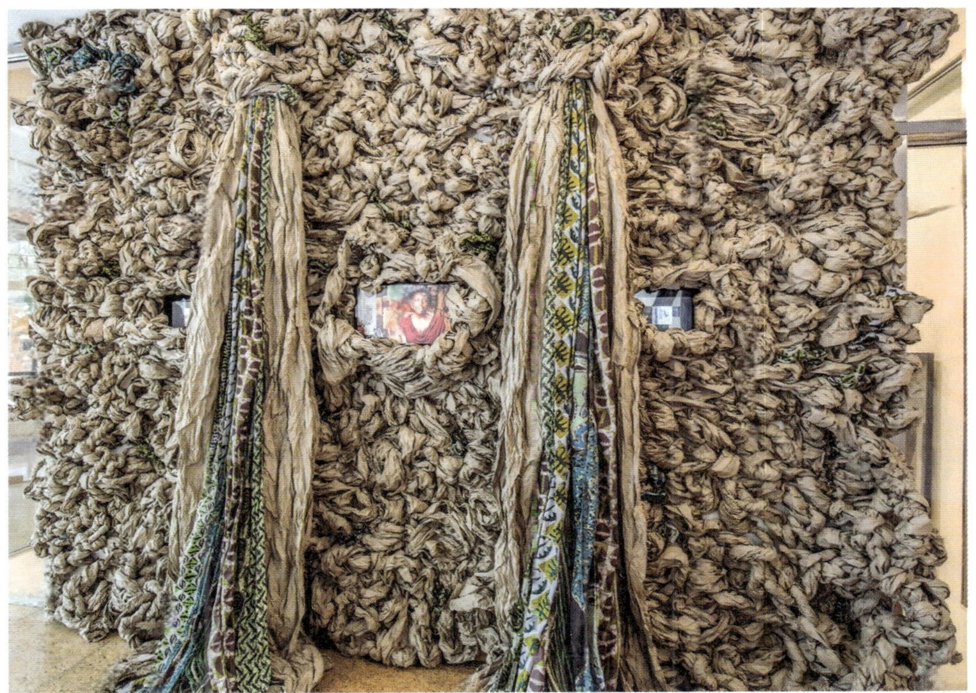

Dianne Smith. *Stuff*. 2015. Butcher paper, West African wax prints, rope, and video. Schomburg Center for Research in Black Culture, New York.

simultaneously ill. When Smith discovered her own illness, it caused her to advocate for the appropriate testing and to be present, which she attributes to another approach to wellness. The loss of loved ones, illnesses, and police killings of unarmed Black people have been turning points for many people, regardless of race and identity. This is what makes Smith's artistic expressions of wellness so accessible. The same can be said about her visual commentary on domestic violence.

Like Amber Robles-Gordon, Diane Smith also showed work at the Schomburg Center exhibit *i found god in myself*, which celebrated the fortieth anniversary of *For Colored Girls*. Smith was commissioned to reinterpret visually the lady in green's choreopoem, "somebody almost walked off wid alla my stuff."[59] At that time Smith was experiencing a domestic violence issue with her then boyfriend. This poem is one of Smith's favorites, and when the domestic violence incident occurred, Smith decided that she could not create work without being transparent and honest about what had just happened to her. In the installation *Stuff*, she chronicled her experience, along with the experiences of a small group of women, in three videos that are surrounded by knotted butcher paper. The video on the left shows a picture of her face with the black eye that she received during the altercation. She took the picture with her iPhone and started recording her face that night and for days afterwards, capturing the swelling and bruising. Then she found domestic violence statistics. In the first video installation viewers can hear her reading these statistics while images of her face flash across the screen. The video is raw and unedited. While Smith reads the statistics, she also hits her fist against her hand. Viewers hear that in the background, like the sound of someone is being slapped. This portion of the installation is deeply personal and was part of Smith's healing processing of trauma.

In the second video, Smith included six other women talking about somebody walking off with all their stuff. These are women who trusted Smith to present their stories; in turn, the stories gave them a reclamation. One woman was nine when she lost her mother; the loss of a job as an adult triggered that memory and revealed a deep sense of hurt and void. This woman experienced being sent from family member to family member with very little ownership of "stuff." In adulthood she made a promise to herself that she would always be able to take care of herself and that no one was ever going to take anything from her again. When she began telling the story of losing her job, it triggered the memory of losing her mother and the impact that it has had on her life.

Another participant in Smith's second installation video was from Honduras. She talked about immigrating to the United States at eight years old and meeting her mother and siblings for the first time. She also reflected on her experiences going to school and people wanting to change her name. Like Robles-Gordon, this woman recalled that forty-plus years ago, a little Black girl speaking Spanish was very foreign to people in her community. Another participant shared the story of being in a long-term relationship. When she was diagnosed with breast cancer, her partner strung her along. Each of these varying stories were about the loss of stuff, physical, emotional, or symbolic. Yet elements of triumph in these women's stories reflect that they did not stay in a space of pain. This reveals Smith's other strategy for wellness, which is to surround yourself with people who are self-aware.

The third video in *Stuff* consists of photographs of Smith's apartment with a voiceover of her reading Ntozake Shange's choreopoem "somebody almost walked off wid alla my stuff." While she reads the poem, photos of her personal belongings in sections of her apartment flash by to convey the idea of the night of Smith's domestic violence experience. After the incident, one of Smith's friends encouraged her to leave her apartment with her boyfriend there, but she was defiant. She remembers saying, "'Wait a minute. Somebody's leaving tonight but it ain't me.' I was like, 'I got stuff to do tomorrow.'"[60] Smith was very clear in the moment, and she opted not to call the police because her then boyfriend, a six-foot-six Black man, had had a couple of cocktails. She feared that the police might break things in her apartment or even kill him if there was an altercation. Smith also wanted to send a clear message to her assaulter that the abuse that just occurred was not a minor infraction, and that they could not return to business as usual. Leaving her home, Smith explained, "would have sent the message that he was still welcome to be there, or that I just needed a moment away. And that's not the message I was intending to send."[61] In the days following the altercation, Smith photographed all her belongings, even things inside her closets. The video montage she created is a very ethereal visual narrative about stuff. The video is guided by the following questions: What is stuff? What does stuff mean? Through reflection, Smith explained, "There're your tangible things, right? And then there's your spiritual, mental, and emotional stuff. But when people take your tangible things, it causes that emotional . . . that, that emotional stuff."[62] Stuff was Smith's way of talking about healing, reclaiming what belongs to her, and holding on to the stuff she values, which might easily get lost in the process of trauma. For Smith, this is not an option.

All three videos in *Stuff* are surrounded by a wall of brown butcher paper that forms a throughline connecting them. At the same time, it provides a level of reverence via the scale of the butcher-paper wall and the elegance of its twisted and knotted texture. It also symbolizes the mark making and imprinting that results from situations that are part of these women's journeys and their lived experiences. It symbolizes the "stuff" that stays with them and life's complexity, much as for the women who are portrayed in Ntozake Shange's choreopoems. Among African diasporic people, part of what comes with life's complexity is the ability to dream despite insurmountable odds.

Creating Black Joy through Abstraction

For the past few years Smith has brought light to Black joy by creating art for Juneteenth celebrations. In 2021 the artist created an immersive experience titled *I Dream a Dream That Looks Back at Me*. In collaboration with Carl Hancock Rux, Smith took over the entire Lincoln Center Plaza in New York City. There a public art performance took place that focused on the abolitionist Harriet Tubman, who was known for having visions and for the quote, "Every great dream begins with a dreamer."[63] Tubman's dreams, visions, and legacy were connected to the pursuit of liberation for herself and others. Smith posits that Tubman's dream still looks back at us as the nation still tries to grapple with this idea of what freedom is, how we constitute freedom, and how we talk about freedom. Movements like Black Lives Matter were highlighted during this immersive exhibition.

For the exhibit, Smith created ball gowns and headdresses made from brown butcher paper. Wearing one of the gowns was the esteemed artist Helga Davis,

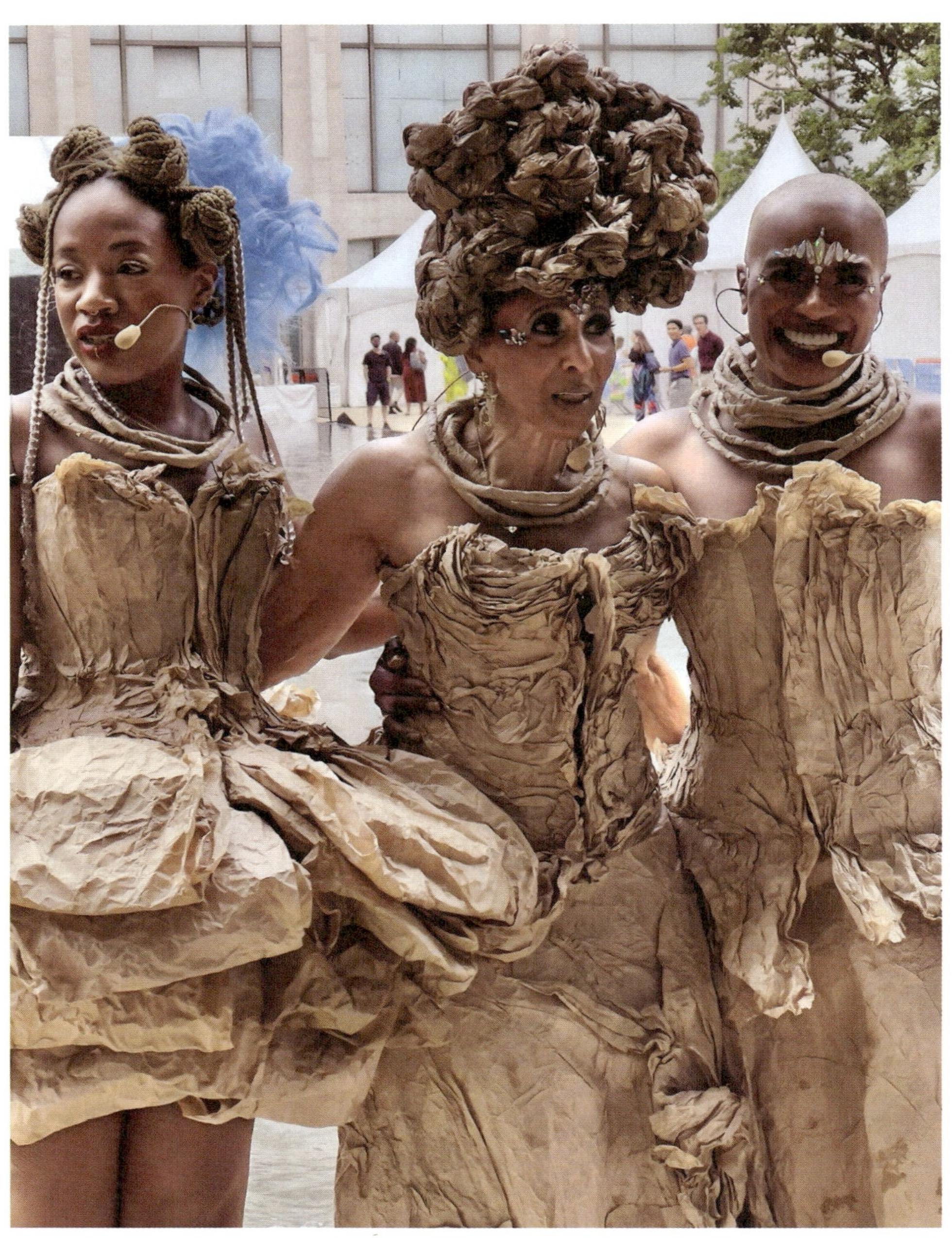

Dianne Smith. *I Dream a Dream That Looks Back at Me (Nona Hendryx, Marcelle Davies-Lashley, and Kimberly Nichole)*. 2021. Butcher paper dresses. Site-specific performance, Lincoln Center Juneteenth.

who was hoisted up on a lift representing America and what America should be, reciting poetry. The renowned singers Nona Hendryx, Marcelle Davies-Lashley, and Kimberly Nichole waded through water while wearing the paper costumes and sang songs commemorating Juneteenth and freedom, such as the "Water Song," written by the two-time Pulitzer Prize winner for drama Lynn Nottage. The participants were surrounded by Smith's mixed media sculptural installation, which became part of the ambiance of the festivities that evening. The next Juneteenth at the Lincoln Center, Smith created paper sculptural dresses for Nona Hendryx, Marcelle Davies-Lashley, Kiki Hawkins, and Patrice Johnson Chevannes, who embodied America and sang and spoke a deconstructed version of the American national anthem and "Lift Ev'ry Voice and Sing," mostly in Jamaican patois. Johnson Chevannes performed while wearing a vibrant blue afro wig and red, white, and blue eyelashes, all while hoisted on a huge lift.

These designs, along with related installations and videos at the Park Avenue Armory and Lincoln Center, are examples of how Smith creates art to celebrate the African diaspora through material, texture, and large-scale artwork that commands viewers' attention. Dianne Smith's artistic expressions, exemplified by her creation of ball gowns and headdresses from brown butcher paper, transcend the boundaries of conventional art forms in a profound display of ritualistic performance. The deliberate incorporation of rituals, such as wading through water while wearing these symbolic gowns and singing songs of liberation, connects Smith's work to the principles of ancestral memory, spirituality, and cognitive wellness within BWAEs. These performances, set against the backdrop of Smith's mixed-media sculptural installations, become immersive experiences that blend material, texture, and scale to celebrate the rich tapestry of the African diaspora. This intentional fusion of ritual and artistic expression reinforces the spiritual essence embedded in BWAEs, where the creative process becomes a sacred act of commemoration and empowerment. Similar celebratory work can be found in installation work like *Jankunu Come Out* on Governors Island.

The installation *Jankunu Come Out* (2019) is an homage to a nonsatirical festival called Junkanoo that originated several centuries ago among enslaved Africans and their descendants on the plantations of Jamaica. It quickly spread throughout the Caribbean with a strong presence in the Bahamas and among Afro-Caribbeans such as the Garífuna people of Belize.[64] The Garífuna people are a small community within the African diaspora. According to Smith, they have not been treated well in Belize and have low social status. Specifically, "the West African transplants were either shipwrecked or escaped from the Caribbean islands of Barbados, St. Lucia, and Grenada, depending on the source. They intermarried with local populations of Arawaks and Carib Indians (Caribs), immigrants from South America, to become known as Garifunas

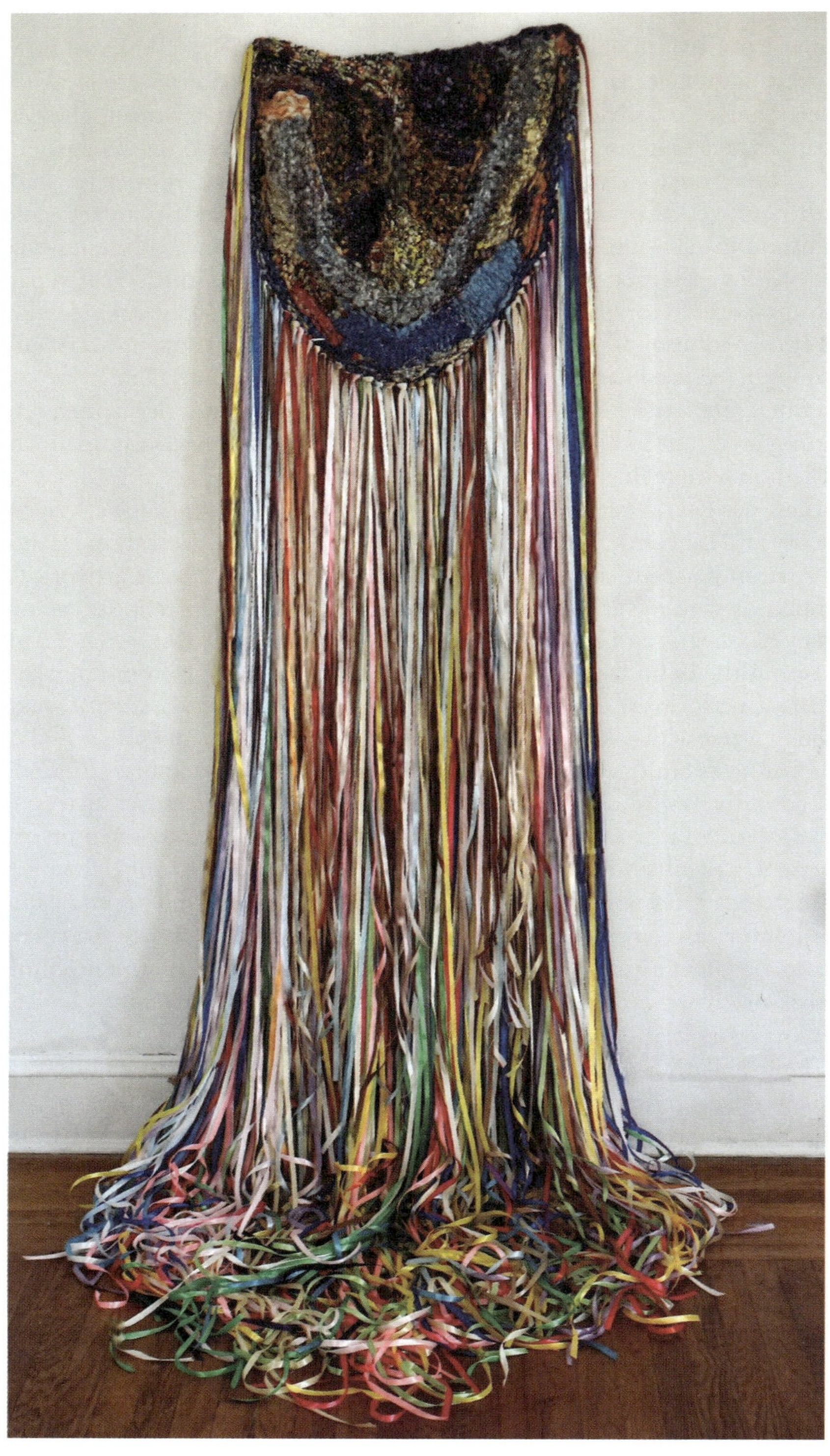

Dianne Smith. *Jankunu Come Out*. 2019. West African textiles, upcycled clothing, ribbons. Courtesy of the artist.

or Black Caribs."[65] Some members of the Garífuna community immigrated to parts of the United States and brought with them traditional African roots and food and language, as well as traditions like the Junkanoo festival. The festival dances are performed to the beat of goatskin drums and often occur in celebration of December 26 (Boxing Day) and January 1. Men and women dress up in beautiful and colorful regalia, pom-poms, and masks. While visiting Summer Stage at Crotona Park, New York, Smith came across Garífuna dancers and a Garífuna band. She photographed and filmed some of the dancers. This inspired her to create an exhibition based on the Garífuna culture. Through research she discovered that there are only five hundred thousand Garífuna people worldwide, with the majority in New York, even more than in the Caribbean. The rich Afro-Caribbean traditions of Garífuna culture resonate with Smith, who tries to capture the multitude of Blackness that exists globally. *Jankunu Come Out* consisted of hanging sculptures made of silk flowers, pom-poms, and vibrantly colored sisal ribbons. This aesthetic is inspired by the costumes worn by Junkanoo performers. The exhibition also included sculpted West African textiles hanging from the walls, along with the photos that Smith took at the Junkanoo festival in Crotona Park.

Dianne Smith's body of work is too vast to cover in its totality, yet ending a discussion of her work with the *Jankunu Come Out* exhibition highlights the key aspects of wellness within her work. Through abstraction, Smith cultivates wellness by creating an homage to Afrocentricity and aesthetics. She brings visibility and voice to ancestral memory, and she exposes the hidden beauty and complexities that shape African diasporic people to decenter our collective trauma.

As abstract artists, both Dianne Smith and Amber Robles-Gordon create work that pushes viewers to seek understanding beyond the recognizable narrative we garner from figurative art. Their artwork also draws attention to the transnational characteristics of BWAEs that contribute to their biodiversity and cultural enrichment. By engaging with abstract forms, they challenge traditional perspectives and encourage a deeper exploration of cultural identities and histories. Their works highlight the interconnectedness of global Black experiences, emphasizing the rich tapestry of influences that shape their art. This approach not only enriches the viewers' experience but also fosters a greater appreciation for the complexity and diversity within the Black art community. Moreover, Smith's and Robles-Gordon's use of unconventional materials and innovative techniques are testaments to the resilience and creativity inherent in Black women's artistic practices. Through their abstract work, they invite viewers to engage in a dialogue about the multifaceted nature of identity, heritage, and artistic legacy, ultimately contributing to a more inclusive and dynamic art world.

8

Community-Based Arts and Socioenvironmental Wellness

In the winter of 2019, I began my role as a professor in the Department of African American Studies at Syracuse University and as the executive director of the Community Folk Art Center (CFAC). CFAC is a unit of the university's Department of African American Studies, founded in 1972 during the Black Arts Movement. At the grassroots level, Herbert T. Williams, a professor specializing in African American studies and sculpture, worked in partnership with fellow Syracuse University faculty and students, alongside local artists and residents of Syracuse.[1] Williams saw the need to establish a platform where artists of the African diaspora could showcase their work and build opportunities to share knowledge through the development of community-based art classes and workshops. The goal was to create a "setting for dialogue and interaction among emerging, mid-career and professional artists in Central New York. In addition to Williams, CFAC's cofounders include Shirley Harrison, Jack White, George Campbell Jr., Mary Schmidt Campbell, David MacDonald, and Basheer Alim."[2] All of these people collectively and individually have carved out opportunities through the arts and community engagement.

In the beginning, the organization was called the Community Folk Art Gallery and was located in a small storefront on the corner of South Salina Street and Wood Avenue. Evidence of robust community engagement through visual and performing arts and art classes for youth and adults has been documented through photos showing people drumming, painting, and creating art with clay, and numerous children engaging in making arts and crafts. After a fire broke out at the South Salina location, the organization relocated to a converted auditorium on the East Side, finally settling into its current space at 805 East Genesee Street, where it expanded in size and programming to function as a multidisciplinary and African diaspora community art center with a corresponding name change to the Community Folk Art Center. Currently

CFAC is both an entity connected to Syracuse University and a nonprofit 501c3. Its current location is easily accessible to both the university community and the local community, making it a bridge between the two through the vehicle of the arts.

Regardless of its different locations, CFAC has mainly been situated near what was once the Fifteenth Ward, a prosperous, predominantly Black neighborhood in Syracuse.[3] Given CFAC's goal of being "a vibrant cultural and artistic hub committed to the promotion and development of artists of the African diaspora," it is clear why CFAC was established there.[4]

Throughout its existence, the Community Folk Art Center has been a unique force in the Syracuse community, specializing in exhibiting and promoting works by African American artists and artists from other underrepresented groups. Through exhibitions, adult and youth arts classes, film screenings, and youth summer arts and literacy camps programming, CFAC realizes its mission and engages the community through the arts and humanities. In addition to these public-facing services, the center has a strong archive collection. The Community Folk Art Center has loosely documented and archived historical records, artworks, and periodicals that document not only the history of the organization but also of historic and predominantly African diasporic neighborhoods like Syracuse's Fifteenth Ward. These are among the community members that CFAC has served over the years and that have primarily supported the organization.

The founding of CFAC and its sustainability are grounded in the preservation of African diaspora culture in a city in which this culture has historically been under attack. The center is not unique; many Black art spaces were established during the Black Arts Movement. However, it is unique within its location, as it is the only African diaspora arts center in the city of Syracuse and surrounding areas. To date, there are no other Black art museums or galleries in the region. For this reason, and because the Department of African American Studies has tied its curriculum to the center, and the economic backing of the university, CFAC has been able to survive for more than fifty years. Still, it takes more than money and politics for an organization like the Community Folk Art Center to keep going. CFAC is still a viable organization because of the will of communities that believe that the space demonstrates their intrinsic values. These values are not exclusive to art but include other things that the center provides, such as the building of community and a safe space where citizens can authentically express themselves and gather for cultural, social, and political programs.

One strong example of CFAC's value to various surrounding communities is the Creative Arts Academy (CAA). Previously, the program was named Kuumba, a Swahili word meaning "creativity." CAA is a free, year-long visual and performing arts immersion program for young creatives from eight to sixteen who are interested in pursuing a career in the arts or who are just looking for a creative outlet. The instructors are local teaching artists who guide students in developing cultural and artistic expression through engagement in and an examination of freedom, activism, and community. Participants can take classes in African drumming, step drill, ballet or tap, piano, stringed instruments, drawing and painting, ceramics, theater and poetry writing, and fiber arts. One of the pedagogical goals of CAA is to implement what the art educators Jacqueline Chanda and Vesta Daniel call "recognizing," a suggested way of teaching that explores the nexus between historical and cultural content in works of art, using examples of African-descended art as a paradigm.[5] The implementation of this strategic pedagogy aims to deepen students' understanding of the rich cultural and historical contexts that inform African-descended art, fostering a more inclusive and comprehensive approach to art education.

When I became executive director of CFAC, I was charged with revitalizing the center, which had been under interim leadership for a few years. As someone who had been engaged with Black cultural center work for many years, I had many ideas, but one deficit that I faced was not intimately knowing the community. Yet being a transplant in the area also was a strength, because I had not been entangled in the past drama and deep wounds that come with every community-serving space. With a healthy dose of optimism and a huge learning curve, I embraced this new professional challenge in my life with the clarity that the Creative Arts Academy was a vital program for the organization's visibility in the community and its continued growth. If you capture patrons at an early age, then you have a generation of students who will grow with the organization, adding to a continuum of support. As valuable as CAA has been to the Community Folk Art Center, the funding for the academy was significantly reduced over the years through budget cuts or by administrators who didn't see its value. In time, the CAA was reduced from being an after-school program offered five days a week to a one-week program during the winter break and a two-week program during the summer break. One of the first administrative changes I made was restoring the Creative Arts Academy to a five-day program, funded by grants and in-kind donations in addition to the operating budget provided by the College of Arts and Sciences.

By March 2020, the Community Folk Art Center, along with other public spaces, faced another challenge, this one brought on by COVID-19. As the world shut down due to a virus that was killing millions of people globally, so did CFAC's regular operations. During this time, we saw the creative sector severely damaged as organizations had to shut their doors with no indication of when they could reopen. Museum galleries, theater spaces, dance studios, and other public arts spaces became ghost towns; many professional artists lost their main source of income. As an arts administrator, I was eager to keep up CFAC's momentum in engaging the community, despite what seemed to be insurmountable odds.

With the help of staff and technology, CFAC pivoted to having an online presence through an online gallery that was developed by a Black woman-owned firm, Collective.ly Digital.[6] At this time, Black Lives Matter protests were springing up around the country. In Syracuse, local artists captured the protests through photography. Among them was Cherilyn Beckles, a graduate student in strategic communications at Syracuse University. While protesting, she decided to use her photographic skills and interview other protesters to capture the movement. CFAC's online gallery was desperately needed once our planned exhibition for the spring 2020 season was suspended. Beckles's photography, along with audio of protesters she interviewed, became one of CFAC's first online exhibitions. I also curated online exhibitions by the local artist Jaleel Campbell, whose digital art and fiber-arts dolls reflect the Syracuse African American community that he grew up in. It was also during this tumultuous time that CFAC streamed several online art classes for the Creative Arts Academy and livestreamed an in-house concert, "For the Love of Justice," featuring the singer-songwriter Danielle Ponder.[7] Ponder, a Rochester native, was a public defender and later a diversity, equity, and inclusion officer before returning to her first love, music.[8] Along with a five-person band, Ponder delivered a mix of pop, rhythm and blues, and rock with a social justice message that the community needed as it grappled with race-based social justice protests amid a global health crisis.

Reflecting on my role as an arts administrator, I take pride in the work I have accomplished along with the dedicated staff and university students during a time of uncertainty and limitations. In hindsight, I probably needed to take this time to rest. Regarding my own understanding of wellness, I sometimes regret not doing so. However, the work we did at CFAC during the height of the pandemic was on trend. Other creatives used their gifts to connect the masses who faced depression and isolation. I am speaking of artists such as Debbie Allen, who offered free dance classes on social media platforms; the DJ D-Nice, who connected people from around the world by DJing for hours on Instagram; online spoken-word poetry events; online artists' talks; virtual gallery exhibitions, live outdoor theater performances, and musical performances. A violinist performed a balcony concert for neighboring apartments in Bologna, Italy, while the country was in strict lockdown measures.[9] These creatives, along with many others, used art to facilitate wellness and emotional healing during the pandemic by fostering a sense of community that made many of us aware that at the core we are connected by our humanity.

Black women artists didn't miss a beat. In the summer of 2020, the Community Folk Art Center participated in a national public service art project spearheaded by the internationally renowned artist Carrie Mae Weems. Weems is a MacArthur Fellowship recipient and the first African American woman to have a retrospective at the Guggenheim Museum, among many other prestigious historic accomplishments. She is a resident of Syracuse and was the first artist in residence for Syracuse University at large. A few months into the pandemic, Weems created the public service announcement project *Resist COVID-19/Take 6*.[10] This included some of her most iconic photographic images of Black people and other people of color. The photos were juxtaposed with text about the disproportionate impact of COVID-19 on community members who got sick and died due to misinformation. Weems displayed her artwork throughout the country at local community centers, grocery stores, and testing sites; her images were reproduced on billboards, buttons, paper fans, pictures, and bags. CFAC participated by hanging huge posters of Weems's work in our gallery storefront windows and by displaying an assortment of buttons and fans for people to take when we gathered publicly outside. When asked to elaborate on her national campaign, Weems explained, "The whole point is to make people aware. To give people information on the deadly implications of COVID-19, and the necessity to mask up, to back up, to wash up. . . . COVID-19 is not a hoax. It's deadly real and it has to be taken seriously. If you don't want to protect yourself, at least protect others."[11] Energized by Weems's words and campaign, CFAC participated in *Resist COVID/Take 6*. The PSA was in alignment with the organization's mission. CFAC was part of a discourse through art that addressed life-threatening issues disproportionately affecting the African diaspora and other underrepresented groups.

The organization safely engaged the Syracuse community by hosting a Black Lives Matter paint party for adults and children at Kirk Park in collaboration with 100 Black Men of Syracuse. While 100 Black Men of Syracuse provided masks, hand sanitizer, voter registration information, and snacks, the Community Folk Art Center displayed Weems's *Resist COVID-19/Take 6* merchandise and managed the paint party. Participants sat safely distanced apart and painted on canvases that were created by Danielle Leveston, a Black woman artist and art educator based in Chicago. I spoke with Leveston and requested predesigned canvases featuring Black people in protest and wearing masks to reflect the experiences of Syracuse and other cities across the United States and around the world, facing both a global health pandemic and a social injustice crisis rooted in anti-black racism and bias. The collaboration yielded a great turnout and demonstrated that community-based organizations could foster dialogue and promote wellness through the visual arts. By utilizing a park, an open public space, we provided a gathering place for people at a time when most of society was sequestered in their homes.

So far, my reflection on the years 2019 and 2020 is anchored in the challenges and triumphs I faced as an administrator of a Black arts organization.

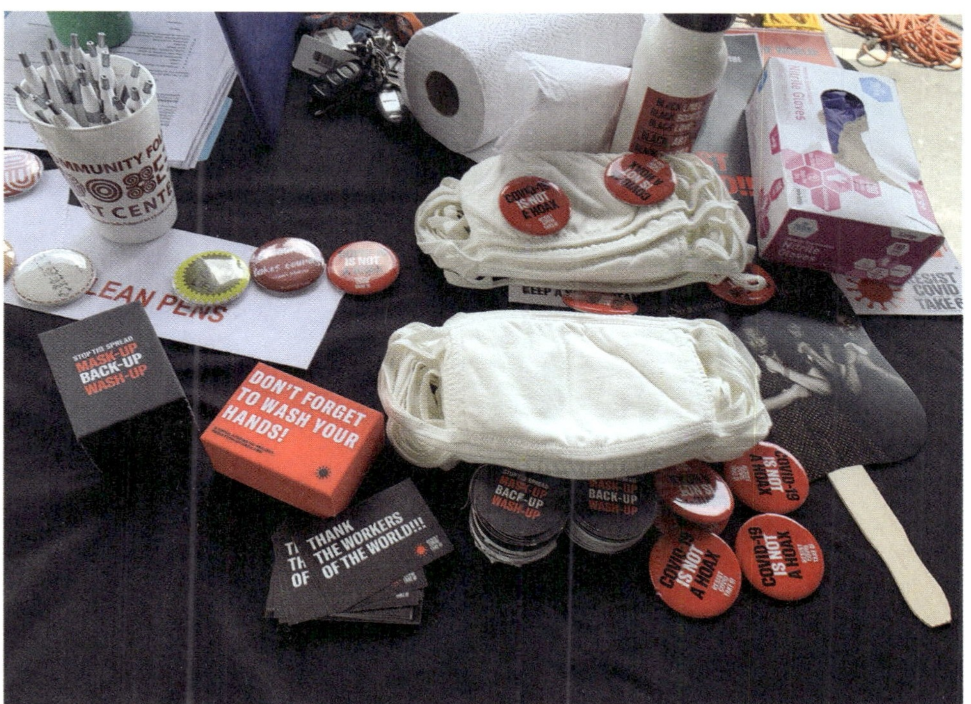

Carrie Mae Weems. Table display of assorted materials from *Resist COVID-19 Take 6!* Paraphernalia were distributed at CFAC's Black Lives Matter paint party at Kirk Park, Syracuse, NY, 2021. Photo by Tanisha Jackson.

I mention experiences and events that occurred at the Community Folk Art Center to convey the significance of Black art ecosystems. The organization exemplifies how a twentieth-century model of community-based and culturally relevant art space, rooted in the Black Arts Movement, remains viable in the twenty-first century. It possesses the power to support communities through contemporary social justice movements such as Black Lives Matter and Say Her Name. However, what I am most proud of is the continuity of initiatives that began before my leadership, such as the Creative Arts Academy and the Competitive Teenage Art Show.

The Competitive Teenage Art Show was established at CFAC in partnership with the Syracuse (NY) chapter of The Links, Incorporated, an international nonprofit corporation consisting of seventeen thousand professional women of color in 299 chapters in forty-one states, the District of Columbia, the Commonwealth of the Bahamas, and the United Kingdom.[12] The Syracuse chapter of The Links was chartered in 1959. In 1972, the same year CFAC was founded, it partnered with the organization to establish a citywide, jur-

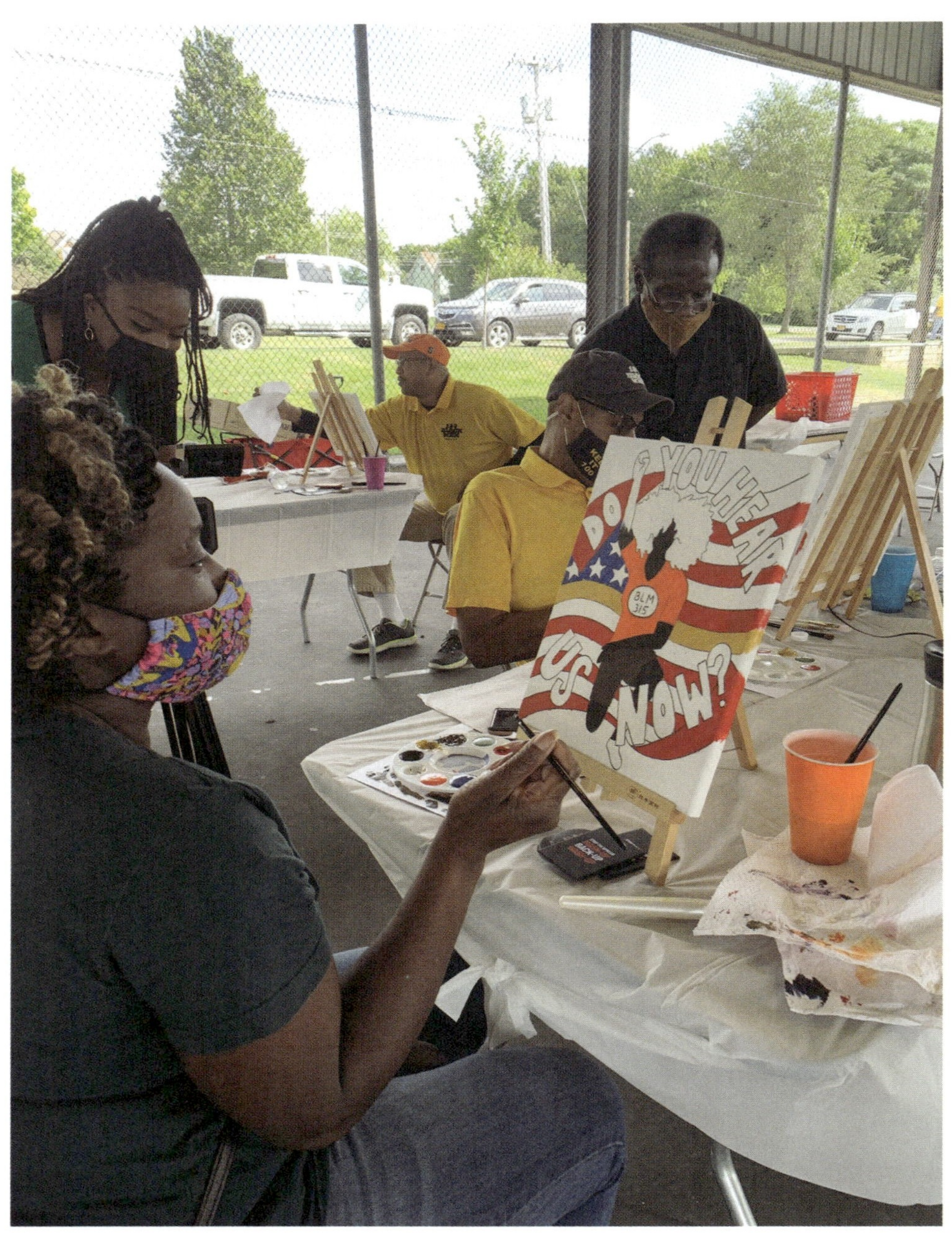

Black Lives Matter Paint Party participants at Kirk Park in Syracuse, NY, 2021. Photo by Tanisha Jackson.

ied art show that awarded college scholarships and provided an opportunity for underrepresented teenagers. African American, Asian, Latino and Native American students attending high schools in the Syracuse area had the opportunity to showcase their artwork in a professional gallery. For more than fifty years, this exhibition has always engaged and continues to engage student artists from all racial and cultural backgrounds who attend high schools from surrounding areas.

The annual exhibition was in jeopardy during the spring of 2020, due to the onset of the pandemic. The two organizations were determined not to break the continuity of such a long tradition. Using CFAC's newly established online art gallery, with tremendous efforts from both CFAC and The Links, we collected and displayed art both in the in-house gallery at CFAC and online, where exhibitions beginning in July 2020 are posted in perpetuity.[13] The artwork that students created while enrolled in school online is an example of their tenacity and how they also were still able to create during a difficult time. It was for this reason, also, that the Community Folk Art Center and the Syracuse chapter of The Links wanted to celebrate some of the community's most creative future art leaders in the area.

One of two submitted artworks that placed in the 2020 Competitive Teenage Art Show was the digital painting by Kelly, an eighth grader at Roberts Middle School, who created a portrait of an Asian woman painted in yellow with visible tears running down her face while the silhouettes of ghost-like figures stand behind her with angry grimaces. In the backdrop of this digital painting are texts that are racial epithets like Chink, Dog-eater, and Ching-Chong. This painting placed second in the digital art category and shows the critical thinking about racism that young artists express through art. Likewise, a portrait titled *All Eyes On Me* by the eleventh- grade student Caitlin shows a Black woman under the gaze of six phenotypical European eyes that are floating around her. This surreal painting captured the attention of all the art judges, who awarded the artwork first place and Best in Show, based on the composition of the work as well as the concept that the artist explained in her artist's statement. Caitlin writes:

> My name is Caitlin S., and I am a junior at C. W. Baker High School. I was inspired to make this piece as I began to research the effects the media, societal pressure, and society as a whole can have on a person. Since the treatment people of color have received throughout history is becoming more recognized and spoken about, I knew that I could relate my piece to these ideas. While I know that as a White woman, I will never know the experiences these people have experienced, I want to capture the emotions one may feel in the best way I could. In my work, the eyes represent the

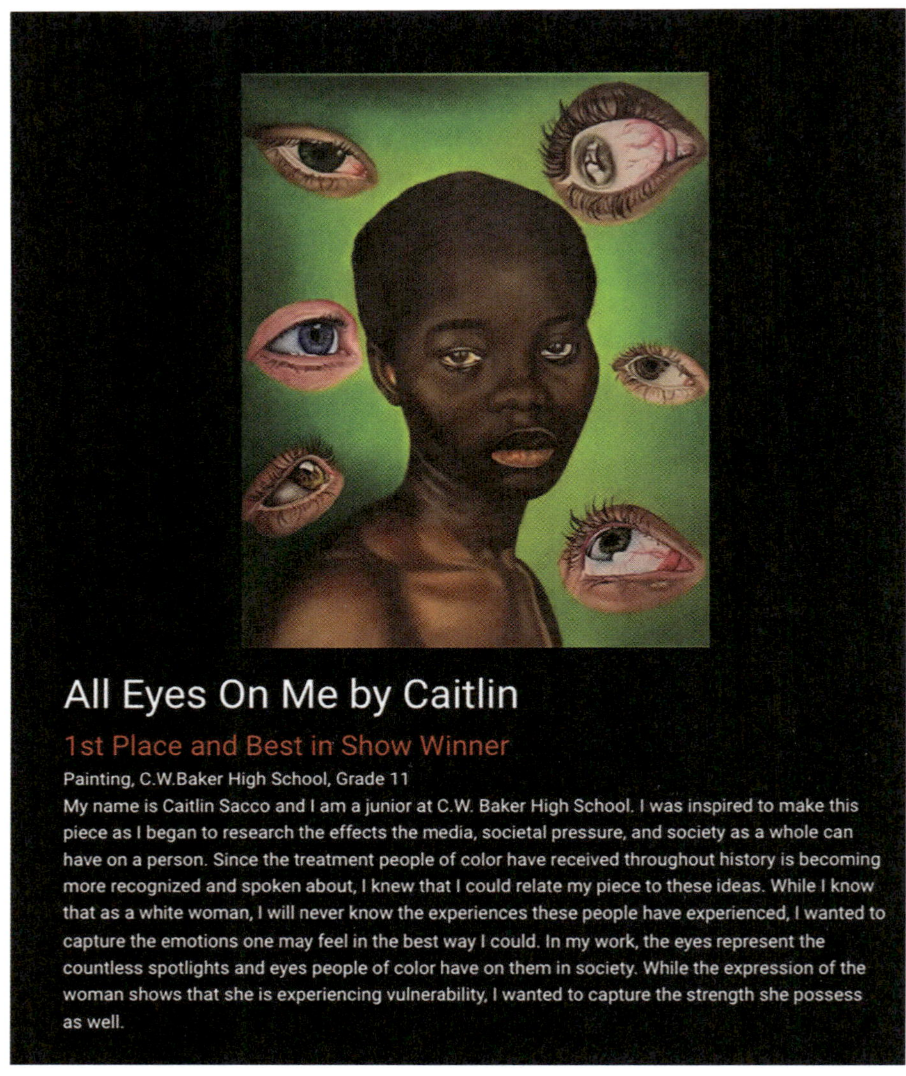

Caitlin Sacco. *All Eyes On Me*. 2021. Acrylic. Photo by Tanisha Jackson.

countless spotlights and eyes people of color have on them in society. While the expression of the woman shows that she is experiencing vulnerability, I wanted to capture the strength she possesses as well.[14]

Caitlin's painting and artist's statement reveal how art can be a tool for developing empathy and intellectual curiosity among those outside the African diaspora so they can investigate institutional racism and perhaps their own implicit bias. Moreover, Black art ecosystems such as the Community Folk Art

Center and the annual Competitive Teenage Art Show Exhibit have provided a platform for diverse groups to share ideas and artistic skills with a much larger community that also values socially engaged art and community engagement.

Since the Competitive Teenage Art Show in 2020, the Community Folk Art Center has hosted many other in-house gallery and online gallery exhibitions that have expanded its audience beyond the Central New York region. Since public spaces have reopened, we have had a few years to reflect on our experiences during the COVID-19 pandemic and adapt to a new normal. Once a systematic approach to implementing good public health measures was established as guided by the Centers for Disease Control and Prevention (CDC), in fall 2021, CFAC opened its doors first to the Syracuse University community and later, to the community at large. During the 2021–22 academic year, the Creative Arts Academy was able to operate as an in-person program, except now temperatures were taken at the door and recorded, and students, teachers, and staff all wore masks. It was also during this time that a surge of local, regional, and federal grants, along with foundation grants, created opportunities for artists and arts institutions to apply for funding that addressed the economic devastation of the pandemic on the creative arts sector. One foundation, the Central New York Community Foundation (CNYCF), established the Black Equity and Excellence Fund. This initiative committed to investing at least 1 million dollars over several years to support Black-led nonprofit organizations and projects that counteract systemic racism.[15] Seeing the need to increase support for the Creative Arts Academy and the center's strategic approach to expanding our footprint through technology, I wrote and submitted a grant application to CNYCF. The Community Folk Art Center was one of many inaugural recipients of a grant of twenty thousand dollars. With it I developed digital storytelling projects that amplified the voices of African diaspora artists. I was not the only one thinking about amplifying artists' voices. Another organization, Sankofa's N.E.S.T. Project, along with the Syracuse artist Vanessa Johnson, would later receive funding to support a project that involved the storytelling of young people in the Syracuse community.[16]

Unwrapping Vanessa Johnson: Socially Engaged Art through Fiber Arts and Storytelling

Vanessa Johnson is a teaching artist at the Community Folk Art Center. Before exploring the details of her partnership with the organization, it is important to introduce her legacy in the Syracuse community. Johnson is known as Syracuse's griot, a storyteller, writer, actor, and visual artist who works with fiber arts and everyday objects to create story quilts. She uses African-influenced iconography, patterns, colors, and symbols to tell new and old stories of the

African diaspora experience in general as well as personal and regional Black history, for example, the impact of Harriet Tubman, who eventually settled in Auburn, New York, a town not far from Syracuse and where the Tubman Home is located.[17] Her relationship to CFAC is important to understanding her journey as an artist. On her website in the visual art section, Johnson posted a fiber artwork titled *Mentor Series 3* from her 2017 solo exhibition *Unwrapping Vanessa: Fiber Memory Art by Vanessa Johnson* at Art Rage Gallery, another local gallery in Syracuse. Below the image is a poem she wrote honoring women visual artists such as the Women of the Beauchamp Library Sankofa Piecemakers Quilting Circle and two past CFAC directors, Megan White and Lauren Austin, who helped her to find her voice as an artist. Johnson writes:

> As Directors of the Community Folk Art [Center], Megan and Lauren created a place for women to gather on Saturday mornings and birth art, sometimes under opposition from those who wanted to control women's expressions. It was there I created my first art pieces. And as a member of the Sankofa Piecemakers, Lauren taught me to find my own voice in the Quilt World . . . to break all the rules![18]

A play on words, the group's name suggests that through quilting and piecing together fabric, they can cultivate peace and facilitate other forms of wellness through art and by gathering or association. This collective also is a continuum of a prominent tradition of both Black and white women's quilting bees in the United States, where women and girls in families or large communities came together to create quilts that celebrated life events such as weddings, births, and other milestones experienced in their respective communities.[19]

Like past CFAC directors, I met Johnson not long after assuming my role as CFAC's executive director, and I learned about her work in the community. Johnson has a history of exhibiting in culturally diverse art spaces throughout the Central New York region. She also is part of the National League of American Pen Women in Central New York, which is the oldest women's arts organization in the country.[20] Through visual art and the exploration of some of Johnson's uploaded video performances, in which she impersonates historical Black history makers, I instantly understood the value that she would bring to CFAC as a teaching artist.

Through conversation, I learned that Johnson worked for many years with organizations throughout the city to facilitate and sometimes administrate youth programming. Johnson also led a travel-abroad project for community members to visit Ghana, West Africa. It is evident that the trajectory of her life's work is anchored in facilitating wellness and centering women and girls through art. In her artist's statement for *Unwrapping Vanessa Johnson*, Johnson explains:

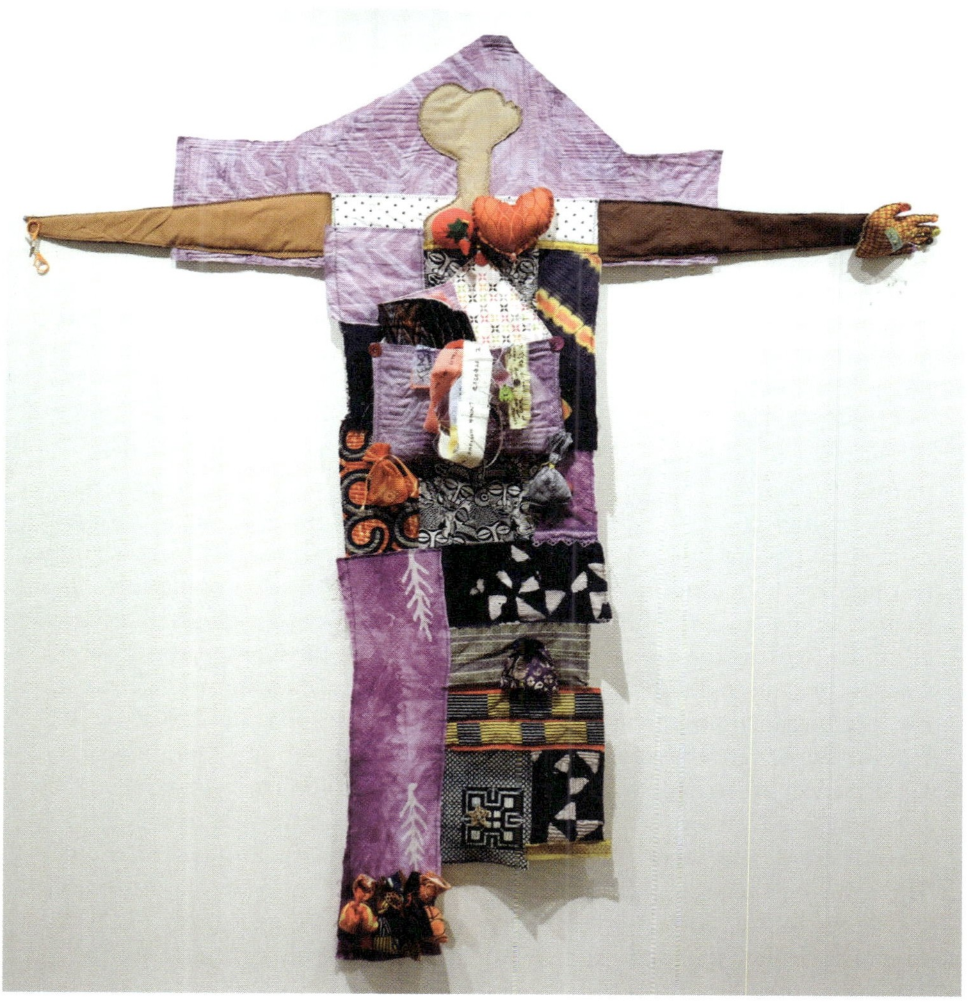

Vanessa Johnson. *Mentor Series 3*. 2017. Mixed-media quilt. From the exhibition *Unwrapping Vanessa Johnson*. Courtesy of the artist.

I am a quilt of all the Women and Girls that I have met on my life journey, the telling of their struggles, triumphs, and defeats. I learned who I was through their testimonies and used their stories to develop how I fought my own battles in creating an Identity as a Woman of African Descent living in the United States. These stories shaped my definition of Social Justice and influenced my own activism. Without these Voices, these Stories, I would not be who I am today.[21]

Johnson's self-reflection highlights the collaborative yet deeply personal nature of her art. Through her extensive involvement with women's groups, she collects and retells women's stories through performance, writing, and visual art, celebrating the strength and vulnerability of her community. For Black women, her role as a griot is crucial, as she breathes life into stories that are often marginalized or erased. As a curator, I was intrigued by the idea of showcasing her visual artwork in a solo exhibition at CFAC's gallery. As our discussions about her partnership with CFAC progressed, it became evident that Vanessa Johnson is a contemporary Black woman artist functioning as a wellness worker in our shared community. This led me to propose a community-based arts project to Johnson, aimed at introducing storytelling and material culture to breast cancer survivors in Syracuse.

October is Breast Cancer Awareness month in the United States. In 2021, it had been two months shy of a year since I lost my grandmother to the disease. Previously, I had never been personally affected by breast cancer, but by December 2020, the disease would take one of the most important and influential people in my life. A self-confessed "grandma's girl," I was going through my own emotional healing, and I wanted to use my platform as a creative and as an arts administrator to support survivors and others who are currently fighting the disease. On October 16, 2021, the Community Folk Art Center hosted a doll-making workshop led by Vanessa Johnson. We invited the local organization Shades of Inspiration, a nonprofit established in 2012 by nine breast cancer survivors who met in a support group. Members of the organization initially gathered together because it was their experience that African American women and other minorities had no one to talk to and ask questions outside of the incredible support of their family and friends. These women recognized the power of association, and the comfort from and necessity for women breast cancer survivors of color to gather in a safe space where they could share their experiences and support one another. As part of its mission, Shades of Inspiration provides "individual, family and group support. We are also here to listen; encourage and help you navigate the medical process. . . . The ladies felt if there was a support group of women that women could relate to their journey through breast cancer it would be easier and less stressful on the person, their caregivers, family, and friends." The doll-making workshop took place in CFAC's gallery, which was decorated in pink, including an arch of pink balloons, and a catered lunch. The participants were asked to come with a story that centered on wellness and to bring small memorabilia items that would help personalize and tell the story of their wellness journey. Before the participants engaged in the workshop, I greeted them and introduced them to the BREATHE model to give them context about how their organization demonstrated all the principles and facilitated wellness throughout the community.[22] CFAC also donated a check for the organization to continue their work of supporting others throughout the community. Specifically, "One of the unique and thoughtful touches [Shades of Inspiration] provide is the 'Lady in Pink Bags.' These specially curated bags are filled with items that help provide comfort and convenience. Inside, you'll find a range of essentials including Bibles, journals, hand sanitizer, lotion, tissues, socks, and neck pillows—everything to make you feel at ease. This meaningful gesture is just one of the ways [they] try to make a positive impact."[23] It was empowering to hear many of the women voluntarily share their stories of finding out they had cancer and their journey toward emotional and physical healing as survivors. They also shared that some members along the way lost their fight with the disease; the memories of their comrades propel the organization to continue working in the community. These stories made a nice transition as I facilitated a brief writing exercise that asked for the women to think of a short story they wanted to write on the cloth dolls they would soon make. For clarity, Vanessa Johnson introduced the idea of having participants reflect and tell their stories of wellness through the making of a flat story doll. The goal was for the women to celebrate health and wellness and to create artwork that highlights the significance of breast cancer awareness, screenings, and support. I titled the workshop *MeTelling Dolls: Telling Our Stories about Wellness through Art*. Johnson had stationed tables with fabric, sewing machines, buttons, yarn, and an array of other art material that the women used to create their dolls.

Traditionally, dolls are toys given to children, particularly girls, so that they can practice caregiving and become socialized into motherhood. We wanted to connect the idea of creating a doll that represents the self metaphorically and caring for it to the advocating for women diagnosed with breast cancer and breast cancer survivors taking care of themselves. The MeTelling Doll workshop was met with enthusiasm because it centered Black women's wellness, along with that of other women of color, through art making. In the fall of 2021 Johnson also began her tenure as a teaching artist at the Creative Arts Academy. As an organization we were excited to order fiber art supplies and use the new sewing machines that we purchased at the beginning of the pandemic for the Griot Guides project.

Sankofa's N.E.S.T. is a 501c3 nonprofit and community-based organization (CBO) whose mission is to "energize urbanites to survive and thrive in urban core neighborhood environments."[24] During the second cycle of the CNYCF Black Equity & Excellence Fund, the organization was awarded a CNYCF Black Equity & Excellence Fund grant during 2020 for a project titled Griot Guides. When the award was publicly announced, teaching artist Vanessa Johnson explained on her Facebook post how this project, geared toward ten- to fourteen-year-old Black Syracuse youth, offered the following pathway toward wellness:

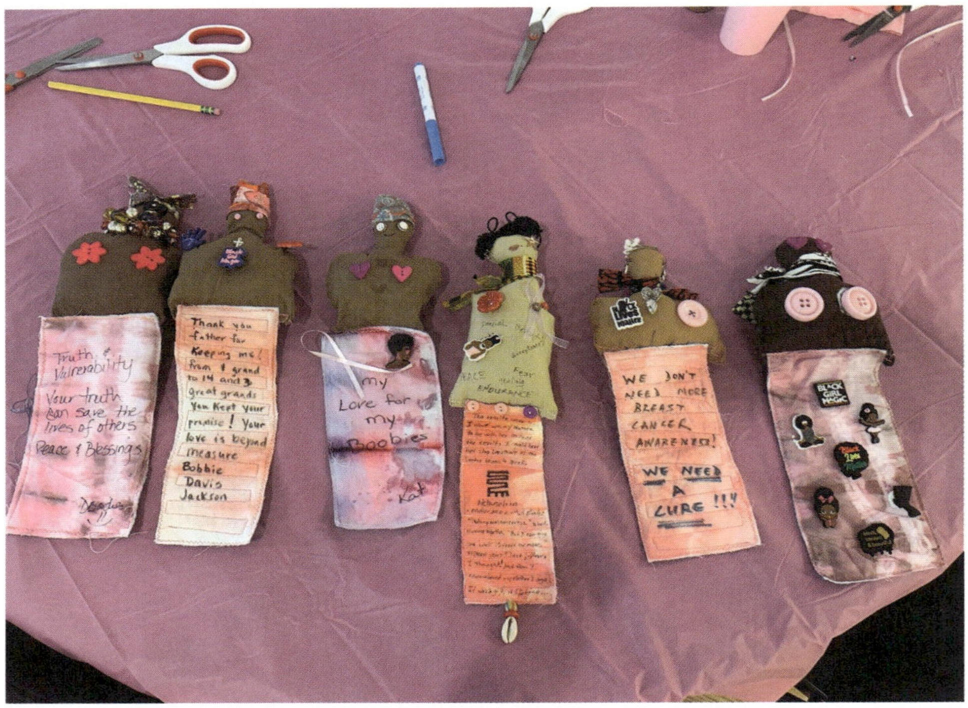

MeTelling dolls made at the Community Folk Art Center, Syracuse, NY, for Breast Cancer Awareness Month. October 2021. Mixed media quilt. Photo by Tanisha Jackson.

"GRIOT GUIDES" will collect and tell the stories of Black Syracuse's Past and Present. They will become the Griots of Syracuse's Black Community! The program fosters personal agency, self knowledge, self confidence, and creative self expression. Youth will explore African-American History and Black Literature, Interview Black Syracuse residents, gather local Oral Histories, and Document their family stories of courage and excellence—and then perform and TELL them![25]

The Community Folk Art Center became a collaborative partner in the Griot Guides Project when the project's lead artist, Vanessa Johnson, asked if she could introduce the curriculum in the Creative Arts Academy. I was excited about the potential outcomes of this partnership and for students in the Creative Arts Academy to merge visual art with literacy. Within the span of an academic year, the Griot Guides met several times a week to share historic, cultural and social justice stories of their families, city, and country. I asked Johnson why she called the participants Griot Guides. She explained that traditionally the griots of societies would pass down the art of storytelling and stories to their children, adding to the continuum of the griot society. However, Johnson does not have biological children; she considers the children whom she teaches the art of storytelling as her legacy and future griots. Part of the curriculum of the program is to teach students how to analyze the themes of their stories through the lens of Black history. From this instruction, the young griots created artwork and wrote stories that they performed in a closing ceremony and ultimately published in a book of short stories, *High-Flown Words: Griot Guide Youth Storytelling Created during the COVID Pandemic.*[26]

Johnson introduced the young griots to the work of Faith Ringgold, especially her picture book *Tar Beach.*[27] As mentioned earlier, Ringgold was one of the cofounders of Where We At and was an influential artist since the Black Power Movement and Women's Rights Movement. Ringgold was particularly known for her art quilts, which often reflected political commentary as well as the Harlem, New York, community where she grew up. Set in Harlem in 1939, *Tar Beach* details the life of an eight-year-old Black girl named Cassie who, like many in the city, went to the rooftop of her building with her family for leisure and relaxation; thus the name of the space is Tar Beach. Cassie's dream was to go wherever she wanted to go; her dream comes true with the help of the stars that help her to fly across the sky over the rooftops of the city.[28] Introducing the Griot Guides participants to Ringgold's work was very timely; the book was quite accessible to its demographic of learners.

In addition to reading the story, students also learned about Ringgold's quilt work and how to make their own quilts using traditional quilt patterns from African American traditions or mixed-media collages with paper and other materials. Like Cassie in *Tar Beach*, Johnson's Griot Guides were asked to expand their imaginations and create visual and written stories in response to the question, "If you could fly anywhere in the Universe, where would you go?"[29] This question and the art project that the Griot Guides were asked to complete were "situated in a truly poignant era of the COVID pandemic's isolation and restriction of movement."[30] The Griot Guides workshops mirror Johnson's art-making process. In addition to observing her work in community-based arts, I became curious about how Johnson might use art to facilitate wellness for herself. Near the end of the Griot Guides workshops, I invited Johnson to a sit-down interview to talk about her art-making process and her earliest memories of creating art.

Johnson remembered that her choice to become an artist developed gradually. Her first art form was that of storyteller. In fact, Johnson still sees herself as someone who uses visual art to tell stories. On deeper reflection, Johnson remembered that she began drawing at an early age, only to hit a turning point in life that would cause her to stop drawing in the third grade. The artist shared the memory of a friend of hers in class who exclusively received recognition for being a talented visual artist. This Caucasian girl got all the praise for her work. The rest of the students, including Johnson, were doing good work but still did not receive recognition or praise. Johnson recalls, "I can remember thinking I wasn't good enough, and I stopped drawing."[31]

Johnson's experience of not being validated as an artist was compounded by another painful experience with art. When Johnson and her family moved from the inner city of Syracuse, New York, to the suburbs of Camillus, New York, she was met with the experience of being one of only two Black children in her school; the other Black child was her brother. There she recalled being constantly called "nigger" and harassed and made fun of. Although Johnson did not hate being Black, she was affected by the racism and mockery to the point that she tried to disappear and not be seen. For example, when she was given the assignment to draw a self-portrait, she avoided doing so. When her parents came to school for parents' night, all the other self-portraits were up except hers. This prompted Johnson's mother to talk to her about her feelings about the art assignment. Johnson recalls, "It wasn't so much me hating being Black. I've never hated being Black, but it was not wanting to stand differently and to use that brown crayon to color me in. When it became about my brownness, creating art became a weapon and so I didn't do it, and I didn't do art unless it was in our class, and I had to do it. I did the minimum."[32] Consequently, the last school art class Johnson took was in high school, where she was able to make choices about the classes she could take. In fact, Johnson didn't take art until her senior year, and that was a handicrafts art class where she learned needlepoint, crochet, and other hand arts. Without calling it art, Johnson always made gifts for family and friends. Regarding storytelling, she recalled that her father's family were big storytellers who would tell stories at family reunions and gatherings. They even had storytelling tell-offs. Although Johnson herself never participated, she was influenced by her family's storytelling and the preservation of family history.

Johnson's engagement with making visual artwork came in the 1990s, when she got involved with local theater. A friend of Johnson's was producing *The People Could Fly* as a full play and needed a prop master and a prop maker; Johnson committed to the role. She remembers this as her first piece of art making as an adult: "I tie-dyed a whole ocean across the whole stage, the whole full stage. And I created wooden buckets and that kind of stuff. A prop that we couldn't find, that were period pieces, I made. And it was really the first art that I made as an adult, and then I was working on another play."[33] Johnson was supposed to be helping with cutting sound, but she became the costume designer. When an actor dropped out of the play, Johnson ended up acting, assuming the roles of Queenie in *Showboat*, dancing and singing. This experience led to others that Johnson describes as "accidents that happened along the way."[34] These "accidents" brought her to art and to storytelling. Storytelling helped create the visual work that she was doing. Johnson was inspired by

Faith Ringgold to tell the stories of what she was seeing in her life and around her. Accordingly, her earliest forms of storytelling were autobiographical.

I asked Johnson what impact biographical storytelling has had on her establishing wellness and creating visual art. She replied, "It was a way of me healing family history. I'm kind of all over the place but things happen at the same time and there was a transition I was going through in the nineties that brought me to doing artwork." While Johnson was making costumes for a very small play production, a local Syracuse artist named Lori Leonard said that she wanted to learn how to make clothes. Johnson replied, "Yeah, me too." Together they found the quilting group at Beauchamp Library. "And I called her. 'Oh. Let's go.'" First Lori began attending the group; three months later, Johnson finally joined her and began working on what she calls "lottery quilts."[35]

Johnson's lottery quilt was made of old paper lottery tickets. She was inspired by a friend who worked at a corner store. Every Friday when her friend got paid, she would buy twenty, thirty, forty, or fifty dollars' worth of lottery tickets. But she didn't have money to pay for art lessons for her kids or other things. Working from that memory, Johnson made a quilted coat out of old lottery tickets and titled it *A Dollar and a Dream*. The coat has little paper figures that are stamped with the commodities they were traded for. Facing them are the things that African-descended people were historically traded for, and or that they were enslaved to produce, such as cotton, rice, and indigo. Also sewn in the coat are figures facing those figures for drugs and cars and the things that Johnson observed people in her community spending money on. Johnson explained, "We don't have investments in our community, in our stores, and our banks. We rent furniture. You know, it's how we use our money, and for this reason I created the whole background of the quilted coat with lottery tickets."[36] The lottery tickets that Johnson incorporated into her quilted coat are orange, red, black, and green, folded into various shapes. This was the first quilt she ever made.

From there, Johnson was encouraged to exhibit her work in several local shows, and she gained new skills such as paper making. At numerous festivals and arts venues, including Plowshares, Central New York's premiere multicultural crafts fair, Johnson also began selling her work. She also saw an increased demand for her art. This encouraged Johnson to create more art and the exposure also brought on notoriety which led to her first solo exhibition, *Unwrapping Vanessa Johnson,* at Art Rage. Johnson's fiber art has become a visual commentary on local, national, and global phenomena. Often, her work centers on women. For example, Johnson created three quilts that reflect her being divided between Africa and the United States. One quilt showed her mother on one side and Winnie Mandela on the other to represent the strength and tenacity of Black women, who often support Black men, families, and nations at the risk of being maligned and forgotten by the community. Johnson addresses Black women's experiences through various art forms, but quilting is her favorite medium.

Vanessa Johnson developed a love for fabric in her formative years. Her dad owned a furniture upholstery shop, and her mother was a seamstress. Before she even knew how to sew or had any plans for using fabric to make art, she would collect pieces of fabric from her parents' work spaces. To date, Johnson has an extensive collection of fabric. She also does batik on white fabric to create her own designs according to the visual narratives she wants to tell.

As with many of the artists I have interviewed as a curator and researcher, I asked Johnson, "When you create art, who are you creating it for?" And like many if not all, Johnson answered, "Me. It's my stories. It's my life. It's my world."[37] With the hope that other people can relate to the stories she tells, Johnson makes it clear that her oral and visual storytelling are centered around African American history and cultural experiences. She hopes that her art will connect with people emotionally and that people from other racial communities "will gain some information from it too." Regardless, her main goal is to tell our stories. Johnson does this with the understanding that these stories are part of her and part of her community. She states, "I am a part of my community. We all—we are not a monolithic community, so we don't see everything the same. But our stories need to be told. And so that is what I do visually with my work. I tell our stories."[38]

One of the stories that Vanessa Johnson is committed to telling is one in which Black women claim who they are. It took a while for her to call herself an artist, but through the encouragement of other Black women in her community who challenged her to see herself as such, Johnson says, "I have embraced the call on my life of being a griot and artist."[39] Another story that Johnson has been public about is her survival of sexual abuse and the consequent abandonment and disbelief of family members. Over the years, Johnson has created art to heal herself and to retrieve memories of the past that she suppressed as a means of survival.

She credits storytelling and her artwork with making it possible for her to be healthy and not to be silenced. Throughout her art, the artist addresses the pain of abuse and of not being believed, and the silence she believes occurs "especially in Black families; we've been taught to keep our mess in our community and our business at home."[40] Johnson's trauma seemed to be compounded by the fact that she was abused by a family member. However, visually and through storytelling and playwriting, her art has been about her own healing. Reflecting on my previous question—"Who do you create art for?"—the artist expounded, "So when you say who I do it for, it is for me; it is to give my eyes, a voice for myself, so that I am not silent. So, you'll see in the narrative and a lot of my visual artwork that I do have narrative that addresses healing."[41] Some of her latest body of visual artwork is about silence, about not being silenced, not being forced into silence as a community, including the banning of books. Here Johnson extends the conversation of silence beyond her personal experience as a sexual assault survivor and to other ways people are silenced systemically, socially, and politically. She addresses the stifling of educators not allowed to teach about race, or what some politicians erroneously label Critical Race Theory, and other forms of silencing that impinge on people's civil and human rights. Her intentions are "to visually put out in the world through art the words that we're not supposed to say, to give it to you visually, to give it to you narratively, to give it to you through performance."[42] As much as creating art is connected to Johnson's personal healing and wellness, she also believes that her work contributes to collective healing, too.

Johnson feels that she "stands naked in the world." She believes that when she tells her stories, she gives the people who hear them an opportunity to heal. When she first publicly shared narratives about sexual abuse in a one-woman show, Johnson was embraced and hugged by many audience members after the show. Some of them whispered in her ear. "Me too" and "Don't tell anyone" and "That's my story." Their whispers are examples of what happens when one voice, the artist's voice, becomes a voice for many. Despite the pain and the nakedness, Johnson feels that in her visual artwork and in her storytelling, "it's a responsibility to other women of all colors and particularly Black women, and to my community to stand in that nakedness."[43] Within BWAEs, this artist cultivates socioenvironmental wellness opportunities for others not only to heal but also to give them permission to tell their stories. When I reflect on the trajectory of Vanessa Johnson's work and how she engages the community to help her create art and tell stories as a collective, I am reminded of other artists working with textiles and mixed media to bring personal and collective healing through art. This act of community-based art sometimes creates unique opportunities for site-specific installations that democratize and empower voices that are not always heard through such visual language.

Delving into the narrative of my own experiences, shaped by multifaceted roles within academia and cultural curation, is a conduit for understanding the symbiotic relationship between individual growth and the collective educational well-being of the community. This nuanced exploration traverses the intersections of scholarship, curation, and executive leadership within the realm of Black studies, offering insights into how these roles contribute synergistically to educational wellness. Commitment to community-based arts emerges as a central tenet, emphasizing not only the impact on individual participants but also the transformative influence on the broader community. By leveraging artistic and educational initiatives, this approach recognizes the potential for art to be a catalyst for learning and to foster intellectual curiosity, cultural understanding, and a sense of belonging among diverse community members. In essence, the alignment with community-based arts illuminates the profound role of socioenvironmental wellness within the broader framework of artistic engagement. This narrative thread underscores the interconnectedness between the artist's personal journey and broader BWAEs, emphasizing the reciprocal relationship between individual enrichment and the collective educational vitality fostered by community-based arts.

Conclusion

The preface of this book begins with my personal story of healing and cultivating wellness through art making. That experience taught me patience and how to connect to who I was at my core, a creative. It provided a sense of normality and a space to prove that I was in fact healing: if I could draw and paint, then the temporary trauma I experienced could be decentralized within my life's narrative and counted as one of many turning points. That previous experience of healing, along with my current responsibilities of teaching Black studies and leading an African diaspora arts center, is the nexus of how I see some Black women artists as wellness workers within Black Women's Art Ecosystems. Ours is an important role in society that has not been comprehensively explored and is the reason I wrote this book.

Black Women's Art Ecosystems systematically aligns with the six ecological principles mentioned in the introduction, culminating in a nuanced exploration of the pivotal role played by Black women artists as wellness workers within the realm of BWAEs. This comprehensive narrative unfolds across chapters, strategically organized to delve into various dimensions of wellness within the artistic community. Chapters 1 and 2 lay the groundwork by examining the historical significance of Black women's artist collectives such as Where We At, participants in the House/Full of Blackwomen project, and the evolution of African American art galleries and museums such as the Ekundayo Gallery and The Colored Girls Museum. These chapters elucidate the systemic barriers faced by Black women artists, emphasizing the importance of collective empowerment and curated spaces in fostering environmental wellness within BWAEs.

In the culmination of this exploration into the transformative power of Black women artists within their respective ecosystems, a resounding theme emerges—the profound impact on wellness, community, and cultural narratives. vanessa german's Love Front Porch and The ArtHouse exemplify the malleability of spaces, showcasing the adaptability required for wellness work that spans transient and permanent domains. Through her endeavors, german provides a blueprint for Black women artists not only to organize and be resources for their communities but also to amplify marginalized voices, sparking awareness and dialogue through visual and performative narratives.

As we traverse the chapters, the continuum of Black women artists as wellness workers unfolds, harking back to the legacies of Augusta Savage and Elizabeth Catlett. In navigating the complexities of contemporary movements, vanessa german and Lava Thomas are catalysts for cultural transformation, resonating with both the Black community and mainstream institutions. Their work explores memorial art as a vehicle for mourning, empowerment, and healing, aligning with the cyclical nature of creativity in ecological systems. Thomas and german use their work to advocate for social justice and contribute to transformative healing.

Lavett Ballard steps into this continuum, positioning herself at the intersection of individual wellness and artistic flourishing. Her impact delves into the broader context of Black women artists reshaping communities, transforming perspectives, and influencing the political landscape. This analysis emphasizes the interconnectedness of individual well-being with the vibrancy of the collective artistic community, aligning with the ecological principles of biodiversity and intersectionality.

Delita Martin and Shanequa Gay, with their commitment to nurturing cultural and spiritual wellness, move beyond visual aesthetics. Their art becomes a conduit for exploring identity, heritage, and spirituality, fostering shared experiences that contribute to the well-being of individuals and communities alike. These symbiotic roles between artists as cultural stewards and spiritual facilitators resonates with the interconnectedness and collaboration principles.

The photographic realms of Tawny Chatmon and Tokie Rome-Taylor delve into generational wellness and ancestral memory. Through intricate embellishments and the deliberate interplay of materials, these artists transcend mere representation, offering a timeless testament to the enduring vitality of generational wellness and the power of ancestral memory. Their art is a bridge between past, present, and future, creating a narrative thread that weaves through generations, fostering a profound sense of identity and well-being within the community. This exploration of ancestral memory becomes a transformative act, connecting individuals to their roots and contributing to a collective sense of resilience and cultural richness.

The abstract artists Dianne Smith and Amber Robles-Gordon draw attention to the transnational characteristics of Black women's art ecosystems. Their work not only challenges viewers to seek understanding beyond recognizable narratives but also cultivates opportunities for healing and storytelling within the community. These abstract artists contribute to cognitive wellness within BWAEs. The examination of nonrepresentational forms and expressions aligns with the cyclical nature of creativity, fostering mental well-being within the community.

In revisiting my autobiographical narrative, I interweave my personal journey as I occupy roles as a Black studies professor, curator, and executive director at the Community Folk Art Center. This journey forms a tapestry that threads through the socioenvironmental wellness of both individual participants and community leaders such as artist Vanessa Johnson and the broader community. Such an exploration aligns with the foundational principle of community-based arts and underscores their instrumental role in fostering wellness.

Relevance to Scholarship on Black Women and Wellness

Taking into consideration the narratives presented, *Black Women's Art Ecosystems* resonates deeply with the scholarship on Black women and wellness, offering a unique and vital contribution to the discourse surrounding the intersection of art, identity, and holistic well-being. This book matters for several reasons, providing insights and perspectives that enrich existing scholarship and contribute to the broader understanding of Black women's experiences in the realms of art and health. First, the book's exploration of Black women artists as wellness workers within BWAEs expands the existing literature on the multifaceted dimensions of wellness. It moves beyond traditional discussions of physical health to emphasize the interconnectedness of physical, emotional, and creative well-being. By acknowledging the nuanced ways in which Black women artists contribute to the wellness of both individuals and communities, this book adds a layer of complexity to the scholarly understanding of wellness in the context of Black women's lives.

Second, this book's engagement with ecological principles and their application to BWAEs offers a novel theoretical framework for examining the intricate relationships within artistic communities. This framework not only enriches discussions in the field of art studies but also contributes to interdisciplinary conversations on the intersections of ecology, identity, and cultural production. By drawing parallels between ecological principles and the dynamics of artistic ecosystems, this book provides a fresh perspective with implications for scholars in fields ranging from art history to environmental studies.

Furthermore, *Black Women's Art Ecosystems* matters because it amplifies the voices and experiences of Black women artists, who have often been marginalized or overlooked in mainstream narratives. The emphasis on community-based arts, memorial art, abstract art, and other forms of artistic expression within BWAEs reclaims and celebrates the agency of Black women in shaping their narratives and fostering wellness. This contribution is significant in challenging historical underrepresentation and promoting a more inclusive understanding of the diverse ways in which Black women contribute to wellness through their artistic endeavors.

This book addresses a critical gap in the scholarship by highlighting the role of Black women artists in nurturing wellness within their communities. It invites scholars, practitioners, and enthusiasts alike to reconsider the value of art not just as a form of aesthetic expression but as a transformative force that influences the well-being of individuals and society at large. This shift in perspective is particularly relevant, given the increasing recognition of the importance of holistic approaches to health and wellness.

Innovation and Advancement in the Field of Black Studies

Black Women's Art Ecosystems also stands as a groundbreaking contribution to the field of Black Studies, extending the boundaries of traditional scholarship and innovatively advancing the discourse. This book transcends conventional frameworks within Black studies by providing a nuanced exploration of the intersections among art, wellness, and Black women's experiences.

Black Women's Art Ecosystems departs from traditional disciplinary silos within Black Studies by integrating art education, art history, ecology, and wellness studies. Its interdisciplinary approach recognizes the complexity of Black women's experiences and offers a more holistic understanding of their contributions to both the artistic and wellness realms.

This innovative integration of diverse fields within Black studies sets a precedent for future scholarship that embraces intersectionality and multidimensional analyses. By applying ecological principles to the study of BWAEs, the manuscript introduces ecofeminist perspectives into the realm of Black studies. This innovative framework facilitates a deeper exploration of the interconnectedness among environmental health, social justice, and Black women's artistic expressions. It invites scholars in Black studies to engage with environmental discourses, fostering a more comprehensive understanding of the ways in which Black women contribute to and are affected by broader ecological contexts.

Black Women's Art Ecosystems redefines agency within the context of these ecosystems, challenging traditional notions of empowerment and representation. Through the lens of wellness work, this book underscores how Black women artists actively shape their narratives, create supportive communities, and contribute to the well-being of individuals and collectives. This redefinition of agency expands the scope of Black studies by emphasizing the dynamic and transformative power embedded in artistic practices and community-building efforts.

Traditionally, Black studies has grappled with issues of representation and visibility in academic discourse. This book takes an approach that not only acknowledges the diverse contributions of Black women to the field but also positions their experiences as crucial to the broader discourse within Black studies. *Black Women's Art Ecosystems* introduces innovative methods, particularly in its examination of Black women artists as wellness workers. Interviews, curatorial analyses, and an ecological framework showcases a diversity that challenges traditional research approaches. I hope it will be an inspiration for scholars within and beyond Black studies, encouraging a more expansive toolkit for researching and documenting Black women's experiences.

Implications for Future Research

Black Women's Art Ecosystems not only illuminates the multifaceted roles of Black women artists as wellness workers within art ecosystems but also points to areas where further exploration and research are warranted. Identifying these gaps in the existing literature opens avenues for future scholarship, providing a roadmap for continued inquiry into the complex intersection of art, wellness, and Black women's experiences. The existing literature often centers on the intersectionality of gender and race. Future scholarship should expand this scope to include a more nuanced examination of intersecting identities, such as sexuality, ability, and socioeconomic status. Exploring how these aspects intersect with gender and race in the context of wellness work will offer a more comprehensive understanding of the diverse experiences within BWAEs.

Black Women's Art Ecosystems primarily focuses on the experiences of Black women artists in the United States. Future scholarship should incorporate global perspectives, examining how Black women artists engage in wellness work in different cultural, social, and political contexts. This wider lens will contribute to a more inclusive and expansive understanding of Black women's contributions to art ecosystems on a global scale. Whereas this book emphasizes the importance of wellness work, future research could assess the tangible impacts of wellness initiatives begun by Black women artists. Understanding how these initiatives affect individuals, communities, and the broader art ecosystem longitudinally will provide valuable insights into the efficacy and transformative potential of such endeavors.

This book briefly touches on the impact of technology on art exhibitions, particularly in the context of the global COVID-19 pandemic. Future scholarship could explore how Black women artists navigate digital and virtual spaces, examining the implications for wellness work, community building, and the accessibility of art. This area gains significance as technology continues to shape the landscape of artistic expression.

Black Women's Art Ecosystems examines community-based arts in the context of education. Future research could specifically explore the educational initiatives undertaken by Black women artists within art ecosystems. This could include examining mentorship programs, art education projects, and initiatives aimed at fostering the next generation of Black women artists. In addressing these gaps, future scholarship has the potential to further enrich our understanding of the intricate relationships among Black women, art, and wellness. Through continued exploration and inquiry, the scholarly landscape surrounding BWAEs can evolve, becoming more inclusive, dynamic, and reflective of the diverse experiences within this vibrant community.

The labor of the Black women artists discussed in this book is a continuum of the overall legacy of Black women's labor, as their work addresses issues that affect their daily lives. Black women have made profound contributions to the art world throughout history, and their artistic expressions continue to shape and enrich contemporary art. These artists are wellness workers within these ecosystems, employing their creativity to promote healing, empowerment, and social change. These talented individuals challenge systemic inequalities, dismantle stereotypes, and elevate marginalized voices through their artwork. Furthermore, by addressing issues such as race, gender identity, and mental health, they provide vital spaces for dialogue, reflection, and transformation.

Black women artists take an integrative approach to wellness, acknowledging the connection between individual and collective well-being. Their art is a form of self-care that helps individuals navigate and transcend complex experiences while building community and solidarity among Black women and other marginalized groups.

Further, Black women artists actively explore the intersections of art, culture, and activism. Utilizing their platforms as advocates for social justice by amplifying historically silenced voices, their artwork becomes an agent for change by challenging dominant narratives and sparking dialogue around racial and gender equity issues.

Black women artists contribute significantly to community well-being by creating spaces of healing within their local areas through workshops, therapeutic art experiences, or other initiatives designed to encourage healing and resilience. Doing so creates connections, empathy, and personal growth opportunities that contribute to overall wellness in individuals and their local areas.

However, it is essential to recognize the unique challenges Black women artists face in both the art world and the wellness industry. They often face underrepresentation, tokenism, and limited resources, yet remain resilient and determined enough to continue making a significant contribution and creating transformative change in society. It is equally essential to recognize that Black women artists cannot shoulder sole responsibility for addressing societal wellness issues; instead, they should be supported and upheld by institutions, communities, and individuals who recognize their contributions and value them. By creating inclusive spaces, providing resources, amplifying voices, and compensating fairly, they will play an essential role as wellness workers.

Black women artists stand at the forefront of wellness work, employing their creativity, resilience, and lived experiences to foster healing, empowerment, and social transformation. Art provides them with a powerful vehicle for self-expression, community building, and reimagining inclusive and equitable wellness practices; by acknowledging and supporting their work, we can foster a fair understanding of wellness that benefits us all.

Black Women's Art Ecosystems presents the stories of contemporary Black women artists and helps both to reconnect and advance the Black community's overarching aspiration to move beyond a history of subjugation in Western society—particularly in the United States—to a celebratory and sustainable space of survival.

Epilogue

One of the major causes of death
for Black women is obedience.
—Simone Leigh

The introduction of this book began with the story of Sonia Boyce as an example of a Black woman artist cultivating wellness through art. Her historic win was accompanied by that of another Black woman artist, Simone Leigh, who also made history at the Venice Biennale. Simone Leigh was selected to represent the United States at the 59th International Art Exhibition of the Venice Biennale. Leigh was the first Black woman awarded the commission to create art for the US pavilion. She was awarded the Golden Lion for being the best participant in the *Milk of Dreams* exhibition, which featured a 16ft-tall sculpture titled *Brick House* (2019), portraying a Black female figure without eyes, standing at the entrance of the Arsenale exhibition.[1] "Brick House" is also the title of a popular 1977 song by the Commodores. It now is an idiom for a woman with a desirable figure, usually with big breasts and voluptuous curves.

More important, this term describes a woman who is sturdy and well built. Leigh gave her sculpture this title to signal that women, specifically Black women, are "solid and enduring instead of fragile and weak."[2] This narrative is the impetus for how the artist represents Black women in her work relating to their labor and contribution to the community. In the summer of 2022, I encountered Leigh's work up close. It was an experience that inspired a great sense of pride and awe as I marveled at her work's layered and textured characteristics. The large scale of Simone Leigh's sculptures puts her visual narratives right in your face. You can't evade it, and I instantly understood her remark that "Black women are the primary audience of [her] work." I observed what Leigh calls "a process of formal creolization," where she combines domestic vessels, Black women's bodies, and African vernacular architecture to discuss Black women's labor, community, and resistance to the colonial gaze.[3] Leaning on Benin bronzes, as well as early twentieth-century African American sculpture and portraiture of the seventeenth-century Spanish painter Diego

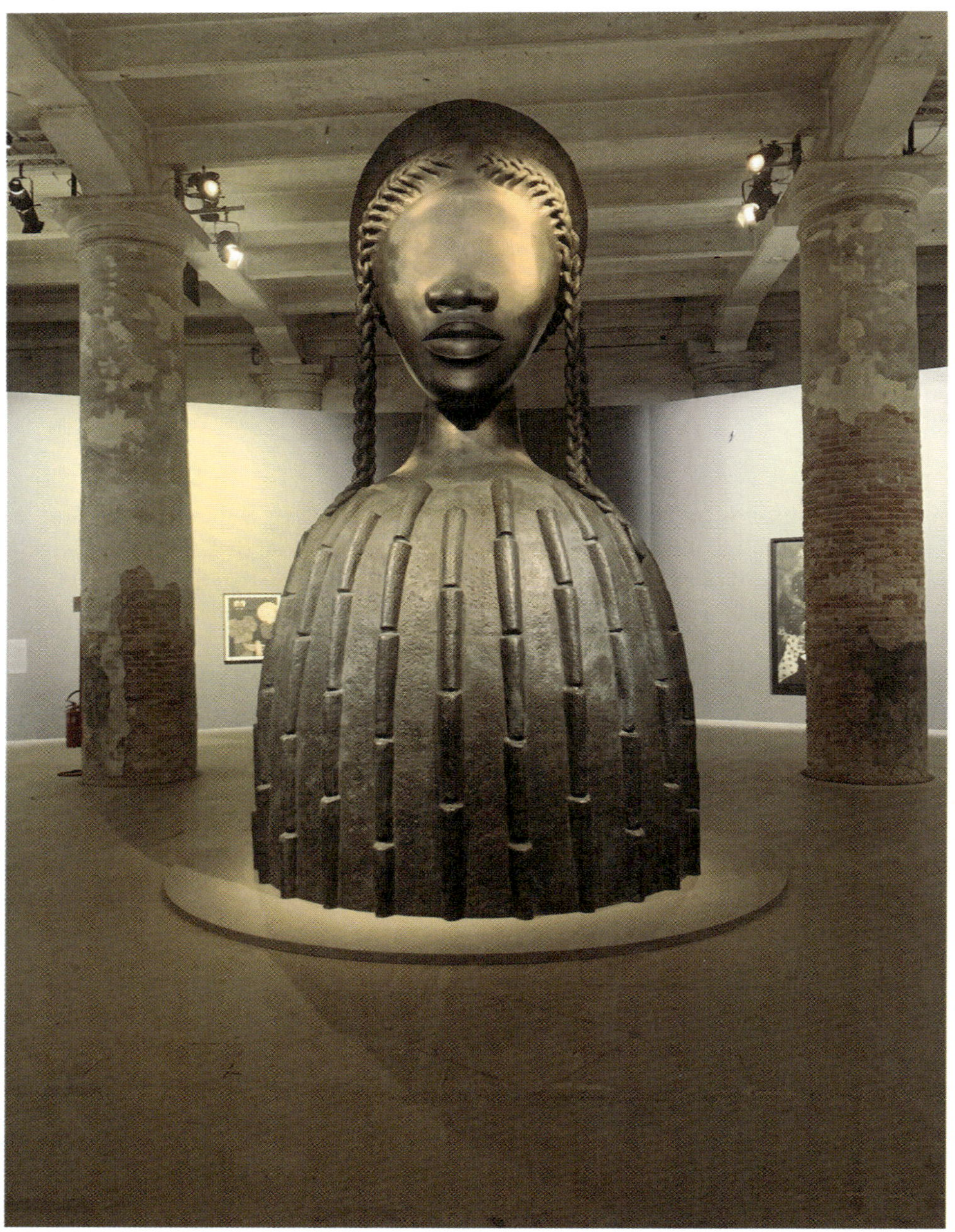

Simone Leigh. *Brick House*. 2019. Bronze, 196 x 114 x 114 inches. Fifty-ninth International Art Exhibition of the Venice Biennale (*The Milk of Dreams*). Photo by Tanisha Jackson. © Simone Leigh, Courtesy Matthew Marks Gallery.

Velázquez, Leigh's creolized forms make plain that the work of Black women's wellness must challenge the racist tropes that confine us while also recognizing the reality of our strength and agency, which has aided our survival, from these narratives.

Connecting history to the present, Leigh converted the exterior of the US pavilion into a hut with a corrugated thatched roof. This transformation recalls the 1931 Paris Colonial Exposition, a contentious exhibition that, even in its time, faced criticism for replicating aspects of African and Asian societies under colonial rule by European countries and was primarily a spectacle for bourgeois audiences.[4] Leigh's exhibition *Sovereignty*, inside the edifice, visually articulates one of the grounding principles of Black power: self-determination. Self-determination is one of the most important strategies for African-descended people's liberation and wellness; Leigh explores this concept through Black female subjectivity. She posits, "To be sovereign is not to be subject to another's authority, another's desires, or another's gaze but rather to be the author of one's history."[5] This highlighting of Black women's agency has been a consistent thread in Leigh's work.

In her Hugo Boss Prize 2018 exhibition, *Loophole of Retreat*, the artist created a body of artwork. She took the title of her exhibition from the writings of a formerly enslaved abolitionist, Harriet Jacobs, who used the term in her 1861 slave narrative to describe a crawl space under the rafters of her grandmother's house. For seven years, Jacobs hid from her enslavers in a crawl space as a form of resistance and agency so she could stay close to her children. Eventually she escaped by ship to the free Northern states. Drawing inspiration from Jacobs's story, Leigh created art that reflects the "long-standing commitment to honoring the agency of Black women and their power to inhabit worlds of their own creation."[6]

Four years before her *Loophole of Retreat*, Leigh was one of four artists commissioned by the Creative Time and Weeksville Heritage Center for a community-based art project called *Funk, God, Jazz, and Medicine: Black Radical Brooklyn*. A walkable, month-long art exhibition, Leigh's contribution was the Free People's Medical Clinic (FPMC), which brought together uniformed nurses, performers, and DJs in the Stuyvesant Mansion in Weeksville. Now within the present Bedford-Stuyvesant neighborhood, Weeksville was founded by James Weeks in 1838 and "was one of the first free [B]lack communities in the nation."[7] Also, Stuyvesant Mansion, where the free clinic took place, was the home of Dr. Josephine English, the first Black female OB-GYN in New York. As with the artists amara tabor-smith and Vashti DuBois, we see Leigh creating opportunities for community-based arts that address community members' health and wellness needs. By virtue of being a Black woman artist, Leigh cultivated a Black women's art ecosystem that not only "paid tribute to the historical legacy of these Black doctors and nurses, but also provided allopathic healing services, yoga and Pilates classes, and free HIV screenings for members of the community."[8] Leigh creates the same BWAEs in many of her exhibitions. In *Sovereignty* and the trajectory of all her artwork, she advances my argument that Black women artists cultivate wellness not only through making art. Through socially engaged art practices, she also strategically addresses and redresses histories that distort Black womanhood. A reflection on Simone Leigh's exhibition at the Venice Biennale brings me to the overall purpose of this book, which is to recognize Black women artists and creatives who are laboring as wellness workers.

Notes

Introduction

1. When referring to people, the words *Black* and *Blackness* will be capitalized as proper nouns to establish empowerment and a shared culture. Jim Beckerman, "To B, or Not to b? Why Capitalize the 'B' in Black?" Northjersey.com, October 13, 2021, https://www.northjersey.com/story/opinion/columnists/2021/10/13/why-capitalize-b-black/5980347001/, retrieved November 22, 2023.

2. Sonia Boyce, "Let frustration fuel inspiration," Daily Inspiration. Inspiring Quotes, https://www.inspiringquotes.com/inspiration/63b48f6c1559f6000930003b?liu=bfb99dadf51e2d85f3443cda78c57e07, retrieved November 21, 2023.

3. "British artist Sonia Boyce's powerful exhibition explores the potential of collaborative play as a route to innovation. Boyce's installation brings together video works featuring five Black female musicians (Poppy Ajudha, Jacqui Dankworth MBE, Sofia Jernberg, Tanita Tikaram and composer Errollyn Wallen CBE) who were invited to improvise, interact and play with their voices." "Explore the 2022 exhibition at the British Pavilion: Feeling Her Way," British Council, 2022, https://venicebiennale.britishcouncil.org/feeling-her-way.

4. Gareth Harris, "Sonia Boyce's British Pavilion Wins Venice Biennale's Coveted Golden Lion for Best National Exhibition," *The Art Newspaper*, April 23, 2022, https://www.theartnewspaper.com/2022/04/23/great-britain-gets-the-coveted-golden-lion-for-best-national-pavilion-in-venice.

5. Harris, "Sonia Boyce."

6. Nadia Khomami, "Sonia Boyce's Venice Biennale winner to be exhibited in UK next year," *The Guardian,* October 26, 2022, https://www.theguardian.com/artanddesign/2022/oct/26/sonia-boyces-venice-biennale-winner-to-be-exhibited-in-uk-next-year.

7. Harris, "Sonia Boyce."

8. National Wellness Institute, "Six Dimensions of Wellness," https://nationalwellness.org/resources/six-dimensions-of-wellness/, accessed July 30, 2020.

9. Black Women's Health Imperative, "An Open Letter on Health Disparities to President Biden, Vice President Harris, and Members of Your National Health Care Team," February 23, 2021, https://bwhi.org/2021/02/23/an-open-letter-on -health-disparities-to-president-biden-vice-president-harris-and-members-of-your -national-health-care-team/.

10. Treva B. Lindsey, *America, Goddam: Violence, Black Women, and the Struggle for Justice* (Berkeley: University of California Press, 2023), 152.

11. Stephanie Y. Evans, Sarita K. Davis, Leslie R. Hinkson, and Deanna J. Wathington, *Black Women and Public Health: Strategies to Name, Locate, and Change Systems of Power* (Albany: State University of New York Press, 2022).

12. World Health Organization, "Determinants of Health," October 4, 2024, https://www.who.int/news-room/questions-and-answers/item/determinants-of -health.

13. Black Women's Health Imperative, https://bwhi.org/.

14. Black Women's Health Imperative.

15. Black Women's Health Imperative.

16. Carmen Braun Williams and Marsha I. Wiggins, "Womanist Spirituality as a Response to the Racism-Sexism Double Bind in African American Women," *Counseling and Values* 54, no. 2 (2010): 175–86, https://doi.org/10.1002/j.2161-007x.2010 .tb00015.x.

17. Williams and Wiggins, "Womanist Spirituality."

18. Williams and Wiggins, "Womanist Spirituality."

19. Janis V. Sanchez-Hucles, "Womanist Therapy with Black Women," in *Womanist and Mujerista Psychologies*, 69–92.

20. Danielle Drake-Burnette, Bravada Garrett-Akinsanya, and Thelma Bryant-Davis, "Womanism, Creativity, and Resistance: Making a Way Out of 'No Way,'" in *Womanist and Mujerista Psychologies*, 173–93.

21. Drake-Burnette, Garrett-Akinsanya, and Bryant-Davis, "Womanism."

22. Shanee Stepakoff, "The Healing Power of Symbolization in the Aftermath of Massive War Atrocities: Examples from Liberian and Sierra Leonean Survivors," *Journal of Humanistic Psychology* 47, no. 3 (2007): 400–12, https://doi.org/10 .1177/0022167807301787.

23. John Bowles, "'Acting Like a Man': Adrian Piper's Mythic Being and Black Feminism in the 1970s," *Signs* 2 (2007): 621–47.

24. Evans, Bell, and Burton, *Black Women's Mental Health*.

25. Evans, Bell, and Burton, *Black Women's Mental Health*.

26. Evans, Bell, and Burton, *Black Women's Mental Health*.

27. Evans, Bell, and Burton, *Black Women's Mental Health*, 6.

28. Evans, Bell, and Burton, *Black Women's Mental Health*.

29. Fritjof Capra, "From the Parts to the Whole: Systems Thinking in Ecology and Education," *The Web of Life* (New York: Anchor Books, 1994).

30. A. G. Tansley, "The Use and Abuse of Vegetational Concepts and Terms," *Ecology: Ecological Society of America* 16, no. 3 (1935): 284–307, https://doi.org/10 .2307/1930070

31. Ecosystem (n.d.). Nationalgeographic.org, https://education.national geographic.org/resource/ecosystem/, retrieved November 21, 2023.

32. Biology Online, "Abiotic Factor." Biology Online Dictionary, https://www
.biologyonline.com/dictionary/abiotic-factor, retrieved November 21, 2023.

33. Nathan Hare, "Black Ecology," *Black Scholar* 1, no. 6 (1970): 2–8, https://
doi.org/10.1080/00064246.1970.11728700.

34. Keelah E. G. Williams, Oliver Sng, and Steven L. Neuberg, "Ecology-
Driven Stereotypes Override Race Stereotypes," *Proceedings of the National Academy of Sciences of the United States of America* 113, no. 2 (2016): 310–15, https://doi
.org/10.1073/pnas.1519401113.

35. Justin Hosbey and J. T. Roane, "A Totally Different Form of Living: On the
Legacies of Displacement and Marronage as Black Ecologies," *Southern Cultures*
27, no. 1 (2021): 68–73, https://doi.org/10.1353/scu.2021.0009.

36. Malcolm Ferdinand and Romy Opperman, "Decolonial Ecologies," In
What Matters Most: Conversations on the Art of Living, ed. Anthony Morgan (Newcastle upon Tyne: Agenda Publishing, 2023), 91–98, https://doi.org/10.2307/jj
.1357297.15.

37. Tiffany Lethabo King, "Racial Ecologies: Black Landscapes in Flux," in *Racial
Ecologies*, ed. Leilani Nishime and Kim D. Hester Williams (Seattle: University of
Washington Press, 2018), 65–75, http://www.jstor.org/stable/j.ctvcwnm95.9.

38. Sacha Jérôme Kagan, "The Practice of Ecological Art," [Plastik], February 15, 2014, https://www.researchgate.net/publication/274719395_The_practice
_of_ecological_art.

39. Ann T. Rosenthal, "Teaching Systems Thinking and Practice through Environmental Art," *Ethics and the Environment* 8, no. 1 (2003): 152–68, https://doi
.org/10.2979/ETE.2003.8.1.152.

40. "Françoise d'Eaubonne's Le Féminisme ou la mort," Environment & Society Portal, https://www.environmentandsociety.org/tools/keywords/francoise
-deaubonnes-le-feminisme-ou-la-mort, accessed January 2, 2024.

41. Lori Gruen and Greta Gaard, "Ecofeminism: Toward Global Justice and
Planetary Health," *Society and Nature* 2, no. 1 (1993): 1–35, https://www.academia
.edu/32438639/Ecofeminism_Toward_Global_Justice_and_Planetary_Health.

42. Ariel Salleh, *Ecofeminism as Politics: Nature, Marx, and the Postmodern* (London: Zed Books, 1997), 12.

43. Alexis K. Karon, "Ecowomanism: A Solution to Climate and Social Injustice," *Theological Investigations*, 2020, https://digitalcommons.augustana.edu/relg
theology/1.

44. Dorceta E. Taylor, "Women of Color, Environmental Justice, and Ecofeminism," in *Ecofeminisim: Women, Culture, Nature,* ed. Karen J. Warren (Bloomington: Indiana University Press, 1997), 38–81; Roger S. Gottlieb, *This Sacred Earth:
Religion, Nature, Environment,* 2nd ed. (New York: Routledge, 2004); Sofía Betancourt, "Between Dishwater and the River: Toward an Ecowomanist Methodology,"
Worldviews: Environment, Culture, Religion 20, no. 1 (2016): 64–75, https://doi.org/
10.1163/15685357-02001006.

45. Melanie L. Harris, "Ecowomanism: An Introduction," *Worldviews* 20, no.
1 (2016): 5–14, https://www.jstor.org/stable/26552243.

46. "What Is Ecosystem–Javatpoint," n.d., www.javatpoint.com, https://www
.javatpoint.com/what-is-ecosystem.

47. Biodiversity BC, sitemap, 2007, http://www.biodiversitybc.org/EN/topnav/31 .html.

48. Ö. Şentürk and K. Özkan, "Calculating Landscape Diversity with Alpha Diversity Indices," *Journal of Environmental Biology* 38, no. 5(SI)(2017): 931–36, https://doi.org/10.22438/jeb/38/5(si)/gm-09.

49. Jouni Paavola, Andrew Gouldson, and Tatiana Kluvánkova-Oravská, "Interplay of Actors, Scales, Frameworks and Regimes in the Governance of Biodiversity," *Environmental Policy and Governance* 19, no. 3 (2009): 148–58, https://doi.org/ 10.1002/eet.505.

50. Komalsingh Rambaree, Stefan Sjöberg, and Päivi Turunen, "Ecosocial Change and Community Resilience: The Case of 'Bönan' in Glocal Transition," *Journal of Community Practice,* 27, no. 3–4 (2019): 231–48, https://doi.org/10.10 80/10705422.2019.1658005.

51. Grazia Brunetta, Rosario Ceravolo, Carlo Alberto Barbieri, et al., "Territorial Resilience: Toward a Proactive Meaning for Spatial Planning," *Sustainability* 11, no. 8 (2019): 2286, https://doi.org/10.3390/su11082286.

52. Chaitanya S. Gokhale, Mariana Velasque, and Jai A. Denton, "Ecological Drivers of Community Cohesion," *mSystems* 8, no. 1 (2023): e0092922, https:// doi.org/10.1128/msystems.00929-22.

53. Somsack Inthasone, Nicolas Pasquier, Andrea G. B. Tettamanzi, and Célia da Costa Pereira, "The BioKET Biodiversity Data Warehouse: Data and Knowledge Integration and Extraction," in *Advances in Intelligent Data Analysis XIII: 13th International Symposium,* IDA 2014, Leuven, Belgium, October 30–November 1, 2014. *Proceedings 13* (Cham, Switzerland: Springer International, 2014), 131–42.

54. Chelsey Walden-Schreiner, Yu-Fai Leung, Tim Kuhn, et al., "Environmental and Managerial Factors Associated with Pack Stock Distribution in High Elevation Meadows: Case Study from Yosemite National Park," *Journal of Environmental Management* 193 (2017): 52–63. https://doi.org/10.1016/j.jenvman.2017.01.076.

55. Alaina Kinol, Elijah Miller, Hannah Axtell, et al., "Climate Justice in Higher Education: A Proposed Paradigm Shift towards a Transformative Role for Colleges and Universities," *Climatic Change* 176, no. 2 (2023), https://doi.org/10.1007/ s10584-023-03486-4.

56. This research study was approved and designated a "Determination of Exemption from Regulations" status on March 18, 2020, by the Institutional Review Board at Syracuse University, IRB# 20-007.

57. Charlie Parker, Sam Scott, and Alistair Geddes, "Snowball Sampling," in *Sage Research Methods Foundations*, ed. Paul Atkinson, Sara Delamont, Alexandru Cernat, Joseph W. Sakshaug, and Richard A. Williams (London: SAGE Publications Ltd., 2019), https://doi.org/10.4135/9781526421036831710.

58. Leo A. Goodman, "Comment: On Respondent-Driven Sampling and Snowball Sampling in Hard-to-Reach Populations and Snowball Sampling Not in Hard-to-Reach Populations," *Sociological Methodology* 41, no. 1 (2011): 347–53, https://doi .org/10.1111/j.1467-9531.2011.01242.x.

59. The participants in this research were furnished with an electronically administered consent form approved by the Institutional Review Board (IRB); they signed the form prior to the commencement of their respective interviews.

60. I used a semistructured interview method combining structured and unstructured elements. This approach involved a set of predetermined questions while also allowing for follow-up inquiries and participant-driven discussions. The interviews were conducted either online via Zoom or in person, according to the location and accessibility of the interviewee.

61. Kay Brown, "The Emergence of Black Women Artists: The Founding of 'Where We At,'" *NKA*, 2011, no. 29 (2011): 118–27, https://doi.org/10.1215/10757163 -1496399.

62. Shelley Esaak, "What Are the Visual Arts?" ThoughtCo, October 1, 2009, https://www.thoughtco.com/what-are-the-visual-arts-182706.

63. Brittney C. Cooper, *Beyond Respectability: The Intellectual Thought of Race Women* (Urbana: University of Illinois Press, 2017), 12.

64. Leigh Raiford, "Photography and the Practices of Critical Black Memory," *History and Theory* 48, no. 4 (2009): 112–29, http://www.jstor.org/stable/25621443.

65. Cheryl Finley, "Visual Legacies of Slavery and Emancipation," *Callaloo* 37, no. 4 (2014): 1023–32, http://www.jstor.org/stable/24265081.

66. Sarah Elizabeth Lewis, "Visual Studies Questionnaire: How Do You Engage with the Visual, and What Is Its Importance in the Twenty-First Century?" *Visual Studies* 36, no. 3 (2021): 223–25.

67. Deborah Willis, "Visualizing Memory: Photographs and the Art of Biography," *American Art* 17, no. 1 (2003): 20–23, http://www.jstor.org/stable/3109414.

68. Deborah Willis, "Carrie Mae Weems: Rehistoricizing Visual Memory," in *Women Mobilizing Memory*, ed. Ayşe Gül Altýnay, María José Contreras, Marianne Hirsch, et al. (New York: Columbia University Press, 2019), 277–84, http://www.jstor .org/stable/10.7312/alti19184.19.

69. Krista A. Thompson, *Shine: The Visual Economy of Light in African Diasporic Aesthetic Practice* (Durham, NC: Duke University Press, 2015).

70. Lisa E. Farrington, *Creating Their Own Image: The History of African-American Women Artists* (Oxford: Oxford University Press, 2005).

71. Nell Irvin Painter, *Old in Art School: A Memoir of Starting Over* (Berkeley: Counterpoint, 2018), 317.

72. Tanisha M. Jackson, "MeTelling: Recovering the Black Female Body," *Visual Culture and Gender* 8 (2013): 48–56, https://vcg.emitto.net/index.php/vcg/article/ view/75/74.

73. Patricia Hill Collins, *Black Feminist Thought* (New York: Routledge, 2000), 69.

74. Collins, "Black Feminist Epistemology," in *Black Feminist Thought*, 267–88.

75. Collins, "Black Feminist Epistemology."

76. Brenda J. Allen, "Feminist Standpoint Theory: A Black Woman's (Re)View of Organizational Socialization," *Communication Studies* 47, no. 4 (1996): 257–71, https://doi.org/10.1080/10510979609368482.

77. Allen, "Feminist Standpoint Theory."

78. Patricia Hill Collins, "Distinguishing Features of Black Feminist Thought," in *Black Feminist Thought* (New York: Routledge, 2000), 26.

79. Uri McMillan, *Embodied Avatars: Genealogies of Black Feminist Art and Performance* (New York: New York University Press, 2015) .

80. Joni Boyd Acuff, "Black Feminist Theory in 21st-Century Art Education Research," *Studies in Art Education* 59, no. 3 (2018): 201–14, https://doi.org/10.1080/00393541.2018.1476953.

81. Thema Bryant-Davis and Lillian Comas-Díaz, "Introduction," in *Womanist and Mujerista Psychologies: Voices of Fire, Acts of Courage* (Washington, DC: American Psychological Association, 2016).

82. Alice Walker, *In Search of Our Mothers' Gardens: Womanist Prose* (San Diego: Harcourt Brace Jovanovich, 1983), xi.

83. EbonyJanice Moore, *All the Black Girls Are Activists: A Fourth Wave Womanist Pursuit of Dreams as Radical Resistance* (New York: Rowhouse Publishing, 2023), xvii.

84. "The term 'site-specific art' was promoted and refined by the Californian artist Robert Irwin, but it was actually first used in the mid-1970s by young sculptors, such as Patricia Johanson, Dennis Oppenheim, and Athena Tacha, who had started executing public commissions for large urban sites." Pritika Chowdhry, "Five Pioneering Site-Specific Artists You Should Know," Pritika Chowdhry Art, November 6, 2021. https://www.pritikachowdhry.com/post/site-specific-art.

85. Allen, "Feminist Standpoint Theory."

86. Raymond Doswell, "Evaluating Educational Value in Museum Exhibitions: Establishing an Evaluation Process for the Negro Leagues Baseball Museum," (EdD dissertation, Kansas State University, 2008), https://krex.k-state.edu/items/f32f207f-d8e1-4e8e-a02e-cbaecb4c1849/full.

87. Amina J. Dickerson, "African American Museums and the New Century: Challenges in Leadership," in *Leadership for the Future: Changing Directorial Roles in American History Museums and Historical Societies; Collected Essays*, ed. Bryant Franklin Tolles, 167–82 (Nashville: American Association for State and Local History, 1991).

88. Centers for Disease Control and Prevention, "About COVID-19," May 11, 2023, https://archive.cdc.gov/#/details?q=About%20COVID-19&start=0&rows=10&url=https://www.cdc.gov/coronavirus/2019-ncov/your-health/about-covid-19.html/, retrieved January 10, 2025.

89. Galerie Myrtis, *Women Heal through Rite and Ritual*, http://galeriemyrtis.net/women-heal-through-rite-and-ritual/, retrieved July 31, 2021.

90. Located in Baltimore, Galerie Myrtis was established in 2006 by Myrtis Bedolla. The gallery has six exhibitions a year and has a national and international presence, showcasing twenty-first-century American art with a focus on African American artists.

91. Myrtis Bedolla, *Women Heal through Rite and Ritual* catalogue (Galerie Myrtis, 2020).

92. Bedolla, *Women Heal through Rite and Ritual*, 7.

93. Bedolla, *Women Heal through Rite and Ritual*, 7.

Chapter 1. Collective Empowerment and Wellness

1. Osman Can Yerebakan, "Dindga McCannon," Artforum, September 29, 2021, https://www.artforum.com/interviews/dindga-mccannon-on-where-we-at-and-the-women-of-the-blues-86788, retrieved September 29, 2021.

2. "Black Power," National Archives, https://www.archives.gov/research/african-americans/black-power, retrieved August 25, 2016.

3. Lisa E. Farrington, *African American Art: A Visual and Cultural History* (New York: Oxford University Press, 2016), 184.

4. Farrington, *African American Art*, 246.

5. Shira Wolfe, *The Life and Legacy of the Spiral Group*, Artland Magazine, November 27, 2020, https://magazine.artland.com/the-life-and-legacy-of-the-spiral-group/.

6. Weusi Artist Collective—Home (n.d.), https://www.weusiartistcollective.gallery/home, accessed January 2, 2024.

7. "Culture Conscious in Chicago," *Negro Digest* 16, no. 10 (1967): 85–87.

8. Catherine Morris and Rujeko Hockley, eds., *We Wanted a Revolution: Black Radical Women, 1965–85; New Perspectives* (Durham, NC: Duke University Press 2018), 27.

9. Morris and Hockley, *We Wanted a Revolution*, 28.

10. *We Wanted a Revolution: Black Radical Women, 1965–85*, Brooklyn Museum, https://www.brooklynmuseum.org/opencollection/exhibitions/3347.

11. *We Wanted a Revolution*.

12. Kay Brown, "'Where We At': Black Women Artists," *Feminist Art Journal* 1, no. 1(1972): 25.

13. Kay Brown, "The Emergence of Black Women Artists: The Founding of 'Where We At,'" *NKA* 2011, no. 29 (2011): 118–27, https://doi.org/10.1215/10757163-1496399.

14. Anna Julia Cooper, *A Voice from the South* (New York: Oxford University Press, 1988), 31.

15. Beverly Guy-Sheftall, "Black Feminist Studies: The Case of Anna Julia Cooper," *African American Review* 43, no. 1 (2009): 11–15, http://www.jstor.org/stable/27802555.

16. Interview with Dindga McCannon, July 9, 2024.

17. Brown, "The Emergence of Black Women Artists," 125.

18. Brown, "The Emergence of Black Women Artists," 125.

19. Brown, "The Emergence of Black Women Artists," 123.

20. The WWA members Dindga McCannon and Kay Brown were also members of the Weusi collective.

21. Brown, "'Where We At': Black Women Artists," 125.

22. Brown, "The Emergence of Black Women Artists," 120.

23. Brown, "'Where We At': Black Women Artists," 25.

24. Brown, "The Emergence of Black Women Artists," 121.

25. Interview with Dindga McCannon, July 9, 2024.

26. Linda Charlton, "'South 40' Tries to Aid Convicts," *New York Times,* April 23, 1972. South Forty Corporation was a nonprofit organization spearheaded by the

former Rhode Island governor William H. Vanderbilt and his wife, Helen, along with working participants. They provided in-prison and out-of-prison educational and rehabilitation programs that were focused on demonstrating that recidivism is not inevitable. The name of the organization is a rural allusion to the plot of land that farmers neglect or get around to last that could be cultivated if properly attended to.

27. Interview with Dindga McCannon, July 9, 2024.

28. Cultural Correspondence (Organization), *We Will Not Be Disappeared! Directory of Arts Activism* (New York: Cultural Correspondence, 1984), http://www.darkmatterarchives.net/wp-content/uploads/2011/12/Directory-of-Arts-Activism.pdf.

29. Cultural Correspondence (Organization), *We Will Not Be Disappeared!* 73.

30. Interview with Dindga McCannon, July 9, 2024.

31. Linda Cousins, *"Where We At" Black Women Artists: A Tapestry of Many Fine Threads*, National Gallery of Art, 1986. https://ia601600.us.archive.org/15/items/where-we-at-exhibit-brochure/Where%20We%20At%20-%20Exhibit%20Brochure_text.pdf.

32. Cousins, *"Where We At" Black Women Artists*, 3.

33. Cousins, *"Where We At" Black Women Artists*, 5.

34. Cousins, *"Where We At" Black Women Artists*, 5, 8.

35. Cousins, *"Where We At" Black Women Artists*, 8.

36. Cousins, *"Where We At" Black Women Artists*, 11.

37. Cousins, *"Where We At" Black Women Artists*, 11.

38. Cousins, *"Where We At" Black Women Artists*, 14.

39. Cousins, *"Where We At" Black Women Artists*, 14.

40. Cousins, *"Where We At" Black Women Artists*, 14.

41. Cousins, *"Where We At" Black Women Artists*, 14.

42. Brown, "The Emergence of Black Women Artists."

43. Stewart Burns, "Living for the Revolution: Black Feminist Organizations, 1968–1980," *Journal of American History* 93, no. 1 (2006): 296–97, https://doi.org/10.2307/4486214.

44. Eve Modzelewski, "Face to Face: Women of Visions Exhibit Revolves around African Mask Theme," *Pittsburgh Post-Gazette,* May 3, 2001, https://www.proquest.com/newspapers/face-women-visions-exhibit-revolves-around/docview/391197159/se-2.

45. Shannon Morris, "Women of Visions Art Exhibit by Black Women," *New Pittsburgh Courier*, September 19, 1998, https://www.proquest.com/newspapers/women-visions-art-exhibit-black/docview/368007889/se-2.

46. Morris, "Women of Visions."

47. "About wov," Women of Visions Inc., https://www.womenofvisionspgh.org/aboutwov, accessed March 9, 2025.

48. This is Ashara Ekundayo's preferred spelling for the word *woman*. Especially in intersectional feminism, the term *womxn* is used, as an alternative spelling to avoid the suggestion of sexism perceived in the spelling sequences *m-a-n* and *m-e-n*, and to include trans women and nonbinary people. Dictionary.com, https://www.dictionary.com/browse/womxn, accessed June 25, 2023.

49. Interview with Ashara Ekundayo, July 8, 2020.

50. "SFAC Apologizes to Lava Thomas for Mishandling Maya Angelou Monument," KQED, August 3, 2020. https://www.kqed.org/arts/13884238/sfac-apologizes -to-lava-thomas-for-mishandling-maya-angelou-monument, accessed January 9, 2022.

51. Interview with Ashara Ekundayo. July 8, 2020.

52. "Our Story," Cite Black Women, https://www.citeblackwomencollective .org/our-story.html, accessed December 5, 2023.

53. Christen A. Smith, "About Us," #CiteASista: Today & Everyday, 2018, Christen https://citeasista.com/about/, accessed February 1, 2017.

54. Ekundayo, personal communication, 2020.

55. The artist amara tabor-smith styles her name all-lowercase. amara tabor-smith, personal communication, 2024.

56. tabor-smith, personal communication.

57. tabor-smith, personal communication.

58. Jacob K. Olupona, "The Study of Yoruba Religious Tradition in Historical Perspective," *Numen* 40, no. 3 (1993): 240–73, https://doi.org/10.1163/ 156852793X00176.

59. tabor-smith, personal communication.

60. "Urban Bush Women is a groundbreaking Black women-led theatrical dance company and social activism ensemble, founded in 1984 by visionary choreographer Jawole Willa Jo Zollar as an engine and an amplifier for the unheard stories of Black Women+. Today, under the artistic leadership of Chanon Judson and Mame Diarra Speis, UBW combines revolutionary performance, deep-healing community engagement, and ancestral knowledge from the African diaspora into a cultural force that is urgent, forward-looking, and essential." "About UBW," n.d., Urban Bush Women, https://www.urbanbushwomen.org/about-ubw, accessed March 10, 2025.

61. tabor-smith, personal communication.

62. tabor-smith, personal communication.

63. tabor-smith, personal communication.

64. tabor-smith, personal communication.

65. tabor-smith, personal communication.

66. tabor-smith, personal communication.

67. House/Full of Blackwomen, Deep Waters Dance Theater, https://www .deepwatersdance.com/housefullofblackwomen, accessed November 27, 2023.

68. tabor-smith, personal communication.

69. This is the terminology used to describe an area where girls are prostituting in the Bay Area community.

70. The Eastside Arts Alliance & Cultural Center is an organization of "Third World artists, cultural workers, and community organizers of color committed to advocating for progressive, systemic social change." https://www.eastsideartsalliance .org.

71. Quoted in Bryant-Davis and Comas-Díaz, "Introduction: Womanist and Mujerista Psychologies," 15.

72. Interview with Ashara Ekundayo, July 8, 2020.

73. "Regina Y. Evans," Shade Movement, n.d., https://www.shademovement .org/regina-evans.

74. "Regina Evans," LaPeña, n.d., https://lapena.org/regina-evans/.

75. House/Full of Blackwomen, Deepwatersdance.com, http://www.deepwaters dance.com/portfolio/housefullofblackwomen-2/, accessed January 10, 2022.

76. House/Full of Blackwomen, http://www.deepwatersdance.com/portfolio/ housefullofblackwomen-2/, accessed January 10, 2022.

77. Amelia Williams, "House/Full of Black Women Delivers 'Rituals' Outside the Confines of a Theater," Local News Matters, August 7, 2020, https://localnewsmatters.org/2020/08/07/house-full-of-blackwomen-delivers -rituals-outside-the-confines-of-a-theater/

78. Williams, "House/Full of Black Women Delivers 'Rituals.'"

79. Neyat Yohannes, "House/Full of Women Present Black Women Dreaming— A Ritual Rest in Oakland," East Bay Express, March 28, 2017, https://eastbayexpress .com/housefull-of-blackwomen-present-black-women-dreaming-a-ritual-rest-in -oakland-2–1/, accessed February 5, 2022.

80. Sarah Burke, "A House Full of Black Women Gets a Week of Rest," KQED Culture cue, March 30, 2017, https://www.kqed.org/arts/12959678/a-house-full -of-black-women-a-week-of-rest.

81. Burke, "A House Full of Black Women Gets a Week of Rest."

Chapter 2. Community Engagement and Environmental Wellness

1. LaTanya Autry and Mike Murawsky, "Museums Are Not Neutral: We Are Stronger Together," *Panorama* 5, no. 2 (2019), https://journalpanorama.org/article/ public-scholarship/museums-are-not-neutral/.

2. *Black Art: In the Absence of Light*, directed by Sam Pollard, HBO Documentary Films and Two Dollars and a Dream, 2020.

3. Yvonne Bynoe, "HBCUs: The First Patrons of African-American Art," Black Art in America, https://www.blackartinamerica.com/blogs/news/hbcus -the-first-patrons-of-african-american-art.

4. David W. Young, "Historic Germantown: New Knowledge in a Very Old Neighborhood," Encyclopedia of Greater Philadelphia, https://philadelphiaencyclopedia .org/essays/historic-germantown-new-knowledge-in-a-very-old-neighborhood-2/, accessed December 22, 2009. Germantown is one of America's most historic neighborhoods, sitting six miles northwest of downtown Philadelphia. It was originally a township established by German settlers in 1683. It also attracted Quakers, Mennonites, Dunkards and other groups looking to live in a religiously tolerant community. In 1688, "four Germantown settlers drafted a protest against slavery within the Dutch-German Quaker community that is considered to be the earliest antislavery document made public by whites in North America. The American Revolution saw one of the largest engagements of the war sprawl over Germantown's streets in 1777." These revolutionary ideas and acts make Germantown a fitting location for TCGM, whose existence alone is also revolutionary.

5. Collins, *Black Feminist Thought*.

6. The 2018 Andrew W. Mellon Foundation, Ithaka S+R, the Association of Art Museum Directors (AAMD) and the American Alliance of Museums (AAM) found that museum employees were more racially homogenous than the US population at large: 72 percent were white and 28 percent people of color, compared with 62 percent and 38 percent in the general population. https://www.theartnewspaper.com/2021/05/25/exclusive-survey-what-progress-have-us-museums-made-on-diversity-after-a-year-of-racial-reckoning.

7. Interview with Vashti Dubois, June 19, 2020.

8. Interview with Vashti Dubois.

9. Interview with Vashti Dubois.

10. Interview with Vashti Dubois.

11. Interview with Vashti Dubois.

12. Collins, *Black Feminist Thought*, 67.

13. Interview with Vashti Dubois.

14. CNN, September 11 Terror Attacks Fast Facts, August 21, 2024, https://www.cnn.com/2013/07/27/us/september-11-anniversary-fast-facts/index.html.

15. Interview with Vashti Dubois.

16. Interview with Vashti Dubois.

17. Interview with Vashti Dubois.

18. Interview with Vashti Dubois.

19. Interview with Vashti Dubois.

20. Cheryl L. Woods-Giscombé, "Superwoman Schema: African American Women's Views on Stress, Strength, and Health," *Qualitative Health Research* 20, no. 5 (2010): 668–83, doi: https://doi.org/10.1177/1049732310361892.

21. Interview with Vashti Dubois.

22. Interview with Vashti Dubois.

23. Interview with Vashti Dubois.

24. "Small Museum of the Month: The Colored Girls Museum," SP Ghost, December 1, 2017, https://spghostcom.wordpress.com/2017/12/01/small-museum-of-the-month-the-colored-girls-museum/, accessed March 10, 2025.

25. Interview with Vashti Dubois.

26. Interview with Vashti Dubois.

27. Federal Bureau of Investigation. "NCIC Missing Person and Unidentified Person Statistics, 2022, https://www.fbi.gov/file-repository/2022-ncic-missing-person-and-unidentified-person-statistics.pdf/view, accessed March 10, 2025.

28. Interview with Vashti Dubois.

29. Jim Beckerman, "'Washington Crossing the Delaware,' Reimagined, at Montclair Art Museum," *Bergen Record*, March 21, 2023, https://www.northjersey.com/story/entertainment/arts/2023/03/21/washington-crossing-the-delaware-is-reimagined-at-montclair-museum/69994053007/. "The artist vanessa german . . . styles her name all-lowercase, like bell hooks and e.e. cummings ('it is a way I level myself without hierarchy')."

30. vanessa german, Kasmin Gallery, https://www.kasmingallery.com/artist/vanessa-german, accessed December 5, 2021.

31. Screen Prism, "Rachel Maddow Goes to America's Most Dangerous Neighborhood (Part 1/2)," YouTube, May 26, 2011, https://www.youtube.com/watch?v=KTbDvAL51HI, accessed December 5, 2021.

32. Justin Vellucci, "Homicides, Shootings Down in '24 in Pittsburgh, Reflecting Nationwide Trends, Data Shows," TribLive, March 8, 2025, https://triblive.com/local/regional/homicides-shootings-down-in-24-in-pittsburgh-reflecting-nationwide-trends-data-shows/, accessed March 10, 2025.

33. Maggie Bullock, "The Future of Work: The 'Citizen Artist' Bringing Hope to Pittsburgh's Homewood," Shondaland, April 17, 2019, https://www.shondaland.com/inspire/a27168640/vanessa-german-citizen-artist-pittsburgh-homewood/.

34. vanessa german, "Poem," TEDxPittsburgh, December 5, 2011, https://www.youtube.com/watch?v=Dngr3s72i18.

35. german, "Poem."

36. german, "Poem."

37. Martin Luther King, Jr., "Loving Your Enemies," sermon delivered at Dexter Avenue Baptist Church, November 17, 1957, Martin Luther King, Jr., Research and Education Institute, https://kinginstitute.stanford.edu/king-papers/documents/loving-your-enemies-sermon-delivered-dexter-avenue-baptist-church.

38. german, "Poem."

39. german, "Poem."

40. german, "Poem."

41. german, "Poem."

42. Bullock, "The Future of Work."

43. Camila Arbelaez, "vanessa german's Art House: A Stronghold Against Gentrification." Brown Political Review, November 13, 2017, https://brownpoliticalreview.org/vanessa-germans-art-house-stronghold-gentrification/.

44. "Rebuilding the 'ArtHouse' in Homewood Following Fire That Left Serious Damage," WTAE, February 19, 2021, https://www.wtae.com/article/rebuilding-the-arthouse-in-homewood-following-fire-that-left-serious-damage/35569980.

45. vanessa german [@vanessalgerman], High. Greetings, Instagram, December 7, 2023, https://www.instagram.com/p/C0jr6fJswAG/.

46. Arbelaez, "vanessa german's Art House."

47. Tyler Dague, "ArtHouse donations surpass \$115K after fire in Homewood," *Pittsburgh Post-Gazette*, March 3, 2021, https://www.post-gazette.com/ae/art-architecture/2021/03/03/Homewood-ArtHouse-fire-Vanessa-German/stories/202102250138.

48. Dague, "ArtHouse donations surpass \$115K."

49. Arbelaez, "vanessa german's Art House."

Chapter 3. Communal Mourning and Collective Wellness through Memorial Art

1. Farrington, *African American Art*, 161.

2. Farrington, *African American Art*, 151.

3. Dan Burley, "Augusta Savage Realizes Dream: Artistic Hands Did This." *New York Amsterdam News*, December 18, 1937, 24, https://www.proquest.com/historical-newspapers/augusta-savage-realizes-dream/docview/226180974/se-2.

4. Farrington, *African American Art*, 161.

5. Dan Burley, "Augusta Savage Realizes Dream," 24.

6. Farrington, *African American Art*, 163.

7. Jacqueline Trescott, "The 'Lively Renaissance' of Elizabeth Catlett," *Washington Post*, March 4, 1977, https://www.washingtonpost.com/archive/lifestyle/1977/03/04/the-lively-renaissance-of-elizabeth-catlett/58a1333c-221c-4bf3-8eb3-2ee787eeeeb5/.

8. Jacqueline Trescott, "Going with the Grain: The Warm, Deep Dignity of Elizabeth Catlett's Art," *Washington Post,* May 22, 1993, https://www.washingtonpost.com/archive/lifestyle/1993/05/22/going-with-the-grain/b92d093d-b74e-44fd-a936-04030edd0e25/?isMobile=1.

9. Pavel Zoubok Fine Art, ADAA The Art Show 2020: vanessa german, Booth A23, http://pavelzoubok.com/exhibition/adaa-the-art-show-2020-vanessa-german/pressrelease/.

10. *Mangaaka Power Figure (Nkisi N'Kondi)*, Metropolitan Museum of Art, New York, https://www.metmuseum.org/art/collection/search/320053.

11. *Power Figure (Nkisi Nkondi).* Brooklyn Museum, https://www.brooklynmuseum.org/opencollection/objects/2957.

12. *Mangaaka Power Figure (Nkisi N'Kondi)*, Metropolitan Museum of Art.

13. Pavel Zoubok Fine Art, ADAA The Art Show 2020: vanessa german, Booth A23.

14. Joanne Klimovich Harrop, "Artist vanessa german to Lead Pittsburgh Walk for George Floyd, Others Lost to Violence," Trib Live, May 25, 2021, https://triblive.com/aande/museums/artist-vanessa-german-to-lead-pittsburgh-walk-for-george-floyd-others-lost-to-violence/.

15. Tyler Dague, "George Floyd," *Pittsburgh Post-Gazette,* May 28, 2021, https://www.proquest.com/docview/2533106209/C6315956F4ED48EAPQ/7?accountid=14214&parentSessionId=DhEP5ns2XpyEgiB%2Fq2NQjiJGv1BSIgNeKEhsrv1lMYM%3D.

16. *Reckoning: Grief and Light*, November 7, 2021, Commonwealth of Oakland, https://www.oaklandcommonwealth.com/event-details-2/reckoning-grief-and-light.

17. *Reckoning: Grief and Light.*

18. *Reckoning: Grief and Light.*

19. *Reckoning: Grief and Light.*

20. Dague, "George Floyd."

21. "sometimes.we.cannot.be.with.our.bodies," Fralin Museum of Art at the University of Virginia, https://uvafralinartmuseum.virginia.edu/exhibitions/sometimeswecannotbewithourbodies.

22. "sometimes.we.cannot. be.with.our.bodies," Union For Contemporary Art, Omaha, https://www.u-ca.org/exhibition/sometimes-we-cannot-be-with-our-bodies.

23. "sometimes.we.cannot. be.with.our.bodies."

24. France Ntloedibe, "A Question of Origins: The Social and Cultural Roots of African American Cultures," *Journal of African American History* 91, no. 4 (Fall 2006): 401–12, https://www.jstor.org/stable/20064123.

25. vanessa german [@vanessalgerman], "THE BLUE WALK is next Thursday evening, MAY 27TH. This is a reckoning ritual of Love, Healing, Grief, Grace and Gratitude," Instagram, March 31, 2021, https://www.instagram.com/p/CPLStYkFPD0/?utm_source=ig_web_copy_link.

26. Dague, "George Floyd."

27. Harrop, "Homewood Artist vanessa german."

28. Dague, "George Floyd."

29. Dague, "George Floyd."

30. Judith Butler, "Between Grief and Grievance, a New Sense of Justice," in *Grief and Grievance: Art and Mourning in America (from Civil Rights to Black Lives Matter)*, edited by Okwui Enwezor (London: Phaidon, 2020), 11–15.

31. german [@vanessalgerman], "Tonight I make poems for the people who wrote me stories of their lost loved ones," Instagram, May 20, 2022, https://www.instagram.com/p/CPF9gm2lH-z/?utm_source=ig_web_copy_link.

32. Tyler Dague, "Vanessa German's Grief Over Black Deaths Reaches the Frick," *Pittsburgh Post-Gazette*, April 11, 2021, https://www.proquest.com/newspapers/reckoning-vanessa-germans-grief-over-black-deaths/docview/2510658277/se-2?accountid=14214.

33. Frick Pittsburgh, *vanessa german—Reckoning: Grief and Light, nothing can separate you from the language you cry in*, YouTube, May 17, 2021, https://www.youtube.com/watch?v=IwVHmI5FQPU.

34. Dague, "Vanessa German's Grief."

35. Kerr Houston, "How Mining the Museum Changed the Art World," *Bmore Art*, May 3, 2017, https://bmoreart.com/2017/05/how-mining-the-museum-changed-the-art-world.html. Fred Wilson's *Mining the Museum* (1992) has been described as a seminal intervention at the Maryland Historical Society (now the Maryland Center for History and Culture), which included working with objects in the museum's collection and juxtaposing them with local histories of Black and Native Americans that cultivated complex and uncomfortable dialogue about institutions' acquisitions and curatorial practices.

36. german [@vanessalgerman], "I found out today that someone killed the little boy who sold waters out of a cooler on the street corner," Instagram. March 31, 2022, https://www.instagram.com/p/CbytpRBsHDZ/?utm_source=ig_web_copy_link.

37. WPXI.com News Staff, "Residents Mourn 15-Year-Old Killed in Wednesday Shooting in Homewood," WPXI, March 31, 2022, https://www.wpxi.com/news/local/allegheny-county/juvenile-critically-injured-after-being-shot-head-pittsburghs-homewood-neighborhood/WPEG7LNXPBALBKB6IX2XFPPLL4/.

38. german [@vanessalgerman], "made a sculpture for the boy," Instagram, April 21, 2022, https://www.instagram.com/p/CcnqrdGLx11/?igshid=MTc4MmM1YmI2Ng%3D%3D.

39. german, "made a sculpture for the boy."

40. german, "made a sculpture for the boy."

41. german, "made a sculpture for the boy."

42. Virginia Hamilton, "The People Could Fly," in *The People Could Fly: American Black Folktales* (New York: Knopf, 1985).

43. Lava Thomas, "Past," http://www.lavathomas.com/past.

44. Felicia Feaster, "Ordinary People, Powerful Drawings: Visual Arts Review Lava Thomas," *Atlanta Journal-Constitution*, November 11, 2022, https://www.proquest.com/newspapers/ordinary-people-powerful-drawings-visual-arts/docview/2735007951/se-2.

45. Interview with Lava Thomas, June 9, 2020.

46. Kevin Everod Quashie, *The Sovereignty of Quiet: Beyond Resistance in Black Culture* (New Brunswick, NJ: Rutgers University Press, 2012), 75.

47. Interview with Lava Thomas.

48. Rena Bransten Gallery, *Lava Thomas Mugshot Portraits: Women of the Montgomery Bus Boycott*, https://renabranstengallery.com/wp-content/uploads/2020/08/Thomas-2018-Press-Kit.pdf.

49. Interview with Lava Thomas.

50. "Heroines of the Montgomery Bus Boycott Celebrated in New Exhibition," *Montgomery Advertiser*, April 13, 2022, https://libezproxy.syr.edu/login?url=https://www.proquest.com/newspapers/new-exhibit-celebrates-heroines-montgomery-bus/docview/2649458396/se-2.

51. "Heroines of the Montgomery Bus Boycott Celebrated."

52. Interview with Lava Thomas.

53. Zachary Small, "San Francisco Reinstates Winning Design for Maya Angelou Monument," *New York Times*, November 5, 2020, https://www.nytimes.com/2020/11/03/arts/design/san-francisco-maya-angelou-monument.html.

54. Chloe Veltman and Sarah Hotchkiss, "SFAC Apologizes to Lava Thomas for Mishandling Maya Angelou Monument," KQED, August 3, 2020, https://www.kqed.org/arts/13884238/sfac-apologizes-to-lava-thomas-for-mishandling-maya-angelou-monument.

55. Veltman and Hotchkiss, "SFAC Apologizes to Lava Thomas."

56. Small, "San Francisco Reinstates Winning Design."

57. Veltman and Hotchkiss, "SFAC Apologizes to Lava Thomas."

58. Small, "Artist's Monument to Angelou Will Finally Stand."

59. Christina Capatides, "South Carolina Church Shooting Victims," CBS News, June 18, 2015, https://www.cbsnews.com/pictures/church-shooting-victims/16/.

60. Claudia Rankine, "The Condition of Black Life Is One of Mourning," in *Grief and Grievance: Art and Mourning in America (from Civil Rights to Black Lives Matter)*, ed. Okwui Enwezoe (London: Phaidon Press, 2020), 17–21.

61. Rankine, "The Condition of Black Life Is One of Mourning," 20.

62. Thomas, "Past."

63. Kelli Moore, "Techniques of Abstraction in Black arts," *Meridians* 21, no. 2 (2022): 413–35. https://doi.org/10.1215/15366936-9882119.

64. https://www.merriam-webster.com/dictionary/requiem.

65. Lava Thomas, *Resistance Reverb: Movements 1 & 2*, http://www.lavathomas.com/resistance-reverb.

66. Interview with Lava Thomas.

67. Interview with Lava Thomas.

68. Interview with Lava Thomas.

69. Interview with Lava Thomas.

70. Interview with Lava Thomas.

71. Interview with Lava Thomas.

72. Allissa V. Richardson, *Bearing Witness While Black: African Americans, Smartphones, and the New Protest #Journalism* (New York: Oxford University Press, 2020), 155.

73. Richardson, *Bearing Witness While Black*.

74. Interview with Lava Thomas.

75. Christina Sharpe, *In the Wake: On Blackness and Being* (Durham: Duke University Press, 2016), 21.

76. Elizabeth Alexander, *The Black Interior* (Minneapolis: Graywolf Press, 2001), 177.

77. Okwui Enwezor, Naomi Beckwith, and Massimilliano Gioni, eds., *Grief and Grievance: Art and Mourning in America* (London: Phaidon, 2020), 7.

78. Enwezor, Beckwith, and Gioni, *Grief and Grievance*.

79. Interview with Lava Thomas.

80. Six Bible verses about Lamb Of God, https://bible.knowing-jesus.com/topics/Lamb-Of-God.

81. Psalm 100:1.

82. Interview with Lava Thomas.

83. Quashie, *The Sovereignty of Quiet*.

Chapter 4. Individual Wellness and Artistic Flourishing

1. Maia Heguiaphal, "Lavett Ballard's African American and Female Narratives," Daily Art Magazine, March 4, 2025, https://www.dailyartmagazine.com/lavett-ballard/.

2. August Wilson, *Fences* (New York: Penguin, 1985), 61.

3. bell hooks, *Art on My Mind: Visual Politics* (New York: New Press, 1995).

4. Interview with Lavett Ballard, 2020.

5. Interview with Lavett Ballard.

6. Lineage Asset Advisors, "What Is a Legacy Property?" February 14, 2018, https://lineageasset.com/what-is-a-legacy-property-series/. For clarity, "a legacy property is a real estate asset that has maintained its historical and cultural significance over multiple generations."

7. Interview with Lavett Ballard.

8. Interview with Lavett Ballard.

9. "Community Folk Art Center Presents Exhibition 'Stories My Grandmother Told Me,'" January 27, 2021, https://news.syr.edu/blog/2021/01/27/community-folk-art-center-presents-exhibition-stories-my-grandmother-told-me/.

10. Gloria J. Browne-Marshall, *The Voting Rights War: The NAACP and the Ongoing Struggle for Justice* (Lanham, MD: Rowman & Littlefield, 2017).

11. Michael Lieberman, "Group Exhibition at African American Museum in Philadelphia Tackles Social Justice Issues with Powerful Imagery and Passion," The Art Blog, July 3, 2018, https://www.theartblog.org/2018/07/group-exhibition-at-african-american-museum-in-philadelphia-tackles-social-justice-issues-with-powerful-imagery-and-passion/.

12. Scott Ellsworth, *Death in a Promised Land: The Tulsa Race Riots of 1921* (Baton Rouge: Louisiana State University Press, 1992).

13. Sophie A. Schuit and Jon C. Rogowski, "Race, Representation, and the Voting Rights Act," *American Journal of Political Science* 61, no. 3 (2016): 513–26, https://doi.org/10.1111/ajps.12284.

14. American Experience, Freedom Riders: Jim Crow Laws, PBS, n.d., https://www.pbs.org/wgbh/americanexperience/features/freedom-riders-jim-crow-laws/.

15. Abby Weiss, "Art Exhibit Portrays the Black Experience Through Lens of One Family," Daily Orange, March 2, 2021, http://dailyorange.com/2021/03/art-exhibit-portrays-black-experience-lens-one-family/.

16. "Out on a Limb: Philadelphia's Dancers, Musicians, Artists, and Actors Can't Imagine When They'll Work Again," *Philadelphia Inquirer*, April 26, 2020, https://www.proquest.com/newspapers/out-on-limb/docview/2395069647/se-2.

17. Rebekah Barber, "Say Her Name Campaign Targets Police Killings of Black Women and Girls," Facing South, July 15, 2020, https://www.facingsouth.org/2020/07/say-her-name-campaign-targets-police-killings-black-women-and-girls.

18. Peter Dobrin, "Stories of Courage: '#SayTheirNames' Remembers the Black Women Who Fought for Justice," *Philadelphia Daily News,* January 18, 2021, https://www.proquest.com/newspapers/stories-courage/docview/2478461650/se-2.

19. Stephanie Y. Evans, *Black Women's Yoga History* (Albany: State University of New York Press, 2021), 382.

20. As cited in Evans, *Black Women's Yoga History,* 382–83.

21. Evans, *Black Women's Yoga History,* 382.

22. Interview with Lavett Ballard, 2020.

23. Interview with Lavett Ballard, 2020.

24. Evans, *Black Women's Yoga History*, 70.

25. Interview with Lavett Ballard, 2020.

26. "It's Handled," Power In Black Tees, n.d., https://www.instagram.com/powerinblacktees/p/CECZtg1gJKy/.

27. Interview with Lavett Ballard, 2020.

28. Collins, *Black Feminist Thought.*

29. Carolyn M. West, "Mammy, Jezebel, Sapphire, and Their Homegirls: Developing an 'Oppositional Gaze' Toward the Images of Black Women," in *Lectures on the Psychology of Women*, ed. Joan C. Chrisler, Carla Golden, and Patricia D. Rozee, 286–99. New York: McGraw-Hill, 2008.

30. Collins, *Black Feminist Thought.*

31. Cheryl L. Woods-Giscombé and Angela R. Black, "Mind-Body Interventions to Reduce Risk for Health Disparities Related to Stress and Strength among African American Women: The Potential of Mindfulness-Based Stress Reduction, Loving-Kindness, and the NTU Therapeutic Framework," *Complementary Health Practice Review* 15, no. 3 (2010): 115–31, https://doi.org/10.1177/1533210110386776.

32. Interview with Lavett Ballard.

33. West, "Mammy, Jezebel, Sapphire."

34. Leeja Carter and Amerigo Rossi, "Superwoman: Exploring Stress, Coping, and Physical Activity among African American Women," paper presented at the Association for Applied Sport Psychology, Phoenix, Arizona, September 2016.

35. Tamara Beauboeuf-Lafontant, *Behind the Mask of the Strong Black Woman: Voice and the Embodiment of a Costly Performance* (Philadelphia: Temple University Press, 2009), 2.

36. National Wellness Institute, Six Dimensions of Wellness, n.d., https://national wellness.org/resources/six-dimensions-of-wellness/.

37. Siraad Dirshe, "What Does It Mean to 'Center Black People'?" *New York Times*, June 19, 2020, https://www.nytimes.com/2020/06/19/style/self-care/centering-blackness.html.

38. Lavett Ballard, *The Bus Riders (1955)*. *Time*, March 5, 2020, https://time.com/5793559/the-bus-riders-100-women-of-the-year/. The *Time* article gives the title of this artwork as *The Bus Riders (1955)*."

39. Rowan College at Burlington County, "RCBC Arts Alum Created TIME Magazine Cover Reimagining Rosa Parks." TAP into Bordentown, March 1, 2021, https://www.tapinto.net/towns/bordentown/articles/rcbc-alum-created-time-magazine-cover-reimagining-rosa-parks.

40. Celeste E. Whittaker, "Her Art Is in Time Magazine Again. What to Know about South Jersey's Lavett Ballard," *Cherry Hill Courier-Post*, February 21, 2023, https://www.courierpostonline.com/story/news/local/2023/02/21/willingboro-nj-lavett-ballard-artist-featured-in-time-magazine/69903289007/.

41. Martha S. Jones, *Vanguard: How Black Women Broke Barriers, Won the Vote, and Insisted on Equality for All* (New York: Basic Books, 2020).

42. Interview with Lavett Ballard.

43. https://www.merriam-webster.com/dictionary/shadow.

44. Tate, "Claudette Johnson: 'Giving Space to the Presence of a Black Woman,'" May 25, 2021, https://www.tate.org.uk/art/artists/claudette-johnson-15861/giving-space-presence-black-woman.

45. Long-Sharp Gallery represented Lavett Ballard as a client at this time.

46. *Lavett Ballard: When She Roars*, Artnet, n.d., https://www.artnet.com/galleries/long-sharp-gallery/when-she-roars.

47. Kimberlee Buck, "The 1963 Birmingham Children's Crusade, A Turning Point for the Civil Rights Movement," *Los Angeles Sentinel*, April 25, 2019, https://lasentinel.net/the-1963-birmingham-childrens-crusade-a-turning-point-for-the-civil-rights-movement.html.

48. Heguiaphal, "Lavett Ballard's African American and Female Narratives."

49. Stephanie Y. Evans, Kanika Bell, and Nsenga K. Burton, eds., *Black Women's Mental Health: Balancing Strength and Vulnerability* (Albany: State University of New York Press, 2018).

50. Interview with Lavett Ballard.

51. Interview with Lavett Ballard.

52. Interview with Lavett Ballard.

53. Interview with Lavett Ballard.

54. Interview with Lavett Ballard.

55. Interview with Lavett Ballard.

56. Interview with Lavett Ballard.

57. Octavia E. Butler, *Kindred* (New York: Doubleday, 1979), 252.

58. Isabel Wilkerson, *The Warmth of Other Suns: The Epic Story of America's Great Migration* (New York: Vintage Books, 2014).

59. Unknown photographer, *A Negro Family Just Arrived in Chicago from the Rural South*, 1922, Schomburg Center for Research in Black Culture, Jean Blackwell Hutson Research and Reference Division, New York Public Library, https://digitalcollections.nypl.org/items/510d47de-1a10-a3d9-e040-e00a18064a99.

60. Interview with Lavett Ballard.

61. "Flower Meaning & Symbolism—Here Is What You Didn't Know about Sunflowers," Bloom This, September 20, 2013, https://bloomthis.co/blogs/facts/flower-meaning-symbolism-the-meaning-of-sunflowers.

62. Helen T. Gray, "Church Mothers Are Pillars of Faith," *Orlando Sentinel*, August 5, 2021, https://www.orlandosentinel.com/news/os-xpm-2002-06-08-0206070454-story.html. "The term 'mothers of the church' means they were mostly older women, faithful, who were looked upon as very godly ladies who served as an example to the people. They gave stability to the church. They are regarded as mothers to the entire congregation and are addressed as 'mother' and then their last name. Not 'sister,' 'Mrs.' or 'Ms.' and certainly never by just their first names."

63. Interview with Lavett Ballard.

64. Interview with Lavett Ballard.

65. "Women in the Visual Arts." Oxford Art Online, n.d., https://www.oxfordartonline.com/page/women-in-the-visual-arts.

66. Interview with Lavett Ballard.

67. Collins, *Black Feminist Thought*, 72.

68. Interview with Lavett Ballard.

69. "The Legacy of Henrietta Lacks," Johns Hopkins Medicine, n.d., https://www.hopkinsmedicine.org/henriettalacks/.

70. Henrietta Lacks's extracted cells were named the HeLa line after the first two letters of her first and last names. They proved to be a valuable contribution to the development of the polio vaccine development have been used to study cancer, HIV-AIDS, gene mapping, and human sensitivity to various household and cosmetic products.

71. Rebecca Skloot, *The Immortal Life of Henrietta Lacks* (New York: Crown, 2010).

72. Lorena Blas, "Oprah Winfrey to star in HBO's 'Henrietta Lacks' movie." USA Today, May 2, 2016, https://www.usatoday.com/story/life/tv/2016/05/02/oprah-winfrey-hbo-the-immortal-life-of-henrietta-lacks/83833298/.

73. "National Portrait Gallery Presents a Portrait of Henrietta Lacks, a Co-Acquisition with the National Museum of African American History and Culture," May 8, 2018, https://www.si.edu/newsdesk/releases/national-portrait-gallery-presents-portrait-henrietta-lacks-co-acquisition-national-museum-.

74. Interview with Lavett Ballard.

75. Sheena M. Morrison and Elizabeth Fee, "Nothing to Work with but Cleanliness: The Training of African American Traditional Midwives in the South," *American Journal of Public Health* 100, no. 2 (2010): 238–39. https://doi.org/10.2105/AJPH.2009.182873.

76. Interview with Lavett Ballard.

77. Interview with Lavett Ballard.

78. Interview with Lavett Ballard.

79. Interview with Lavett Ballard.

80. Interview with Lavett Ballard.

81. Toni Morrison, *Beloved* (New York: Knopf, 1987), 87.

82. In this literary scene, consider the following: First, Morrison presents a spiritual ritual led by an empowered Black woman with spiritual wisdom. Baby Suggs demonstrates her empowerment through personal prayer and celebration. Then she advocates for others in the community to gather and practice self-care through the pursuit of self-love. The act of collective gathering for a healing ritual of prayer places further emphasis on the influential role of women as healers. "Finally [Baby Suggs] called the women to her. 'Cry,' she told them. 'For the living and the dead. Just cry.' And without covering their eyes, the women let loose." Here Morrison suggests that Black women hold a particular role in travailing for their community. Morrison, *Beloved*, 88.

83. Interview with Lavett Ballard.

Chapter 5. Nurturing Cultural and Spiritual Wellness

1. April Hardwick, "On a Mission to Change Hearts and Minds through Art and Activism," Luxe Interiors + Design, January 19, 2021, https://luxesource.com/artist-delita-martin-change-hearts-minds-art-activism/.

2. Robert Farris Thompson, *Flash of the Spirit: African and Afro-American Art and Philosophy* (New York: Vintage, 1984).

3. Interview with Delita Martin, 2020.

4. Interview with Delita Martin.

5. Interview with Delita Martin.

6. Interview with Delita Martin.

7. Interview with Delita Martin.

8. Interview with Delita Martin.

9. Interview with Delita Martin.

10. Interview with Delita Martin.

11. Interview with Delita Martin.

12. Jon Kabat-Zinn, *Full Catastrophe Living: How to Cope with Stress, Pain, and Illness* (New York: Delacorte, 1990).

13. Interview with Delita Martin.

14. Interview with Delita Martin.

15. Jonathan C. David, *Together Let Us Sweetly Live: The Singing and Praying Bands* (Champaign: University of Illinois Press, 2007).

16. Ann Harris, "Ring Shout Across America," *Triangle Tribune* (Durham, NC), September 23, 2012, https://www.proquest.com/newspapers/ring-shout-across-america/docview/1220468312/se-2.

17. Thompson, *Flash of the Spirit*.

18. Interview with Delita Martin.

19. Interview with Delita Martin.

20. Laurie A. Wilkie, "Magic and Empowerment on the Plantation: An Archaeological Consideration of African-American World View," *Southeastern Archaeology* 14, no. 2 (1995) 136–48.

21. Patricia Samford, "The Archaeology of African-American Slavery and Material Culture," *William and Mary Quarterly* 53, no. 1 (1996): 87–114, https://doi.org/10.2307/2946825.

22. Maulana Karenga, *Introduction to Black Studies* (Los Angeles: University of Sankore Press, 2010).

23. Georges Niangoran-Bouah, *Akan World of Gold Weights: Abstract Design Weights* (New York: Hacker Art Books, 1988).

24. Interview with Delita Martin.

25. Micah Issitt and Carlyn Main, *Hidden Religion: The Greatest Mysteries and Symbols of the World's Religious Beliefs* (Santa Barbara: ABC-CLIO, 2014).

26. Khelli Willets, "Beyond the Tangible," in *Shadows in the Garden*, ed. Delita Martin (Huffman, TX: Black Box Press Studio, LLC, 2019): 12–14.

27. Interview with Delita Martin.

28. Interview with Delita Martin.

29. Willets, "Beyond the Tangible," 12–14.

30. Caitlin Albritton, "Women Who Can Fly," *Creative Loafing*, February 9, 2017, https://libezproxy.syr.edu/login?url=https://www.proquest.com/newspapers/women-who-can-fly/docview/1870210040/se-2.

31. ROUX, Galveston Arts Center, n.d., https://www.galvestonartscenter.org/roux.

32. Interview with Delita Martin.

33. Interview with Delita Martin.

34. Very few of Martin's subjects' smile. The artist states that this is not intentional, and the women are not angry. It just happens that she does not portray that characteristic in her work.

35. Willets, "Beyond the Tangible," 12–14.

36. Willets, "Beyond the Tangible," 12–14.

37. Interview with Delita Martin, 2020.

38. Stephen Hamilton, "Alaro: Indigo and the Power of Women in Yorubaland." Squarespace, n.d., https://tinyurl.com/yc88aths.

39. Georgene Bess Montgomery, *The Spirit and the Word: A Theory of Spirituality in Africana Literary Criticism* (Trenton, NJ: Africa World Press, 2008).

40. Interview with Delita Martin, 2020.

41. Interview with Delita Martin, 2020.

42. Interview with Shanequa Gay, 2020.

43. Felicia Feaster, "Artist Mixes Hometown Pride with Sadness: Artwork Originates in Childhood Experiences Growing Up in Atlanta," *Atlanta Journal-Constitution*, January 30, 2022, https://www.proquest.com/newspapers/artist-mixes-hometown-pride-with-sadness-artwork/docview/2623653490/se-2.

44. Interview with Shanequa Gay.

45. Personal communication, 2021.

46. Interview with Shanequa Gay.

47. Shanequa Gay, *Creative Mornings Atlanta*, April 24, 2020, https://www.youtube .com/watch?v=p3I_RFfWAxs.

48. Interview with Shanequa Gay.

49. Kelley D. Evans, "Artist Shanequa Gay Brings Inspiring Black Experiences to Canvas in New Exhibition." Andscape, March 6, 2017, https://andscape.com/ features/artist-shanequa-gay/.

50. "The Cosby Show," Encyclopaedia Britannica, https://www.britannica.com/ topic/The-Cosby-Show.

51. William Grimes, "Varnette Honeywood, Whose Art Appeared on 'Cosby Show,' Dies at 59," *New York Times*, September 16, 2010, https://www.nytimes.com/2010/ 09/16/arts/design/16honeywood.html.

52. Interview with Shanequa Gay.

53. Interview with Shanequa Gay.

54. Interview with Shanequa Gay.

55. Michael A. Antonucci, review of *The Chitlin' Circuit and the Road to Rock 'n' Roll*, by Preston Lauderbach, *American Studies* 53, no. 1 (2014): 202–4, http://dx .doi.org/10.1353/ams.2014.0057.

56. Interview with Shanequa Gay.

57. Carolyn Desalu, "Things to Do: Art Explores Culture, Issues," *Atlanta Journal-Constitution,* February 26, 2015, https://www.proquest.com/newspapers/ things-do-art-explores-culture-issues/docview/1658361453/se-2.

58. Interview with Shanequa Gay.

59. Shantay Robinson, "Studio Visit with Shanequa Gay." Burnaway, August 17, 2016, https://burnaway.org/magazine/shanequa-gay-studio-visit/.

60. "About: Overview," Art Basel, n.d., https://www.artbasel.com/about. "Founded by gallerists in 1970, Art Basel is the leading global platform connecting collectors, galleries, and artists. Art Basel's fairs in Basel, Hong Kong, Paris, and Miami Beach, as well as its Online Viewing Rooms, are a driving force in supporting galleries as they nurture the careers of artists. Our publication *The Art Market*, co-published with our Lead Partner UBS, is a commitment to increasing the transparency of the art market. Art Basel's Initiatives strive to create unique artist-led experiences and strengthen local art scenes."

61. Interview with Shanequa Gay.

62. "bell hooks & Gloria Steinem at Eugene Lang College," YouTube, October October 8, 2014, https://www.youtube.com/watch?v=tkzOFvfWRn4

63. Heather Williams, "bell hooks Speaks Up," *Sandspur* 112, no. 17 (2013), https:// issuu.com/thesandspur/docs/112–17. Inspired by bell hooks, who purposely uses lowercase for proper nouns, Gay has also adopted this style when she titles her work.

64. Interview with Shanequa Gay.

65. William R. Black, "How Watermelons Became a Racist Trope," *The Atlantic*, December 8, 2014, https://www.theatlantic.com/national/archive/2014/12/ how-watermelons-became-a-racist-trope/383529/; Gene Demby, "Where Did That Fried Chicken Stereotype Come From?" *Code Switch*, NPR, May

22, 2013, https://www.npr.org/sections/codeswitch/2013/05/22/186087397/where-did-that-fried-chicken-stereotype-come-from.

66. Interview with Shanequa Gay.

67. Feaster, "Artist Mixes Hometown Pride with Sadness."

68. Malik Simba, "The Three-Fifths Clause of the United States Constitution (1787)," BlackPast, October 3, 2014, https://www.blackpast.org/african-american-history/events-african-american-history/three-fifths-clause-united-states-constitution-1787/.

69. Interview with Shanequa Gay.

70. Hannah Drake628, "Why Are Black Women Always the Clean Up Woman?" Writesomeshit, February 27, 2018, https://writesomeshit.com/2018/02/27/why-are-black-women-always-the-clean-up-woman/.

71. Feaster, "Artist Mixes Hometown Pride with Sadness."

72. Interview with Shanequa Gay.

73. Interview with Shanequa Gay.

74. Menah Pratt-Clarke, "A Radical Reconstruction of Resistance Strategies: Black Girls and Black Women Reclaiming Our Power Using Transdisciplinary Applied Social Justice©, Ma'at, and Rites of Passage," *Journal of African American Studies* 17, no. 1 (2013): 99–114, https://doi.org/10.1007/s12111-012-9221-6.

75. Keith A. Alford, "Cultural Themes in Rites of Passage: Voices of Young African American Males," *Journal of African American Studies* 7, no. 1 (2003): 3–26, https://doi.org/10.1007/s12111-003-1000-y.

76. Mark Strauss, "The 5,000-Year Secret History of the Watermelon." National Geographic, April 29, 2020, https://www.nationalgeographic.com/history/article/150821-watermelon-fruit-history-agriculture.

77. Audrey Stanton, "The Somewhat Sinister and Rebellious History behind Your Striped Shirt," The Good Trade, March 1, 2019, https://www.thegoodtrade.com/features/history-of-stripes.

78. Interview with Shanequa Gay.

79. Kevin Everod Quashie, *Black Women, Identity, and Cultural Theory: (Un)Becoming the Subject* (New Brunswick, NJ: Rutgers University Press, 2004).

80. Interview with Shanequa Gay.

81. Interview with Shanequa Gay. This is a reference to Matthew 18:20 (KJV): "For where two or three are gathered together in my name, there am I in the midst of them."

82. Interview with Shanequa Gay.

83. Associated Press, "Timeline of Key Events in Eric Garner Chokehold Death," AP, July 16, 2019, https://apnews.com/general-news-ec7ac5a664d74cdab852d639c0da08f4.

84. Interview with Shanequa Gay.

85. Interview with Shanequa Gay.

86. Interview with Shanequa Gay.

87. Interview with Shanequa Gay.

88. Interview with Shanequa Gay.

89. Interview with Shanequa Gay.

90. Interview with Shanequa Gay.

91. Galerie Myrtis, *Shanequa Gay—The Crooked Room 2018*, YouTube, March 27, 2020, https://www.youtube.com/watch?v=f4LIJAXz6Og.

92. Melissa V. Harris-Perry, *Sister Citizen: Shame, Stereotypes, and Black Women in America* (New Haven: Yale University Press, 2011).

93. Myrtis Bedolla, *Tea with Myrtis: Artistically Speaking with Shanequa Gay*, YouTube, March 27, 2020, https://www.youtube.com/watch?v=jSyNyZbgf_g&t=2s.

94. Galerie Myrtis, *Shanequa Gay—The Crooked Room 2018*.

95. Paul Laurence Dunbar, "We Wear the Mask," Poetry Foundation, https://www.poetryfoundation.org/poems/44203/we-wear-the-mask

96. Interview with Shanequa Gay.

97. Interview with Shanequa Gay.

98. Associated Press, "Heartbreaking: Alexis Crawford, 21, found dead," EEW Magazine, November 8, 2019, https://www.eewmagazineonline.com/latest-news/2019/11/8/pray-for-the-family-missing-clark-atlanta-university-student-alexis-crawford-found-dead-police-call-it-heartbreaking.

99. Interview with Shanequa Gay.

100. "Ex-Cops Apologize for Deadly Drug Raid Ahead of Sentencing," CNN, February 23, 2009, https://www.cnn.com/2009/CRIME/02/23/atlanta.police.sentencing/index.html.

101. A "proverbial altar" typically is a symbolic or figurative altar, rather than a literal one. In literature or conversation, it often alludes to a place where something is metaphorically sacrificed or offered, usually for a cause, belief, or principle.

Chapter 6. Ancestral Memory and Generational Wellness through Photography

1. Tawny Chatmon, "About," https://www.tawnychatmon.com/about.

2. Tawny Chatmon, "About."

3. Rebecca Epstein, Jamilia J. Blake, and Thalia González, "Girlhood Interrupted: The Erasure of Black Girls' Childhood," Center on Poverty and Inequality, Georgetown Law, June 27, 2017, https://www.law.georgetown.edu/poverty-inequality-center/wp-content/uploads/sites/14/2017/08/girlhood-interrupted.pdf.

4. Mark Jenkins, "An Intimate Panorama of Video Art's Variety and Breadth," *Washington Post*, June 27, 2021, https://www.proquest.com/newspapers/intimate-panorama-video-arts-variety-breadth/docview/2545295022/se-2.

5. Quashie, *The Sovereignty of Quiet*, 6.

6. Jenkins, "An Intimate Panorama."

7. Interview with Tawny Chatmon, 2021.

8. Lizette Alvarez and Cara Buckley, "Zimmerman Is Acquitted in Trayvon Martin Killing," *New York Times*, July 13, 2013, https://www.nytimes.com/2013/07/14/us/george-zimmerman-verdict-trayvon-martin.html. Trayvon Martin, a seventeen-year-old African American, was fatally shot by George Zimmerman, a neighborhood watch volunteer, on February 26, 2012, in Sanford, Florida. Zimmerman claimed self-defense under Florida's Stand Your Ground law. The case sparked nationwide

protests and ignited discussions about racial profiling, gun laws, and justice in America.

9. Leslie Gray Streeter, "Maryland Painter Tawny Chatmon Frames Her Black Subjects in Gold," *Washington Post*, February 13, 2022, https://www.proquest.com/newspapers/maryland-painter-tawny-chatmon-frames-her-black/docview/2628017410/se-2.

10. Interview with Tawny Chatmon, 2021.

11. Errin Whack, "Black Women at the Forefront in Fight for Racial Equality," NBC News, May 8, 2017, https://www.nbcnews.com/news/nbcblk/black-women-move-forefront-fight-racial-equality-n756416.

12. "About," Humanize My Hoodie, https://www.humanizemyhoodie.com/. The following quote is from the "About" section of the website: "The Humanize My Hoodie Movement originated from a demand to end the killing of Black and Indigenous People across the world. We recognize how hoodies have been used to amplify the myth of Black criminality. Our mission is to debunk that stereotype by designing revolutionary social justice campaigns for Black and Indigenous People of Color to be HUMANIZED, not criminalized."

13. Tanisha C. Ford, *Liberated Threads: Black Women, Style, and the Global Politics of Soul* (Chapel Hill: University of North Carolina Press, 2015), 3.

14. The section about Tawny Chatmon was first published in Tanisha Jackson, "What I Want You to Know: Chatmon's Visual Love Letter to Black Children," in *If I'm No Longer Here, I Wanted You to Know . . .* exh. cat. (Baltimore: Gallerie Myrtis, 2021).

15. Interview with Tokie Rome-Taylor.

16. Leigh Raiford, "Photography and the Practices of Critical Black Memory," *History and Theory* 48, no. 4 (2009): 112–29, http://www.jstor.org/stable/25621443.

17. Interview with Tokie Rome-Taylor.

18. Michael Muata Moss, *Sankofa: Kemetamorphing Black to the Future: The Reclamation of African-Centered Healing and Wellness* (North Charleston, SC: Createspace Independent Publishing Platform, 2018).

19. Interview with Tokie Rome-Taylor.

20. Interview with Tokie Rome-Taylor.

21. Molefi Kete Asante, *The History of Africa: The Quest for Eternal Harmony* (London: Routledge, 2024), 14.

22. Interview with Tokie Rome-Taylor.

23. Interview with Tokie Rome-Taylor.

24. Interview with Tokie Rome-Taylor.

25. Maya Angelou, "Our Grandmothers" (New York: Limited Editions Club, 1994).

26. Interview with Tokie Rome-Taylor.

27. Interview with Tokie Rome-Taylor.

28. Samford, "The Archaeology of African-American Slavery," 87.

29. John Noble Wilford, "Slave Artifacts under the Hearth," *New York Times*, August 27, 1996, https://www.nytimes.com/1996/08/27/science/slave-artifacts-under-the-hearth.html.

30. Krish Seetah, "Objects Past, Objects Present: Materials, Resistance and Memory from the Le Morne Old Cemetery, Mauritius," *Journal of Social Archaeology* 15, no. 2 (2015): 233–53, https://doi.org/10.1177/1469605315575124.

31. Interview with Tokie Rome-Taylor.

32. Jessica Smith, "#NotAStereotype," *Flagpole* 35, no. 20, May 19, 2021, https://www.proquest.com/magazines/notastereotype/docview/2532201163/se-2.

33. Anita Strezova, "The Icon of the Trinity by Andrei Rublev," in *Hesychasm and Art: The Appearance of New Iconographic Trends in Byzantine and Slavic Lands in the 14th and 15th Centuries* (Canberra: ANU Press, 2014), 173–232, http://www.jstor.org/stable/j.ctt13www4f.13.

34. Interview with Tokie Rome-Taylor.

35. Interview with Tokie Rome-Taylor.

36. Thompson, *Flash of the Spirit*, xiii.

37. Interview with Tokie Rome-Taylor.

38. P. A. Mullins, "Appropriating Black Africa," in *Black Africa and the US Art World in the Early 20th Century: Aesthetics, White Supremacy*, 73–98 (London: Anthem Press, 2024), https://doi.org/10.2307/jj.9941117.7.

39. Interview with Tokie Rome-Taylor.

40. Interview with Tokie Rome-Taylor.

41. Interview with Tokie Rome-Taylor.

42. Interview with Tokie Rome-Taylor.

43. Interview with Tokie Rome-Taylor.

44. Attr. to Francis Bacon, *Meditationes sacrae* (London: Excusum impensis Humfredi Hooper, 1597).

45. Gaspésie Literary Council, "Types of Literacy," n.d., https://gaspelit.ca/types-of-literacy/.

46. Imani Perry, *South To America : A Journey Below the Mason-Dixon to Understand the Soul of a Nation* (New York: ECCO Press, 2022), 253; "Igbo Landing," Brittanica, n.d., https://www.britannica.com/place/Igbo-Landing. Perry discusses how *The People Could Fly* is a tale about the Ibo landing on St. Simons Island, Georgia. According to historical records, a group of Ibo people arrived in Savannah, Georgia, in 1803 aboard a slave ship called the *Wanderer*. They were purchased by merchants and subsequently resold to plantations on St. Simons Island. During their transfer to the island, the Ibo people revolted, drowned their captors, and ran the ship aground. They then disembarked, singing and marching into the sea to escape a life of slavery. One legend has it that they changed into buzzards and flew back to Africa. Perry asserts that the inhabitants of St. Simons have preserved the memory of the flying Ibo, creating a unique blend of African and Black American culture known as Gullah Geechee. Additionally, they blurred the line between life and death in their quest for freedom.

47. Thompson, *Flash of the Spirit*, 235.

48. Geoffrey Batchen, Richard Beard, Mark Haworth-Booth, Curtis Moffat, Charlotte Cotton, Arthur Ou, Brian Dillon, et al., "Who Are You Looking At?" *Art on Paper* 12, no. 4 (2008): 48–75, http://www.jstor.org/stable/24556754.

Chapter 7. Abstract Art and Cognitive Wellness

1. *Alma W. Thomas: A Retrospective Exhibition, 1959–1966* (Howard University Gallery of Art, 1966), Alma Thomas papers, Smithsonian Institution, Washington, DC, https://collections.si.edu/search/results.htm?q=record_ID=AAA.thomalma_ref799&repo=DPLA.

2. Tate, "Minimalism," https://www.tate.org.uk/art/art-terms/m/minimalism.

3. Eleanor Munro, "The Late Springtime of Alma Thomas: Conversations with the Washington Colorist, from an Absorbing New Book," *Washington Post,* April 15, 1979, https://www.proquest.com/historical-newspapers/late-springtime-alma-thomas/docview/147004338/se-2.

4. Aleia N. Brown, "Alma Woodsey Thomas," National Women's History Museum, 2021, https://www.womenshistory.org/education-resources/biographies/alma-woodsey-thomas.

5. Grace Glueck, "Art: Studio Museum Exhibits Alma Thomas," *New York Times,* April 29, 1983, https://www.nytimes.com/1983/04/29/arts/art-studio-museum-exhibits-alma-thomas.html.

6. "Category: Abstraction," Ultrawolvesunderthefullmoon, December 29, 2020, https://ultrawolvesunderthefullmoon.blog/category/abstraction/.

7. Farrington, *African American Art: A Visual and Cultural History* (Oxford University Press, 2016).

8. Munro, "The Late Springtime of Alma Thomas."

9. Leigh Raiford, "Burning All Illusion: Abstraction, Black Life, and the Unmaking of White Supremacy," *Art Journal* 79, no. 4 (2020).): 76–91, https://doi.org/10.1080/00043249.2020.1779550.

10. Raiford, "Burning All Illusion."

11. "Abstract Art by Black Women Artists from 1960s to Today at Women's Museum in DC," ArtfixDaily, September 6, 2017, https://www.artfixdaily.com/artwire/release/4563-abstract-art-by-black-women-artists-from-1960s-to-today-at-women%E2%80%99.

12. Tate, "Abstract Art," https://www.tate.org.uk/art/art-terms/a/abstract-art.

13. Interview with Amber Robles-Gordon, 2022.

14. Frantz Fanon, *Black Skin, White Masks*, trans. Richard Philcox, 37 (New York: Penguin Classics, 2021).

15. Interview with Amber Robles-Gordon, 2022.

16. Shantella Sherman, "D.C. Artist Fits all the Pieces Together," *Afro-American Red Star,* January 28, 2006, https://www.proquest.com/newspapers/d-c-artist-fits-all-pieces-together/docview/369568816/se-2.

17. Interview with Amber Robles-Gordon, 2022.

18. Amber Robles-Gordon, "Heal Thyself," Amber Robles-Gordon, n.d., https://www.amberroblesgordon.com/heal-thyself-series.

19. Robles-Gordon, "Heal Thyself."

20. Charles H. Rowell, "Amber Robles-Gordon," *Callaloo* 38, no. 4 (2015): 855–57. https://doi.org/10.1353/cal.2015.0112.

21. Ntozake Shange, *For Colored Girls Who Have Considered Suicide When the Rainbow Is Enuf: A Choreopoem* (New York: Bantam Books, 1981); Lamia Khalil Hammad, "Black Feminist Discourse of Power in *For Colored Girls Who Have Considered Suicide*," *Rupkatha Journal on Interdisciplinary Studies in Humanities*, 3, no. 2 (2011): 258–67, https://rupkatha.com/V3/n2/05_For_Colored_Girls_Who_Have_Considered_Suicide.pdf.

22. Shange, *For Colored Girls*.

23. Shange, *For Colored Girls*.

24. Luke 4:40; Acts 8:14–19.

25. Interview with Amber Robles-Gordon 2022.

26. Shange, *For Colored Girls*.

27. Rowell, "Amber Robles-Gordon."

28. Rowell, "Amber Robles-Gordon."

29. Rowell, "Amber Robles-Gordon."

30. Rowell, "Amber Robles-Gordon."

31. "Gee's Bend Quilting Collective," https://www.geesbendquiltingretreats.com/gees-bend-quilting-collective.html. "The women of Gee's Bend, a small remote black community in Alabama, have created hundreds of quilt masterpieces dating from the early 20th century to the present. Gee's Bend quilts carry forward an old and proud tradition of textiles made for home and family. Gee's Bend quilts transform recycled work clothes and dresses, feed sacks and fabric remnants into sophisticated design vessels of cultural survival and continuing portraits of the women's identities"; Rowell, "Amber Robles-Gordon."

32. Rowell, "Amber Robles-Gordon."

33. Rowell, "Amber Robles-Gordon."

34. S. Angelin Sheeja, "Mapping the Black Culture in Alice Walker's *The Temple of My Familiar*," *Journal for English Language and Literary Studies* 3, no. 4 (2013): 9–15, https://brbs.tjells.com/index.php/tjells/article/view/125/205.

35. Rowell, "Amber Robles-Gordon."

36. Rowell, "Amber Robles-Gordon."

37. Interview with Dianne Smith, March 14, 2023.

38. Interview with Dianne Smith, March 14, 2023.

39. Interview with Dianne Smith, March 14, 2023.

40. Interview with Dianne Smith, March 14, 2023.

41. Interview with Dianne Smith, March 14, 2023.

42. Interview with Dianne Smith, March 14, 2023.

43. Interview with Dianne Smith, March 14, 2023.

44. Interview with Dianne Smith, March 14, 2023.

45. Interview with Dianne Smith, March 14, 2023.

46. Interview with Dianne Smith, March 14, 2023.

47. Interview with Dianne Smith, March 14, 2023.

48. Tim Higgins, "Community Connection: Allentown Art Museum Artist-in-Residence Dianne Smith Tells Stories of City Residents and Their Struggles and Hopes in 'Intersections' Exhibit," *Morning Call*, October 16, 2016, https://www.proquest

.com/newspapers/community-connection-allentown-art-museum-artist/docview/
1829332636/se-2.

49. Interview with Dianne Smith, March 14, 2023.

50. Harry Brunius, "African Burial Ground under New York Streets," *Christian Science Monitor,* June 17, 1999, https://www.proquest.com/newspapers/african
-burial-ground-under-new-york-streets/docview/405654088/se-2.

51. Interview with Dianne Smith, March 14, 2023.

52. Interview with Dianne Smith, March 14, 2023.

53. Interview with Dianne Smith, March 14, 2023.

54. Interview with Dianne Smith, March 14, 2023.

55. Interview with Dianne Smith, March 14, 2023.

56. Interview with Dianne Smith, March 14, 2023.

57. Higgins, "Community Connection: Allentown Art Museum Artist-in-Residence."

58. Interview with Dianne Smith, March 14, 2023.

59. Shange, *For Colored Girls.*

60. Interview with Dianne Smith, March 14, 2023.

61. Interview with Dianne Smith, March 14, 2023.

62. Interview with Dianne Smith, March 14, 2023.

63. Harriet Tubman, Goodreads.com, https://www.goodreads.com/quotes/
5935-every-great-dream-begins-with-a-dreamer-always-remember-you.

64. Jerrilyn McGregory, "Junkanoo/Jankunú," in *One Grand Noise: Boxing Day in the Anglicized Caribbean World,* 55–78 (Jackson: University Press of Mississippi, 2021).

65. Global Sherpa, Garifuna People, History and Culture, http://globalsherpa.org/
garifunas-garifuna/

Chapter 8. Community-Based Arts and Socioenvironmental Wellness

1. Syracuse University Community Folk Art Center, "History," n.d., https://
communityfolkartcenter.org/history/.

2. CFAC, "History."

3. WSYR-TV, "Throwback Thursday: The Long-Gone 15th Ward in Syracuse," Local SYR, February 4, 2021, https://www.localsyr.com/throwback-thursday/
throwback-thursday-the-long-gone-15th-ward/. "The 15th Ward was a section of Syracuse that sat between downtown Syracuse and the University Hill area. Much of the largely African American neighborhood was destroyed to make way for the construction of Interstate 81." When President Dwight D. Eisenhower signed the Federal-Aid Highway Act in June 1956, it authorized the construction of "a 41,000-mile network of interstate highways that would span the nation." This included the construction of I-81 in the heart of Syracuse. It became evident that many of the highways were being built through Black and brown communities. In Syracuse, Interstate 81 "came with the forced displacement of nearly 1,300 residents from the city's 15th Ward." Surrounding areas were destroyed due to urban renewal in the 1960s, resulting

in the relocation of 75 percent of the African American neighborhood, "devastat[ing] a historic Black community, severing the social fabric of the community and razing swaths of buildings, and with them, affordable housing options. Neighborhood deterioration, a glut of surface parking lots, and citywide population loss followed."

4. CFAC, "History."

5. Jacqueline Chanda and Vesta Daniel, "Recognizing Works of Art: The Essences of Contextual Understanding," *Art Education* 53, no. 2 (2000): 6–11, https://doi.org/10.2307/3193844.

6. Syracuse CFAC | Virtual Museum, http://cfacgallery.org. Eri O'Diah is the founder and former CEO of Collective.ly Digital, a digital marketing agency, and also the founder of SIID Technologies, a tech startup focused on mitigating biases in systems and institutions through AI SaaS solutions. Collective.ly Digital designed the initial version of cfacgallery.org

7. Danielle Ponder, "Danielle Ponder Presents: For the Love of Justice," n.d., https://danielleponder.com/for-the-love-of-justice.

8. Daniel Kushner, "Danielle Ponder—A Singer Who Was Once a Lawyer—Enjoys Critical Raves," NPR, September 17, 2022, https://www.npr.org/2022/09/17/1123657145/danielle-ponder-a-singer-who-was-once-a-lawyer-enjoys-critical-raves.

9. Isobel van Hagen and Matthew Mulligan, "Violinist Performs Balcony Concert in Locked-Down Italy," NBC News, March 14, 2020, https://www.nbcnews.com/health/health-news/live-blog/coronavirus-updates-live-house-approves-coronavirus-aid-bill-n1158821/ncrd1158866.

10. Carrie Mae Weems is the artist in residence at Syracuse University. Her Social Studies 101 initiative spearheaded the *Resist COVID/Take 6!* campaign. The "Take 6!" in the title referred to the six feet of social distancing recommended for safety. Launched in 2020, this project aimed to encourage preventive actions, counter misinformation, and recognize the contributions of front-line and essential workers. The campaign was featured in Atlanta, Dallas, Detroit, Johannesburg, London, Los Angeles, New York City, and Philadelphia. For additional details, please visit http://socialstudiesproject.org.

11. Jessica Houghtaling, "Syracuse Art Campaign Highlights COVID's Impact on Minorities," Spectrum News 1 Central NY, July 9, 2020, https://spectrumlocalnews.com/nys/central-ny/coronavirus/2020/07/09/syracuse-art-campaign-highlights-covid-s-impact-on-minorities.

12. The Links, Incorporated, https://linksinc.org/the-links-incorporated/. Since 1946, The Links, Inc. has been "one of the nation's oldest and largest volunteer service organizations of extraordinary women who are committed to enriching, sustaining and ensuring the culture and economic survival of African Americans and other persons of African ancestry."

13. Syracuse Community Folk Art Center, *Teen Art Competition Exhibit 2021*, https://www.cfacgallery.org/teen-art-competition-exhibit-2021/.

14. Syracuse Community Folk Art Center, *Teen Art Competition Exhibit 2021*.

15. Central New York Community Foundation, "Black Equity & Excellence," n.d., https://cnycf.org/receive/grants/black-equity-excellence/.

16. Central New York Community Foundation, "First Grants Awarded from Black Equity & Excellence Fund," September 29, 2020, https://cnycf.org/first-grants-awarded-from-black-equity-excellence-fund/.

17. Harriet Tubman Home, Harriet Tubman National Historical Park, https://www.nps.gov/places/harriettubmanhome.htm. "The Tubman Home was designated a National Historic Landmark on May 30, 1974, and added to the National Register of Historic Places on April 2, 1999. It was later designated Harriet Tubman National Historical Park, under the National Park Service, Department of the Interior, on January 10, 2017."

18. Unwrapping Vanessa Johnson, *Mentor Series 3*, https://www.vanessajohnsonstoryteller.com/mentor-series-3.

19. Quilts as a Visual History, Clio History, https://www.cliohistory.org/visualizingamerica/quilts/visualhistory.

20. Jeanne Albanese, "CNY Chapter of American Pen Women celebrates More Than 95 Years of Supporting Women in Art," Syracuse, March 25, 2022, https://www.syracuse.com/living/2022/03/cny-chapter-of-american-pen-women-celebrates-more-than-95-years-of-supporting-women-in-art.html.

21. ArtRage, "UNWRAPPING VANESSA: Fiber memory art by Vanessa Johnson," https://artragegallery.org/unwrapping-vanessa-fiber-memory-art-by-vanessa-johnson/.

22. Evans, Bell, and Burton, *Black Women's Mental Health*.

23. "Who We Are . . .," Shades of Inspiration, n.d., https://www.shadesofinspiration.org/about-us-1.

24. Linh Le, "Foundation Awards Grants for Initiatives That Improve Black Communities," Daily Orange, October 21, 2020, https://dailyorange.com/2020/10/foundation-awards-grants-initiatives-improve-black-communities/.

25. Vanessa Johnson, "Sankofa N. E. S. T. is excited to announce," Facebook, October 5, 2020, https://www.facebook.com/share/19PYPtFUjt/?mibextid=wwXIfr.

26. *High-Flown Words: Griot Guide Youth Storytelling Created During the COVID Pandemic* (New York: Wildebeest Publishing, 2022).

27. Faith Ringgold, *Tar Beach* (New York: Crown, 1991).

28. Kathleen Hunter, "Putting Books to Work: TAR BEACH," International Literacy Association, February 18, 2014, https://www.literacyworldwide.org/blog/literacy-now/2014/02/18/putting-books-to-work-tar-beach.

29. Interview with Vanessa Johnson, 2022.

30. Interview with Vanessa Johnson, 2022.

31. Interview with Vanessa Johnson, 2022.

32. Interview with Vanessa Johnson, 2022.

33. Interview with Vanessa Johnson, 2022.

34. Interview with Vanessa Johnson, 2022.

35. Interview with Vanessa Johnson, 2022.

36. Interview with Vanessa Johnson, 2022.

37. Interview with Vanessa Johnson, 2022.

38. Interview with Vanessa Johnson, 2022.

39. Interview with Vanessa Johnson, 2022.
40. Interview with Vanessa Johnson, 2022.
41. Interview with Vanessa Johnson, 2022.
42. Interview with Vanessa Johnson, 2022.
43. Interview with Vanessa Johnson, 2022.

Epilogue

Epigraph. Creative Time Summit NYC | A Curriculum's Content: Simone Leigh, YouTube, December 8, 2015, https://www.youtube.com/watch?v=2v0Tc5aQ8fo.

1. Harris, "Sonia Boyce's British Pavilion."

2. "Artist Dossier: Simone Leigh," Penn Arts & Sciences: Architecture, https://architecture.sas.upenn.edu/student-work/architecture-university/arch-401 -advanced-design/arch-401-gallery-african-american-11.

3. Guggenheim Museum, "Simone Leigh: *Loophole of Retreat* at the Guggenheim," Gotham To Go—Art & Culture, May 2, 2019, https://gothamtogo.com/ simone-leigh-loophole-of-retreat-at-the-guggenheim/.

4. "In Venice, Simone Leigh Reimagines Colonial Narratives," *Economist*, May 3, 2022, https://www.economist.com/culture/2022/05/03/in-venice-simone -leigh-reimagines-colonial-narratives.

5. Grace Ebert, "Artist Simone Leigh Embodies Self-Determination in the Historic 'Sovereignty' at the Venice Biennale," Colossal, May 3, 2022, https://www. thisiscolossal.com/2022/05/simone-leigh-sovereignty/.

6. Guggenheim Museum, "Simone Leigh: *Loophole of Retreat*."

7. BOTWC staff, "Here's Everything You Never Learned about Weeksville, the Once Thriving Black Community in Brooklyn," Because of Them We Can, January 20, 2023, https://www.becauseofthemwecan.com/blogs/culture/here-s-everything-you-never-learned-about-weeksville-the-once-thriving-black-community-in-brooklyn.

8. Rizvana Bradley, "Going Underground: An Interview with Simone Leigh." Art in America, August 20, 2015, https://www.artnews.com/art-in-america/interviews/going-underground-an-interview-with-simone-leigh-56438/.

"Abstract Art by Black Women Artists from 1960s to Today at Women's Museum in DC." ArtfixDaily, September 6, 2017. https://www.artfixdaily.com/artwire/release/4563-abstract-art-by-black-women-artists-from-1960s-to-today-at-women%E2%80%99.

Acuff, Joni Boyd. "Black Feminist Theory in 21st-Century Art Education Research." *Studies in Art Education* 59, no. 3 (2018): 201–14.

Albanese, Jeanne. "CNY Chapter of American Pen Women Celebrates More than 95 Years of Supporting Women in Art." Syracuse, March 25, 2022. https://www.syracuse.com/living/2022/03/cny-chapter-of-american-pen-women-celebrates-more-than-95-years-of-supporting-women-in-art.html.

Albritton, Caitlin. "Women Who Can Fly." *Creative Loafing*, February 9, 2017. https://www.proquest.com/newspapers/women-who-can-fly/docview/1870210040/se-2.

Alexander, Elizabeth. *The Black Interior*. Minneapolis: Graywolf Press, 2001.

Alexander, Michelle. *The New Jim Crow: Mass Incarceration in the Age of Colorblindness*. New York: New Press, 2010.

Alford, Keith, Patrick McKenry, and Stephen Gavazzi. "Enhancing Achievement in Adolescent Black Males: The Rites of Passage Link." In *Educating Our Black Children: New Directions and Radical Approaches*, edited by Richard Majors, 141–56. London: RoutledgeFalmer, 2001.

Alford, Keith A. "Cultural Themes in Rites of Passage: Voices of Young African American Males." *Journal of African American Studies* 7, no. 1 (2003): 3–26. https://doi.org/10.1007/s12111-003-1C00-y.

Allen, Brenda J. "Feminist Standpoint Theory: A Black Woman's (Re)View of Organizational Socialization." *Communication Studies* 47, no. 4 (1996): 257–71. https://doi.org/10.1080/10510979609368482.

Alvarez, Lizette, and Cara Buckley. "Zimmerman Is Acquitted in Trayvon Martin Killing." *New York Times*, July 13, 2013. https://www.nytimes.com/2013/07/14/us/george-zimmerman-verdict-trayvon-martin.html.

American Experience. "Freedom Riders: Jim Crow Laws." PBS, n.d. https://www
.pbs.org/wgbh/americanexperience/features/freedom-riders-jim-crow-laws/.

Antonucci, Michael A. Review of *The Chitlin' Circuit and the Road to Rock 'n' Roll*,
by Preston Lauderbach. *American Studies* 53, no. 1 (2014): 202–4. http://dx.doi
.org/10.1353/ams.2014.0057.

Arbelaez, Camila. "Vanessa German's Art House: A Stronghold against Gentrification." *Brown Political Review*. November 13, 2017. https://brownpoliticalreview
.org/2017/11/vanessa-germans-art-house-stronghold-gentrification/.

Art Basel. "About: Overview." N.d. https://www.artbasel.com/about.

"Artist Dossier: Simone Leigh." Penn Arts & Sciences: Architecture. https://
architecture.sas.upenn.edu/student-work/architecture-university/arch-401
-advanced-design/arch-401-gallery-african-american-11.

ArtRage, "UNWRAPPING VANESSA: Fiber memory art by Vanessa Johnson," https://
artragegallery.org/unwrapping-vanessa-fiber-memory-art-by-vanessa-johnson/.

Arts Impact Explorer. "We Will Not Be Disappeared! Directory of Arts Activism." 1983. http://ww2.americansforthearts.org/publications/we-will-not-be
-disappeared-directory-arts-activism.

Asante, Molefi Kete. *The History of Africa: The Quest for Eternal Harmony*. London:
Routledge, 2024.

Associated Press. "Heartbreaking: Alexis Crawford, 21, Found Dead." *EEW
Magazine,* November 8, 2019. https://www.eewmagazineonline.com/latest
-news/2019/11/8/pray-for-the-family-missing-clark-atlanta-university-student
-alexis-crawford-found-dead-police-call-it-heartbreaking.

Associated Press. "Timeline of Key Events in Eric Garner Chokehold Death," AP,
July 16, 2019. https://apnews.com/general-news-ec7ac5a664d74cdab852d639
c0da08f4.

Autry, LaTanya, and Mike Murawsky. "Museums Are Not Neutral: We Are Stronger
Together," *Panorama* 5, no. 2 (2019), https://journalpanorama.org/article/public
-scholarship/museums-are-not-neutral/.

Bacon, Francis. "Meditationes Sacrae." London: Excusum impensis Humfredi
Hooper, 1597.

Barber, Rebekah. "Say Her Name Campaign Targets Police Killings of Black Women
and Girls." *Facing South*, July 15, 2020. https://www.facingsouth.org/2020/07/
say-her-name-campaign-targets-police-killings-black-women-and-girls.

Batchen, Geoffrey, Richard Beard, Mark Haworth-Booth, Curtis Moffat, et al. "Who
Are You Looking At?" *Art on Paper* 12, no. 4 (2008): 48–75. http://www.jstor
.org/stable/24556754.

Beauboeuf-Lafontant, Tamara. *Behind the Mask of the Strong Black Woman: Voice
and the Embodiment of a Costly Performance*. Philadelphia: Temple University
Press, 2009.

Beckerman, Jim. "To B, Or Not to b? Why Capitalize the 'B' in Black?" Northjersey.com,
October 13, 2021, https://www.northjersey.com/story/opinion/columnists/2021/
10/13/why-capitalize-b-black/5980347001/.

Beckerman, Jim. "'Washington Crossing the Delaware,' Reimagined, at Montclair
Art Museum," *Bergen Record*, March 21, 2023, https://www.northjersey.com/

story/entertainment/arts/2023/03/21/washington-crossing-the-delaware-is
-reimagined-at-montclair-museum/69994053007/.

Bedolla, Myrtis. *Tea with Myrtis: Artistically Speaking with Shanequa Gay.* YouTube,
March 27, 2020. https://www.youtube.com/watch?v=SyNyZbgf_g&t=2s.

"bell hooks & Gloria Steinem at Eugene Lang College." YouTube, October 8, 2014.
https://www.youtube.com/watch?v=tkzOFvfWRn4.

Betancourt, Sofía. "Between Dishwater and the River." *Worldviews: Environment,
Culture, Religion* 20, no. 1 (2016): 64–75. https://doi.org/10.1163/15685357
-02001006.

Bianchi, Mike, and Scott Maxwell. "Church Mothers Are Pillars of Faith." *Sentinel*, June 8, 2002. https://www.orlandosentinel.com/news/os-xpm-2002-06-08
-0206070454-story.html.

Biodiversity BC. Sitemap. 2007. http://www.biodiversitybc.org/EN/topnav/31.html.

Biology Online. "Abiotic Factor." Biology Online Dictionary. https://www.biology
online.com/dictionary/abiotic-factor, retrieved November 21, 2023.

Black Art: In the Absence of Light. Directed by Sam Pollard. HBO Documentary
Films and TwoDollars and a Dream, 2020.

"Black Power." National Archives. https://www.archives.gov/research/african
-americans/black-power.

Black Power. In "It's Handled." https://www.powerinblack.com/products/its
-handled?variant=8775564001329.

Black, William R. "How Watermelons Became a Racist Trope." *The Atlantic*,
December 8, 2014. https://www.theatlantic.com/national/archive/2014/12/
how-watermelons-became-a-racist-trope/383529/.

Black Women's Health Imperative. "An Open Letter on Health Disparities to
President Biden, Vice President Harris, and Members of Your National Health
Care Team." February 23, 2021. https://bwhi.org/2021/02/23/an-open-letter
-on-health-disparities-to-president-biden-vice-president-harris-and-members
-of-your-national-health-care-team/.

Blackartinamerica.com. April 19, 2021. https://www.blackartinamerica.com/index
.php/2021/04/19/hbcus-the-first-patrons-of-african-american-art/.

Blas, Lorena. "Oprah Winfrey to Star in HBO's 'Henrietta Lacks' Movie." USA
Today, May 2, 2016. https://www.usatoday.com/story/life/tv/2016/05/02/
oprah-winfrey-hbo-the-immortal-life-of-henrietta-lacks/83833298/.

Bowles, John. "Acting Like A Man": Adrian Piper's Mythic Being and Black Feminism in the 1970s." *Signs* 2 (2007): 621–47.

BOTWC staff. "Here's Everything You Never Learned about Weeksville, the Once
Thriving Black Community in Brooklyn." Because of Them We Can, January 20,
2023. https://www.becauseofthemwecan.com/blogs/culture/here-s-everything
-you-never-learned-about-weeksville-the-once-thriving-black-community-in
-brooklyn.

Boyce, Sonia. "Daily Inspiration." Inspiring Quotes. Accessed January 2, 2024.
https://www.inspiringquotes.com/inspiration/63b48f5c1559f6000930003b?liu
=bfb99dadf51e2d85f3443cda78c57e07.

Bradley, Rizvana. "Going Underground: An Interview with Simone Leigh." Art in

America, August 20, 2015. https://www.artnews.com/art-in-america/interviews/going-underground-an-interview-with-simone-leigh-56438/.

"Brooklyn Museum." Brooklynmuseum.org. https://www.brooklynmuseum.org/opencollection/exhibitions/3347.

Brown, Aleia N. "Alma Woodsey Thomas." National Women's History Museum, 2021. https://www.womenshistory.org/education-resources/biographies/alma-woodsey-thomas.

Brown, Kay. "The Emergence of Black Women Artists: The Founding of 'Where We At.'" *Nka 2011, no.* 29 (2011): 118–27, https://doi.org/10.1215/10757163-1496399.

Brown, Kay. "Where We at': Black Women Artists." *Feminist Art Journal* 1, no. 1 (1972): 25.

Browne-Marshall, Gloria J. *The Voting Rights War: The NAACP and the Ongoing Struggle for Justice.* Lanham, MD: Rowman & Littlefield, 2017.

Brunetta, Grazia, Rosario Ceravolo, Carlo Alberto Barbieri, Alberto Borghini, Francesca de Carlo, et al. "Territorial Resilience: Toward a Proactive Meaning for Spatial Planning." *Sustainability* 11, no. 8 (2019): 2286, https://doi.org/10.3390/su11082286.

Brunius, Harry. "African Burial Ground under New York Streets." *Christian Science Monitor,* June 17, 1999. https://www.proquest.com/newspapers/african-burial-ground-under-new-york-streets/docview/405654088/se-2.

Bryant-Davis, Thema, and Lillian Comas-Díaz. "Introduction: Womanist and Mujerista Psychologies." In *Womanist and Mujerista Psychologies: Voices of Fire, Acts of Courage,* 3–25. Washington, DC: American Psychological Association, 2016.

Buck, Kimberlee. "The 1963 Birmingham Children's Crusade, A Turning Point for the Civil Rights Movement." *Los Angeles Sentinel,* April 25, 2019. https://lasentinel.net/the-1963-birmingham-childrens-crusade-a-turning-point-for-the-civil-rights-movement.html.

Bullock, Maggie. "The Future of Work: The 'Citizen Artist' Bringing Hope to Pittsburgh's Homewood." Shondaland, April 17, 2019. https://www.shondaland.com/inspire/a27168640/vanessa-german-citizen-artist-pittsburgh-homewood/.

Burke, Sarah. "A House Full of Black Women Gets a Week of Rest." KQED. March 30, 2017. https://www.kqed.org/arts/12959678/a-house-full-of-black-women-a-week-of-rest.

Burley, Dan. "Augusta Savage Realizes Dream: Artistic Hands Did This." *New York Amsterdam News,* December 18, 1937, 24. https://www.proquest.com/historical-newspapers/augusta-savage-realizes-dream/docview/226180974/se-2.

Burns, Stewart. "Living for the Revolution: Black Feminist Organizations, 1968–1980." *Journal of American History* 93, no. 1 (2006): 296–97. https://doi.org/10.2307/4486214.

Butler, Judith. "Between Grief and Grievance, a New Sense of Justice." In *Grief and Grievance: Art and Mourning in America (from Civil Rights to Black Lives Matter),* edited by Okwui Enwezor, Naomi Beckwith, and Massimiliano Gioni, 11–15. London: Phaidon, 2020.

Butler, Octavia E. *Kindred.* New York: Doubleday, 1979.

Bynoe, Yvonne. "HBCUs: The First Patrons of African-American Art." Black Art in America. https://www.blackartinamerica.com/blogs/news/hbcus-the-first -patrons-of-african-american-art.

Bynoe, Yvonne. "How Public Art Projects Expanded Opportunities for a Generation of Black Artists, Part 1." Black Art In America™ Gallery & Gardens. October 10, 2021. https://www.blackartinamerica.com/blogs/news/how-public -art-projects-expanded-opportunities-for-a-generation-of-black-artists-part-1.

Campagna, Anna. "Roya Marsh—'Blk Joy'." Button Poetry. May 31, 2021. https:// buttonpoetry.com/roya-marsh-blk-joy/.

Capatides, Christina. "South Carolina Church Shooting Victims." CBS News, June 18, 2015. https://www.cbsnews.com/pictures/church-shooting-victims/16/.

Capra, Fritjof. *From the Parts to the Whole: Systems Thinking in Ecology and Education.* New York: Anchor Books, 1994.

Carter, Leeja, and Amerigo Rossi. "Superwoman: Exploring Stress, Coping, and Physical Activity among African American Women." Paper presented at the Association for Applied Sport Psychology, Phoenix, Arizona, 2016.

"Category: Abstraction." Ultrawolvesunderthefullmoon, December 29, 2020. https://ultrawolvesunderthefullmoon.blog/category/abstraction/.

Centers for Disease Control and Prevention. "About COVID-19." May 11, 2023. https://archive.cdc.gov/#/details?q=About%20COVID-19&start=0 &rows=10&url=https://www.cdc.gov/coronavirus/2019-ncov/your-health/ about-covid-19.html/.

Central New York Community Foundation. "Black Equity & Excellence." N.d. https://cnycf.org/receive/grants/black-equity-excellence/.

Central New York Community Foundation. "First Grants Awarded from Black Equity & Excellence Fund." September 29, 2020. https://cnycf.org/ first-grants-awarded-from-black-equity-excellence-fund/.

Chanda, Jacqueline, and Vesta Daniel. "Recognizing Works of Art: The Essences of Contextual Understanding." *Art Education* 53, no. 2 (2000): 6–11. https://doi.org/ 10.2307/3193844.

Charlton, Linda. "'South 40' Tries to Aid Convicts." *New York Times*, April 23, 1972.

Chatmon, Tawny. "About." N. d. https://www.tawnychatmon.com/about.

Chowdhry, Pritika. "Five Pioneering Site-Specific Artists You Should Know." Pritika Chowdhry Art. November 6, 2021. https://www.pritikachowdhry.com/post/ site-specific-art.

Cite Black Women. "Our Story." n.d. https://www.citeblackwomencollective.org/ our-story.html.

CNN. "Ex-Atlanta Officers Get Prison Time for Cover-up in Deadly Raid." February 24, 2009.

CNN. "Ex-Cops Apologize for Deadly Drug Raid Ahead of Sentencing." February 23, 2009.

CNN. "September 11 Terror Attacks Fast Facts." August 21, 2024. https://www.cnn .com/2013/07/27/us/september-11-anniversary-fast-facts/index.html.

Collins, Patricia Hill. "Black Feminist Epistemology." In *Black Feminist Thought*, 267–88. New York: Routledge, 2000.

Collins, Patricia Hill. *Black Feminist Thought: Knowledge, Consciousness, and the Politics of Empowerment*. New York: Routledge, 2000.

The Colored Girls Museum. "Urgent Care." https://www.facebook.com/events/the-colored-girls-museum/tcgm-presents-urgent-carea-social-care-experience/473116809723365/?ref=110.

Comas-Díaz, Lillian, ed. *Womanist and Mujerista Psychologies: Voices of Fire, Acts of Courage*. Washington, D.C., DC: American Psychological Association, 2016.

"Community Folk Art Center Presents Exhibition 'Stories My Grandmother Told Me.'" January 27, 2021. https://news.syr.edu/blog/2021/01/27/community-folk-art-center-presents-exhibition-stories-my-grandmother-told-me/.

Community Folk Art Center. "History." 1972. https://communityfolkartcenter.org/history/.

Cooper, Anna Julia. *A Voice from the South*. New York: Oxford University Press, 2005.

Cooper, Brittney C. *Beyond Respectability : The Intellectual Thought of Race Women*. Urbana: University of Illinois Press, 2017.

"The Cosby Show." *Encyclopedia Britannica,* 2023. https://www.britannica.com/topic/The-Cosby-Show.

Cousins, Linda. "'Where We At' Black Women Artists : A Tapestry of Many Fine Threads." National Gallery of Art, 1986. https://ia601600.us.archive.org/15/items/where-we-at-exhibit-brochure/Where%20We%20At%20-%20Exhibit%20Brochure_text.pdf.

Creative Time Summit NYC | A Curriculum's Content: Simone Leigh. YouTube, December 8, 2015. https://www.youtube.com/watch?v=2v0Tc5aQ8fo.

"Culture Conscious in Chicago." *Negro Digest* 16, no. 10 (1967): 85–87.

Dague, Tyler. "ArtHouse Donations Surpass $115K after Fire in Homewood." *Pittsburgh Post-Gazette*, March 3, 2021. https://www.post-gazette.com/ae/art-architecture/2021/03/03/Homewood-ArtHouse-fire-Vanessa-German/stories/202102250138.

Dague, Tyler. "George Floyd." *Pittsburgh Post-Gazette*, May 28, 2021. https://www.proquest.com/docview/2533106209/C6315956F4ED48EAPQ/7?accountid=14214&parentSessionId=DhEP5ns2XpyEgiB%2Fq2NQjiJGv1BSIgNeKEhsrv1lMYM%3D.

Dague, Tyler. "Vanessa German's Grief Over Black Deaths Reaches the Frick." *Pittsburgh Post-Gazette,* April 11, 2021, https://www.proquest.com/newspapers/reckoning-vanessa-germans-grief-over-black-deaths/docview/2510658277/se-2?accountid=14214.

Dague, Tyler. "vanessa german's Grief over Black Deaths the Subject of a Powerful Museum Show," *Pittsburgh Post-Gazette*, April 11, 2021. https://www.post-gazette.com/ae/art-architecture/2021/04/11/Vanessa-German-The-Frick-Pittsburgh-art-Reckoning-Grief-Light-George-Floyd-Breonna-Taylor-Elijah-McClain/stories/202104050084." Danielle Ponder." n.d. Danielleponder.com. https://danielleponder.com/bio.

David, Jonathan C. *Together Let Us Sweetly Live: The Singing and Praying Bands*. Champaign: University of Illinois Press, 2007.

Davis, Angela. "Reflections on the Black Woman's Role in the Community of Slaves." *Journal of Black Studies and Research* 13, no. 1/2 (1972): 3–15.

Demby, Gene. "Where Did That Fried Chicken Stereotype Come From?" *Code Switch*, NPR, May 22, 2013. https://www.npr.org/sections/ codeswitch/2013/05/22/186087397/where-did-that-fried-chicken-stereotype -come-from.

Desalu, Carolyn. "Things to Do: Art Explores Culture, Issues," *Atlanta Journal-Constitution,* February 26, 2015, https://www.proquest.com/newspapers/ things-do-art-explores-culture-issues/docview/1658361453/se-2.

Diamond, Irene. *Reweaving the World: The Emergence of Ecofeminism.* Sierra Club Books, 1990.

Dickerson, Amina J. "African American Museums and the New Century: Challenges in Leadership." In *Leadership for the Future: Changing Directorial Roles in American History Museums and Historical Societies; Collected Essays,* edited by Bryant Franklin Tolles, 167–82. Nashville: American Association for State and Local History, 1991.

Dirshe, Siraad. "What Does It Mean to 'Center Black People'?" *New York Times,* June 19, 2020, https://www.nytimes.com/2020/06/19/style/self-care/centering -blackness.html.

Dobrin, Peter. "Stories of Courage: '#SayTheirNames' Remembers the Black Women Who Fought for Justice." *Philadelphia Daily News,* January 18, 2021. https:// www.proquest.com/newspapers/stories-courage/docview/2478461650/se-2.

Doswell, Raymond. "Evaluating Educational Value in Museum Exhibitions: Establishing an Evaluation Process for the Negro Leagues Baseball Museum." EdD dissertation, Kansas State University, 2008, https://krex.k-state.edu/items/ f32f207f-d8e1-4e8e-a02e-cbaecb4c1849/full.

Drake-Burnette, Danielle, Bravada Garrett-Akinsanya, and Thelma Bryant-Davis. "Womanism, Creativity, and Resistance: Making a Way Out of 'No Way.'" In *Womanist and Mujerista Psychologies: Voices of Fire, Acts of Courage,* edited by Thema Bryant-Davis and Lillian Comas-Díaz, 173–93. Washington, DC: American Psychological Association, 2016.

Dunbar, Paul Laurence. "We Wear the Mask." Poetry Foundation, https://www .poetryfoundation.org/poems/44203/we-wear-the-mask.

Ebert, Grace. "Artist Simone Leigh Embodies Self-Determination in the Historic 'Sovereignty' at the Venice Biennale." Colossal, May 3, 2022. https://www.thisis colossal.com/2022/05/simone-leigh-sovereignty/.

Ellsworth, Scott. *Death in a Promised Land: The Tulsa Race Riots of 1921.* Baton Rouge: Louisiana State University Press, 1992.

Enwezor, Okwui, Naomi Beckwith, and Massimilliano Gioni, eds. *Grief and Grievance: Art and Mourning in America.* London: Phaidon, 2020.

Epstein, Rebecca, Jamilia J. Blake, and Thalia González. "Girlhood Interrupted: The Erasure of Black Girls' Childhood." Center on Poverty and Inequality, Georgetown Law, June 27, 2017. https://www.law.georgetown.edu/poverty-inequality -center/wp-content/uploads/sites/14/2017/08/girlhood-interrupted.pdf.

Esaak, Shelley. "What Are the Visual Arts?" ThoughtCo, October 1, 2009, https://www.thoughtco.com/what-are-the-visual-arts-182706.

Evans, Kelley D. "Artist Shanequa Gay Brings Inspiring Black Experiences to Canvas in New Exhibition." Andscape, March 6, 2017. https://andscape.com/features/artist-shanequa-gay/.

Evans, Stephanie Y. *Black Women's Yoga History: Memoirs of Inner Peace*. Albany: State University of New York Press, 2021.

Evans, Stephanie Y., Kanika Bell, and Nsenga K. Burton, eds. *Black Women's Mental Health: Balancing Strength and Vulnerability*. Albany: State University of New York Press, 2018.

Evans, Stephanie Y., Sarita K. Davis, Leslie R. Hinkson, and Deanna J. Wathington. *Black Women and Public Health: Strategies to Name, Locate, and Change Systems of Power*. Albany: State University of New York Press, 2022.

"Ex-Cops Apologize for Deadly Drug Raid Ahead of Sentencing." CNN, February 23, 2009. https://www.cnn.com/2009/CRIME/02/23/atlanta.police.sentencing/index.html.

"Explore the 2022 Exhibition at the British Pavilion: Feeling Her Way." British Council, 2022. https://venicebiennale.britishcouncil.org/feeling-her-way.

Fanon, Frantz. *Black Skin, White Masks*. Translated by Richard Philcox. New York: Penguin Classics, 2021.

Farrington, Lisa E. *African American Art: A Visual and Cultural History*. New York: Oxford University Press, 2017.

Farrington, Lisa E. *Creating Their Own Image : The History of African-American Women Artists*. Oxford: Oxford University Press 2005.

Feaster, Felicia. "Artist Mixes Hometown Pride with Sadness: Artwork Originates in Childhood Experiences Growing Up in Atlanta." *Atlanta Journal-Constitution,* January 30, 2022. https://www.proquest.com/newspapers/artist-mixes-hometown-pride-with-sadness-artwork/docview/2623653490/se-2.

Feaster, Felicia. "Ordinary People, Powerful Drawings: Visual Arts Review Lava Thomas." *Atlanta Journal-Constitution,* November 11, 2022.

Ferdinand, Malcom, and Romy Opperman. "Decolonial Ecologies." In *What Matters Most*, edited by Anthony Morgan, 91–98. Newcastle upon Tyne: Agenda Publishing, 2023, https://doi.org/10.2307/jj.1357297.15.

Finley, Cheryl. "Visual Legacies of Slavery and Emancipation." *Callaloo* 37, no. 4 (2014): 1023–32, http://www.jstor.org/stable/24265081.

"Flower Meaning & Symbolism—Here Is What You Didn't Know about Sunflowers." *Bloom This*, September 20, 2018. https://bloomthis.co/blogs/facts/flower-meaning-symbolism-the-meaning-of-sunflowers.

Ford, Tanisha C. *Liberated Threads: Black Women, Style, and the Global Politics of Soul*. Chapel Hill: University of North Carolina Press, 2015.

"Françoise d'Eaubonne's Le Féminisme Ou La Mort." Environment & Society Portal. https://www.environmentandsociety.org/tools/keywords/francoise-deaubonnes-le-feminisme-ou-la-mort.

Frick Pittsburgh. *vanessa german—Reckoning: Grief and Light, nothing can separate you from the language you cry in.* YouTube, May 17, 2021. https://www.youtube .com/watch?v=IwVHmI5FQPU.

Galerie Myrtis. *Shanequa Gay—The Crooked Room 2018.* YouTube, March 27, 2020. https://www.youtube.com/watch?v=f4LIJAXz6Og.

Galerie Myrtis. *Women Heal through Rite and Ritual.* January 27, 2020. http:// galeriemyrtis.net/women-heal-through-rite-and-ritual/.

Gaspésie Literary Council. "Types of Literacy." N.d. https://gaspelit.ca/types-of- literacy/.

Gay, Shanequa. *Creative Mornings Atlanta*, April 24, 2020. https://www.youtube .com/watch?v=p3I_RFfWAxs.

german, vanessa [@vanessalgerman]. "Allow me to introduce myself." Instagram, n.d. https://www.instagram.com/p/C0jr6fJswAG/.

german, vanessa [@vanessalgerman]. "THE BLUE WALK Is Next Thursday Eve- ning, MAY 27TH. This Is a Reckoning Ritual of Love, Healing, Grief, Grace and Gratitude." Instagram, March 31, 2021. https://www.instagram.com/p/ CPLStYkFPD0/?utm_source=ig_web_copy_link.

german, vanessa [@vanessalgerman]. "High. Greetings." Instagram. December 7, 2023. https://www.instagram.com/p/C0jr5fJswAG/.

german, vanessa [@vanessalgerman]. "I Found out Today That Someone Killed the Little Boy Who Sold Waters Out of a Cooler on the Street Corner." Ins- tagram, March 31, 2022. https://www.instagram.com/p/CbytpRBsHDZ/ ?utm_source=ig_web_copy_link.

german, vanessa [@vanessalgerman]. "made a Sculpture for the Boy." Instagram. April 21, 2022. https://www.instagram.com/p/CcnqrdGLx11/?igshid=MTc4 MmM1YmI2Ng%3D%3D.

german, vanessa [@vanessalgerman]. "Poem." TEDxPittsburgh, December 5, 2011. https://www.youtube.com/watch?v=Dngr3s72i18.

german, vanessa [@vanessalgerman]. "Tonight I Make Poems for the People Who Wrote Me Stories of Their Lost Loved Ones." Instagram, May 20, 2022. https:// www.instagram.com/p/CPF9gm2lH-z/?utm_source=ig_web_copy_link.

Global Sherpa. "Garifuna People, History and Culture." Global Sherpa. http:// globalsherpa.org/garifunas-garifuna/.

Glueck, Grace. "Art: Studio Museum Exhibits Alma Thomas." *New York Times*, April 29, 1983. https://www.nytimes.com/1983/04/29/arts/art-studio-museum -exhibits-alma-thomas.html.

Gokhale, Chaitanya S., Mariana Velasque, and Jai A. Denton. "Ecological Drivers of Community Cohesion." *mSystems* 8, no. 1 (2023): e0092922. https://doi.org/ 10.1128/msystems.00929-22.

Goodman, Leo A. "Comment: On Respondent-Driven Sampling and Snowball Sampling in Hard-to-Reach Populations and Snowball Sampling Not in Hard-to- Reach Populations." *Sociological Methodology* 41 no. 1 (2011): 347–53. https://doi .org/10.1111/j.1467-9531.2011.01242.x.

Gottlieb, Roger S. *This Sacred Earth: Religion, Nature, Environment.* 2nd ed. New York: Routledge, 2004.

Gray, Helen T. "Church Mothers Are Pillars of Faith." *Orlando Sentinel*, August 5, 2021. https://www.orlandosentinel.com/news/os-xpm-2002-06-08-0206070454 -story.html.

Grimes, William. "Varnette Honeywood, Whose Art Appeared on 'Cosby Show,' Dies at 59." *New York Times*, September 16, 2010. https://www.nytimes.com/ 2010/09/16/arts/design/16honeywood.html.

Gruen, Lori, and Greta Gaard. "Ecofeminism: Toward Global Justice and Planetary Health." *Society and Nature* 2, no. 1 (1993): 1–35. https://www.academia .edu/32438639/Ecofeminism_Toward_Global_Justice_and_Planetary_Health.

Guggenheim Museum. "Simone Leigh: *Loophole of Retreat* at the Guggenheim." GothamToGo—Art & Culture, May 2, 2019. https://gothamtogo.com/simone -leigh-loophole-of-retreat-at-the-guggenheim/.

Guy-Sheftall, Beverly. "Black Feminist Studies: The Case of Anna Julia Cooper." *African American Review* 43 no. 1 (2009): 11–15. https://doi.org/10.1353/afa.0 .0019.

Hamilton, Stephen. "Alaro: Indigo and the Power of Women in Yorubaland." Squarespace, n.d. https://tinyurl.com/yc88ath

Hamilton, Virginia. "The People Could Fly." In *The People Could Fly: American Black Folktales*. New York: Knopf, 1985.

Hammad, Lamia Khalil. "Black Feminist Discourse of Power in *For Colored Girls Who Have Considered Suicide*." *Rupkatha Journal on Interdisciplinary Studies in Humanities* 3, no. 2 (2011): 258–67, https://rupkatha.com/V3/n2/05_For_ Colored_Girls_Who_Have_Considered_Suicide.pdf.

Hancock, C. [@carlhancockrux]. July 5, 2021. "More Photos from #carlhancockrux's I DREAM A DREAM THAT DREAMS BACK AT ME (a Juneteenth Celebration) @lincolncenter. [Photo]." Instagram. 2021, July 5. https://www .instagram.com/p/CQ_Ex1yFPl-/?igshid=MTc4MmM1YmI2Ng==.

Hannahdrake628. "Why Are Black Women Always the Clean Up Woman?" Writesomeshit, February 27, 2018. https://writesomeshit.com/2018/02/27/why -are-black-women-always-the-clean-up-woman/.

Hardwick, April. "On A Mission to Change Hearts and Minds through Art and Activism." Luxe Interiors + Design, January 19, 2021. https://luxesource.com/ artist-delita-martin-change-hearts-minds-art-activism/.

Hare, Nathan. "Black Ecology." *Black Scholar* 1, no. 6 (1970): 2–8, https://doi.org /10.1080/00064246.1970.11728700.

Harris, Ann. "Ring Shout Across America." *Triangle Tribune* (Durham, NC), September 23, 2012. https://www.proquest.com/newspapers/ring-shout-across-america/ docview/1220468312/se-2.

Harris, Gareth. "Sonia Boyce's British Pavilion Wins Venice Biennale's Coveted Golden Lion for Best National Exhibition." Art Newspaper, April 23, 2022. https://www.theartnewspaper.com/2022/04/23/great-britain-gets -the-coveted-golden-lion-for-best-national-pavilion-in-venice.

Harris, Gareth. "Missed It in Venice? See It in Margate: Sonia Boyce's Golden Lion Exhibition Tours to Two UK Venues." Art Newspaper, October 27, 2022. https://

www.theartnewspaper.com/2022/10/27/miss-it-in-venice-see-it-in-margate
-sonia-boyces-golden-lion-exhibition-tours-to-two-uk-venues.

Harris, Melanie L. "Ecowomanism: An Introduction." *Worldviews: Environment,
Culture, Religion* 20, no. 1 (2016): 5–14. https://www.jstor.org/stable/26552243.

Harris-Perry, Melissa V. *Sister Citizen: Shame, Stereotypes, and Black Women in
America*. New Haven: Yale University Press, 2011.

Harrop, Joanne Klimovich. "Artist vanessa german to Lead Pittsburgh Walk for
George Floyd, Others Lost to Violence." Trib Live, May 25, 2021. https://triblive
.com/aande/museums/artist-vanessa-german-to-lead-pittsburgh-walk-for-george
-floyd-others-lost-to-violence/.

Heguiaphal, Maia. "Lavett Ballard's African American and Female Narratives."
Daily Art Magazine, March 4, 2025. https://www.dailyartmagazine.com/lavett
-ballard/.

Higgins, Tim. "Community Connection: Allentown Art Museum Artist-in-Residence Dianne Smith Tells Stories of City Residents and Their Struggles and Hopes
in 'Intersections' Exhibit." *Morning Call,* October 16, 2016. https://www.proquest
.com/newspapers/community-connection-allentown-art-museum-artist/
docview/1829332636/se-2.

*High-Flown Words: Griot Guide Youth Storytelling Created During the COVID Pan-
demic*. New York: Wildebeest Publishing, 2022.

"Hoboken, New Jersey, Mayor Orders Curfew." NBC News. March 14, 2020.
https://www.nbcnews.com/health/health-news/live-blog/coronavirus
-updates-live-house-approves-coronavirus-aid-bill-n1158821/ncrd1158866.

"Homewood Artist vanessa german on a Journey of Healing." May 25, 2021. https://
www.proquest.com/docview/2531921492/4825E3D39E2F4202PQ/1?account
id=14214.

hooks, bell. *Art on My Mind: Visual Politics*. New York: New Press, 1995.

hooks, bell. *Black Looks: Race and Representation*. London: Turnaround Books, 1992.

Hosbey, Justin, and J. T. Roane. "A Totally Different Form of Living: On the Legacies of Displacement and Marronage as Black Ecologies." *Southern Cultures* 27,
no. 1 (2021): 68–73, https://doi.org/10.1353/scu.2021.0009.

Houghtaling, Jessica. "Syracuse Art Campaign Highlights COVID's Impact on
Minorities." Spectrum News 1 Central NY, July 9, 2020. https://spectrumlocal
news.com/nys/central-ny/coronavirus/2020/07/09/syracuse-art-campaign
-highlights-covid-s-impact-on-minorities.

House Full of Blackwomen. Deep Waters Dance Theater. https://www.deepwaters
dance.com/housefullofblackwomen.

Houston, Kerr. "How Mining the Museum Changed the Art World." *Bmore
Art,* May 3, 2017. https://bmoreart.com/2017/05/how-mining-the-museum
-changed-the-art-world.html.

Humanize My Hoodie. "About." N.d. https://www.humanizemyhoodie.com/.

Hunter, Kathleen. "Putting Books to Work: TAR BEACH." International Literacy Association, February 18, 2014. https://www.literacyworldwide.org/blog/
literacy-now/2014/02/18/putting-books-to-work-tar-beach.

"Igbo Landing." Brittanica, n.d. https://www.britannica.com/place/Igbo-Landing.

"In Venice, Simone Leigh Reimagines Colonial Narratives." *Economist*, May 3, 2022. https://www.economist.com/culture/2022/05/03/in-venice-simone -leigh-reimagines-colonial-narratives

Inthasone, Somsack, Nicolas Pasquier, Andrea G. B. Tettamanzi, and Célia da Costa Pereira. "The BioKET Biodiversity Data Warehouse: Data and Knowledge Integration and Extraction." In *Advances in Intelligent Data Analysis XIII: 13th International Symposium*, IDA 2014, Leuven, Belgium, October 30–November 1, 2014. *Proceedings 13*. Cham, Switzerland: Springer International Publishing, 2014.

Issitt, Micah, and Carlyn Main. *Hidden Religion: The Greatest Mysteries and Symbols of the World's Religious Beliefs: The Greatest Mysteries and Symbols of the World's Religious Beliefs*. Santa Barbara: ABC-CLIO, 2014.

Jackson, Tanisha M. "MeTelling: Recovering the Black Female Body." *Visual Culture and Gender* 8 (2013): 48–56, https://vcg.emitto.net/index.php/vcg/article/view/75/74.

Jackson, Tanisha M. "What I Want You to Know: Chatmon's Visual Love Letter to Black Children" In *If I'm No Longer Here, I Wanted You to Know. . . .* Baltimore: Gallerie Myrtis, 2021. Exhibition catalog.

Jaeger, Edmund Carroll. *A Source-Book of Biological Names and Terms*. 3rd ed. Springfield, IL: Charles C. Thomas, 1978.

Jenkins, Mark. "An Intimate Panorama of Video Art's Variety and Breadth." *Washington Post*, June 27, 2021. https://www.proquest.com/newspapers/intimate-panorama-video-arts-variety-breadth/docview/2545295022/se-2.

"Jim Crow Laws." History. February 28, 2018. https://www.history.com/topics/early-20th-century-us/jim-crow-laws.

Johnson, Vanessa. "Sankofa N. E. S. T. is excited to announce." Facebook, October 5, 2020. https://www.facebook.com/share/19PYPtFUjt/?mibextid=wwXIfr).

Johnson Chevannes, Patrice. [@cpatricejohnsonchevannes]. "Big up oonu self!!! And No Matter Where You Are, Memba Dis. . . . Oonu FREE!! [Video]." Instagram, July 4, 2022. https://www.instagram.com/p/CfnYqiBMtOf/?igsh id=MTc4MmM1YmI2Ng==.

Jones, Martha S. *Vanguard: How Black Women Broke Barriers, Won the Vote, and Insisted on Equality for All*. New York: Basic Books, 2020.

Jordan, June. *Some of Us Did Not Die: New and Selected Essays of June Jordan*. New York: Basic/Civitas Books, 2002.

Jordan-Zachery, Julia S. *Black Women, Cultural Images, and Social Policy*. New York: Routledge, 2009.

Kabat-Zinn, Jon. *Full Catastrophe Living: How to Cope with Stress, Pain, and Illness*. New York: Delacorte, 1990.

Kagan, Sacha Jérôme. "The Practice of Ecological Art." [Plastik], February 15, 2014. https://www.researchgate.net/publication/274719395_The_practice_of_ecological_art.

Karenga, Maulana. *Introduction to Black Studies*. Los Angeles: University of Sankore Press, 2010.

Karon, Alexis K. "Ecowomanism: A Solution to Climate and Social Injustice." *Theo-*

logical Investigations, 2020. https://digitalcommons.augustana.edu/relgtheology/1.

Kasmin Gallery. "vanessa german." https://www.kasmingallery.com/artist/vanessa-german.

Kenney, Nancy. "Exclusive Survey: What Progress Have US Museums Made on Diversity, after a Year of Racial Reckoning?" *Art Newspaper*, May 25, 2021. https://www.theartnewspaper.com/2021/05/25/exclusive-survey-what-progress-have-us-museums-made-on-diversity-after-a-year-of-racial-reckoning.

Khomami, Nadia. "Sonia Boyce's Venice Biennale Winner to Be Exhibited in UK Next Year." *The Guardian*, October 26, 2022. https://www.theguardian.com/artanddesign/2022/oct/26/sonia-boyces-venice-biennale-winner-to-be-exhibited-in-uk-next-year.

King, Martin Luther, Jr. "Loving Your Enemies." Sermon delivered at Dexter Avenue Baptist Church, November 17, 1957. Martin Luther King, Jr., Research and Education Institute. https://kinginstitute.stanford.edu/king-papers/documents/loving-your-enemies-sermon-delivered-dexter-avenue-baptist-church.

King, Tiffany Lethabo. "Racial Ecologies: Black Landscapes in Flux." In *Racial Ecologies*, edited by Leilani Nishime and Kim D. Hester Williams, 65–75. Seattle: University of Washington Press, 2018. http://www.jstor.org/stable/j.ctvcwnm95.9.

Kinol, Alaina, Elijah Miller, Hannah Axtell, Lana Hirschfeld, et al. "Climate Justice in Higher Education: A Proposed Paradigm Shift towards a Transformative Role for Colleges and Universities." *Climatic Change* 176, no. 2 (2023). https://doi.org/10.1007/s10584-023-03486-4.

Knowing-jesus.com. "6 Bible Verses about Lamb Of God." https://bible.knowing-jesus.com/topics/Lamb-Of-God.

Kushner, Daniel. "Danielle Ponder—A Singer Who Was Once a Lawyer—Enjoys Critical Raves." NPR, September 17, 2022. https://www.npr.org/2022/09/17/1123657145/danielle-ponder-a-singer-who-was-once-a-lawyer-enjoys-critical-raves.

"Latest Updates." The Metropolitan Museum of Art Collection API. https://metmuseum.github.io/.

Lavett Ballard: When She Roars. Artnet, n.d. https://www.artnet.com/galleries/long-sharp-gallery/when-she-roars.

Le, Linh. "Foundation Awards Grants for Initiatives That Improve Black Communities." *Daily Orange*, October 21, 2020. https://dailyorange.com/2020/10/foundation-awards-grants-initiatives-improve-black-communities/.

Lee, Shayne. *Erotic Revolutionaries: Black Women, Sexuality, and Popular Culture*. Lanham, MD: Hamilton, 2010.

"The Legacy of Henrietta Lacks." Johns Hopkins Medicine, n. d. https://www.hopkinsmedicine.org/henriettalacks/.

Lewis, Sarah Elizabeth. "Visual Studies Questionnaire: How Do You Engage with the Visual, and What Is Its Importance in the Twenty-First Century?" *Visual Studies* 36, no. 3 (2021): 223–25.

Lieberman, Michael. "Group Exhibition at African American Museum in Philadelphia Tackles Social Justice Issues with Powerful Imagery and Passion." Art Blog, July 3, 2018. https://www.theartblog.org/2018/07/group-exhibition-at-african

-american-museum-in-philadelphia-tackles-social-justice-issues-with-powerful
-imagery-and-passion/.

Lineage Asset Advisors, "What Is a Legacy Property?" February 14, 2018. https://
lineageasset.com/what-is-a-legacy-property-series/.

Lindsey, Treva B. *America, Goddam: Violence, Black Women, and the Struggle for
Justice.* Berkeley: University of California Press, 2023.

Long-Sharp Gallery. "Lavett Ballard's Work Featured on Time Magazine for
a Second Time." February 3, 2023. https://www.longsharpgallery.com/
ballard-when-she-roars-addl-info.

Lorde, Audre. *A Burst of Light: And Other Essays.* Mineola, NY: Ixia Press, 2017.

Martin, Delita. *Shadows in the Garden.* Huffman, TX: Black Box Press, 2019.

McGregory, Jerrilyn. "Junkanoo/Jankunú." In *One Grand Noise: Boxing Day in the
Anglicized Caribbean World,* 55–78. Jackson: University Press of Mississippi,
2021.

McMillan, Uri. *Embodied Avatars: Genealogies of Black Feminist Art and Performance.*
New York: New York University Press, 2015.

Modzelewski, Eve. "Face to Face: Women of Visions Exhibit Revolves around African
Mask Theme." *Pittsburgh Post-Gazette,* May 3, 2001. https://www.proquest.com/
newspapers/face-women-visions-exhibit-revolves-around/docview/391197159/
se-2.

Montgomery, Georgene Bess. *The Spirit and the Word: A Theory of Spirituality in
Africana Literary Criticism.* Trenton, NJ: Africa World Press, 2008.

Moore, EbonyJanice. *All the Black Girls Are Activists: A Fourth Wave Womanist
Pursuit of Dreams as Radical Resistance.* New York: Rowhouse Publishing, 2023.

Moore, Kelli. "Techniques of Abstraction in Black Arts." *Meridians* 21, no. 2 (2022):
413–35. https://doi.org/10.1215/15366936-9882119.

Morris, Catherine, and Rujeko Hockley, eds. *We Wanted a Revolution: Black Radical Women, 1965–85: New Perspectives.* Durham: Duke University Press, 2018.

Morris, Shannon. "Women of Visions Art Exhibit by Black Women." *New Pittsburgh Courier,* September 19, 1998. https://www.proquest.com/newspapers/
women-visions-art-exhibit-black/docview/368007889/se-2.

Morrison, Sheena M., and Elizabeth Fee. "Nothing to Work with but Cleanliness:
The Training of African American Traditional Midwives in the South." *American
Journal of Public Health* 100, no. 2 (2010): 238–39.

Morrison, Toni. *Beloved.* Plume, 1998.

Moss, Michael Muata. *Sankofa: Kemetamorphing Black to the Future: The Reclamation of African-Centered Healing and Wellness.* North Charleston, SC: Createspace
Independent Publishing Platform, 2018.

Mullins, P. A. "Appropriating Black Africa." In *Black Africa and the US Art World
in the Early 20th Century: Aesthetics, White Supremacy,* 73–98. London: Anthem
Press, 2024.

Munro, Eleanor. "The Late Springtime of Alma Thomas: Conversations with the
Washington Colorist, from an Absorbing New Book." *Washington Post,* April
15, 1979. https://www.proquest.com/historical-newspapers/late-springtime
-alma-thomas/docview/147004338/se-2.

National Black Church Initiative. "The National Black Church Initiative Invites African American Men Back to Church." July 22, 2011. https://www.naltblackchurch.com/pdf/invite-mentochurch.pdf.

National Geographic. "Ecosystem." n.d. Nationalgeographic.org. Accessed January 2, 2024. https://education.nationalgeographic.org/resource/ecosystem/.

"National Portrait Gallery Presents a Portrait of Henrietta Lacks, a Co-Acquisition with the National Museum of African American History and Culture." Smithsonian Institution. May 8, 2018. https://www.si.edu/newsdesk/releases/national-portrait-gallery-presents-portrait-henrietta-lacks-co-acquisition-national-museum-.

National Wellness Institute. Six Dimensions of Wellness. N.d. https://national wellness.org/resources/six-dimensions-of-wellness/.

Niangoran-Bouah, Georges. *Akan World of Gold Weights: Abstract Design Weights*. New York: Hacker Art Books, 1988.

Nishime, Leilani, and Kim D. Hester Williams. *Racial Ecologies*. Washington, DC: University of Washington Press, 2018.

Ntloedibe, France. "A Question of Origins: The Social and Cultural Roots of African American Cultures." *Journal of African American History* 91, no. 4 (Fall 2006): 401–12. https://www.jstor.org/stable/20064123.

Olupona, Jacob K. "The Study of Yoruba Religious Tradition in Historical Perspective." *Numen* 40, no. 3 (1993): 240–73. https://doi.org/10.1163/156852793X00176.

Osaka, Naomi, and Mikey Williams. "Mikey Williams In Conversation With Naomi Osaka: 'We're Young Black Athletes. We Have Spotlights On Us.'" Time.com. August 20, 2020. https://time.com/5880993/naomi-osaka-mikey-williams-black-athletes/.

"Out on a Limb: Philadelphia's Dancers, Musicians, Artists, and Actors Can't Imagine When They'll Work Again." *Philadelphia Inquirer*, April 26, 2020. https://www.proquest.com/newspapers/out-on-limb/docview/2395069647/se-2.

Paavola, Jouni, Andrew Gouldson, and Tatiana Kluvánková-Oravská. "Interplay of Actors, Scales, Frameworks and Regimes in the Governance of Biodiversity." *Environmental Policy and Governance* 19, no. 3 (2009): 148–58, https://doi.org/10.1002/eet.505.

Painter, Nell Irvin. *Old in Art School: A Memoir of Starting Over*. Berkeley: Counterpoint, 2019.

Parker, Charlie, Sam Scott, and Alistair Geddes. "Snowball Sampling." In *Sage Research Methods Foundations*, edited by Paul Atkinson, Sara Delamont, Alexandru Cernat, et al. London: SAGE Publications Ltd., 2019. https://doi.org/10.4135/9781526421036831710.

Pavel Zoubok Fine Art. ADAA The Art Show 2020: vanessa german, Booth A23. http://pavelzoubok.com/exhibition/adaa-the-art-show-2020-vanessa-german/pressrelease/

Perry, Imani. *South to America: A Journey Below the Mason-Dixon to Understand the Soul of a Nation*. New York: Ecco, 2022.

Ponder, Danielle. "Danielle Ponder Presents: For the Love of Justice." N.d. https://danielleponder.com/for-the-love-of-justice.

Pratt-Clarke, Menah. "A Radical Reconstruction of Resistance Strategies: Black Girls and Black Women Reclaiming Our Power Using Transdisciplinary Applied Social Justice©, Ma'at, and Rites of Passage." *Journal of African American Studies* 17, no. 1 (2013): 99–114. https://doi.org/10.1007/s12111-012-9221-6.

Quashie, Kevin Everod. *Black Women, Identity, and Cultural Theory: (Un)Becoming the Subject.* New Brunswick, NJ: Rutgers University Press, 2004.

Quashie, Kevin Everod. *The Sovereignty of Quiet: Beyond Resistance in Black Culture.* New Brunswick, NJ: Rutgers University Press, 2012.

Quilts as Visual History. Clio History, n.d. https://www.cliohistory.org/visualizing america/quilts/visualhistory.

Raiford, Leigh. "Burning All Illusion: Abstraction, Black Life, and the Unmaking of White Supremacy." *Art Journal* 79, no. 4 (2020): 76–91. https://doi.org/10 .1080/00043249.2020.1779550.

Raiford, Leigh. "Photography and the Practices of Critical Black Memory." *History and Theory* 48, no. 4 (2009): 112–29. http://www.jstor.org/stable/25621443.

Rambaree, Komalsingh, Stefan Sjöberg, and Päivi Turunen. "Ecosocial Change and Community Resilience: The Case of 'Bönan' in Glocal Transition." *Journal of Community Practice* 27, no. 3–4 (2019): 231–48. https://doi.org/10.1080/ 10705422.2019.1658005.

Rankine, Claudia. "The Condition of Black Life Is One of Mourning." In *Grief and Grievance: Art and Mourning in America (from Civil Rights to Black Lives Matter)*, edited by Okwui Enwezoe, Naomi Beckwith, and Massimiliano Gioni, 17–21. London: Phaidon, 2020.

"Rebuilding the 'ArtHouse' in Homewood Following Fire That Left Serious Damage." WTAE. February 19, 2021. https://www.wtae.com/article/rebuilding-the -arthouse-in-homewood-following-fire-that-left-serious-damage/35569980.

"Reckoning: Grief and Light." Commonwealth of Oakland, n.d. https://www .oaklandcommonwealth.com/event-details-2/reckoning-grief-and-light.

"Regina Evans." LaPeña. https://lapena.org/regina-evans/.

"Regina Y. Evans." Shade Movement. https://www.shademovement.org/regina -evans.

Rena Bransten Gallery. *Lava Thomas Mugshot Portraits: Women of the Montgomery Bus Boycott.* https://renabranstengallery.com/wp-content/uploads/2020/08/ Thomas-2018-Press-Kit.pdf.

Richardson, Allissa V. *Bearing Witness While Black: African Americans, Smartphones, and the New Protest #Journalism.* New York: Oxford University Press, 2020.

Ringgold, Faith. *Tar Beach.* New York: Crown, 1991.

Robinson, Shantay. "Studio Visit with Shanequa Gay." Burnaway, August 17, 2016, https://burnaway.org/magazine/shanequa-gay-studio-visit/

Robles-Gordon, Amber. "Heal Thyself." N.d. Amber Robles-Gordon. https://www .amberroblesgordon.com/heal-thyself-series.

Rosenthal, Ann T. "Teaching Systems Thinking and Practice through Environmental Art." *Ethics and the Environment* 8, no. 1 (2003.): 152–68. https://doi .org/10.2979/ete.2003.8.1.152.

ROUX. Galveston Arts Center, n.d. https://www.galvestonartscenter.org/roux.

Rowan College at Burlington County, "RCBC Arts Alum Created TIME Magazine Cover Reimagining Rosa Parks." TAP into Bordentown, March 1, 2021. https://www.tapinto.net/towns/bordentown/articles/rcbc-alum-created-time-magazine-cover-reimagining-rosa-parks.https://www.tapinto.net/towns/bordentown/articles/rcbc-alum-created-time-magazine-cover-reimagining-rosa-parks.

Rowell, Charles H. "Amber Robles-Gordon." *Callaloo* 38, no. 4 (2015.): 855–57. https://doi.org/10.1353/cal.2015.0112.

Salleh, Ariel. *Ecofeminism as Politics: Nature, Marx, and the Postmodern.* London: Zed Books, 1997.

Samford, Patricia. "The Archaeology of African-American Slavery and Material Culture." *William and Mary Quarterly* 53, no. 1 (1996): 87–114. https://doi.org/10.2307/2946825.

Sanchez-Hucles, Janis V. "Womanist Therapy with Black Women." In *Womanist and Mujerista Psychologies: Voices of Fire, Acts of Courage,* edited by Thema Bryant-Davis and Lillian Comas-Díaz, 69–92. Washington, DC: American Psychological Association, 2016.

Schuit, Sophie A., and Jon C. Rogowski. "Race, Representation, and the Voting Rights Act." *American Journal of Political Science* 61, no. 3 (2016): 513–26. https://doi.org/10.1111/ajps.12284. Screen Prism. "Rachel Maddow Goes to America's Most Dangerous Neighborhood (Part 1/2)." YouTube, May 26, 2011. https://www.youtube.com/watch?v=KTbDvAL51HI. Seetah, Krish. "Objects Past, Objects Present: Materials, Resistance and Memory from the Le Morne Old Cemetery, Mauritius." *Journal of Social Archaeology* 15, no. 2(2015.): 233–53. https://doi.org/10.1177/1469605315575124.

Şentürk, Ö., and K. Özkan. "Calculating Landscape Diversity with Alpha Diversity Indices." *Journal of Environmental Biology* 38, no. 5(SI, 2017): 931–36. https://doi.org/10.22438/jeb/38/5(si)/gm-09.

"SFAC Apologizes to Lava Thomas for Mishandling Maya Angelou Monument." KQED, August 3, 2020. https://www.kqed.org/arts/13884238/sfac-apologizes-to-lava-thomas-for-mishandling-maya-angelou-monument, accessed January 9, 2022.

Shades of Inspiration. "Who We Are . . ." N.d. https://www.shadesofinspiration.org/about-us-1.

Shange, Ntozake. *For Colored Girls Who Have Considered Suicide When the Rainbow Is Enuf: A Choreopoem.* New York: Bantam Books, 1981.

Sharpe, Christina. *In the Wake: On Blackness and Being.* Durham: Duke University Press, 2016.

Sheeja, Angelin. "Mapping the Black Culture in Alice Walker's *The Temple of My Familiar.*" *Journal for English Language and Literary Studies* 3, no. 4 (2013): 9–15. https://brbs.tjells.com/index.php/tjells/article/view/125/205.

Sherman, Shantella. "D.C. Artist Fits all the Pieces Together." *Afro-American Red Star,* January 28, 2006. https://www.proquest.com/newspapers/d-c-artist-fits-all-pieces-together/docview/369568816/se-2.

Simba, Malik. "The Three-Fifths Clause of the United States Constitution (1787)." BlackPast, October 3, 2014. https://www.blackpast.org/african

-american-history/events-african-american-history/three-fifths-clause-united
-states-constitution-1787/.

Skloot, Rebecca. *The Immortal Life of Henrietta Lacks*. New York: Crown, 2010.

"Small Museum of the Month: The Colored Girls Museum." SP Ghost, December 1, 2017. https://spghostcom.wordpress.com/2017/12/01/small-museum-of-the -month-the-colored-girls-museum/, accessed March 10, 2025.

Smith, Cherranda. This Website Honors the Stories of Tens of Thousands of Missing Black Women. Black Information Network, September 24, 2021. https://www .binnews.com/content/2021-09-24-this-website-honors-the-stories-of-tens-of -thousands-missing-black-women.

Smith, Christen A. "About Us." #CiteASista: Today & Everyday. February 1, 2017. https://citeasista.com/about/.

Smith, Jessica. "#NotAStereotype," *Flagpole*, 35, no. 20, May 19, 2021, https://www .proquest.com/magazines/notastereotype/docview/2532201163/se-2.

"sometimes.we.cannot.be.with.our.bodies," Fralin Museum of Art at the University of Virginia, https://uvafralinartmuseum.virginia.edu/exhibitions/sometimeswe cannotbewithourbodies.

"sometimes.we.cannot. be.with.our.bodies." Union For Contemporary Art, Omaha. https://www.u-ca.org/exhibition/sometimes-we-cannot-be-with-our-bodies.

Stanton, Audrey. "The Somewhat Sinister and Rebellious History behind Your Striped Shirt." *The Good Trade*, March 1, 2019. https://www.thegoodtrade.com/ features/history-of-stripes.

Steiger, Johann Anselm. "Die Meditationes Sacrae (1606/07) Des lutherischen Theologen Johann Gerhard im Lichte des philologischen und hermeneutischen Phänomens von, Übersetzung." In *Edition und Übersetzung*, 367–76. Berlin: De Gruyter, 2002.

Stepakoff, Shanee. "The Healing Power of Symbolization in the Aftermath of Massive War Atrocities: Examples from Liberian and Sierra Leonean Survivors." *Journal of Humanistic Psychology* 47, no. 3 (2007): 400–12. https://doi.org/ 10.1177/0022167807301787.

Straub, Kellie. "Six Dimensions of Wellness." National Wellness Institute. April 29, 2020. https://nationalwellness.org/resources/six-dimensions-of-wellness/.

Strauss, Mark. "The 5,000-Year Secret History of the Watermelon." *National Geographic*, August 21, 2015. https://www.nationalgeographic.com/history/ article/150821-watermelon-fruit-history-agriculture.

Streeter, Leslie Gray. "Maryland Painter Tawny Chatmon Frames Her Black Subjects in Gold." *Washington Post*, February 13, 2022. https://www.proquest .com/newspapers/maryland-painter-tawny-chatmon-frames-her-black/docview/ 2628017410/se-2.

Strezova, Anita. "The Icon of the Trinity by Andrei Rublev." In *Hesychasm and Art: The Appearance of New Iconographic Trends in Byzantine and Slavic Lands in the 14th and 15th Centuries*, 173–232. Canberra: ANU Press, 2014.

Syracuse Community Folk Art Center. Virtual Museum, http://cfacgallery.org.

Syracuse Community Folk Art Center. "History." n.d. https://communityfolkartcenter .org/history/.

Syracuse Community Folk Art Center. *Teen Art Competition Exhibit 2021*. https://
www.cfacgallery.org/teen-art-competition-exhibit-2021/.

Tate. "Abstract Art." N.d. https://www.tate.org.uk/art/art-terms/a/abstract-art.

Tate. "Claudette Johnson: 'Giving Space to the Presence of a Black Woman.'"
May 25, 2021, https://www.tate.org.uk/art/artists/claudette-johnson-15861/
giving-space-presence-black-woman.

Tate. "Minimalism." https://www.tate.org.uk/art/art-terms/m/minimalism.

Tavana, Ali Mehrabi. "Does the Health of Individuals Have a Mathematical Code?"
International Journal of Preventive Medicine 4, no. 7 (2013): 849–51. https://pmc
.ncbi.nlm.nih.gov/articles/PMC3775227/.

Taylor, Dorceta E. "Women of Color, Environmental Justice, and Ecofeminism."
In *Ecofeminisim: Women, Culture, Nature*, edited by Karen J. Warren, 38–81.
Bloomington: Indiana University Press, 1997.

Thomas, Alma. *Alma W. Thomas: A Retrospective Exhibition, 1959–1966*. Howard
University Gallery of Art, 1966). Alma Thomas papers, Smithsonian Institu-
tion, Washington, DC. https://collections.si.edu/search/results.htm?q=record_
ID=AAA.thomalma_ref799&repo=DPLA.

Thomas, Lava. "Past." http://www.lavathomas.com/past.

Thomas, Lava. *Resistance Reverb: Movements 1 & 2*. http://www.lavathomas.com/
resistance-reverb.

Thompson, Krista A. *Shine: The Visual Economy of Light in African Diasporic Aesthetic
Practice*. Durham: Duke University Press, 2015.

Thompson, Lisa B. *Beyond the Black Lady: Sexuality and the New African American
Middle Class*. Urbana: University of Illinois Press, 2009.

Thompson, Robert Farris. *Flash of the Spirit: African and Afro-American Art and
Philosophy*. New York: Vintage, 1984.

Timesupnow. Meet the Artist: Regina Evans. Instagram, April 14, 2021. https://
www.instagram.com/p/CNphZEygS6_/.

Trescott, Jacqueline. "Going with the Grain: The Warm, Deep Dignity of Elizabeth
Catlett's Art." *Washington Post*, May 22, 1993. https://www.washingtonpost
.com/archive/lifestyle/1993/05/22/going-with-the-grain/b92d093d-b74e
-44fd-a936-04030edd0e25/?isMobile=1.

Trescott, Jacqueline. "The 'Lively Renaissance' of Elizabeth Catlett." *Washington Post*,
March 4, 1977. https://www.washingtonpost.com/archive/lifestyle/1977/03/04/
the-lively-renaissance-of-elizabeth-catlett/58a1333c-221c-4bf3-8eb3-2ee787
eeeeb5/.

Tubman, Harriet. https://www.goodreads.com/quotes/5935-every-great-dream
-begins-with-a-dreamer-always-remember-you.

Ubiñas, Helen. "Naomi Osaka Did What Many Women of Color Have to Do:
Choose Themselves, at a Cost." *Inquirer*, June 2, 2021. https://www.inquirer.com/
opinion/naomi-osaka-french-open-mental-health-tennis-helen-ubias-20210602
.html.

Unknown photographer. *A Negro Family Just Arrived in Chicago from the Rural South*. 1922.
Schomburg Center for Research in Black Culture, Jean Blackwell Hutson Research
and Reference Division, New York Public Library Digital Collections. https://
digitalcollections.nypl.org/items/510d47de-1a10-a3d9-e040-e00a18064a99.

Unwrapping Vanessa Johnson, *Mentor Series 3*, https://www.vanessajohnsonstoryteller.com/mentor-series-3.

van Hagen, Isobel, and Matthew Mulligan. "Violinist Performs Balcony Concert in Locked-Down Italy." NBC News, March 14, 2020. https://www.nbcnews.com/health/health-news/live-blog/coronavirus-updates-live-house-approves-coronavirus-aid-bill-n1158821/ncrd1158866.

"vanessa german's Grief over Black Deaths the Subject of a Powerful Museum Show." *Pittsburgh Post-Gazette*, April 11, 2021. https://www.post-gazette.com/ae/art-architecture/2021/04/11/Vanessa-German-The-Frick-Pittsburgh-art-Reckoning-Grief-Light-George-Floyd-Breonna-Taylor-Elijah-McClain/stories/202104050084.

Vellucci, Justin. "Homicides, Shootings Down in '24 in Pittsburgh, Reflecting Nationwide Trends, Data Shows." TribLive, March 8, 2025. https://triblive.com/local/regional/homicides-shootings-down-in-24-in-pittsburgh-reflecting-nationwide-trends-data-shows/, accessed March 10, 2025.

Veltman, Chloe, and Sarah Hotchkiss. "SFAC Apologizes to Lava Thomas for Mishandling Maya Angelou Monument." KQED, August 3, 2020. https://www.kqed.org/arts/13884238/sfac-apologizes-to-lava-thomas-for-mishandling-maya-angelou-monument.

Walden-Schreiner, Chelsey, Yu-Fai Leung, Tim Kuhn, Todd Newburger, and Wei-Lun Tsai. "Environmental and Managerial Factors Associated with Pack Stock Distribution in High Elevation Meadows: Case Study from Yosemite National Park." *Journal of Environmental Management* 193 (2017): 52–63. https://doi.org/10.1016/j.jenvman.2017.01.076.

Walker, Alice. *In Search of Our Mothers' Gardens: Womanist Prose*. San Diego: Harcourt Brace Jovanovich, 1983.

Weiss, Abby. "Art Exhibit Portrays the Black Experience through Lens of One Family." Daily Orange, March 3, 2021. http://dailyorange.com/2021/03/art-exhibit-portrays-black-experience-lens-one-family/.

West, Carolyn M. "Mammy, Jezebel, Sapphire, and Their Homegirls: Developing an 'Oppositional Gaze' Toward the Images of Black Women." In *Lectures on the Psychology of Women*, edited by Joan C. Chrisler, Carla Golden, and Patricia D. Rozee, 286–99. New York: McGraw-Hill, 2008.

Weusi Artist Collective—Home (n.d.). https://www.weusiartistcollective.gallery/home, accessed January 2, 2024.

Whack, Errin. "Black Women at the Forefront in Fight for Racial Equality." NBC News, May 8, 2017. https://www.nbcnews.com/news/nbcblk/black-women-move-forefront-fight-racial-equality-n756416

"What Is Ecosystem—Javatpoint." javatpoint.com. Accessed January 2, 2024. https://www.javatpoint.com/what-is-ecosystem.

Whittaker, Celeste E. "Her Art Is in Time Magazine Again. What to Know about South Jersey's Lavett Ballard," *Cherry Hill Courier-Post*, February 21, 2023, https://www.courierpostonline.com/story/news/local/2023/02/21/willingboro-nj-lavett-ballard-artist-featured-in-time-magazine/69903289007/.

Wilford, John Noble. "Slave Artifacts under the Hearth." *New York Times*, August

27, 1996. https://www.nytimes.com/1996/08/27/science/slave-artifacts-under
-the-hearth.html.

Wilkerson, Isabel. *The Warmth of Other Suns: The Epic Story of America's Great Migration*. New York: Vintage, 2014.

Wilkie, Laurie A. "Magic and Empowerment on the Plantation: An Archaeological Consideration of African-American World View." *Southeastern Archaeology* 14, no. 2 (1995): 136–48.

Willets, Khelli. "Beyond the Tangible." In *Shadows in the Garden*, edited by Delita Martin, 12–14. Huffman, TX: Black Box Press Studio, 2019.

Williams, Amelia. "House/Full of BlackWomen Delivers 'Rituals' Outside the Confines of a Theater." Local News Matters. August 7, 2020. https://localnewsmatters.org/2020/08/07/house-full-of-blackwomen-delivers-rituals-outside-the-confines-of-a-theater/.

Williams, Carmen Braun, and Marsha I. Wiggins. "Womanist Spirituality as a Response to the Racism–Sexism Double Bind in African American Women." *Counseling and Values* 54, no. 2 (2010): 175–86. https://doi.org/10.1002/j.2161-007x.2010.tb00015.x.

Williams, Heather. "bell hooks Speaks Up." *Sandspur* 112, no. 17 (2013). https://issuu.com/thesandspur/docs/112–17.

Williams, Keelah E. G., Oliver Sng, and Steven L. Neuberg. "Ecology-Driven Stereotypes Override Race Stereotypes." *Proceedings of the National Academy of Sciences of the United States of America* 113, no. 2 (2016): 310–15, https://doi.org/10.1073/pnas.1519401113.

Williams, Serena. "Serena Williams Poses Unretouched for Harper's BAZAAR." *Harper's BAZAAR*, July 9, 2019. https://www.harpersbazaar.com/culture/features/a28209579/serena-williams-us-open-2018-essay/.

Willis, A. J. "Forum: The Ecosystem; An Evolving Concept Viewed Historically." *Functional Ecology* 11, no. 2 (1997): 268–71. https://doi.org/10.1111/j.1365-2435.1997.00081.x.

Willis, Deborah. "Carrie Mae Weems: Rehistoricizing Visual Memory." In *Women Mobilizing Memory*, edited by Ayşe Gül Altýnay, María José Contreras, Marianne Hirsch, et al., 277–84. New York: Columbia University Press, 2019. http://www.jstor.org/stable/10.7312/alti19184.19.

Willis, Deborah. "Visualizing Memory: Photographs and the Art of Biography." *American Art* 17, no. 1 (2003): 20–23, https://doi.org/10.1086/444679.

Willis, Deborah, and Carla Williams. *The Black Female Body: A Photographic History*. Philadelphia, PA: Temple University Press, 2002.

Wilson, August. *Fences*. New York: Penguin Books, 1985.

Wolfe, Shira. "The Life and Legacy of the Spiral Group." *Artland Magazine*, November 27, 2020. https://magazine.artland.com/the-life-and-legacy-of-the-spiral-group/.

"Women in the Visual Arts." Oxford Art Online, n.d. https://www.oxfordartonline.com/page/women-in-the-visual-arts.

Women of Visions Inc. "Our Herstory." https://www.womenofvisionspgh.org/aboutwov.

Woods-Giscombé, Cheryl L. "Superwoman Schema: African American Women's

Views on Stress, Strength, and Health." *Qualitative Health Research* 20, no. 5 (2010): 668–83. https://doi.org/10.1177/1049732310361892.

Woods-Giscombé, Cheryl L., and Angela R. Black. "Mind-Body Interventions to Reduce Risk for Health Disparities Related to Stress and Strength among African American Women: The Potential of Mindfulness-Based Stress Reduction, Loving-Kindness, and the NTU Therapeutic Framework." *Complementary Health Practice Review* 15, no. 3 (2010): 115–31. https://doi.org/10.1177/1533210110386776.

World Health Organization. "Determinants of Health." October 4, 2024. https://www.who.int/news-room/questions-and-answers/item/determinants-of-health.

WPXI.com News Staff. "Residents Mourn 15-Year-Old Killed in Wednesday Shooting in Homewood." WPXI., March 31, 2022. https://www.wpxi.com/news/local/allegheny-county/juvenile-critically-injured-after-being-shot-head-pittsburghs-homewood-neighborhood/WPEG7LNXPBALBKB6IX2XFPPLL4/.

WSYR-TV. "Throwback Thursday: The Long-Gone 15th Ward in Syracuse." Local SYR, February 4, 2021. https://www.localsyr.com/throwback-thursday/throwback-thursday-the-long-gone-15th-ward/.

Yerebakan, Osman Can. "Dindga McCannon." Artforum, September 29, 2021. https://www.artforum.com/interviews/dindga-mccannon-on-where-we-at-and-the-women-of-the-blues-86788.

Yohannes, Neyat. "House/Full of Blackwomen Present Black Women Dreaming—A Ritual Rest in Oakland." East Bay Express, March 28, 2017. https://eastbayexpress.com/housefull-of-blackwomen-present-black-women-dreaming-a-ritual-rest-in-oakland-2-1/, accessed February 5, 2022.

Young, David W. "Historic Germantown: New Knowledge in a Very Old Neighborhood." Encyclopedia of Greater Philadelphia. https://philadelphiaencyclopedia.org/essays/historic-germantown-new-knowledge-in-a-very-old-neighborhood-2/, accessed December 22, 2009.

Harrison, Shirley, 216
Harris-Perry, Melissa, 157–59
Hawkins, Kiki, 213
Heckler Report on Black and Minority
	Heath (1985), 3
HeLa cell, 125–27
Hendryx, Nona, 212, 213
historically Black colleges and universi-
	ties (HBCUs), art museums at, 22,
	57–58
HIV/AIDS epidemic, 46, 79–80
Honeywood, Varnette P., 144
hoodies, 83, 170, 171
hooks, bell, 102, 147
Horne, Lena, 67
Hosbey, Justin, 7
House/Full of Blackwomen (Oakland),
	22, 42, 45, 48–55, 237; *Black Women
	Dreaming* series, 49, 53, 55, 63, 64;
	episodes, 47, 49, 51–55, 63; healing
	and wellness, 49–55; origin, 49; sex
	trafficking project, 49–50, 51
Howard Harris, Mattie, 117–18
Howard University, 57–58, 191, 194
Huerta, Dolores, 95
Humanize My Hoodie Movement, 170
Hurd, Cynthia, 92

Ibo people, 188
identity construction for Black women,
	12
Ifa religion, 142
The Immortal Life of Henrietta Lacks
	(Skloot), 125
imposter syndrome, 204
Instagram. *See* social media
interconnectedness: of Black women
	artists with communities, 17; of eco-
	logical systems, 11, 13
intersectionality: of arts, culture, and
	activism, 242; of ecological systems,
	9–10, 238; lack of, in the women's
	liberation movement, 29; of race and
	gender, 4, 16, 62, 241
In the Wake (Sharpe), 98
invisibility/erasure: of African Ameri-
	cans in early archives, 128; of African
	Americans in museums and galleries,
	175–76; of Black women and girls,

40–41, 60, 65–67, 162, 231–32; of
	Black women artists, 40–41, 44–45,
	58, 90–91, 191–93; of Black women
	scholars, 44–45; of Black women
	victims of violence, 60, 108, 155–56,
	159, 221, 234–36; domestic violence
	victims and, 209–11; of missing Black
	women and girls, 65–67; sexual
	assault victims and, 234–36

Jackson, Mahalia, 75
Jackson, Susan, 92
Jackson, Tanisha: autobiographical/auto-
	ethnographic narrative, xiii–xv, 12–13,
	75–76, 97, 235, 237; MeTelling Nar-
	ratives (Jackson), 18, 228–29, 230. *See
	also* Community Folk Art Center
Johns Hopkins Medical Center, 125
Johnson, Ann "Sole Sister," 139
Johnson, Harvey, 132
Johnson, James Weldon, 73
Johnson, John Rosamond, 73
Johnson, Vanessa, 225–36; African
	diaspora and, 225–26; background,
	234; community-based arts activi-
	ties, 226–29, 234–36; *A Dollar and
	a Dream* lottery quilt, 233; fiber arts,
	226–28, 231, 233–34; as griot/story-
	teller, 225, 228, 231–36; *Mentor Series
	3*, 226, 227; in the National League of
	American Pen Women, 226; as prop
	master and actor in plays, 232–34;
	quilts and quilting, 226, 231, 233;
	Unwrapping Vanessa solo exhibition,
	226–28, 233–34; wellness through
	art, 234–36
Johnson Chevannes, Patrice, 213
Johnston, Kathryn, 159
Jones, Martha S., 92, 113
Jordan, June, 20
Juneteenth celebrations, 211–13

Kemet, 150
Kindred (Butler), 120
King, Martin Luther, Jr.: assassination,
	88; fiftieth anniversary of assassina-
	tion, 88; Montgomery bus boycott
	and, 88; transforming power of love
	and, 68–69

American Art, 191; Washington Color School and, 191–92

Thomas, Lava, 23, 87–101, 162, 238; *Homecoming* exhibition, 88–90; *Mugshot Portraits: Women of the Montgomery Bus Boycott* exhibition, 87–90; protests of San Francisco Arts Commission, 90–91; *Requiem for Charleston* installation, 91, 92–94, 98, 99–100; *Resistance Reverb: Movements 1 & 2* installation, 95–97; sculpture design for Maya Angelou monument, 44, 90–91; solo exhibit at the Museum of the African Diaspora, 96; as wellness worker, 87–101

Thompson, Krista, 14, 16

Thompson, Myra, 92

Thompson, Robert Farris, 180, 188

Tilla Studios (2017–present), 21

TIME magazine, 112–14

transformative justice, 101

trauma: Emanuel African Methodist Episcopal Church killings, 91, 92–94, 99–100; of gun violence in Pittsburgh, 67, 70, 71, 76, 84–86; of living with anti-Blackness, 91, 92–94, 205–7; of marginalization of Black women artists, 90–91; mass media and, 207–8, 223

Trump, Donald, 87

Tubman, Harriet, 211, 226

Tulsa race massacre (1921), 105–6

Unburied, Unmourned, Unmarked (Wineglass), 84

Union for Contemporary Art (Omaha) *Blue Walk* procession, 80–82, 84–85

University of Arkansas, 132

University of California, Berkeley, 88

Urban Bush Women, 46

Velázquez, Diego, 246–47

Venice Biennale (2022): Golden Lion for *The Brick House* bronze (Leigh), 245–47; Golden Lion for *Feeling Her Way* exhibition (Boyce), 1; *Milk of Dreams* exhibition (Leigh), 245; *Sovereignty* exhibition (Leigh), 247

Vickers, Dayvon "DayDay," 84–86

Vietnam Veterans Memorial (Washington, DC), 99

violence/gun violence: art as counternarrative to, 70 (*see also* memorial art); Tawny Chatmon and, 164, 170; children and, 83–86, 164; domestic violence, 209–11; Emanuel African Methodist Episcopal Church killings, 91, 92–94, 99–100; erasure/invisibility of Black women victims, 60, 108, 155–56, 159, 221, 234–36; Shanequa Gay and, 145–47, 155–56, 159; vanessa german and, 67, 70, 71, 76–80, 84–86; medical violence and health outcomes (Lindsey), 3. *See also* Black Lives Matter movement; police brutality

Voting Rights Act (1965), 106

wake work, 98–99

Walker, Alice, 19–20, 197–99

Walker, Mark, *Love Duality,* 197

Washington, Dinah, 67

Washington Color School, 191–92

Week, James, 247

Weems, Carrie Mae: Guggenheim Museum retrospective, 219–20; *Resist COVID-19/Take 6!* public service announcement project, 219–20, 221; as Syracuse University artist in residence, 219–20

wellness: African indigenous healing practices, 5; agency of Black women and, 2–4, 22, 239–41, 247; artists as wellness workers, 1–2; Black feminist epistemology and, 4–6, 18–19; Black women's health disparities and, 2–4; collective (*see* Black women's collectives and art spaces); collective empowerment and wellness; community-based programming and (*see* community-based arts programming); components of, 2; and dance, 45, 46, 48–49; defined, 2, 112, 133; determinants of quality of health, 3; ecosystems as metaphor for Black women's wellness, 6–9; environmental, 22–23,

wellness (*continued*)
  56 (*see also* Black art galleries and
  museums; environmental wellness);
  mental health practices (*see* mental
  health); as ongoing state of healing,
  25; self-care in (*see* self-care); snowball
  sampling methodology, 12–14; spiritual healing (*see* spirituality); visual art
  as self-reflection, 5, 137, 186, 227–28;
  womanism and, 4–6, 19–20. *See also*
  "laying on of hands"
West, Carolyn, 111–12
Western gaze, 175–76, 184; power over
  the gaze, 155–56; White heteronormative gaze, 60
Weusi Artist Collective (Harlem), 28, 32
Weusi-Nyumba Ya Sanaa gallery
  (Harlem): *Cookin' and Smokin'* exhibition, 32, 33; establishment, 28
"Where We At" Black Women Artists,
  Inc. (1971–85), 20–22, 27, 30–41,
  237; Black Arts Movement and feminist art movement, 20–21, 27–29,
  31–32; *Close Connections* exhibition,
  32; collaboration with Black male
  artists, 32; community-based arts
  programming, 32, 34–36; *Cookin' and
  Smokin'* exhibition, 32, 33; demands
  addressed to the Brooklyn Museum,
  32–34; as example of collective power
  and wellness, 21–22; founded, 13–14,
  20–21, 27, 30, 36, 60, 119, 231;
  growth of, 30, 36; importance of, 41;
  Joining Forces: 1 + 1 = 3 exhibition, 32;
  sister circles, 6, 41; wellness and art,
  36–41; "WHERE WE AT"—BLACK
  WOMEN ARTISTS, 30–32, 60;
  "Where We At" Black Women Artists
  exhibit, 36–41; workshops at cor-
  rectional institutions, 34–35. *See also*
  House/Full of Blackwomen (Oakland)
White, Jack, 216
White, Megan, 226
White supremacy: anti-Blackness as
  requirement for, 112 (*see also* anti-
  Blackness); removing symbols of, 90;
  Donald Trump and, 87
Whitney Museum of American Art, 191
Wideman, John Edgar, 67–68

Wiggins, Marsha I., 4
Wilkerson, Isabel, 113
Willetts, Kheli R., 135–37, 139–40
Williams, Amelia, 51
Williams, Brittany, 44
Williams, Carmen Braun, 4
Williams, Delores, 20
Williams, Herbert T., 216
Williams, Keelah, 7
Willis, Deborah, 14, 15–16, 190
Wilson, August, 102
Wineglass, Jonathan, 84
Winfrey, Oprah, 125
wings/feathers, 188
womanism: defined, 20; wellness and,
  4–6, 19–20
Women Heal through Rite and Ritual
  online exhibition (2020, Galerie
  Myrtis, Baltimore), 23–24; Lavett
  Ballard and, 24, 120–30; curator,
  23–24, 120, 122, 158; exposure on
  social media, 24; Shanequa Gay and,
  24, 146, 149–55; Delita Martin and,
  24
Women of the Beauchamp Library
  Sankofa Piecemakers Quilting Circle
  (Syracuse), 226, 233
Women of Vision, Inc. (Pittsburgh):
  Apparition and Destinations exhibition, 41–42; founded, 21, 41; incorporated, 41; as longest-running Black
  women's art collective in the US, 21
women's liberation movement: Black
  Arts Movement and, 20–21, 27–29,
  31–32; first wave of feminism, 30–31;
  nature of, 29; Nineteenth Amend-
  ment and, 112, 113; racism and, 29;
  women's rights movement and, 21,
  112, 113, 231
Women's Marches (2017), 95
Woodruff, Hale A., 28, 29, 58
Woods-Giscombé, Cheryl L., 62
Works Progress Administration (WPA),
  73
World Health Organization (WHO), 3
World's Fair (1939, New York City),
  The Harp ("Lift Every Voice and Sing")
  sculpture (Savage), 73–74
Wright, Peter "Souleo," 196

TANISHA M. JACKSON is an assistant professor of African American studies at Syracuse University.

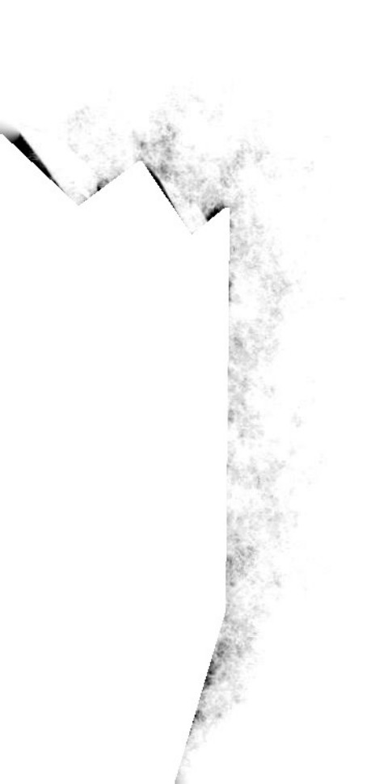

The University of Illinois Press
is a founding member of the
Association of University Presses.

———————————————

Composed in 10.5/13 Adobe Garamond
with Trade Gothic display
by Jim Proefrock
at the University of Illinois Press
Manufactured by Versa Press, Inc.

University of Illinois Press
1325 South Oak Street
Champaign, IL 61820-6903
www.press.uillinois.edu